Academic Writing Instruction for Creole-Influenced Students

Academic Writing Instruction for Creole-Influenced Students

VIVETTE MILSON-WHYTE

THE UNIVERSITY OF THE WEST INDIES PRESS
Jamaica • Barbados • Trinidad and Tobago

The University of the West Indies Press
7A Gibraltar Hall Road, Mona
Kingston 7, Jamaica
www.uwipress.com

© 2015 by Vivette Milson-Whyte

All rights reserved. Published 2015

A catalogue record of this book is available from the National Library of Jamaica.

ISBN: 978-976-640-509-0 (print)
        978-976-640-521-2 (Kindle)
        978-976-640-532-8 (ePub)

Cover design by Robert Harris
Book design by The Beget, India
Printed in the United States of America

Material from Vivette Milson-Whyte, "How Changed Attitudes to Academic Writing and Its Instruction May Enhance WAC", in "Integrating Discourse Communities in the Academy: Writing across the Curriculum", special issue, *Caribbean Journal of Education* 30, no. 2 (2008): 399–423, is reproduced here with permission from the *Caribbean Journal of Education*.

For

Mr King
Eric (David) King
stalwart of Mona's writing programme
champion record keeper
who informed but allowed me to interpret

and

in memory of
"Bell"
Violet Isabel Benjamin (1955–1982)
my mother
whose language habits
and questionable insistence that I "study" and "talk properly"
saved me from linguistic orphanhood

Contents

Acknowledgements	ix
Note on Terms Used in the Book	xi
Abbreviations	xiii
Chapter 1 Literacy Crises and Myths about Creole-Influenced University Students' Writing	1
Chapter 2 Developing Local Leaders without Explicit Academic Writing Instruction Prior to Independence, Pre-1960s	43
Chapter 3 Professionalizing the Aspirant Middle Class through Survey Writing after Independence, 1960s to the Mid-1980s	77
Chapter 4 Nurturing "Linguistic Orphans" with Basic Writing in the Post-National Era, Late 1980s to 2004+	119
Chapter 5 Improving the Graduate's Profile via "Universalist" Writing at the Turn of the Century, 1990s to 2010+	143
Chapter 6 Fashioning Versatile Creole-Influenced Writers through a Transcultural Rhetorical Perspective on Writing in the New Millennium, Beyond 2010	189
Notes	229
References	233
Index	255

Acknowledgements

Many of the ideas in this book first emerged as I pursued doctoral studies at the University of Arizona in Tucson in the United States. Some of these ideas were expressed in the 2008 dissertation that arose from those studies, "A History of Writing Instruction for Jamaican University Students: A Case for Moving Beyond the Rhetoric of Transparent Disciplinarity at the University of the West Indies, Mona". Other ideas emerged following completion of graduate work and reintegration in the writing programme at the University of the West Indies. I therefore wish to express my profound gratitude to the organizations and individuals who facilitated the germination of all of these ideas and contributed to the production of this book:

- the J. William Fulbright Scholarship Board for offering me a Fulbright-LASPAU grant to finance the first two years of my doctoral programme in the United States;
- the University of the West Indies, Mona, for awarding me various forms of leave and a grant to assist with completing doctoral studies between August 2004 and July 2008, and sabbatical leave for 2012–2013 when I was able to profit from uninterrupted time to refine the ideas in this book;
- G.E.A. Falloon who, in his capacity as campus registrar at Mona, granted me permission to use the campus as a site for studying attitudes to academic writing instruction;
- personnel in the Archives, Documentation Centre, Main Library and Registry Records at the University of the West Indies, Mona, for assisting me in locating and reproducing research materials;
- the Department of Language, Linguistics and Philosophy, University of the West Indies, Mona: heads, past and present, for encouragement in ways they may be unaware of; members of the departmental office; lecturers and instructors, past and present, who graciously provided information and encouraged my endeavours; and, especially, Eric (David) King, who was an undergraduate in the 1950s, "Use of English" tutor in the 1960s and later course moderator;

- the University of Arizona: members of the College of Humanities laboratories for technological support in 2007–2008; the Department of English for offering various scholarships and informal subsidies for completing graduate studies; Thomas Miller, Anne-Marie Hall and Geta Leseur Brown for advice on researching, writing and re-envisioning writing; other faculty for their encouragement; graduate colleagues and friends for productive criticism and support;
- the reviewers and editors for their invaluable feedback;
- my family and Jamaican friends who provided support in countless ways and meaningful distraction to keep me grounded;
- my Forever Friend who holds more than my writing hand.

Note on Terms Used in the Book

The term *Creole-speaking* is often used to refer to contexts such as Jamaica where most citizens speak a Creole language as first language. Noted Caribbean language educator Dennis Craig used the term "Creole-influenced vernacular" to refer to the spoken form of language in the Caribbean region. Creoles and other language varieties influenced by the Creoles inform such speech. *Creole-influenced* is used in this book to achieve a broader range than is covered by the more common term "Creole-speaking" and to facilitate presentation of implications of Creole influence for not only spoken and informal situations but also written and formal communication in academic settings.

An *external examiner* vets examination questions and checks final results, grading, and so on in a specific course. This person is usually in another institution (overseas).

A *moderator* is responsible for selection and ongoing training of instructors, coordinating the production of teaching materials, supervising and standardizing the marking of coursework and examinations, revising existing courses, and developing and introducing new ones. A *university/chief moderator* has responsibility for a course on all of the university's campuses. A *campus moderator* oversees a course on a specific campus. Other terms such as *convenor* and *coordinator* are also used.

The *senate* is the university's central policymaking body.

The *sixth form* refers to the two additional years that students spend in high school to prepare for examinations that can qualify them for university studies. In a "graded" system, these years cover grades 12 and 13.

A *tutor* is a faculty member or graduate student who conducts a tutorial (seminar), usually following a large group lecture.

The *University Academic Committee* (institution-wide) and the *Academic Board* (on a campus) have specific responsibilities for decisions related to teaching.

Common terms with *different meanings* in the Jamaican and American academic traditions:

Jamaican	American
course	class
department	department
faculty	college
faculty (academic/s)	professor/s
instructor	lecturer
lecturer (general term)	professor
lecturer (rank)	assistant professor
postgraduate	graduate
professor (an accomplished academic in a field)	professor (of a subject + accomplished academic)
senior lecturer	associate professor

Abbreviations

CAPE	Caribbean Advanced Proficiency Examination
CXC	Caribbean Examinations Council
ELS	English Language Section
GCE	General Certificate of Education
GWSI	general writing skills instruction
MOCAS	mechanics/grammar, organization, content, analysis and style
UCWI	University College of the West Indies
UWI	University of the West Indies
WAC	writing across the curriculum

1 | Literacy Crises and Myths about Creole-Influenced University Students' Writing

In writing are the roots, in writing are the foundations of eloquence; by writing resources are stored up, as it were, in a sacred repository, whence they may be drawn forth for sudden emergencies or as circumstances require. (Quintilian quoted in Bizzell and Herzeberg 2001a, 404)

When student writing is viewed in [a] particularistic, pseudo-scientific way, it gets defined in very limited terms as a narrow band of inadequate behavior separate from the vastly complex composing that faculty members engage in for a living and delve into for work and for play. And such perception yields what it intends: a behavior that is stripped of its rich cognitive and rhetorical complexity. (Rose 1985, 346)

Without a knowledge of history and traditions, we risk running in circles while seeking new paths. Without knowing the traditions, there is no way of knowing which traditions to hold dear and which to discard. (Villanueva 1993, 75)

Sounding the Alarm

"Bloody English! UWI, UTech Students Struggle with the Language" (Virtue 2013), a news article appearing on 27 January 2013 in Jamaica's popular newspaper the *Sunday Gleaner*, would probably have surprised students and faculty had it appeared in the late 1940s. Surprise would have arisen not because there was only one university college in Jamaica then, and the item references the University of the West

Indies (UWI) and the University of Technology, but because the article mentions postsecondary students' "poor communication and language use skills" – forcing introduction of an "English Fix for UWI" students through five recently approved English language foundation courses (ibid.). No such course was offered to Creole-influenced students during the foundation years of higher education that began in 1948 when the University College of the West Indies (UCWI), later the UWI, was established in Jamaica. However, in the over six-decade history of the institution, there have been shifts from no provision of explicit writing instruction through to provision of general and basic writing courses to attempts to teach writing across the curriculum (WAC) and writing based on faculties in tandem with the institution's commendable attempts to shift from selecting and training a few applicants to fostering the individual development of many of the Caribbean region's human resources.

For faculty, like me, who are involved in teaching students advanced written literacy in the new millennium, the news article confuses many issues – albeit inadvertently. Quoting from "UWI sources", the article states, "the University of the West Indies (UWI), Mona campus, said it has been forced to re-evaluate its language-based foundation courses as 'students display abominable use of English in the simplest form'" (Virtue 2013). This statement implies that the new courses – listed as Critical Reading and Writing in Education; Critical Reading and Expository Writing in the Humanities; Critical Reading in the Social Sciences; Critical Reading and Writing in Science and Technology and Medical Sciences; and Critical Reading and Writing in the Disciplines – were meant to address some kind of *English problem*. However, if any of the courses were meant to be an "English Fix", it would be that described as "a six-credit foundation course which is to be offered to students who are unable to meet the university's English language proficiency standards as measured by the score in the UWI, Mona English Language Proficiency Test". Therefore, inclusion of courses meant to teach academic literacies under the heading "English Fix for UWI" suggests misunderstanding of postsecondary level communication requirements and, specifically, of how writing works.

It is unclear if the misunderstanding was on the part of the journalist or the "UWI sources". However, appearing in the new millennium, the news article continues the trend in which the media can be relied on to trigger an alarm about a literacy crisis in higher education – in Jamaica as well as in more developed countries with a longer history of higher education. This trend was set in the first two decades following the institution's establishment: consistent with the Oxbridge tradition, in the early years, entry to the then UCWI was based on the results of very rigorous examinations, entry cohorts were small, all students resided on the campus, and there was no course teaching students to write for academic purposes. However, Jamaica, like the United States, relaxed requirements for commencing higher education in the 1960s to 1970s. In the United States, the change dubbed "open admissions" meant increased access to universities for students considered less prepared in writing than their predecessors, and *basic* writing courses were introduced for many of those nontraditional students. In Jamaica, certain examination requirements remained in place, but the residential requirement was removed to enable students to register for part-time and/or evening programmes at the UWI. At the same time that part-time students were being allowed to pursue an undergraduate degree at the UWI in the 1960s, administrators introduced survey courses, one of which was an *applied* language course called "Use of English". Removal of the residential requirement at the UWI also led to increasing numbers of new admits who were first-generation university students from Creole-speaking (rather than English-speaking) backgrounds. As in the United States and in other countries where critics have commented on any development in language/writing instruction, especially if it is associated with students considered less prepared than others, in Jamaica, many academics and public figures have over the last half-century (and more) criticized the "Use of English" course, other courses in writing instruction and – naturally – student writing in the university.

Although in "Bloody English!" the journalist uses the coarse slang to present "English" as a nuisance, other articles by journalists and academics that I analyse below tend to present the students as the problem. Wherever the problem is located, and although the bells have tolled in each decade since the 1960s, the reactionary furore seems to die as quickly as it begins without the real issue – academic writing development for Creole-influenced students – being addressed.

This book focuses on just that subject, specifically the teaching of academic writing to Creole-influenced students – students who are influenced in one way or another by the country's Creole language but who are not all Creole-speaking. I use the "English Language" programme at the UWI at Mona in Jamaica as a case for exploring the evolution of the theoretical paradigms, curricular practices and general politics of writing instruction for these students in Jamaican higher education. Where possible, I make comparisons with the well-established tradition of teaching composition in the United States and the more recent development of teaching academic writing/literacies in the United Kingdom. Throughout the book, I make necessary connections between writing instruction in the academy, language teaching in schools and language use in Jamaican society. All of these moves are meant to facilitate comprehension of strategies and approaches that would be appropriate for Creole-influenced students who are required to write in English at the postsecondary level – many of whose linguistic and cultural experiences are far removed from prevailing academic conventions because such students have to make wide-ranging connections between what they know and what they need to learn in educational institutions. Drawing on my examination of the evolution of writing instruction for Jamaican students in this university in a Creole-speaking environment where English is the official language, I suggest that, based on historical antecedents and current and changing demands and platforms for writing, desired improvements in writing by Creole-influenced students are likely to follow from dismantling various writing myths and adopting a progressive rhetoric of writing. Before providing a synopsis of this history and proposal, I expand the term "Creole-influenced", give an overview of the UWI, explain what I mean by academic writing, analyse some criticisms of student writing and identify misconceptions about writing that inform these criticisms.

Transculturation: Jamaica's History, Education System and Languages

Views about academic writing and its instruction in Jamaica have to be understood against the background of the country's colonial history, linguistic context and ties with England and other British West Indian colonies. Therefore, in reviewing academic writing and its instruction in Jamaica, I draw on the concept of "transculturation" that Mary Louise Pratt (1991) develops in her explorations of contact zones. Pratt relates this largely historical concept to classrooms, but I wish to focus on her use of the term in relation to history. Contact zones, says Pratt, are "social spaces where cultures meet, clash, and grapple with each other, often in contexts of highly asymmetrical relations of power, such as colonialism, slavery, or their aftermaths as they are lived out in many parts of the world today" (34). However, like other scholars, she argues that the domination and resistance binary that is often associated with such contact zones does not provide a nuanced account of relations in them. In such contact zones, cultures and subcultures interact, exchanging values, terms and attitudes in a process of "transculturation". The latter, she explains, is a term that Cuban sociologist Fernando Ortiz first coined in the 1940s to "replace overly reductive concepts of acculturation and assimilation used to characterize culture under conquest" (Pratt 1991, 36). According to Pratt, transculturation describes "processes whereby members of subordinated or marginal groups select and invent from materials transmitted by a dominant or metropolitan culture.... While subordinate peoples do not usually control what emanates from the dominant culture, they do determine to varying extents what gets absorbed into their own and what it gets used for" (ibid.).

Transculturation is evident in Jamaica in the way in which subjects in contact constitute themselves through interaction and improvisation. The Caribbean region where Jamaica is located is an archetypal contact zone that was balkanized through European expansionism into British, Danish (now US Virgin Islands), Dutch, French and Spanish West Indies. Each Caribbean island's culture is a result of violent contact between Europeans, Amerindians and transplanted peoples from other continents. However, while domination and resistance abound in each culture, transculturation is also evident in the improvisation that Caribbean peoples demonstrate.

The interactive and improvisational nature of contact in Jamaica dates back to the fifteenth century and influenced educational and language patterns in the country. When Christopher Columbus landed in Jamaica in 1494, he secured the island for Spain. In 1655, the English took over Jamaica from the Spanish, rendering the island a British Crown Colony (governed by the Colonial Office in England through its appointed autocratic governors) by 1670. Today, more than 90 per cent of Jamaicans are of predominantly African descent, their/our ancestors forcibly transported by Europeans from the west coast of Africa to plough and populate West Indian sugar plantations. The Spanish left very little, if any, mark on education in Jamaica. Like those of other former British colonies, Jamaica's education system was influenced by England's. Public elementary education was introduced in Jamaica in 1834, public teacher education in 1836, public secondary education in 1879 and public university education only in 1948 (see Figueroa 1971; Gordon 1963; V. Roberts 2003; Whyte 1977). Jamaica's young education system suggests that many of present-day Jamaicans' forebears were not exposed to formal Western concepts of education. After all, during plantation slavery, when planters were property owners and slaves were property, there was very little concern for education. As Philip Sherlock observes in work coauthored with Rex Nettleford, the anglophone Caribbean, of which Jamaica is the largest island, was dominated by a white planter class "that for two centuries resisted intellectual enquiry, despised learning and defined the vast majority of its people as 'pieces of property'" (Sherlock and Nettleford 1990, v). However, as the next two chapters reveal, locals selected and adapted features of British education in their bid to transform the British model university that was established in 1948 as a college of the University of London.

Jamaican Creole, the language spoken by the majority of Jamaicans, is the linguistic embodiment of transculturation. Its development and function in society are germane to discussions of writing instruction in higher education. This language was formed in the crucible of the plantation, from the contact between European, African, and indigenous Caribbean languages. It is testament to the ways in which Jamaicans' ancestors selected from the languages available and reinvented them, as they tried to adapt to the new situation imposed on them in the Caribbean. Many Jamaicans are justly proud of this emblem of adaptation, but perhaps more stigmatize it because of the high personal and social prestige associated with "proper" English (Christie 2003, 4–5). Analyses reveal that Jamaican Creole is lexically related to English, but the two languages differ markedly in the other features, especially in terms of phonology and syntax (see Alleyne 1980; Bailey 1966; Cassidy 1961; Cassidy and LePage 1980). Some educators believe that the close lexical relationship poses a problem for some learners, manifesting in Creole interference in writing in English (see Craig 1999; Pollard 1998). For a long time, higher education was reserved for a few for whom proficiency in English was considered a mark of distinction. Students considered literate in English could write without interference from Jamaican Creole. Hence, comfort in using this code and resultant difficulties in using English are at the heart of some of the errors that have informed complaints about student writing at the UWI at Mona and about graduates' communication skills in general.

Given this history and the resultant linguistic peculiarities, Jamaicans' linguistic behaviours can appear enigmatic. Some Jamaicans are English-only speakers who understand Creole; some are English-dominant bilinguals; some are Creole-dominant bilinguals; some may be equally bilingual in Creole and English; some are Creole-only speakers who may or may not understand English; some slide between the shifting poles in ways yet to be named; some do not acknowledge their linguistic profiles and behaviours, but all encounter Jamaican Creole. Since all Jamaicans are influenced in one way or another by the Creole, but are not all Creole-speaking, I refer to Jamaican students as *Creole-influenced* students.

The University of the West Indies

Jamaican Creole-influenced students have been receiving higher education for over six decades at the UWI. This institution was established as the UCWI in 1948 as part of a British imperial system of elite universities that emphasized excellence. This oldest university and premier provider of higher education in the anglophone Caribbean, a region with few such local institutions, was established after years of negotiation between the British government and passionate advocates of higher education in the region (Sherlock and Nettleford 1990, v). Located in a suburb of Kingston, the island's capital, this university college of the University of London was to function as a regional institution, transforming students from the British colonies across the Caribbean into local leaders (Great Britain Commission 1945, 16). By 1962, the UCWI became the UWI, an independent research university. Today, the UWI is a multicampus, multinational institution, with three fixed physical campuses (the two others established in 1960 in Trinidad and 1963 in Barbados), a branch campus of Mona launched in 2008 in western Jamaica, an open online campus launched in 2008 and operating from over forty-five Caribbean site locations – some of which are former intramural centres located in the non-campus contributing territories, and a School of Tourism located in the Bahamas. Students can also take UWI-approved courses at various tertiary-level affiliate institutions in the region. Overall, the university serves three campus and thirteen non-campus countries. This institution, which began with thirty-three students, now has a combined enrolment of over forty-seven thousand (UWI 2012, vii), and no longer operates as it was conceived as a small, centralized, residential institution.

The Mona campus in Jamaica, which is my focus, has offered its changing cohorts of students academic writing courses which have contributed generally to the language development and specifically the academic writing development of its Creole-influenced constituents. However, while facilitating students' initiation into the academy, these courses and the resources allocated to academic writing instruction reflect assumptions about writing and learning that, I propose, need to be reassessed in light of changing groups of students in order to yield versatile writers and disassociate the courses and writing from the alarmist rhetoric that often emerges in the media and in academe. These changing cohorts are adequately significant to warrant inclusion in the institution's strategic plans. The UWI's *Draft Strategic Plan 2007–2012* specifies that although the institution has accepted "successive cohorts of the brightest and the best" from secondary schools in the Caribbean region, "today the student intake represents a much broader range of aptitudes and abilities as enrolment has expanded to facilitate access to higher education" (2007b, 11). In this document is admission that the student body is no longer the homogenous group of students from upper- or middle-income backgrounds that obtained in the 1940s when the institution was established. This document expresses the change in terms of *diversity*: "While the UWI continues to compete for the brightest and the best students who are very well prepared to undertake University level work, the expansion of student intake has led to greater diversity in terms of abilities, learning styles, levels of preparation, etc." (13). However, the strategic plan for 2012–2017 acknowledges a negative impact of the change. It lists "student intake quality" (UWI 2012, 2) as a threat to realization of institutional goals: "The declining average student entrant scores will negatively affect the University's throughput and retention rates" (18). Another concern for the institution is that the university's "regional character" continues to be undermined by "overwhelming and increasing dominance of students from the host country on each campus" (UWI 2007b, 37). One consequence of this shift in demographics is that there are increasing numbers of Jamaican Creole-influenced students requiring academic writing instruction on the Mona campus.

Academic Writing

I use the term "academic writing" to mean the written scholarly discourses that academics produce in conformity with the conventions and expectations of their respective disciplines. Most of the knowledge creation and distribution in the academy takes place through such writing. Students – in their quest to increase their learning in new subjects – are expected to comprehend, evaluate, challenge and eventually produce such discourses in order to communicate effectively in writing in the university and beyond. Courses that provide explicit instruction in student academic writing have differing emphases. Some emphasize general shared academic conventions, sometimes with reference to forms and ways of writing that are inflected differently in specific disciplines, while others address discipline-specific writing requirements in terms of teaching the conventions and assumptions or expectations that govern a particular discipline or specific disciplines. I believe that students *should* learn both shared academic conventions and discipline-specific strategies. Whatever the focus with regard to writing, increasingly these courses tend to include elements of critical thinking and reading. These courses are also called different terms in different traditions: (English) composition or general writing and WAC or writing in the disciplines in the United States and academic writing or academic literacies in the United Kingdom and some of its former colonies. A range of terms such as *communication, use of English, English for academic purposes* or *English language* is used in these places and in various other countries including Jamaica.

Specifically at the UWI at Mona academic writing instruction is offered in courses referred to as foundation "English Language" courses in the English Language Section (ELS) of the Department of Language, Linguistics and Philosophy in the Faculty of Humanities and Education. Mona's writing programme (called English Language programme) bears vestiges of its beginning in the 1960s, but it also reflects features selected from US programmes and reinvented in the local context. Ideas about process writing and portfolios in teaching from the United States have intersected with local ones, mainly through faculty members' education, attendance at conferences, or subscription to English and US composition journals. The ELS coordinator (the head of the ELS) is supported by individual course coordinators (this writer being one such) who are tenured or tenure-track faculty and writing "instructors" who are usually employed full-time on two-year renewable contracts. The faculty members and most of the instructors have at least a master's degree, usually in literature, linguistics or education, and at least two members (this writer being one) completed doctoral degrees in rhetoric and composition. The unit does not offer specialist graduate writing courses, so graduate students are not usually involved in teaching academic writing. In the recent past, one or two graduate students in English, French or Spanish literature or linguistics were employed along with a few part-time facilitators to meet last minute needs.

I also use the term "academic writing" because it is convenient, but I acknowledge that it is problematic, misleading even, since it can suggest *one* kind of writing. The reality is that there is no easily defined entity called academic writing, especially when its synonym, "academic discourse", is invoked. The latter term usually ignores the plural discourses of the academy. My intention, however, is to foreground that plurality. What I want to emphasize, therefore, is *kind*. My focus is on writing done in the academy for the academy or professions as opposed to writing done for popular magazines, for example. I am also focusing on written literacy because, as the first epigraph says, in it are "the foundations of eloquence" (Quintilian, quoted in Bizzell and Herzeberg 2001a, 404). In his extended treatment of the utility of and procedures for writing, Quintilian promotes its importance to the development of oratorical powers. My interest is in teaching students to be more than mere consumers or reproducers of disciplinary knowledge so that they can become shapers of texts or producers of knowledge. As writing researcher Charles Bazerman (2007, 1) asserts, "It is by writing that we inscribe our place in the literate world and all the social systems that depend on literacy."

Additionally, my focus is on advanced written literacy instruction in *Jamaica* – only one of the many territories served by the UWI. This focus is to be understood not as a move against regionalization, but as a personal desire to understand the link between Jamaica's intriguing linguistic context and other issues that have bedevilled the education of Creole-influenced Jamaicans. Because I focus on the Mona campus, it may seem that I am excluding those Jamaican students who study law in Barbados, engineering or agriculture in Trinidad, tourism in the Bahamas, or other subjects on either of those campuses. Significantly, although my focus is Jamaica, sometimes what I provide are statements about other English-speaking Caribbean island countries that represent or are intertwined with the Jamaican situation and for whose peoples the UWI was established. Relevant reports from other territories, therefore, include Jamaicans who may be studying on those campuses. Readers can also readily draw parallels with respect to other Caribbean students or institutions. Additionally, while the focus is on Jamaican students in a Caribbean university, researchers and educators working with other Creole-influenced students, or in contexts where language boundaries are blurred, or where the vernaculars impact significantly on the language(s) of instruction, may find germane the history unveiled and the suggestions for providing academic writing instruction for their students.

The reader should also bear in mind that, as Mikhail Bakhtin ([1934–35] 1981, 293) says, "each word tastes of the context and contexts in which it has lived its socially charged life". Some of the terms that I use with reference to the Caribbean or the UWI will, therefore, reflect inevitable "contextual overtones" (ibid.). As an example, the traditional description of Jamaica and other similar Caribbean countries as "English-speaking" is, as Creole linguist Lawrence Carrington (1978, 85) writes, "a convenient inexactitude which excuses itself simply because English is the official language of the states". Also, in addition to the English terms in the note on terms used in the book, I use the term "writing specialists" to refer to lecturers (full-time tenured or tenure-track faculty members) and instructors (full-time non-tenure-track staff on two-year renewable contracts) in the ELS, and "'content' faculty" or "other content faculty" to refer to faculty in other disciplines. I am tempted to put "content" in quotation marks throughout the book to highlight the misconception that other courses have "content" but writing has none.

In what follows here, I look closely at some journalists' and academics' criticisms of student writing and identify myths that emerge in these criticisms. I then link these myths to attitudes to academic writing instruction in the university to call for a transcultural rhetorical perspective on teaching academic writing to Creole-influenced students.

Crises

When public figures and academics criticize student writing, they often focus on quantifiable errors related to grammar and mechanics (NCTE 2007; Rose 1985). The result is that critics' complaints usually reflect a crisis. However, this focus also serves to highlight critics' ignorance of the complexity of written literacy, for it promotes and perpetuates what literacy educator Mike Rose (1985) defines as the "myth of transience" and a view of writing that I call "the rhetoric of transparent disciplinarity" or the "myth of the transparency of language in all disciplines". I explain these concepts after I present a few cases of criticism of student writing to highlight critics' misconceptions about writing, its instruction, and how writing reveals learning. However, suffice it to say here that, according to the myth of transience, if better teaching is done at lower educational levels, problems in student writing in the university will disappear (Rose 1985, 355–56). I define the rhetoric of transparent disciplinarity based on the work of cross-cultural writing researcher David Russell (2002) who examines the view that writing is a single mechanical, generalizable skill that is learned once and for all. This concept is also alluded to, though not called that term, in the work of various UK writing researchers who critique the workings of "the discourse of transparency" in higher education (see Jones, Turner and Street 1999a; Lea and Street 1998; Lillis 1999, 2001, 2006; and Lillis and Turner 2001). Advocates of this "rhetoric" consider writing as a transparent recording of reality or completed thought that can be taught separate from disciplinary knowledge. Accompanying this rhetoric are views that writing within disciplines is neutral, hardly influenced by persuasion; any instruction in writing at the tertiary level has as its aim remediation; the academy is a single discourse community; and the focus of higher education ought to be excellence rather than equity (Russell 2002, 9–10). These myths are evident in some criticisms of student writing.

Among the criticisms of student writing in the Jamaican print media are statements such as the following that bespeak misunderstanding about writing courses and that even hilariously reflect weaknesses in the critic that are similar to those for which students are criticized. On 8 July 2004, the editorial "Mr Crawford and UWI Fees" in the *Jamaica Observer* stated "If many of those who are now entering UWI are honest about it, they will admit that despite matriculating they carry many deficiencies. Which is why so many remedial English courses are around". Since at the time of writing there would have been only one supposedly "remedial course" on the Mona campus along with various first-year writing courses, this editorial erroneously equates "standard" writing courses with remediation. Needless to say, the fragment ("Which . . . around") included in the editorial instantiates one type of "deficiency" for which students are criticized even though the critic would probably claim to have written acceptable journalistic prose. On the following day, 9 July 2004, the newspaper's editorial "UWI Fees and an Open Mouth" stated, "We have felt that resources should be shifted from the tertiary to the lower reaches of the education totem pole so that there is a better foundation on which to build the tertiary system. We would then be able to drop the courses in remedial English and so on". With no definition of the mentioned "foundation", with treatment of the subject as a matter of "resources", and with the inclusion of "and so on" as probably alluding to other standard courses, this editorial is another reflection of misunderstanding of the university's writing courses, and ignorance of how writing develops at different levels of the education system.

Such misunderstandings do not appear in editorials alone. On 6 May 2007, columnist Mark Wignall would include in his *Sunday Observer* article a personal e-mail communication from a student in the Faculty of Pure and Applied Sciences to demonstrate the student's failure to write a "well-structured" letter with "few grammatical errors" to "invite an intelligent response" about a problem involving a professor in the student's department. Wignall wanted the readers of his "How Did He Enter UWI, Mona" to try to "skirt the surface of a mind that somehow, by a crazy mix of 'turd' [the student's likely spelling] world standards and the need to cram the Math Department with all available students, the university found it useful to admit him". Wignall also asserted that the country's purported 89 per cent literacy rate "makes a mockery of the reality". That assertion, the many errors in the personal communication, and Wignall's association of increased intake with poor writing quality and, therefore, a lowering of standards can only evoke thoughts associated with a crisis. Indeed, Wignall's article is redolent of the popular US publication, Merril Sheils's "Why Johnny Can't Write", which appeared in *Newsweek* on 8 December 1975. This article served to sound the alarm of a literacy crisis in the United States after the Conference on College Composition and Communication (CCCC 1974) had adopted and published the *Students' Right to Their Own Language* resolution. This controversial resolution on language rights called for a de-emphasis of errors due to dialectal differences and for emphasis on content and meaning instead. In the Jamaican case, Wignall's comments seem to be justifiably harsh because meaning seems to be obscured by the many grammatical errors and the student's apparent heavy reliance on instant text-messaging language in the e-mail communication that Wignall cites. However, while the comments *hint* at the way in which a student's writing indicates failure to be able to use grammatical features learned to express and analyse experiences, trends or problems, the comments do not plumb the issue of the process of literacy development for Creole-influenced students.

Similar and harsher comments than Wignall's were also made by Carl Stone, well-known Jamaican pollster, lecturer in the Faculty of Social Sciences, and a regular contributor to Jamaica's oldest newspaper, the *Daily Gleaner*. In a 6 July 1988 piece entitled "The Threat of Mediocrity", Stone listed as problems among new students in his faculty in the 1987–1988 academic year:

- inability to grasp and comprehend fully the reading materials they are expected to
- inability to coherently express themselves in written work
- failure to answer questions adequately because language deficiencies cloud their understanding of what is being taught
- failure to comprehend the meaning of words
- inability to precisely express what they wish to say

Stone did not realize that some of those problems, especially the last three, could have arisen from faculty's failure to explain evaluation terms to new students. He acknowledged that some students often demonstrated some of those weaknesses prior to the 1987–1988 academic year, but noted, "The problem has multiplied in the current year as increased admission of students to the various faculties resulted in an increased proportion of students admitted with deficient and marginal capacity to use the English Language." He emphasized that beyond the problem posed by "bad grammar, poor spelling, clumsy language or inelegant word constructions" is that of "comprehension". He asserted that students understand very little of what is said in lectures or what they read, the result being memorization of course materials that are then "reproduced ritually" in examinations. Stone linked failure rates in general with language deficiency: "As the English problem has increased, failure rates have also increased as the two are organically connected."

Although Stone (1988) spoke of the "English problem", he did not delve into the issue to point to the way that students' understanding may indeed be clouded by an imposed language problem that has plagued generations of Jamaicans. Stone felt that 40 per cent of the students in the first-year course he was teaching then "ought not to be in a university because language deficiencies severely impair their ability to learn and express themselves". Worse, he felt that "intellectually deficient students . . . corrupt and damage the norms and values operating within the student body". Such students, he maintained, "have no real interest in deepening their knowledge and understanding or in enlarging their intellect". In his view, because for such students "University life is just an exam hustle", they eventually "pollute the learning environment with the debris of mediocrity". Although in the latter statements Stone seemed to be broadening his focus to students who were probably lazy and uninterested in education, the reader cannot help connecting them to the students who exhibit the language deficiencies that are the focus of his article. Terms such as "pollute" and "debris of mediocrity" are representative of the language of crisis that emerged in the Jamaican media in the 1980s and has continued into the new millennium.

In the first few years of the new millennium, commentators invoked writing in discussions about the purpose of higher education in Jamaica, but this reference was often in relation to problems in writing (see Chevannes 2005; Holding and Burke 2005; Robotham 2000) – continuing a related trend: beyond the alarm that is often raised in the print media regarding student writing, academics have for generations also criticized student writing without adequately attending to writing instruction. A representative case of criticism of student writing within academic circles in Jamaica appears in "Sprinting Over the Long Distance: Education at a Crossroad". In this book chapter, Barry Chevannes, noted professor of social anthropology and former dean of the Faculty of Social Sciences at the UWI at Mona invokes writing in discussions about quantity/quality at the university level. Chevannes's comments appear in Holding and Burke's *Revisiting Tertiary Education Policy in Jamaica: Towards Personal Gain or Public Good?* (2005) – a collection of the presentations and comments that were made at a three-day conference on the role of tertiary and higher (postsecondary) education in Jamaica in August 2004. Chevannes discusses the tertiary level in general, including community colleges, teacher training colleges, and evening institutes, as well as universities, but focuses on *higher* education, which is traditionally associated with the university.

Chevannes's (2005) pronouncements are representative of those of previous and later commentators (including Stone 1988) who focus on basic grammatical or mechanical correctness and ultimately perpetuate incorrect assumptions about writing. His comments were inspired by those of another leading figure in Jamaican education, then minister of education Maxine Henry-Wilson, who declared that the Jamaican government was committed to increasing access to tertiary institutions to 30 per cent of all eligible applicants to give the country a "competitive edge" (Chevannes 2005, 302). Chevannes felt that it was an opportune time to address *quality* since enrolment had already increased to 15 per cent – indeed, "sprinted from seven percent in 1997 to 15 per cent by 2003" (306). Chevannes's concern was that the country focus on improving quality at the secondary level instead of "continu[ing] the momentum" to reach the new enrolment target of 30 percent" (ibid.). He made this recommendation on the basis that "the strategic considerations we give to the quality of education at tertiary level cannot ignore the state of secondary education" (302), and "quality assurance at the tertiary level begins at the secondary level with the complete and adequate preparation of students" (306). These appear to be fair statements, indicating that what happens at the primary and secondary levels is likely to influence what happens at the tertiary level and should, therefore, never be ignored in any discussion of policy changes at that level. However, some of Chevannes's statements also reflect misunderstanding about writing instruction in the academy. Chevannes asserts that if preparation at the secondary level is "incomplete or inadequate, tertiary institutions will be faced with the need for remedial education to bring their students up to the acceptable level, or with lowered standards of accreditation" (ibid.). Chevannes was aware that no one wants to associate tertiary, especially higher, education with *remedial* instruction. However, he ignored the fact that even if students are considered "good readers and writers" before they start higher education, they are not as mature cognitively as experts in the system and would therefore need help to adjust to the new knowledge making and acquisition experiences that the academy *should* offer.

In emphasizing that the university has had to face the challenge of educating students who come from a secondary system marked by "declining standards", Chevannes (2005, 297) recalls the introduction of an English proficiency test and "Fundamentals of English" (UC010), an attendant basic writing course. He includes writing samples from three proficiency test takers and a final year student in the Faculty of Social Sciences to highlight various errors related to syntax, sentence structure, diction/idiomatic usage, and grammar as regards number and verb forms (300). Since, in Chevannes's view, the secondary population changes only marginally from year to year, "the conclusion is inevitable that the tertiary sector will have to make room for the likes of those who failed the English proficiency test". He contextualizes his comments by pointing to limited resources in Jamaica: "Greater quantity in Jamaica's current context of resource-constraints must mean lower quality", he asserts. He reiterates that "until we begin to record greater successes in the preparation of students for tertiary education, thus reducing the necessity for remedial work at that level, the increase in tertiary enrolment over the course of the next few years is bound to undermine standards" (303). In essence, Chevannes was arguing that in the Jamaican context, quantity and quality cannot be realized simultaneously; that is, more students cannot have access to higher education without lowering standards.

To underscore his claim that administrators in Jamaica should, therefore, focus on quality at the secondary level rather than quantity at the tertiary level, Chevannes (2005, 306) remarks that "education is not about sprinting but about a marathon begun a hundred and sixty years ago and still going". One of my aims in this book is to extend Chevannes's cautionary note to *writing*: I would like to add that writing development is also a marathon, one that endures over the long distance, is not completed as short distance runs, and involves multiple trainers. I extend Chevannes's claim on the basis that he, thankfully, invoked writing in this discussion of quality and quantity at the UWI at Mona.[1] While I am delighted that language issues, specifically writing abilities, are implicated in this debate in Jamaica, I wish to shift the focus of discussions about writing so that policymakers may acknowledge the role that writing could play in enabling a simultaneous realization of quantity and quality in higher education. Indeed, I wish to emphasize that different understandings of writing and its instruction may serve to empower Creole-influenced students notwithstanding their numbers at any given time.

As an example, the nature of writing samples considered is important to modified discussions of writing and how it develops. The first writing sample that Chevannes (2005) discusses as representing writing by a Jamaican is a paper written about Haiti. Based on my experience advising in the English proficiency test unit and supervising instructors who taught Haitian Creole speakers, I perceive that the paper bears the marks of one written by a Haitian Creole-speaking student. As the Department of Language, Linguistics and Philosophy's (DLLP 2004) UC010 Report for 2003–2004 indicates, Haitian Creole-speaking students have significant difficulties – far more than Jamaican Creole speakers – manipulating English in writing. However, very few Haitian Creole–speaking students attend the UWI at Mona. Rather than be an accurate representation of *Jamaican* UWI student writing, Chevannes's sample may reflect a scenario in which the writer was crossing more language boundaries than a Jamaican student would cross. It is also important to note that many students do not take the proficiency test immediately after leaving secondary school (see Robotham 2000). Some of these test takers are already in the workforce and are years removed from any kind of systematic English or writing instruction in a secondary school. Faculty may cringe at the fact that those already in the workforce, in teaching, for example, write in ways that content faculty deplore. However, faculty need to recognize that factors beyond the secondary level are implicated in advanced writing instruction and development.

Of the other two excerpts that he quotes, Chevannes (2005, 300) says the "spelling and grammatical mistakes . . . are not all the result of exam nervousness, but reflect serious language deficiencies which are clearly going to hamper performance at the university level". Chevannes rightly suggests that too much may be asked of a basic writing course when students with certain "language deficiencies" are offered a place in the university:

> In allowing them in, the hope is that the remedial English course will allow the author of Excerpt 2, for example, to recognize the word "neighbouring" [the student used "labouring"] in a sociology text and be able to use it in an essay; or the author of Excerpt 1 to know the difference between "they" and "there", and between capital and common letters – all simple matters which should have been mastered in primary school, corrected at high school, but not left to the tertiary level to remedy. (301)

Identification of some of the problems as "simple matters" seems appropriate for features in writing that, while being distracting or irritating, may not prevent comprehension. What I believe to be graver and require more pressing attention are the larger writing concerns – such as unfamiliarity with disciplinary discourse – that the excerpts manifest and that pose *real* barriers to comprehension.

In treating the final year sample that is riddled with the same kinds of errors mentioned for the first proficiency test sample, Chevannes (2005, 301) emphasizes that "students' performance often falls below acceptable standards of English, whether in speech, essay writing or written exams, and used to be the object of many a good end-of-examinations laugh among academics". He feels however, that "it is hardly a laughing matter" when grave grammatical and mechanical errors appear in a final year student's paper. To my mind, the sample provided portrays what Susan Miller (1989, 90) calls "the garbled syntax of a [student] finding language for new and complex concepts". Readers may ask, however, if the student got beyond the first year, and if the final year writing is unsatisfactory, what kind of feedback were the content faculty providing the student all along? Chevannes (2005, 302) does not address that question. He notes, instead, that the student would get a bare pass degree, but that the problem extends to "many of the brighter graduates who go on to higher degrees [and] take with them the same or a similar degree of incompetence in English". With approximately 10 per cent of the graduate students requiring what Chevannes considers remedial instruction, the Faculty of Social Sciences introduced an advanced writing course for those pursuing masters and doctoral degrees. Chevannes argues that although such a course can be rightly considered a "waste of resources" (ibid.), one must recognize that the graduates' deficiencies will be blamed on the university and not their high schools.

I would not want to seem to be whitewashing the problems that Chevannes (2005) mentions, for various reasons. First, writing faculty tend to complain about deficiencies in papers written by Faculty of Social Sciences students, as in this comment in which a senior writing faculty member indicated in a departmental meeting in January 2002 that students from the Faculty of Social Sciences "form the core of poor essay writing and grammar weaknesses" (DLLP 2002a, 5). In the early 1990s Peter Roberts, another senior faculty member (at Cave Hill), had commented on the disparity in requirements for Social Sciences students and others in the university. P. Roberts (1991, 2) mentioned the grave problem triggered by the Faculty of Social Sciences – "the faculty with the greatest number of students requires no further qualification on the part of its students than a CXC grade II". The university seemed to require a higher level of expertise in English for students graduating from the then Faculties of Arts and General Studies, Natural Sciences, Medicine, Law, and Agriculture than for those in the Faculty of Social Sciences (and Engineering) (ibid.), because the latter were never required to take a first-year writing course until 1998. Second, as UK researchers Christopher Winch and Peter Wells (1995, 78) argue, mastery of the rules of spelling, punctuation, and the like help to create "a clear and attractive style", while the inability to write clearly can "compromise authorship and meaning". Third, and perhaps more important, is the institutional context. As Caroline Dyche (1996c, 144), the ELS coordinator up to 2006–2007, points out "at the UWI, emphasis is placed on grammatical and discourse competence as it affects the writing and not the speaking of English". She explains that this emphasis on students' written English proficiency is related to "the sociopolitical role that English, and particularly written English, plays in what are predominantly oral Creole-speaking societies" (145). She also notes that critics of students' written English often emphasize surface errors that "do not impede transmission of meaning" but usually specify class. She rightly notes, "In Anglo-West Indian societies, however, the functional-communicative value of English is often of secondary importance to its high personal and social prestige value" (ibid.). I am, therefore, not ignoring this "specific UWI academic context" where, as Dyche writes, "students [are] judged specifically on their ability to write grammatical English" (146). However, this focus on "grammatical English" is an unfortunate colonial legacy which reflects a language policy that many stakeholders have uncritically accepted. Writing is about more than mechanical or even syntactic concerns.

I also want to underscore two other points about writing. The first, that eluded Chevannes (2005), is that the mechanical and syntactic confusion suggests the final year student writer could have been experiencing the significant challenge of writing to conform to the disciplinary discourse – a discourse that has remained *new* even though the student is in the final year, because content coverage often takes precedence over discipline-specific writing instruction in content courses. What other content faculty and even some writing specialists often miss or ignore is the learning that is represented in writing – a situation that often arises when academics forget that writing is never fixed but is instead continuously being learned and relearned as students learn more complex forms of knowledge, as indicated in the earlier quotation from S. Miller (1989). As she says, "'missing' verb endings . . . do not demonstrate a writer's hopeless stupidity. Rather, they invite us to look carefully at the relation of the individual to the overwhelming and inescapable grammars constituting the civilized structures of language that we have made dominant" (167). Additionally, students' ignorance of conventions often reveals, as S. Miller suggests, "how arbitrary those conventions are" and the extent to which we aim to "elevate the only, the correct, ways to write" (169). In the Jamaican context, it is unfortunately not only the arbitrary conventions that are elevated but also those who master such conventions, with correspondent stigmatization of other Creole-influenced writers.

The second point is Chevannes's (2005) statement that the students will be seen as *graduates of the university* and not of their high school. And as becomes evident in a book chapter by Don Robotham (2000), former pro-vice chancellor with responsibility for graduate studies at the UWI, the university can be equated to the faculty from which the student graduates. Writing about five years earlier than Chevannes, Robotham addresses the difficulty of simultaneously increasing tertiary enrolment ratios and enhancing quality. In "Changing a University: Reconciling Quantity with Quality – The Case of the University of the West Indies", Robotham observes that the university has been exceeding targets set for increased enrolment. He mentions "the Faculty of Social Sciences, Mona, for example, surpassing its enrolment target for the year 2000 from as early as 1993" (238). In his view, this rapid increase foregrounds the "problem of the *quality* of . . . graduates and the extent to which the UWI educational experience is fostering those qualities in . . . students that fulfil the needs of the community and the individual, broadly conceived" (238; emphasis in the original). Robotham is here questioning the standards of performance of UWI graduates – from Chevannes's (2005) faculty.

Robotham's chapter also demonstrates how when critics express concerns about quality, they often invoke English, communication, and, by extension, writing, and associate writing skills with differences in the modes of thinking needed at work. "On paper," says Robotham, "there is little hard evidence of deteriorating standards" (2000, 238). After all, increasing percentages of students are receiving first and upper second degrees, and those graduates are being admitted in prestigious overseas universities and excelling there. However, concerns about quality arise because employers often complain that graduates are "not sufficiently practical; that they are opinionated and have false expectations; that their command of the English language and other communication skills leave a lot to be desired; that they lack vision and leadership qualities" (239). Robotham admits that some of those complaints are contradictory, but feels they should not be ignored, especially since supporting them are the "whispered reservations of faculty colleagues about . . . the serious deficiencies in English" (239).

Robotham (2000) is careful to make connections with other countries, noting that the United States and United Kingdom have had to address "the quantity/quality dilemma", but have found ways to categorize institutions or, especially in the case of the United States, controversially pass on undergraduate teaching to graduate students in large research universities. He emphasizes how the developing world with fewer institutions is different: "We have to be all things to all persons, with the same institution required to excel at undergraduate and graduate education, teaching and research, elite and mass higher education: in a word – quantity and quality" (240). However, to address the dilemma in Jamaica, Robotham, like Chevannes (2005), propagates a myth about the academy. Robotham (2000, 245–46) proposes that "if we are to resolve the quantity/quality dilemma, then it is fairly clear that we must . . . identify clearly the institutions from which our students come. Having done so, we must . . . work with the other institutions to steadily raise the quality of their educational processes over a definite period of time." He cites data – admittedly flawed, based on the form designed for applicants – that demonstrates that most students admitted to the UWI in 1995–96 were not from the high schools, but rather the community colleges, teacher training colleges, and evening institutes in Kingston. This same point is also made in the Faculty of Arts and General Studies, Cave Hill's (1987) "Report on Faculty Review 1986/87". Much of what is said in this report about the Cave Hill campus in Barbados is also true for Mona. This report mentions that more than three-quarters of the incoming students did not have "genuine 'A' level qualifications" (2), and this number has been increasing steadily. As well, many new students were not coming directly from secondary schools, and more and more faculty members felt that the university was "not receiving the best products" from these schools (2). Robotham (2000, 246) calls for a "coherent programme" to improve quality in preuniversity institutions. Based on his suggestions for change, Robotham feels "it will be possible to ensure that the level of the 'average' student *entering* any tertiary level system, over time, will be raised *prior* to entering" (248; emphasis in the original). In his view, it is only then that standards can be maintained and enhanced simultaneous with expansions in enrolment.

Robotham (2000), like Chevannes (2005), suggests that as long as more is done for students *preuniversity*, excellence can be guaranteed in higher education. I am proposing, however, that their statements should be considered in light of the following recommendations from the Faculty of Arts and General Studies at Cave Hill:

> Clearly the situation is circular. We accept weak students; we turn out poor graduates; and we receive in turn weak students taught by our poor graduates. One consequence is that the UWI degree is devalued in the eyes of the public. . . . But, *the more important point* is an internal one. *Do we fully acknowledge the existence of the problem, and do we persistently search for solutions to it?* It is our effort in this area which will determine whether we are serious about the maintenance of acceptable standards. *We cannot sit back and blame the other levels of the educational system for the existence of the problem; all that does is to perpetuate the problem.* (1987, 7; emphasis added)

It appears that administrators and faculty have largely ignored these recommendations and persisted in locating the writing problem elsewhere – in tandem with perpetuating the myth of transience and promoting the rhetoric of transparent disciplinarity that I explain next.

Indeed, critics' disparaging comments about student writing at the postsecondary level in Jamaica have not only led to alarmist rhetoric in the media and in academe but also often served to obscure issues deserving to be addressed regarding students' writing development. By emphasizing errors in student writing, especially those quantifiable errors related to grammar and mechanics, these critics have effectively elicited a feeling of crisis in student writing without conscientiously addressing the historical dimension of the problem, including the traditional emphasis on summative (evaluative) rather than formative (developmental) writing, attitudes to writing and its instruction, and responsibility for writing development throughout the education system in Jamaica. What has emerged then is a tradition of acrimonious references to student writing and the belief that writing problems belong elsewhere and will disappear from the academy as soon as individuals in preuniversity settings make appropriate changes, or as soon as students get an "English Fix" (Virtue 2013) in one university course.

Misconception 1: The Myth of Transience

Rose (1985) describes the myth that I detect various journalists, Chevannes (2005), Robotham (2000) and others propagate. Rose uses the term "myth of transience" in reference to the way in which administrators and some faculty – including those who teach writing – often perceive writing problems as belonging "elsewhere" rather than in the university. Although Rose's focus is the language used when writing is discussed in institutions in America, his ideas can be usefully applied to the Jamaican and other Creole-influenced situations. In defining the myth of transience, Rose notes, "Despite the accretion of crisis reports, the belief persists in the . . . university that if we can just do *x* or *y*, the problem will be solved – in five years, ten years, or a generation – and higher education will be able to return to its real work" (355). This myth emerges in journalists' recommendations to spend more at lower educational levels in Jamaica in order to spend less on English courses in the university and in Chevannes's suggestion that emphasis be placed on secondary-level preparation for a few years, so that the university will not have to address language, specifically writing, deficiencies. As Rose observes, this myth "blinds faculty members to historical reality and to the dynamic and fluid nature of the educational system that employs them" (356). In other words, because the myth of transience "assures its believers that the . . . source of the problem is elsewhere" (ibid.), faculty often consider the problem as temporary, without recognizing that it endures over generations. The "powerful liability" that accompanies the myth of transience and which Rose observes in the American context is, therefore, true for Jamaica: "Each generation of academicians facing the characteristic . . . shifts in demographics and accessibility sees the problem anew, laments it in the terms of the era, and optimistically notes its impermanence. *No one seems to say that this scenario has gone on for so long that it might not be temporary*" (355; emphasis added). As subsequent chapters will establish, each decade brings a new wave of complaints about student writing in Jamaican higher education. Suffice it to say here that among the complaints about student writing is identification of quantifiable errors of the kind that Chevannes (2005) names and journalists often highlight. However, there is usually more involved than the errors that are noted.

Rose (1985, 344–45) proposes that discussions of error need to include "the social context of error, or of its cognitive-developmental meaning – that is, [an] interpretation of its significance in the growth of the writer". He points to questionable assumptions that "good writing is correct writing, and that correctness has to do with pronoun choice, verb forms, and the like" (345). As indicated in the second epigraph, critics detract attention from the ways in which writing simultaneously aids and reflects learning when they focus on quantifiable errors rather than consider how writers negotiate unfamiliar discourse conventions in their attempts to appropriate them (346). However, Mina Shaughnessy's (1977, 11) work confirms "the intelligence of [students'] mistakes"; that is, as Rose (1985, 357) says, "even the most error-ridden prose arises from the confrontation of inexperienced student writers with the complex linguistic and rhetorical expectations of the academy". Indeed, if faculty reflect on personal writing challenges or adopt a posture of willingness to examine and learn from students' writing, faculty may become self-consciously aware of the situational constraints writers negotiate while working with a discipline's unfamiliar codified conventions.

The myth of transience also "plays itself out against complex social-political dynamics" (Rose 1985, 356), with each higher education institution forever struggling to define its curriculum to distinguish it from the secondary schools'. Institutions of higher education simultaneously attempt to "influence, even determine", the secondary schools' curriculum to "shape it to the[ir] needs" (357). One factor that is often ignored in these struggles is that preparing students for higher education is but *one* of the secondary school's multiple purposes. Required modifications in the university's curriculum (to include writing instruction in all courses) or in institutional purpose (to see writing instruction and development as central concerns) may unfortunately not be considered because of the misconception about the temporary nature of the problem. Therefore, journalists and academics in Jamaica often recommend that secondary schools and other preuniversity institutions prepare students to write effectively in disciplines at university.

Journalists' and academics' recommendation that preuniversity institutions prepare students to write in the university appears to be indisputable, especially in light of a secondary system that has been considered substandard since its beginnings (Parker 1978, 137) – and not merely "declining" as Chevannes (2005, 297) says – and is plagued by weaknesses that require attention. However, policymakers must realize that when written literacy is considered, there needs to be recognition of what academic writing means and what its development requires. More is at stake than mere preuniversity preparation or remedial education at the tertiary level. As well, a recommendation to do more at the secondary level requires some reflection, especially when writing instruction is concerned. After all, students in Jamaica already write a great deal at the secondary level: written examinations are preponderant; some students in the sixth form begin to specialize and could be said to begin to write in specific disciplines before entering the university where they are immediately admitted into a specific faculty; and there is the well-established writing course (general paper) that is still offered in some schools along with the Caribbean Advanced Proficiency Examination (CAPE) Communication Studies that was developed to achieve more relevance to the Caribbean situation than did the general paper examination that is set and graded in England. The unspoken assumption that these writing-intensive subjects and examinations prepared students to write at university is one of the factors that led to neglect of considerations of writing instruction and development in the early years of higher education in the United Kingdom (see Ivanĭc and Lea 2006) and, therefore, in Jamaica.

The Rhetoric of Transparent Disciplinarity or the Myth of the Transparency of Language in All Disciplines

In addition to unintentionally perpetuating the myth of transience, academics and public figures tend to make comments that are redolent of a view of writing as transparent recording – so mechanical, intrinsic, gradually acquired, and plain to content faculty that the latter do not recognize that students may require explicit introduction to disciplinary writing conventions. As UK writing researcher Theresa Lillis says, this view of writing "assumes *transparency* in relation to language and *transmission* in relation to pedagogy" (2006, 32; emphasis in the original). In other words, language is believed to function as a transparent medium, reflecting meaning and knowledge that is accurately verbalized rather than appropriately mediated; and students are believed to learn to produce academic writing in any discipline merely by *hearing* about "the most visible aspects of writing" (ibid.) in some general writing course before entering their discipline. What I call "the rhetoric of transparent disciplinarity" becomes evident as Russell (2002) identifies various views of language and writing that militated against establishing a full WAC programme in US institutions of higher education after more than a century of the introduction of writing instruction in US colleges.

Russell (2002, 9–10) highlights four conflicts related to the nature and acquisition of writing that are useful heuristics for an analysis of the way in which academic writing has been understood and taught at the UWI at Mona. These are

1. academic writing as transparent recording as opposed to visible rhetoric – "writing as a single elementary skill, a transparent recording of speech or thought or physical reality, versus writing as a complex rhetorical activity, embedded in the differentiated practices of academic discourse communities",
2. academic writing instruction as remediation or development – "writing acquisition as remediation of deficiencies in skill versus writing acquisition as a continuously developing intellectual and social attainment tied to disciplinary learning",
3. academic discourse as involving a community or several communities – "academia as single discourse community versus academia as many competing discourse communities", and

4. the goals of writing instruction being excellence or equity – "disciplinary excellence versus social equity as the goal of writing instruction".

The first element in each set reflects a misconception that feeds the myth of the transparency of language while the second element contributes to the view of academic writing as visible rhetoric in the plural academy where writing instruction is for development and social equity. As well, the first element of each of these conflicts reflects what in the recent UK writing tradition are study skills and academic socialization/acculturation approaches to writing, whereas the second element embodies the academic literacies approach that views knowledge as mediated through language and writing as situated rather than being a transparent medium. The study skills approach signifies a view of writing as a set of skills that are learned at an early age and that are easily transferred to varying writing contexts. This view also suggests that any instruction in writing reflects a need for remediation rather than indicates development. The academic socialization model suggests that writing is embedded within disciplinary or professional learning, so that students learn to write at the same time that they are learning disciplinary content. Based on the assumption that students do not need explicit instruction in a disciplinary course or a general writing course, this model renders writing invisible to faculty, students and administrators. Advocates of the academic literacies approach do not embrace the views of the other two orientations. This approach emphasizes the variability, continued development, and centrality of writing in academic disciplines. Therefore, instead of promoting writing as a single, generalizable skill or set of skills or as an unteachable aspect of successful entry into and development in a discipline, the academic literacies approach highlights differences in knowledge creation and writing practices in differing discourse domains (see Jones, Turner and Street 1999a; Lea and Street 1998). As I continue to explicate the conflicts that Russell (2002) addresses, I draw on other UK discussions of the discourse of transparency, where appropriate.[2] The group of first elements constitutes the rhetoric of transparent disciplinarity: academic writing as transparent recording; writing instruction serves the purpose of remediation; the academy is a single discourse community; and the goal of academic writing instruction is (only) disciplinary excellence.

Misconception 2: Academic Writing as Transparent Recording

Russell (2002) asserts that faculty may either consider writing as a neutral transparent medium for accurately and objectively recording ideas or acknowledge that writing is intricately linked to disciplinary writing practices that turn on the writer's desire to influence through persuasive writing. In other words, faculty may see writing as transparent recording or as visible rhetoric. In addressing the tension between these conflicting views, Russell reminds readers of the "old oral conception of writing as transcription" that turns on "blindness to the rhetorical nature of academic writing" (10). Before the 1870s, Russell recalls, "writing was ancillary to speaking" and there was, therefore, "little need for systematic writing instruction" (3). This means that "formal writing instruction essentially amounted to training in handwriting, the mechanical process of transcribing sound to visual form. Literacy meant knowing one's ABCs. Once these orthographic conventions were mastered, 'correct' writing was an ordinary outcome of being raised a gentleman or gentlewoman who spoke 'correct' English, which is to say the language of the upper class" (4). However, as academe changed, as professionals increased in a new print age, and as education was separated into subsystems/levels, writing's role changed. As Russell observes, "writing was no longer a single, generalizable skill learned once and for all at an early age; rather it was a complex and continuously developing response to specialized text-based discourse communities, highly embedded in the differentiated practices of those communities" (5). Despite such changes, there was a general understanding in the system that writing was "a way to examine students, not to teach them, . . . a means of demonstrating knowledge rather than of acquiring it" (6). Because writing was used for evaluative and not pedagogical purposes, when students did write, they were often responding to examination questions, and writing and learning of content were kept separate (7).

Coupled with the epistemological contradiction that writing is a single mechanical skill is a long tradition of deploring student writing and futile attempts to find a comprehensive solution. As Russell (2002, 6) writes, "Because academics and other professionals assumed that writing was a generalizable skill and that academia held a universal, immutable standard of literacy, they were constantly disappointed when student writing failed to measure up to the local, and largely tacit, standards of a particular social class, institution, discipline, or profession by which they were in fact judging that writing." Since academics considered writing as a mechanical transferable skill, they applied a deficit model to students' writing. Since, based on this model, weaknesses in writing meant that the student was lacking in basic skills, educators always sought "a single solution to a specific educational problem" (7). And they often felt that the solution lay in preuniversity institutions or situations. In other words, educators considered good writing to be "generalized, transparent – a matter of prior instruction, aptitude, intelligence, or dedication rather than of conscious, discipline-specific teaching" (28). Educators clung to and perpetuated what Rose (1985) describes as the myth of transience when they located the fault elsewhere when students failed to write by the discipline's standards. Russell (2002) notes that S. Miller's research into classical rhetoric reveals, as she writes, that academics "still in many ways long for [the oral] curriculum" (1989, 65) when they talk about what should be learned prior to higher education. S. Miller asserts, "The idea that 'reading and writing' should be mastered before the main business of education begins is an ironic trace from oral curricula that persisted to the end of the eighteenth century and beyond" (65).

Russell (2002, 10) reminds readers that "the naïve view of language as transparent recorder of thought or physical reality" is tied to the scientific method that flourished in the eighteenth and nineteenth centuries. On account of the "ethics of scientific objectivity", academics hardly acknowledged how persuasion functioned in their scholarly activities and considered their disciplines as "vehicles discovering the bare facts and immutable laws of nature". Additionally, as Russell observes, specialization of knowledge resulted in "powerful institutional barriers to seeing the differentiated and rhetorical nature of academic writing" (11). Because many academics have learned the writing conventions of their discipline over time, they take them for granted, believing writing ability is intrinsic, even forgetting that most of the writing they do involves much thought, complex abilities and persuasion, and is tied to specific contexts whose requirements students will need to be taught. These misconceptions abound because, as Rose (1985, 348) notes, "to view writing as a skill in the university context reduces the possibility of perceiving it as a complex ability that is continually developing as one engages in new tasks with new materials for new audiences".

UK writing researchers Theresa Lillis and Joan Turner help to explicate what Russell (2002, 11) calls the "ethics of scientific objectivity". In "Student Writing in Higher Education: Contemporary Confusion, Traditional Concerns", Lillis and Turner (2001) focus on "the discourse of transparency in evaluation". They point out that in the discourse of transparency, "language is treated as ideally transparent and autonomous" (58), and writing as "a self-evidently transparent medium and, therefore, non-problematic" (62). They argue that the view of "language as a transparent conduit" (66) informs the academic discourse of scientific rationality which became institutionally embedded in the seventeenth and eighteenth centuries and prevails today in attitudes to writing in the academy even though we are living in different social circumstances and in an era that promotes different epistemological assumptions than universality and essentialism that were prevalent then.

Lillis and Turner (2001) remind readers that the roots of the discourse of transparency are in Lockean empiricism and Cartesian rationalism, specifically in the conduit model of language. This model of language is illustrated in Locke's *Essay Concerning Humane Understanding*: "For Language being the great Conduit, whereby Men convey their discoveries, Reasonings and Knowledge, from one to another, he that makes an ill use of it, though he does not corrupt the Fountains of Knowledge, which are in Things themselves; yet he does, as much as in him lies, break or stop the Pipes, whereby it is distributed to the publick use and advantage of Mankind" ([1689] 1695, 290). In the conduit model, meaning/knowledge is separated from language, with language functioning only to convey discoveries clearly and correctly, and emphasis being on avoiding error and stating only what is true. As Lillis and Turner argue, seventeenth-century emphasis on rigour in science and correctness in the language transmitting thought and knowledge is still deeply embedded in Western academic culture. These notions have led to the creation of "an ideology of clarity for the inter-relationship between language and thought" and this ideology "continues to fuel the discourse of transparency" (2001, 63). This ideology of clarity drives faculty's expectations of student writing as well as faculty's assumptions that their metalanguage on student writing is easily accessible. The operations of the discourse of transparency therefore emerge as "double-edged" (ibid.).

This transparency model of language often leads teachers to assume that the terms and guidelines used in evaluation – in questions to which students should respond and in teacher comments on student writing – are "transparently meaningful" (Lillis and Turner 2001, 58) when in fact the meanings are highly situated, meaning different things in different contexts. In their research, Lillis and Turner have found that whereas students are usually trying to determine the "particular configuration of conventions" in which they are to write, tutors often take it for granted that students know what these conventions are and deny the situatedness of the meanings of such terminology as *"write an introduction", "cite authorities", "avoid plagiarism", "faulty grammar", "faulty punctuation", "argument", "structure",* and *"define key term"*, or such wordings as *"state clearly, spell it out, be explicit, express your ideas clearly, say exactly what you mean"* (58; emphasis in the original). As other UK writing researchers Mary Lea and Brian Street (1998, 164) observe, teachers often present such conventions as "self-evidently the correct way in which things should be done", when in reality, as Carys Jones, Joan Turner and Brian Street (1999a, xxii) remind, academic writing is "an expression of cultural values and beliefs of epistemological standpoints that often remain hidden".[3] Lillis and Turner observe that students often challenge claims about transparency through their complaints about the quirks of each teacher, but such complaints that each teacher wants something different are often not read as a challenge to this discourse. Instead of acknowledging different epistemic conventions in disciplines and the consequent situatedness of language and meaning, "tutors work within a discourse of transparency which both underplays the importance of language and potentially excludes from successful participation in academic discourse those participants who do not already take the norms of this discourse for granted" (Lillis and Turner 2001, 61–62). It is hardly surprising then, as Lillis (2001, 168) states, that "the routine enactment" of this transparency model of language marginalizes nontraditional students whose confusion and complaints about what conventions mean expose an ideologically inscribed "institutional practice of mystery [which] works against those least familiar with the conventions surrounding academic writing, thus limiting their participation in [higher education] as currently configured" (Lillis 1999, 127).

As Lillis and Turner (2001) explain, the conduit assumption denies the rhetorical ordering of language; that is, it denies the fact that neither are audiences neutral nor is information ever presented neutrally in real contexts. However, studies (such as Bazerman 1988) in the sociology of knowledge demonstrate the influence of language in the construction of knowledge. To counter the conduit assumption, Lillis and Turner (2001) recall Bazerman's discussion of Newton's work. The latter demonstrates a concern for explicating not only the experiment but also the reasoning process involved in conducting and relaying the experiment. Drawing on Newton's attention to language because of the need to persuade his readers, Lillis and Turner (2001, 65) argue that "rhetorical organisation is highly significant, but also . . . socioculturally situated and, hence, subject to change". In other words, the sociocultural norms to which Newton subscribed were peculiar to his era: "They privileged, in linguistic form, the values of the time which included a desire for universality, for certainty, and for rational and epistemic clarity." Although academics today – in the postmodern world – question the values of universality and essentialism, "their rhetorical norms have become so ideologically powerful, in the wake of the cultural prestige accruing to enlightenment science, that they are embedded, yet invisible, within higher education practices" (ibid.). As Lillis and Turner emphasize, the discourse of transparency is preserved – unfortunately – because of this invisibility of the cultural history and rhetorical nature of the values of universality and essentialism.

Misconception 3: Academic Writing Instruction as Remediation

When faculty consider writing as either transparent recording or visible rhetoric, they hold a corresponding view of writing instruction as either remediation or development. In distinguishing between writing instruction for remediation and for development, Russell asserts that "modern mass education carried over a premodern view of writing as a single, generalizable skill, learned once and forever. Students whose writing did not conform to a particular community's standards were thought to exhibit some deficit, which had to be remedied *before* they could be admitted to the community" (2002, 15; emphasis in the original). In this deficit model, basic skills are, as Roz Ivanič and Mary Lea (2006, 12) say, "conceptualised as decontextualised", with content faculty believing that once students learn these skills they can be transferred to other contexts. This model ignores writing's relation to knowledge making in academia, for it virtually equates learning to write with learning to ride a bicycle, rather than promotes it as the nonhierarchical, recursive process that it is (see NCTE 2007, 2). However, if faculty recognize that writing is not a single, generalizable, elementary skill, but is instead a complex ability whose development is ongoing and which is tied to disciplinary practices, they may understand instruction in writing as developmental – that is, writing instruction as "a process of socialization or acculturation, analogous to a young child learning to speak" (Russell 2002, 15).

Such reconceptions of instruction in writing become clear in Russell's (2002) use of Vygotsky's theory of first-language acquisition. Russell uses Vygotsky's theory to "illuminate the process of acquiring advanced literacy in an academic or professional community" (15) that can be understood as a language community in which members grow up over time. In "linguistic initiation", initiates observe and model experts, often receiving feedback in a process that "requires the neophyte to use the language of the community *while* participating in its activity not *before* participating, as the remedial view would have it" (16; emphasis in the original). The student gradually develops what Vygotsky calls "an internal language", that functions to guide the student's thought and actions, which increasingly resemble those of an experienced member of the discourse community. US WAC advocate Mark Waldo (1996, 7) reports the negative but exact description of experts as "automatons": in each discipline, which can be read as a language community, experts have gradually assimilated the discipline's language which eventually – almost unconsciously – directs their reception and construction of oral and written texts. Russell (1995, 70) also observes that over time "these conscious actions become automatic and unconscious" to the extent that experts believe they are "'natural', although they only seem natural" (70). The result is that "writing tends to become transparent, automatic, and beneath the level of conscious activity for those who are thoroughly socialized into it" (ibid.), and newcomers are expected to fall in line.

This theory of writing acquisition reveals, as Russell (2002) proposes, how the process of learning to write *seems* transparent or unconscious because of the gradual nature of newcomers' *active, participatory* learning. Accordingly, a discipline's scholars and researchers "come to view the particular genres that the disciplinary community has evolved (and each member has internalized) not as rhetorical strategies, conventional – but gradually changing – means of persuasion; instead, the community's genres and conventions appear to be unproblematic renderings of the fruits of research" (Russell 2002, 16–17). Researchers in the area of student academic writing in the United Kingdom refer to faculty's apparently tacit knowledge of disciplinary conventions as "academic 'common sense'" – the feeling that all conventions and writing requirements are transparent and unproblematic (see Coffin et al. 2003; Jones, Turner and Street 1999a, 1999b; Lillis 1999; Lillis and Turner 2001). These researchers dispute that assumption by demonstrating that although in subjects requiring a formal laboratory report "the overt rhetorical purpose is to recount research experiments and results", there usually is a "more hidden purpose ... to persuade the reader of the viability of the report or claims" (Coffin and Hewings 2003, 51). Like Lillis and Turner (2001), Russell (2002, 17) draws on Bazerman's (1988) research to show that, indeed, persuasion infuses all academic disciplines; and that the tacit knowledge and conventions that are so deeply embedded in each discipline that members acquire through subtle learning ought to be seen as elements requiring explicit instruction, especially to previously excluded groups of students (see also Curry and Lillis 2003).

The UK researchers and Russell's (2002) work confirm that since each academic discipline has its unique topics, vocabulary, values, concepts, processes of inquiry, and forms of writing, students need explicit instruction in each if they are to become successful writers who can "go native" (Kuhn 1970, 204) in the discipline's language. However, because faculty have often not articulated their discipline's conventions and values and how they are acquired, they have often associated writing instruction with remediation – a task to be completed in a general writing course. Such attitudes have served to marginalize writing instruction and the discipline of writing. As Russell (2002, 17) asserts, the "transparency of rhetoric in the academic disciplines also helps explain why writing instruction has so often been marginalized". If academics do not have a conscious awareness of their discipline's rhetorical conventions, they are likely to feel that a general first-year writing course or preuniversity preparation is equivalent to discipline-specific writing instruction. They, therefore, marginalize writing by expecting the general writing course to instruct students in general skills that students should then generalize to all disciplines or by expecting preuniversity preparation to enable students to write *within* the discipline. Consequently, academics tend to reinforce the myths of transience and transparency by "mistak[ing] the inevitable struggles of students to acquire the rhetorical conventions of a discipline for poor writing or sheer ignorance" (Russell 2002, 18). Instead of gradually assisting students in appropriating the strategies of a new discourse community, faculty may encourage students to attend to – what faculty consider remedial – instruction in general writing courses.

What happens is, as educator Michael Carter (2007, 386) writes, the "conception of the disciplines as domains of specialized knowledge, reinforced by the assumption that a writing course outside the disciplines could somehow improve students' writing in the disciplines, has led . . . to a specialized conception of disciplinary knowledge combined with a generalized conception of writing". Content faculty consider their "disciplines as domains of specialized knowledge and writing as general across disciplines" (408). In explaining this misconception, Carter juxtaposes knowledge and knowing – disciplines as "repositories of knowledge" (declarative/ conceptual knowledge) and disciplines as "active ways of knowing" (procedural/ process knowledge). Carter argues that "because the organizing principle of knowledge in the disciplines is typically perceived as conceptual knowledge, faculty and students tend to understand learning in a discipline as a process of obtaining, at least in short-term memory, the particular knowledge base of the discipline". As well, because faculty consider writing to be "universally generalizable", they do not "conceptualize writing in the disciplines in a way that is grounded in the disciplines themselves" (387). In fact, this view is linked to content faculty's perception of their discipline as "domains of declarative knowledge" rather than also "ways of doing" (388) that are often expressed in and through writing. As Carter observes, the "relationship among knowing, doing, and writing is concealed by the disciplinary focus on conceptual knowledge" (389). Because of this emphasis on content, content faculty also fail to articulate the ways in which "writing gives shape to the ways of knowing and doing in a discipline" (391). Like other researchers, Carter uses the lab report to demonstrate that faculty should "see that their responsibility for teaching the ways of knowing and doing in their disciplines also extends to writing, which is not separate from but essential to their disciplines" (408). His work, like Russell's (2002), which he draws on, illustrates the point that disciplines and disciplinary knowledge are socially constructed through writing, but faculty do not usually/ always admit this to students or help students appreciate how writing does the work of disciplines.

Even when content faculty seem to acknowledge their responsibility in teaching disciplinary writing and design programmes geared to initiating students into the strategies needed to understand and navigate the discipline's codified conventions, such programmes seem limited. Russell (2002) acknowledges that despite their general tendency to marginalize writing instruction by implying that writing programmes/departments can provide all the instruction that students need, content faculty sometimes develop research methods courses for graduate students to become familiar with discipline-specific writing conventions. However, because these are *graduate* courses, only a small percentage of students in an institution benefit from them. This limited reach is evident in the writing course for graduate students that Chevannes (2005) mentions. With that course taught by faculty from the Department of Language, Linguistics and Philosophy, a message is conveyed – albeit inadvertently: as Russell says of graduate education in the United States, "others had failed to teach students to write; others must solve the problem" (246). The recently approved faculty-specific[4] writing courses at Mona may also convey the same message – that others are to handle the problem of *writing in faculties* to prepare students to write *within* disciplines. Faculty may also claim, as Russell acknowledges, that many students have learned to write even without deliberate instruction. However, a compelling counterargument is Russell's assertion that such learning has occurred "perhaps less consciously or less rapidly or less effectively than with direct instruction" (19). Sadly, the common occurrence is that, instead of faculty's taking the time to identify their discipline's rhetorical strategies in order to be able to teach them, faculty often complain about problems in student writing and transfer the responsibility to other individuals and institutions whose worth and work may be undervalued, simultaneous with the unacknowledged importance of writing to the existence, acquisition, investigation, creation and communication of disciplinary knowledge.

Misconception 4: Academia as Single Discourse Community

Faculty's transference of the responsibility for writing development to first-year general writing courses or preuniversity institutions is often an extension of the misconception that the academy is a single discourse community and, therefore, there is a unified or universal academic discourse that can be taught. In addressing this misconception, Russell (2002, 20) recalls the beginnings of higher education in the United States – before the modern university – when education was unified and students were selected primarily based on social class, which "guaranteed linguistic homogeneity". However, by the early twentieth century, faculties reorganized along disciplinary departmental lines, and broadening access destroyed linguistic homogeneity. Additionally, increasing specialization meant that the university was "an aggregate of competing discourse communities; it was not a single community" (22). Russell rightly concludes that "to speak of the academic community as if its members shared a single set of linguistic conventions and traditions of inquiry is to make a categorical mistake" (ibid.). This is so because although teaching, research and service may unite disparate disciplines in a common mission, disciplines differ markedly in terms of epistemic conventions, including their nature of inquiry and strategies for documenting knowledge. Academic literacies research in the United Kingdom has been highlighting the complex codes and conventions which faculty in specific disciplines take for granted because faculty mistakenly assume such codes and conventions are universal or transparent, but with which students must become familiar, especially when they take modular courses that cross-disciplinary boundaries (see Ivanīc and Lea 2006; Jones, Turner and Street 1999b; Lea and Street 1998; Lillis 1999, 2001; Lillis and Turner 2001).

Therefore, when faculty promote "a single advanced literacy" (Russell 2002, 24) in academia, they abdicate the responsibility to explain their distinctive discipline-specific conventions, and to consider how they differ from other disciplines' conventions or from language use in the wider society. Russell observes that because "faculty rarely asked their students to struggle with the complexities of entering a specific discourse community through writing, they could more easily maintain the illusion that the university was still one discourse community, that such terms as *reason, the generally educated person,* or *the humanities* referred to single, unitary concepts" (ibid.; emphasis in the original). Consistent with that illusion, first-year general writing or preuniversity courses and their facilitators and content faculty do not always indicate the extent to which the university and the meaning of such terms are as diverse and independent as there are disciplines. What often gets ignored is situatedness or "contextual variability", a concept that Elaine Maimon (2002, x) defines as "recognition that meaning changes as the stance of the reader and writer change from situation to situation".

Misconception 5: Academic Writing Instruction for Disciplinary Excellence

Consistent with faculty's promotion of a "a single advanced literacy" based on their misconception of disciplinary knowledge as specialized and writing as generalized are their efforts to restrict access to their discipline rather than expand it. Drawing on the work of Burton Clarke (1983), Russell (2002, 26) argues that appropriately initiating neophytes into disciplinary discourses has been "marginalized by another fundamental conflict in academia" – "the competing claims of 'equity' and 'excellence' . . . or, more broadly, of inclusion and exclusion". Like Chevannes (2005), Robotham (2000) and others, Russell acknowledges that virtually every society has had to reckon with previously excluded social groups who demand equity in education. However, Russell emphasizes that when such groups succeed in gaining access to educational systems, they usually encounter efforts to "value exclusionary standards of excellence over equity" (26). Russell rightly observes that writing instruction is implicated in this conflict. However, as he asserts, writing is often used as a tool to exclude the undesired and maintain standards:

> To teach students the discourse of a professional elite is often a crucial part of initiating them into the profession; to exclude them from such discourse is to make that initiation more difficult, if not impossible. By relegating systematic writing instruction to the margins of academic work, outside the specific disciplinary contexts where students are taught to enter coveted professional roles, institutions preserve standards of excellence and reduce social equity. (26–27)

When faculty marginalize writing instruction by transferring the responsibility from those most familiar with disciplinary discourse, they restrict access to the discipline. Unfortunately, restricting access is sometimes explained as a way to maintain or raise a discipline's status in the academy, where disciplines often compete for recognition of their excellence in research.

Another educator and historian of rhetoric and English Studies, Thomas Miller (1997), sheds light on the dialectical relationship between access and excellence in his critique of instruction in Oxbridge-type English institutions that encouraged learning through rote repetition. T. Miller rightly asserts that "when a culture is tacitly transmitted rather than formally taught, the cultural capital of the educated is preserved in several ways", one of which is that conventions that are not discussed are "not raised to the level of conscious examination where they can be called into question" (66). Discouraging challenge to conventions serves in such situations to maintain the status quo and remind students that they are of the wrong class. In Freirian terms, what is maintained is formalism over critical reflection. If facilitators can keep students' focus on grammar and mechanics, for example, then students remain enshrined in rules that they cannot get past and which confirm their status. This posture is consistent with Paulo Freire's description of the banking concept of education which "anaesthetizes and inhibits creative power" for it "attempts to maintain the *submersion* of consciousness" (1972, 54; emphasis in the original). The better approach, "problem-posing education", which is meant to yield tangible development, "involves a constant unveiling of reality" to facilitate "*emergence* of consciousness and *critical intervention* in reality" (ibid., emphasis in the original).

In order to avoid being accused of restricting access, administrators may engage in pseudo-egalitarianism. Russell (2002, 27) shows how the American system has been able to accommodate the duality of equity and excellence by "institutionalizing ambiguity in many ways through its approach to writing and its teaching". He explains that designated general composition courses have in one sense been a means of widening access by helping to *prepare* "successive waves of previously excluded students" for college writing. However, he continues, "to the extent that those courses were treated as remedial or purgatorial, they also performed a 'gatekeeping' function by keeping students on the margins of the institution" (ibid.). The UWI English proficiency test and its associated course are analogues of such US manifestations. In both the American and Jamaican contexts, general writing courses stem from and perpetuate the myth of transience and the view that disciplinary writing is transparent. As Russell notes of the United States, in the face of general writing courses, "disciplines were free to set rhetorically based standards tacitly. At the same time they could deny (or leave unexamined) the rhetorical nature of their work and thus the responsibility to articulate or systematically teach their discourse" (30). In tandem with disciplines' denied or unexamined rhetoricality and freedom from articulating or teaching their rhetoric is the emergence of the myth of transience as "adaptive, for it helps to mediate within the institution the deep value conflicts between equity and excellence, but it does so at the expense of a genuine examination of the ways that writing influences higher learning" (ibid.).

I believe in enabling students, once they have matriculated or qualified, to access higher education. However, I also believe that if they are going to enter and succeed in the various disciplines and help those disciplines maintain standards of excellence, the experts will have to participate in appropriately initiating the newcomers as required, especially if the newcomers are first-generation – and Creole-influenced – university students. It is my view that if content faculty systematically study their ways of doing, knowing, and writing and make those visible to students, a country such as Jamaica can achieve "greater social equity – helping those individuals and groups who have not been able to enter certain powerful activity systems to enter them and change them for the better" (Russell 1995, 69). In this way, an egalitarian attitude which promotes opportunities for all to succeed would serve Jamaica better than the traditional elitist approach that has served those most likely to succeed without writing instruction within disciplines because they are from privileged backgrounds or are accustomed to succeeding despite odds.

Historicizing the Myths to be Transcended

Based on my analysis of archival materials and data gathered from questionnaires and interviews with past and current writing specialists, the transparency paradigm has been evident at the UWI at Mona since the institution's earliest years.[5] Evident in statements and actions of academics and administrators at Mona is perpetuation of a certain tacit assumption that writing is a natural process. Academics at Mona have not consistently articulated their knowledge of disciplinary writing strategies. By recalling Jamaica's history of education, I demonstrate how this assumption parallels colonial administrators' determination that Jamaican Creole speakers should naturally learn English to advance in society. I propose that, like the early English language policies, this rhetoric needs to be challenged to a greater degree than is being done with recent developments in writing courses. Even though these recent developments indicate administrators and academics' new and more realistic understandings of writing, such developments suggest that stakeholders have not gone far enough in transforming writing instruction to realize fully its potential and place in higher education. I contend that past and current thinking about writing, in its emphasis on English language and on writing based on "an assumed instinct" (Strickland quoted in Education Department 1899, 401), fails to develop a transformative model of academic writing and its instruction that takes as its aim the development of Creole-influenced students in disciplinary writing. I propose that if academics understand or acknowledge the extent to which disciplinary writing constitutes rhetoric and if they make that rhetoric visible, then instruction in writing will be understood as developmental and necessary within the different disciplines of the plural discourse community that the university is. Such instruction will provide equal opportunities for increasing numbers of neophytes to succeed in disciplines without lowering standards therein.

Ultimately, explicit attention to writing strategies will open up disciplinary and cultural codes for analysis, so students may learn to critically reflect on such codes, develop practical understanding of them, and become engaged in knowledge production (rather than reproduction only). Additionally, such attention will shift the emphasis in discussions of and instruction in writing from formalist to rhetorical concerns, demonstrate the interconnectedness of writing and learning within disciplines and outside the academy, ground instruction in the social context and in responsiveness to increasingly diverse student populations, and help critics understand how writing really works. I, therefore, propose that administrators and academics consider a different attitude to writing in the academy – one that departs from conventional yet largely inaccurate models of writing and that may influence attitudes at other educational levels and elsewhere in the society.

The transparency paradigm at the UWI at Mona and my call for an opposing rhetoric of writing are the focus of the remaining chapters. These are organized by decades – with a few overlaps, focusing on writing and its involvement in the university's development, specifically the UWI's response to changing cohorts of students. Convenience explains this arrangement by decades because what I focus on are continuities in academics' and administrators' attitudes to writing, its instruction, and development rather than on chronological differences. In the next chapter, "Developing Local Leaders without Explicit Writing Instruction Prior to Independence, Pre-1960s", I explore attitudes to writing and its instruction in the periods when the focus in higher education was developing local leaders who were believed to write based on "an assumed instinct" (Strickland quoted in Education Department 1899, 401). Prior to the establishment of the UCWI, higher education for Jamaicans was limited to study in England or the United States and to the overseas programmes of the University of London. With the establishment of a regional university, the focus was on developing leaders who could take over administration of the colony from the English. In this period, besides a series of lectures in logic in the 1950s, there was no explicit writing instruction. The matriculation/entry requirements of the UWI's early years reveal views about students' writing development and the kind of writing instruction which applicants were deemed to have received prior to their university career.

However, as cross-cultural education researcher Robin Alexander (2000, 5) says, "no educational policy . . . can be properly understood except by reference to the web of inherited ideas and values, habits and customs, institutions and world views which make one country, or one region, or one group, distinct from another". David Russell and David Foster (2002, 4) also note in a cross-national study of writing that researchers "must look closely at the cultural-historical factors in each nation that shape writing development" if their intention is to use ideas from other nations to inform writing classroom practices, curriculum development and policymaking. Therefore, to locate the roots of the misconceptions about writing in the regional university, I examined Jamaica's intriguing linguistic context and *implicit* language policies that were implemented at preuniversity levels. The chapter, therefore, highlights the historical developments, national language policies and theories of language that obtained in an era when writing was considered an elementary skill that potential local leaders could unconsciously transfer to writing requirements in the university. I argue that the problems that would emerge in students' writing in the academy are blamed on an education system whose problematic origins are yet to be adequately examined and transformed to yield genuine development.

In chapter 3, "Professionalizing the Aspirant Middle Class through Survey Writing after Independence, 1960s to the Mid 1980s", I outline the circumstances that led to the introduction of the "Use of English" survey course at the UWI. I indicate possible connections to the introduction of evening courses and nonresident students – suggesting broadening access – in an institution that was modelled on the elite English university – marked by concerns for excellence. Through rhetorical analysis of university and course documents available from this period, I considered the views of administrators, writing specialists, and other faculty regarding writing instruction. Eric (David) King, a retired "Use of English" lecturer, facilitated triangulation through questionnaire and interview responses. My analysis reveals administrators' understanding that language and writing instruction to professionalize the aspirant middle class was to be through teaching writing as English language and not necessarily as initiation into disciplinary rhetorical conventions. As well, there was the erroneous view that the necessity for discussion of, and explicit instruction in, language and writing meant a need for remediation rather than for consideration of language use beyond basic English in disciplines. I, therefore, propose that because of limited understanding of writing, administrators and many academics promoted the rhetoric of transparent disciplinarity and perpetuated the myth of transience in the 1960s to mid-1980s.

Chapter 4, "Nurturing 'Linguistic Orphans' with Basic Writing in the Post-National Era, Late 1980s to 2004+", addresses how writing instruction evolved from a survey model to reflect "relevance" for the Caribbean context. This evolution involved introduction in 1988 of "Fundamentals of English", a course that served to "nurture" the linguistic orphans created by government language policies applied at other educational levels. Such students were, like those described by Patricia Irvine and Nan Elsasser (1988, 314) in the US Virgin Islands, "expected to deny the existence of their first language and read and write in a second one". If they failed to give up the conventions of their first language, they often failed to meet the minimum writing requirements for commencing their university career.

The chapter demonstrates, however, that Jamaica, like other developing countries, is not untouched by recent global trends. As the new millennium approached, concerns about declining finances were accompanied by increasing concern for certification (as in qualifications on paper) rather than education (as in development of character or mental powers). The result was an unfortunate shift from *nurturing* to *testing*, with the myth of transience yielding increasing marginalization of groups of students who did not display acceptable levels of mastery in written English. I argue that the development of "Fundamentals of English" marked a necessary response to changing cohorts and diverse abilities of students; however, its management – and that of the writing centre – suggests administrators and faculty ignored the country's distinctive social issues and the interconnectedness of writing and learning in the academy and language learning and use in society.

Chapter 5, "Improving the Graduate's Profile via 'Universalist' Writing at the Turn of the Century, 1990s to 2010+", treats developments in the original "Use of

English" course (following the introduction of "Fundamentals of English"), and the introduction of other "standard" first-year writing courses beginning in the 1990s and a pilot WAC project in 2006–2007. I rely on recent curricula and on interviews with and questionnaires completed by writing course coordinators and instructors to determine the focus of academic writing courses towards the end of the twentieth century. I determine that, while exposing students to process writing and preparing them to write for a general university-level educated audience, the courses seemed to perpetuate formalist concerns, especially through emphasis on exposition. By emphasizing exposition and encouraging development in general writing courses outside of disciplines, faculty continued to keep disciplinary writing knowledge tacit and therefore alienated learning from writing in disciplines. I also analyse documents for the WAC pilot project. This analysis reveals academics' deeper understandings of writing than were exhibited in earlier years; however, like the standard courses, the project did not adequately link Creole-influenced students' language and writing development to development within disciplines. Faculty's primary concern seemed to continue to be students' English language competence rather than actual writing development in disciplines. I argue that the assumptions and motivations of these valuable courses and programme needed to be reassessed so that they could promote the crucial link between writing and learning in disciplines and outside the academy.

In the final chapter, "Fashioning Versatile Creole-Influenced Writers through a Transcultural Rhetorical Perspective on Writing Development in the New Millennium, beyond 2010", I summarize the history and development of writing courses at the UWI at Mona and the writing conventions that they sought to transmit and uphold, even while they perpetuated some myths about writing. I also consider the development of faculty-specific courses in the first few years of the new millennium to indicate how they risk perpetuating myths about writing. To counter the misconceptions, I draw on the report of the first quality assurance review of the ELS and emphasize writing's function as more than a mechanical or intrinsic skill and its "rich relationship with inquiry" (Rose 1985, 359). I also suggest ways for academics to make rhetoric more visible in the disciplines and writing more valuable in realizing quantity and quality in higher education and, by extension, contributing to various forms of development. Ultimately, I propose that in an era marked by widening participation in higher education and concerns for maintaining excellence, an institution such as the UWI that caters to Creole-influenced students is likely to benefit from a transcultural rhetorical perspective on writing. This approach involves

1. acknowledging the attributes of transcultural peoples, especially as concerns how Creole-influenced students *do language*.
2. countering the myth of transience and the rhetoric of transparent disciplinarity by making rhetoric more visible in the disciplines; by promoting

writing instruction as developmental; and by highlighting writing as involving multiple context-dependent skills and abilities that are necessary for participation in multiple socially/rhetorically constructed disciplines and for realization of personal, institutional and national development.

This transcultural rhetorical approach to writing development could help writing specialists, other content faculty, and administrators to be involved in moulding versatile Creole-influenced writers who can conform to as well as critically engage with required conventions and in disassociating writing from the discourses of crisis that often emerge in academe and in the media. This perspective intersects with proposals by scholars in rhetoric and composition in the United States for code-meshing and other translingual approaches in the teaching of language, literacy and writing.[6] However, it remains focused on transculturation because a Jamaican sensibility informs my views on language and academic writing instruction.

It seems opportune to analyse how academic writing has been understood and taught at the UWI at Mona, since language, and specifically writing, is being invoked in discussions about the purpose of higher education in the new millennium (see Chevannes 2005; Robotham 2000). Additionally, alarmist rhetoric in 2012 regarding very weak performance of Jamaican secondary-level students in regional English language examinations and continuing alarm because university students struggle in their use of English (Virtue 2013) suggest that there is need for academics, administrators and the public to understand the nature of writing and the ways in which it reflects learning and can improve learning in education. The first epigraph points readers to the importance of writing abilities. However, I believe that more reflection on the nature of writing and its place in the deeply entrenched conflicts in any educational system is required for Creole-influenced learners.

Russell (2002, 32) cautions that in the American tradition "a narrow focus on the history of composition courses may actually reinforce the myth of transience", resulting in a loss of "institutional perspective that would see composition courses as one of many ways students learn (or fail to learn) written discourse of many kinds". That caution has guided my examination, but so too has my awareness that in light of a preponderance of writing for evaluative purposes and the absence of cross-curricular writing instruction, general writing courses represent the major way in which students have been provided explicit instruction in academic writing at the UWI at Mona. For more than four decades, these courses have, as writing administrators and researchers Yvonne Merrill and Thomas Miller (2002, 214) describe US first-year composition courses, "offer[ed] unparalleled support for learning". Still, as Jeanne Gunner (2004, 264) writes in her caution to those who would seek to write histories of writing programme administrators, I have to "take care to resist what might be called Hail and Interpellate narratives: reconstructions that call into official existence" a history of teaching academic writing at the UWI "without also invoking a critique" of that history. It is, therefore, my wish that the history and recommendations in this book will assist academics and administrators to reflect on how Creole-influenced students *do language* and on "the submerged conflicts that underlie . . . attitudes and approaches to advanced literacy" and address these important questions: "what is academic writing and how is it learned? What is an academic community and who should be admitted?" (Russell 2002, 9). The first set of questions is integral to the second, because how academic writing is defined and learned will influence communal development. If students, especially first-generation Creole-influenced university students, are taught the conventions, they can join the community and contribute to its development; if they are not taught, they are kept out. Students can develop various abilities in a general writing course or in a faculty-specific course, but ultimately remain on the periphery of their discipline of interest. The equality implied in the democratization of education in Jamaica requires all faculty's engagement with the conflict between access to or exclusion from disciplines – a conflict made visible in provisions (or lack thereof) for writing development.

Beyond the reflection that I wish the book will engender, I am intent on engagement with the third epigraph, on gaining and revealing "knowledge of history and traditions" to avoid "running in circles while seeking" development. One of the courses mentioned as new in "Bloody English" looks very much like the basic writing course that the institution offered between 1988–1989 and 2004. It is my view that worthwhile reflection should yield appropriate adaptations in attitudes and practices to better meet academic writing goals. The book will *make transparent* curricular practices at the UWI that can be adapted, but I hope that it will also contribute to disassociating advanced written literacy instruction from the intellectual opprobrium and disdain that it is often shown because of outsiders' ignorance of the discipline of writing. Ultimately, my concern is not so much with improving instruction that is offered daily in classes, but rather more with changing attitudes to and erasing misconceptions that abound about writing instruction and its place in the academy. Surely, if appropriate measures follow changed attitudes, the institution is likely to realize improvements in classes and student writing.

While providing the theoretical underpinnings of curricular practices and highlighting the value of the discipline of writing, the book also addresses the absence of a documented history of writing instruction in Jamaican higher education. Although instruction in writing has been offered at the UWI at Mona since the 1960s (and arguably the 1950s), no full-length book addressing the teaching of academic writing in this Creole-influenced context exists. Available materials usually address language and literacy development at the primary and secondary levels. This is the case with Beverley Bryan's *Between Two Grammars: Research and Practice for Language Learning and Teaching in a Creole-Speaking Environment* (2010), which focuses on language learning and teaching in schools in Jamaica and elsewhere in the Caribbean; and Dennis Craig's *Teaching Language and Literacy:*

Policies and Procedures for Vernacular Situations (1999), which addresses similar concerns though including not just the wider Caribbean context but also African American concerns. *Dialects, Englishes, Creoles, and Education*, which is edited by Shondel Nero (2006) and includes two chapters on educating Caribbean students, addresses considerations for educating linguistic minorities in North American and other classrooms. Caroline Dyche has been doing historical examinations of policymaking regarding English language education, but so far the findings have only appeared in articles (Dyche 2006b, 2007b) that I cite. *Academic Writing Instruction for Creole-Influenced Students* will therefore be a ready reference on the history of, and attitudes to, writing instruction in Jamaican higher education. Its usefulness may extend to recently established Jamaican universities whose faculty can learn from the UWI's experience with academic writing instruction.

Additionally, in addressing the UWI at Mona context, this book references scholarship on writing from the United States and United Kingdom and should contribute to the extant cross-cultural research into writing. As Lisa Ganobcsik-Williams (2006, xxiii) writes in her introduction to the collection *Teaching Academic Writing in UK Higher Education*, "the study of university writing is becoming increasingly trans-national and comparative in nature", moving beyond the long-standing exclusive focus on the United States. This development in writing research arises from expansions in higher education. This democratization of education has meant increasing access for previously excluded groups of students. Consonant with these changes in higher education are calls for increasing institutional awareness of the need to address students' writing development – how well students write and how they learn to write in the academy (see for example Foster 2006; Foster and Russell 2002; Jones, Turner and Street 1999a, 1999b; Lea and Stierer 2000; Lillis and Turner 2001). Some concerns arise from increasing numbers of students who seek help with their writing assignments; however, central to these concerns are first-year writing courses. In places where these courses have existed, they have been criticized as functioning to welcome students to the academy while they simultaneously "decontextualize writing by separating it from knowledge-making contexts" (Foster 2006, 1). Where these courses have not existed, some institutions have begun to attend to the needs of students through various kinds of resource centres or discussion about introductory writing instruction orWAC for students. This book addresses how one institution could bridge the divide between these poles that Foster calls "writing as distinct competence" and "writing as situated knowledge-making" (12). It, therefore, seeks to contribute to that international conversation about student writing and writing instruction in higher education. Hopefully, this conversation will serve to foreground the ways writing makes learning visible and is grounded in codified disciplinary conventions, and its ongoing instruction is, therefore, invaluable in teaching and learning in academic disciplines.

Finally, in his treatise on nationalism, Benedict Anderson (2006, 204) writes, "All profound changes in consciousness, by their very nature, bring with them characteristic amnesias. Out of such oblivions, in specific historical circumstances, spring narratives." In this vein, my interpretation is but one narrative of the many historical reconstructions that are possible regarding writing instruction at the UWI. And this narrative is coloured by my own experiences there. I am a proud alumna and faculty member, but I remember being frustrated as an undergraduate with how to write my first English literature essay after I switched from taking mathematics to pursuing a full Humanities major between 1991 and 1994. I did not understand why French literature essays were to be written in English at the university, and not in French as in the sixth form, and lecturers did not explain in class how they were to be written. I remember that much writing in the postgraduate programme at Mona in the mid- to late 1990s required what Victor Villanueva (1993, 71) calls "Professorial Discourse Analysis". This involved going to the library to see what the lecturer had published to "try to discern a pattern to her writing; try to mimic the pattern" (ibid.). This is not to say that graduate supervisors provided no feedback on writing; some supervisors' feedback was abundant, but mainly about content and not about composing. As a tutor in 1998 and then an assistant lecturer in French literature and comparative Caribbean literature from 1999 to 2001, besides when students attended optional consultation sessions, I did not explicitly address *how to* write the required course essays: in the absence of adequate reflective inquiry into teaching, I continued the tradition of assuming that students knew how to write essays based on prior learning in preuniversity settings or in their English Language foundation courses or, at the very least, on intrinsic ability.

I am, therefore, not exempt from some of the criticisms of this tradition. When I started teaching full time in the English Language programme in September 2001, I thought I had got the opportunity to help students to prepare papers in other courses. However, I quickly became concerned about the focus on general educated audiences, an unstated rule that correct writing is good writing, and the lack of opportunities to help students from different disciplines with real writing opportunities. As the coordinator of basic writing from 2002 to 2004, I was also concerned that most of the measures employed to help basic writing students did not seem to work, because such students were not literate in the language in which they were most comfortable. Still, as a young faculty member, I was not adequately cognizant of some of the cognitive and disciplinary dimensions of writing that I propose in this book to challenge content faculty to articulate their tacit assumptions about writing, and to push beyond teaching general academic writing or teaching formalist conventions in ways that do not have practical relevance for learners. As coordinator of English for Academic Purposes from 2008 to 2012, I was able to contemplate the writing development of students in classes and in research studies as well as engage in the ELS's reassessment of the writing courses. That reassessment has taken the programme to a point where the institution has approved the teaching of faculty-specific writing courses mentioned in the "Bloody English" news article. This approval marks a significant milestone for the ELS, whose members know how difficult it is to get support from colleagues and approval from upper administration to effect changes in writing courses, because misconceptions about writing are deeply ingrained in institutional practices. However, as the chapters will indicate, the results of attitudes to and provisions for writing throughout the institution's history suggest that genuine writing development of Creole-influenced students is likely to follow not so much from faculty-specific writing courses but more from a transcultural rhetorical perspective on teaching writing – *institution-wide*.

2 | Developing Local Leaders without Explicit Academic Writing Instruction Prior to Independence, Pre-1960s

> The key to understanding language in context is to start, not with language but with context.... Only by examining the relationship from the side of contexts can we see an essential part of what is going on when language is taught. (Hymes 1972, xix)

> The English language was not considered merely as a means of communication but as something invested with the ability to re-form subject peoples into replicas of English men and women of a particular class. (Bryan 1998, 2)

> The question of language is one of the most difficult issues to deal with in Caribbean society for it is an area where whenever you attempt to touch it, you touch all the social concerns. (Carrington quoted in Sherlock and Nettleford 1990, 132)

The first cohorts of undergraduates who were being educated at the UCWI to become leaders in postwar Caribbean society did not receive explicit instruction in academic writing. Documents associated with the establishment and early years of this institution suggest that this situation obtained for two main reasons. The first is that administrators largely followed the tradition of English universities on which the UCWI was modelled in the post-World War II era. Faculty could be seen to be advocating a liberal view of education that saw writing as a transparent medium for recording thought, specifically a reflection of *genius*. Russell (2002, 234) writes that liberals consider writing "an unteachable response to inner promptings, a mode of appreciation or an indication of genius. Writing [does] not aid learning; it show[s] the state of mind." In the Jamaican context, writing – specifically *writing in English* – was considered part of the character of an educated person. In other words, mastery of English was considered a mark of education, and the educated was assumed to be able to write well in the language. Faculty also seemed to believe that if writing could indeed be learned, it was learned prior to university studies – usually in the *repeated* writing that was done in preparation for examinations. If writing reflects genius, is inherent in the educated, or is learned in preuniversity settings, its instruction in the academy would be seen to serve a remedial purpose that could not be associated with an elite institution such as the UCWI, which emphasized excellence.

There being insufficient consideration of the context-bound nature of good writing, misconceptions arose and were perpetuated about language and writing. Indeed, language in Jamaica and misconceptions about language are closely connected to probably equally disturbing misconceptions about writing development. As historian of rhetoric James Berlin (1982) reminds, every view of writing presupposes a view of language and its relationship with knowledge. On the one hand, writing may be considered an epistemic activity facilitating development of thought and knowledge *if* knowledge is taken to be socially constructed and persuasively presented in and through language. In this case, writing emerges as an aid to learning and requires careful instruction to help learners create and communicate disciplinary knowledge. If, on the other hand, knowledge is believed to be preexistent and waiting to be retrieved, language serves only as a transparent medium to neutrally record in writing what is retrieved. In this case, instruction in writing emphasizes correctness in language in transmitting what is retrieved from some permanent repository (such as the mind), and such instruction is considered remedial (see also, Berlin 1987, 6–17). These views of language and writing as transparent mediums have persisted in Jamaica.

Although similar observations may be made about writing and language in other countries, as Alexander (2000, 5) asserts, we understand educational developments in specific countries only "by reference to the web of inherited ideas and values, habits and customs, institutions and world views which make one country, or one region, or one group, distinct from another". Also, as the first epigraph in this chapter from world-renowned linguist Dell Hymes (1972) emphasizes, language and context are intertwined: to understand views about language, we should examine context. Indeed, views about writing and language in Jamaica only become clear when considered in light of the development of formal education and the teaching of English in schools in Jamaica, for, as Kathleen Drayton (1990, 207) remarks, this is "the heritage that is blamed for the problems and dilemmas of present-day English teaching". This context, I argue, informs the second reason for the absence of academic writing instruction that would see faculty at UCWI articulating their knowledge of disciplinary writing strategies and conventions: administrators and educators were subscribing to the discourse of transparency that emerged in the 1800s regarding language at preuniversity levels in Jamaica.

In their collection of cross-national studies of writing, Russell and Foster (2002, 43) include a set of questions that could be considered for cross-national research. One of these questions is, "What are the effects of language policy and traditions on writing development?" Russell and Foster propose that "at the level of teaching, national and local language policies and traditions condition writing development in powerful and increasingly contested ways" (ibid.). My examination of the Jamaican situation to determine "how . . . language policies and traditions enable and constrain writing development" (44) reveals that informing the views about writing is the belief that students learn language, specifically English, and write based on "an assumed instinct" (Strickland quoted in Education Department 1899, 401). One assistant inspector of schools R.B. Strickland criticized this faulty assumption that he observed in 1898. This situation arose in the colonial period when English – the language variety of the elite – became the medium of instruction. Colonial administrators seemed to believe that children from privileged backgrounds would write well by virtue of knowing the alphabet and speaking English; and Creole-speaking children would speak and write in English without being explicitly taught it and how to write in it. I argue that this view was one of the guiding forces that were evident in the UCWI in the 1940s and 1950s. However, this view of language kept some knowledge of writing tacit and therefore preserved the cultural capital of the privileged.

The determination to use English as the sole medium of instruction in Jamaica was not an innocent undertaking: it reveals linguistic prejudice. When administrators imposed a language that was not that of the demographic majority, they favoured the children who could claim it – English – as linguistic capital (in Pierre Bourdieu's [1991] terms). Nineteenth-century colonial officials were aware that language transmits ideology, and they distributed official documents reflecting the ideological dimensions of their enterprise. One such document is a *Circular Despatch* from the lieutenant governor of Trinidad to the secretary of state in 1841. This document can be read as a directive to all British West Indian governments. The intent to disseminate English globally is reflected in the policy "to cause the language spoken to be that of the country to which this colony belongs" (quoted in Augier and Gordon 1962, 166). The most telling document, however, is probably an 1847 *Colonial Office Despatch* that instructs governments to maintain social control by indoctrinating a coloured middle class into Britain's cultures and values. The governments were to develop a "native middle class among the negro population . . . by creating a body of men interested in the protection of property, and with intelligence enough to take part in that humbler of machinery of local affairs which ministers to social order" (quoted in Augier and Gordon 1962, 182). More important, they were to "diffuse a grammatical knowledge of the English Language as the most important agent of civilisation for the coloured population of the colonies" (ibid.). As the second epigraph in this chapter highlights, the result was that people considered English as more than a language; they viewed it as "a portable commodity necessary for some measure of success in life" (Bryan 1998, 4). Administrators' intention was for English to disseminate the values of the mother country as superior to local values, becoming what Drayton (1999, 291) terms "the main cultural form of oppression". And what would guarantee such dissemination was the school – that significant bastion of colonialism and custodian of linguistic imperialism.

The directive seems to have been well executed. In emphasizing West Indians' readiness for a university after consultation with *members of the elite* in the various Caribbean territories in 1944, the West Indian Committee of the Commission on Higher Education noted, "the people of the West Indies, unlike those of most other parts of the Colonial Empire, are already literate as regards a high percentage of the population, and literate in English, which has for at least 150 years, and in many instances for longer, been the mother tongue of the great majority" (Great Britain Commission 1945, 51). However, one marked result of the 1847 colonial directive has been widespread failure – a situation that horrified educators when the learning revealed in writing indicated that very little, if anything, had been taught. Certainly, English may have been the language of *the elite*, but it was not the "mother tongue" of the demographic majority. Unfortunately, this mother tongue myth and the idea that one speaks English or writes it based on some inherent quality were present in the establishment and early years of the university when students were expected to write intrinsically – that is, without explicit instruction. Although the problems associated with these misconceptions were apparent, educators never seemed to consider the importance of articulating knowledge that was invisible to outsiders. Instead of articulating codified disciplinary writing conventions, educators remained concerned with the code – English. Since they expected the elementary (and later secondary) schools to teach basic English skills, administrators and academics blamed them and expressed that the writing problems that emerged in the university would disappear following appropriate developments in those institutions and in examinations. I argue, however, that the writing problems at the university level were (and are still being) blamed on a system whose problematic origins have not been adequately examined and transformed to yield genuine language and writing development for local leaders and other Creole-influenced citizens.

Birth of a Regional University for Caribbean Writing "Geniuses"

The nature of the establishment and development of the regional university provides a partial explanation for the misconception that saw educators in Jamaica in the 1940s and 1950s associating writing with genius and something individuals did by virtue of being educated, with that view translated in the absence of academic writing instruction for undergraduates in the early years of the UWI.

What is today the UWI was originally the UCWI, established in 1948 as a publicly funded affiliate of the University of London under the Asquith Plan for colonial universities and located at Mona in Kingston, Jamaica. Various scholars (for example, Cobley 2000; I. Maxwell 1980; Parker 1978) highlight the British tardiness in establishing this local institution of higher learning after "long, terrible years during which a colonial philosophy of education and plantation-values wasted the true wealth of the Indies, the creativity and intellectual ability of the people" (Sherlock and Nettleford 1990, 303).[7] These scholars assert that the ethnicity, limited qualifications, and concern with financial gain of the colonizers who landed in the islands explain the late establishment and paucity of higher education institutions in the anglophone Caribbean. Sherlock, one of the founding members of the UWI, who rose through the ranks to become vice chancellor, and his coauthor Rex Nettleford, scholar and former UWI vice chancellor, observe that unlike the Spanish colonists in Santo Domingo, Mexico and Peru who established universities in the mid-sixteenth century, the British, who had been in the West Indies (in Barbados and St Kitts) since the 1620s, did not establish a university college until more than three centuries following their arrival. Based on the white planters' attitudes, Sherlock and Nettleford (1990, 7) write that the "West Indian sugar-and-slave plantation society could not tolerate a place of light, liberty and learning because it tolerated neither moral principle nor idealism. The motivation force was powerful and destructive, an insatiable greed for riches. Cash came first, Christ a distant second." John Figueroa, former dean of education at UCWI, explains that in contrast to the situation in colonies in the United States, very few university graduates – who would probably be interested in supporting higher education in the region – were among the settlers who arrived in the West Indies (1971, 14–15).

The UCWI was, therefore, established late in a region where the colonizers' main concern was gain. However, it was also located in a region where colonizers and West Indians attended to standards set in England. Alan Cobley (2000), M. Kazim Bacchus (1994, 2005), Millicent Whyte (1977) and others report that over the years several *individuals* had proposed the establishment of a regional university, but Britain seemed to ignore them because colonial officials considered public postsecondary education "premature and inexpedient in the colonies" (I. Maxwell 1980, 3). After all, the settlers felt that "home was elsewhere" and therefore sent their children to pursue education overseas (Figueroa 1971, 14). Later, other students *of means* seeking higher education were sent to Europe and North America. Bright children from the lower middle and working classes competed for a rare island scholarship to Oxford or Cambridge, and others remained in the West Indies, studying on their own or in an affiliated college (such as Jamaica High School) to take and pass external degree examinations offered by the University of London. The island scholarship and an

English education benefited the *almost white* young West Indian males who obtained them (see Great Britain Commission 1945, 6–13). However, as Cobley (2000, 5), then dean of Humanities at Cave Hill writes, they also elevated "an Oxbridge education to the status of Holy Grail for West Indian students, and, by implication, tended to belittle the efforts of local institutions to offer quality education".

When the British colonial administrators decided to establish a university in the West Indies, they concentrated on educating the brightest and best in the region to ensure social control. Cobley (2000), I. Maxwell (1980), Paul Parker (1978) and Sherlock and Nettleford (1990) report that various sociopolitical factors explain why that concentration informed the establishment of the Inter-University Council for Higher Education in the Colonies and the Commission on Higher Education in the Colonies (the Asquith Commission) that investigated the need for such institutions. Among these factors were efforts at social reconstruction evident in increased access to higher education in Britain in the postwar years, changes in the perceived value of the colonies because of reduction in sales of cane sugar on the world market, and pre- and postwar agitation by advocates of local university education. Cobley emphasizes that because the colonies had become liabilities by the mid-twentieth century, England wished to sever ties with them. It saw the university as essential to developing local leaders to take over administration after the world wars and ensure self-government and self-reliance in the Caribbean (6–9). Parker rightly observes in his dissertation on changes in the University of Puerto Rico and UCWI that the focus of the latter was not for mass utilitarian education but training leaders for government and the professions (161). This rationale was heavily criticized. As Nettleford (1986, 7–8) remarks, "many beneficiaries of the 'gift' . . . with the advantage of hindsight" did not consider the UCWI's establishment as a purely innocent undertaking that would facilitate "peaceful orderly transition from colonialism to independence". For Cobley, "indigenous elites would not only receive the training they required for effective leadership, they would remain intellectually and ideologically tied to Britain" (10). The members of the West Indies Committee of the Commission on Higher Education were well aware of this allegiance to English values and culture, but used it to emphasize the region's readiness for an institution of higher learning: "The dominion of English language and culture, viewed, moreover, in conjunction with the proportion of the population which has for long received secondary and higher education, means that the West Indians are more ready than the peoples of some of the other colonies to make immediate use of a University established in their midst" (Great Britain Commission 1945, 51).

Despite the varying motivations for higher education in the region, the focus would be educating leaders in a system that emphasized high standards. Like the other universities established on recommendation by the Asquith Commission, the UCWI was to be "an integral part of an imperial university system" (I. Maxwell 1980, 6). In this system, excellence was emphasized. I. Maxwell, who served as assistant secretary of the Inter-University Council for Higher Education in the Colonies, reports that "high quality and the determination to secure worldwide academic recognition were the characteristics of the institutions founded on the Asquith plan" (62–63). To ensure high standards, the UCWI (and each of the other Asquith institutions) would be a ward of the University of London. This institution was accorded this "maternal role" on account of its experience in offering external degrees to students who prepared for and took its examinations in various British colonies (Parker 1978, 181). The UCWI's (1959) *Calendar 1959-60* emphasizes that examinations were conducted by University of London examiners; that is, UCWI and University of London examiners prepared draft examination papers and did first marking of student scripts, but University of London examiners determined the final draft of examination papers and the final examination results. I. Maxwell recalls, "To emphasise quality from the start was a deliberate choice as well as a recognition that any alternative which countenanced mediocrity would have won no acceptance in the developing world. Britain would not be forgiven there if, on independence, countries found the standards were below their needs; if on the other hand the standards proved too severe, adjustments could be made without recrimination" (13). Although I. Maxwell's statements suggest that emphasis on standards was to prevent postindependence disgruntlement in the colonies by creating an acceptable elite – a group whose elite standing would not be questioned – the predilection for winning academic respect is, perhaps, better explained as a feature of English universities that was transferred to the colonial institutions. As Cobley (2000, 16) notes, "in the anxiety to deliver good quality education, standards had been set at a punitive level, so that many of those who did matriculate found it difficult to progress through the university system. Once this pattern was established, however, faculty members at the UCWI – many of whom were expatriates – seemed to take a perverse pride in holding to it." These standards would attract criticism because excellence seemed to translate into meeting standards that perpetuated the system by getting the best and brightest to define themselves in the system's values.

Because of such arrangements, at its inception, everything about the university college, which began with a single medical faculty, appeared to be *English* in character – a University of London curriculum and an Oxbridge emphasis on elitism. The matriculation requirements (including writing requirements), the faculties and departments, the degree structures, the syllabuses, and the teaching methods were dictated by the University of London. In describing the UCWI's academic requirements and its governing senate and council, Nettleford (1986, 6) writes, "the British 'redbrick university' had come to the Caribbean" but Oxford and Cambridge features were present in the residential requirement. Because the UCWI was modelled on English institutions, its administrators adopted an elitist approach to education, in contrast to US mass-oriented land grant universities. While researchers such as Christopher Hunte (1978) and Parker (1978) merely indicate that the UCWI admitted a very small number of students, others such as Cobley (2000) emphasize that that small number underwent a rigid and rigorous selection process at the end of which they were offered a narrow, scholarly curriculum. As historian and poet Howard Fergus (1998, 21) recalls, "the university [UCWI] itself was rooted in a liberal education tradition and served ... an elite function". It offered "an education not concerned with immediate ends and the efficient adaptation of the individual to existing surroundings but with knowledge capable of being its own end" (Joyce quoted in Fergus 1998, 21–22).

This elitist perspective helps explain the belief that writing is an intrinsic skill. Indeed, because of the UCWI's connections to English universities and because of students' social class and education in the 1940s, administrators assumed that students would be able to write at the university without explicit writing instruction. Most undergraduates were from middle-income groups, and displayed mastery of English befitting their class. Robert LePage (1955), professor of English and pioneer in Caribbean Creole studies, conveys a sense of the social class of students who were usually accepted at UCWI and of their language skills and writing abilities in his call for volunteers to assist with a projected linguistic survey of the British Caribbean region in the early 1950s. LePage used terms such as "white talk" and "Creolese English" to refer to British English and West Indian English respectively.[8] LePage's observations reveal that the majority of the undergraduates then displayed facility in English by virtue of their birth or their parents' education and students' personal interests. LePage found that there was "a very small percentage of children whose native speech approximates to the Southern British dialect of English" (41). These children's parents were usually English administrators or businessmen or West Indians who had spent many years in England where they attended high school and university. Le Page observed that those children who accounted for about 1 to 2 per cent of the school population were often bilingual. He describes a second group of children in each colony: "children from middle-class homes where the natural tongue is an educated Creolese English". Such children's parents used "white talk" among themselves. However, the careful observer would notice that they sometimes included "specifically local words and English words used in a specifically local sense" (ibid.). LePage observed that a significant percentage of the secondary school students and "probably the majority of University undergraduates, at least in Barbados and Jamaica" (42) were from this second group. Children in this group tended to perform well in language and writing because of what may have appeared to be questionable strategies: LePage's description of these children's attitudes reflects Villanueva's (1993, 39) description of "racelessness" as practised by some minority groups in the United States in their attempts to take on mainstream language and culture. LePage (1955, 42) reports that when these children became adults, some self-consciously suppressed "lower-class creolese" while others abandoned it to lead a fully middle-class lifestyle. Various Caribbean writers have criticized this situation in which many students admired the British, imitated them, and adopted their values. These students who uncritically accepted English values were culturally English. In the English-speaking Caribbean, individuals who were considered culturally white but racially black were called "roast breadfruit". This pejorative term is the equivalent of the "sugar cane" metaphor used in the French West Indies where Frantz Fanon (1952) criticized earlier generations for being black on the outside and white inside. These pejorative terms hint at the reality that some Caribbean students in the first few decades of the twentieth century were thought to have mastered the colonial language better than the colonial masters and their descendants – in both speech and writing.[9]

Although students' social class and apparent consequent mastery of English may have led administrators to believe they did not have to articulate writing instruction, what probably confirmed that students could write instinctively were the institution's matriculation and, therefore, writing requirements. Students in the 1940s sat writing-intensive school-leaving and university-qualifying examinations at the end of their five secondary years. Sixteen-year-old secondary-level students who were not considering a university education took the (Cambridge) School Certificate (Ordinary level) examination. Those students who were planning to attend university or obtain a scholarship took the Senior Cambridge and then the Higher Certificate Examination, usually after two additional years. It is to be remembered that because of the special relationship, the UCWI's matriculation requirements were the same as those for the University of London. Parker (1978) observes that there were no detailed statements about requirements in the UCWI *Year Books* for 1947–49, 1949–50, or 1950–51. These catalogues directed students to the University of London's requirements. Before 1952, London required students on the London Matriculation Examination to pass English, elementary mathematics, and three other subjects selected from a list of twenty-nine in one sitting. The English public criticized these rigid requirements, particularly the way in which the very specialized entrance tests that the British universities administered virtually dictated the secondary school curriculum that understandably focused on the examinations' content. Following those criticisms and decisions taken by the British minister of education, one new entry examination, with "Ordinary", "Advanced" and "Scholarship" levels, replaced the two existing examinations. This new General Certificate of Education (GCE) examination would allow all sixteen-year-olds in or out of school to take any number of subjects they wished and receive a single certificate indicating the subjects they had passed and the levels at which they had passed them (Parker 1978, 201–3). Therefore, by 1952, the GCE became the university-qualifying examinations, with London and Cambridge being the most popular in Jamaica. In general, students who applied to the university in the early 1950s were expected to have passes in six subjects, at least two of which had to be at the Advanced (A) level, or have passes in five subjects, at least three of which had to be at the A level. Because taking the A level meant that the student had passed the subject at the Ordinary (O) level, these requirements really meant having at least eight passes. In 1952, students could choose from a wide range of forty-two subjects on the approved list. Drayton (1990, 210) notes that because the GCE was not a single subject examination, students had to study for the five or six required ordinary level subjects (one of which was English language) that they would take in one round of examinations. English language and English literature were treated as separate subjects. For the language examination, students wrote an essay and a précis, and answered comprehension questions in sentences. They also did sentence analysis up to the mid-1960s. The literature examination involved knowledge of set texts – usually a Shakespearian text, novels or short stories, and poetry.

Since these examinations, like their predecessors, that West Indians took were set for students in England, some segments of the local population criticized their use as requirements for university entry in the West Indies (Drayton 1990, 211). It seems that lay practitioners criticized what they perceived to be limited access created by rigid entry schemes and the suggestion that authorities were forcefully protecting the boundaries of educated culture almost in the same way as did the colonial officials who had refused the colonies a university before the war years. Parker notes that one of the significant factors that contributed to slow enrolment growth between 1948 and 1954 was that "the requirement that students present *passes on the GCEs in Latin* was too high for most West Indians" (1978, 227; emphasis added). Requirements in Latin indicate significant boundary restrictions for they suggest that *to be literate meant being familiar with classical languages* and their forms of logic and expression. As well, the UCWI could have had only a small pool of applicants since only those students who could access good secondary schools were likely to succeed in the London Matriculation Examinations (Parker 1978, 229). Parker reminds readers of what is now a known fact – that secondary educational development in the Caribbean often lagged behind Britain's, resulting in students' experiencing grave difficulty in passing the A-level examinations (137).

Still, as Drayton (1990, 211) notes, "the West Indian perennial concern with standards, preferably those set outside, made these examinations, set and marked in the UK, highly valued". Other West Indians, therefore, believed that if a student passed the examinations, that student knew how to demonstrate knowledge in writing. This was because the new A-level requirement meant additional writing experience for university-bound students, and educators seemed to believe that the requirements prepared students to write in the university. The GCE A-level requirement meant that students spent two additional years (in the sixth form) beyond the school-leaving age of sixteen in preparation for more writing-intensive examinations. Following in the English tradition, in which students specialized in established disciplinary areas such as history, chemistry, or law, Jamaican students preparing for higher education would take only about three subjects after the fifth form. Students preparing to specialize in a science subject would take A-level courses and examinations in such subjects as chemistry, zoology, mathematics, or physics, while students preparing to major in law would take history, English literature, and French. Preparation in this small number of subjects would be considered as discipline-specific preparation for the areas in which students would major in the university because A-level preparation involved writing many essays as a form of subject-specific learning in most of these subjects. It is to be understood that the writing involved included *practice by repetition* rather than practice through multiple revisions such as became common in the United States after the 1960s, and the examinations were, as Foster and Russell (2002, 319) observe of some European systems, "grueling tests of early disciplinary mastery".

As well, all students aspiring to do higher studies locally or win a scholarship for study overseas had to take and obtain a good pass in English language, which emphasized essay writing that was *evaluated but not really taught*. Nonetheless, administrators seemed to feel that students were getting more writing practice preuniversity while they were preparing for the new university-qualifying examinations. In addition to their A-level qualifications, applicants had to take an entrance examination (UCWI 1954, 6) in which they displayed their knowledge *in* writing and, therefore, their knowledge *of* writing. Having passed the requisite number of examinations and the entrance test, students were considered ready for the writing tasks of their chosen faculty. As Foster and Russell (2002, 331) observe in some European situations, after preparing for exams in subjects and disciplines that were the focus of their university studies, Jamaican students began their university career as "experienced apprentices in chosen disciplines" and not as novices as is likely to be the situation in the United States, where students start with general studies and do not specialize until late in their undergraduate programme.

Because of the largely unspoken assumption that preparation for (the London Matriculation or Higher Certificate Examination before 1952 and later for GCE) A levels meant students knew how to write for disciplinary audiences, academics did not offer writing instruction in Jamaican higher education. In the Jamaican system, faculty believed that matriculants would continue to write to demonstrate learning in the discipline. However, faculty seemed to forget that although these students were not complete novices, they were "apprentices", and not "experts". As long as faculty neglected to instruct students in how to write, faculty's knowledge of writing was kept tacit, unarticulated, and therefore embedded in shared experiences that were not readily accessible to outsiders. It is probably the fact that this knowledge was also unarticulated in preuniversity settings that some persons criticized "the system" that they did not fully understand for excluding them.

The modes of instruction employed in the UCWI confirm my belief that knowledge of writing remained largely invisible and unarticulated in the institution. Students who were offered a place in the university were accepted into a specific faculty (with a dean as head and comprising the students and lecturers in departments of a specific field) to pursue a five-year degree in Medicine or a three-year degree in Arts, Natural Sciences or Social Sciences.[10] As in the English system, two modes of instruction prevailed in these faculties – large group lectures and small group tutorials. In England, faculty gave the lectures and often masters and doctoral students led the tutorials. Since there were no masters students to begin with at the UCWI and graduate students were not introduced until 1963 (V. Roberts 2003, 44), regular faculty would have conducted the tutorials. Some faculty gave lectures from notes while others read from a fully composed lecture. Lectures were not compulsory at UCWI. They still are not; however, tutorials have always been compulsory. In the mandatory tutorials, one student often presented a paper on a particular topic for peers and the lecturer or tutor to critique it in the lecturer's office. Eric King confirmed that these critiques were related to content and not also "how to write" (personal interview, 16 July 2007). It seems that much rote learning took place since the goal of learning was for students to master the information the lecturers were disseminating rather than for students to critically reflect on it to generate new knowledge (see Figueroa 1957, 1963).

Also consistent with the Oxbridge tradition – the centre of English education, faculty apparently ignored rhetoric and its emphasis on the context-bound nature of discourse. Apparently, there was no discussion of the fact that writing in biology and writing in chemistry, or writing in history and writing in literature, though in the same faculty were based on certain disciplinary conventions. Since, generally, academics disdained rhetoric because rather than being concerned with truth it focused on speakers' invoking shared assumptions when addressing public audiences, academics lost the opportunity to teach students how to claim authority as they positioned themselves as speakers and writers, and how to address audience expectations and other aspects of each situation faced. With no explicit instruction in how to write for varied audiences, students would have continued to write as they knew how, based on what writing practice they would have had in the sixth form. All of this seems ironic since the initial aims of the UCWI included developing local public leaders – and rhetoric was concerned with developing such public figures who would be invested in public life and could ably address the public on public issues. Critics such as Eric Williams ([1950] 1994) protested against any inclusion of an antiquarian English education that focused on the ancient languages, perpetuation of domination by a small, stable social elite through striving for the ideal of Quintilian's good man who speaks well or what T. Miller (1997, 69) calls "the ossified forms of Aristotelianism and Ciceronianism" that pervaded Oxbridge education. However, these critics never seemed to suggest how a rhetorical education could indeed assist in creating the kind of Caribbean man that was envisioned.[11]

This lack of acknowledgement of rhetoric's civic usefulness that was evident in the lack of explicit writing instruction with reference to public, general or disciplinary audiences is linked to the institution's beginnings and its emphasis on excellence rather than also equity. In his description of the founding and first two decades of the university in the book he coauthored with Nettleford, Sherlock quotes from the unpublished personal diary of Raymond Priestly, principal and vice chancellor of the University of Birmingham and one of the members of the Irvine Committee that recommended establishing a university in the British West Indies. In considering changes that he thought should eventually be made to the curriculum, Priestly made some jottings that suggest early considerations of explicit writing instruction. He noted that there should be changes in selection criteria as well as consideration of teaching in the United States. He was particularly interested in general education courses, noting

> The freshman and sophomore years of their university or college courses – which are, it should be remembered, the equivalent of the British VIth Form years – are practically entirely devoted to such general courses with the addition of the *study of the English Language as a vehicle for thought*. There is a strong feeling throughout the academical world today that *something of the same sort is needed to counterbalance and counteract the specialization that is inevitable when experts are being trained*. . . . (Quoted in Sherlock and Nettleford 1990, 19; emphasis added)

What Priestly was drawing on was the US tradition of teaching general education as a means to instil a "common culture" or rather to teach *the previously excluded* to respect *the insiders'* culture. He felt that that kind of foundational period would be valuable to West Indian students' development. However, the university began and continued for more than a decade without any such instruction that seemed to be associated with education that did not stress excellence or quality.

Indeed, locals criticized the institution's emphasis on quality, but local administrators would not relent. Hugh Springer, one of the two local members of the Irvine Committee and first registrar of the UCWI, was among those who defended the institution's emphasis on quality. He noted that criticisms of the university college, most notably from Eric Williams, were based on experiences with the US land grant system – a system that was considered good, "but although we needed a developmental approach we needed also a high-standard one. The public wanted to be assured of our *degree's currency*" (quoted in Sherlock and Nettleford 1990, 26; emphasis added). Springer's use of "developmental" here is in reference to US four-year first degree programmes and the abundance of general writing courses in the initial stages of that scheme that seemed to allow for greater access than in a system that catered to the academically gifted. His use of "public" and his hugely revealing metaphor of "currency" beg the question, "Whose coinage were the degrees valued in?" Since, as expressed, some locals were critical of the rigid requirements, this public was English or *international*, and the currency was that of London, England.

This "currency" indicated that the emphasis on valuing the outside – England – prevailed over criticisms of rigidity or antiquarianism and over calls for general education courses in the form of writing instruction for future local leaders.

Introducing Logic or the Beginnings of Writing Instruction at UCWI?

Despite the assumption that the high quality of students precluded the need for explicit writing instruction for students' development, there was instruction of a sort in academic writing conventions, beginning with a series of lectures in logic in 1954. In fact, the reasons for introducing that series of lectures suggest that explicit instruction in language use and discourse construction began within the first decade of the university's establishment, and not in 1963 with a "Use of English" survey course as Dyche (2006b) proposes. In a paper "prepared at short notice" for the arts faculty in December 1957, Figueroa (1957) described the series of lectures in logic that he had been offering since 1954, gave the reasons for starting the lectures, suggested its benefits, and solicited criticism from members of the arts faculty based on the content and delivery up to that point. The first portion of Figueroa's paper described the very first instantiation of the subject that was offered in four lectures to students in arts and in the department of education in the first part of the 1954 to 1955 academic year. Topics covered in this first offering included formal logic; immediate inference; laws of contradiction, identity, and excluded middle; mediate inference – hypothetical and categorical syllogisms and deduction; "more common fallacies" such as the traditional Ignoratio Flenchi and the undistributed middle; the "traditional four figures;" and precise definitions of such terms as "proposition", "concept", "term", "name" and "universal". Figueroa mentioned that more could be done in the lectures, especially as regards "the problem of Induction" and "Scientific Method", but stressed that students seemed to have enjoyed what was presented. He noted that a "quotation of nearly all of the *Spectator* for December the 4th 1711 amused the students very much" (2). Figueroa also reported that since 1954, the lectures had been "repeated, improved and enlarged" (3), with the first lectures focusing on defining what logic is and identifying the reasons for studying it. His paper explained that logic is a special kind of examination of language, different from the other two elements of the trivium – grammar and rhetoric: it is "concerned with the processes of reasoning aright. It is a science in the sense that it examines right reasoning and establishes norms; it is an art in as much as it teaches us the skill whereby we reason aright." In an apparent attempt to eventually sell the subject to other disciplines and faculties, Figueroa asserted, "Logic is concerned not with truth but with consequence." It is useful, he continued, as a "tool . . . in any sort of discursive, analytic work; . . . the necessary first step in philosophy, as well as in science, law, all argument and reasoning" (ibid.).

This germ of a course that reflects Hugh Blair's ([1783] 1965) ideas seems to have been organized in an ad hoc manner, with topics that appeared to be abstract and lacking in practical relevance. Figueroa (1957, 2) wrote, "I trust that during the next term it will be possible for the Arts Faculty to let me have four more lectures in which we could strengthen and enlarge what we have already done, and introduce one or two new topics." These new topics would probably have included modern symbolic logic that an unnamed colleague had offered to teach. The topics seem to be rather specialized, hardly oriented to what appeared to be the learners' needs. Eric King and other students who attended these lectures did not perceive the relevance to their writing. Some students felt that the lecturer really wanted to display knowledge of logic that was not popular then (King, personal interview, 16 July 2007).

Still, Figueroa's (1957) reason for introducing the lectures is revealing of the roots and persistence of the myth of transience in the Jamaican system. Figueroa felt UCWI students should be introduced to logic because "their writings seem to lack logical insight both creatively and analytically" (3). He started the lectures because many faculty members were "disturbed at the lack of logic, connection and consequence apparent in scholarship essays and in the writing of undergraduates". Figueroa felt that "starting from this clear need we might move to more epistemological questions [and] encourage our arts students to understand something about the nature of scientific research; about the way by which we acquire many premises from which we often proceed to argue illogically; about the degrees of knowledge and certainty; about the meaning of 'is' in many propositions" (4). Herein is the myth revealed: Figueroa and others who frequently visited schools felt that the weaknesses in the students' writings were to be blamed on the sixth forms, which did not adequately prepare students "in the general matters of logical thought and consequential expression, not to mention selective and critical reading" (ibid.). He felt that UCWI students should be exposed to courses that would encourage them to develop the skills that would enable them to "examine and evaluate their attitudes and to deepen their insight into important questions of meaning and existence" (5).

Other UCWI personnel would observe problems in student writing, indicating the extent to which problems in university students' writing are observed in every generation (beginning in the 1950s), but remain without adequate or meaningful treatment. Each observer suggested replacing the qualifying examinations or remedying the problems in schools. As an example, in a reflection on examinations and student preparation, LePage (1959) stated, "It has been apparent to me and to a number of other people for a long time that the quality and preparedness of our intake of students here will not improve very greatly until we can radically change their outlook of the school in the Caribbean, which at present is focussed on cramming for examinations conducted by one or another of the English universities". LePage felt that the UCWI should remodel its entrance and scholarship examination to replace the higher school certificate which he considered "useless as a criterion of ability and preparedness, and which . . . stultifie[d] a great deal of the potential ability of the students by forcing them to cram for the examination". LePage seemed to be addressing subjects that lent themselves to "cramming" and regurgitation. The implication is that students were not expected to question or critique what they were learning. Although the observation is astute, LePage did not seem to consider how the problem could have been addressed *in* the institution. Hector Wynter, the then registrar, would also recognize the problem in the 1950s, to the extent that he would write to the University of London to express the desire to offer English language in the general degree so graduates who became teachers would have general linguistic grounding. Wynter (1959) observed, "The teaching of English Language is very poor generally in the schools of the West Indies, and the students' weak command of Standard English stultifies a great deal of the teaching in other subjects."

What Wynter (1959) labelled a weak command of English was, indeed, becoming evident in students' performance in their external English examination. Based on statistics from the 1950s and early 1960s, Craig (quoted in E. Miller 1981, 374) observed,

> At GCE "O" level, for instance, the failure rate in English for the region as a whole fluctuates between 70 and 80 percent. This is bad enough, but the real size of the problem is revealed by the fact that these failures come from among those children who have been specially selected to go to high school to prepare for this very examination. Among the others who never get to high school and who, it must be remembered, form about 90 per cent of the age group, standards are even lower.

These observations reveal that although many prospective university students were familiar with the language of schooling and of written examinations by virtue of the circumstances of their birth or by shedding the Creole language to increase mastery in English, students did not perform very well in the English language examination. These high failure rates confirm that the country's linguistic realities had begun to affect the institution as early as the 1950s: increasingly students who learned English by virtue of exposure in school rather than because of the circumstances of their birth were accessing secondary and eventually higher education. All of these students had, however, passed through a system which rested on the belief that students could learn English and write in it based on what Strickland rightly labelled "an assumed instinct" (Education Department 1899, 401).

This belief, I argue, is the other reason that administrators and educators expected students to write intrinsically in their disciplines and were reluctant to address the problem within the university college. However, by suggesting that the schools should address the problems that were becoming evident in the institution, administrators and academics were not only propagating the myth of transience. They were also ignoring the problematic aspects of those schools. I am not suggesting that the schools could have taken on the responsibility if situations were different; I am contending that the university was ignoring those students who would have passed through the elementary system or be offspring of Jamaicans who had passed through that system without going on to secondary or postsecondary education. Such students – quite likely first-generation university students – would, therefore, have been further removed from academic discourses than those from more privileged backgrounds. Unfamiliarity with disciplinary discourse in the university setting would have compounded any language weaknesses students may have been deemed to have. Ignoring those students was one instantiation of the linguistic prejudice that was institutionalized in the 1840s when colonial officials imposed English as the medium of instruction in Jamaica, and lack of explicit writing instruction meant that such students would have been kept on the periphery of their disciplines and how adherents make and convey knowledge through writing. Tracing the roots of the underlying misconceptions is what I attempt in the next section.

Historical Roots of the Discourse of Transparency in Jamaica

The social hierarchy and the influence of imported models in the development of education in Jamaica are crucial to understanding the instruction that the local elite received prior to attending the UCWI in the first decade of its existence and that the educated elite would receive in later years. First, the three-tiered hierarchy established during plantation slavery – with white planters and their successors at the top, coloureds occupying the second level, and descendants of black Africans occupying the lowest rung while forming the demographic majority – largely determined who had access to education and to the official language variety. Second, Jamaica's education system, like those of other former British colonies was influenced by England's. In fact, elements of English education were imposed on the local system to the extent that it attracted criticism such as that from then Prime Minister Michael Manley (1974, 21) for being "imported lock, stock and barrel from England without a moment's thought about its relevance to Jamaica's needs and aspirations". This imposition is most marked in terms of language and literacy.

In terms of access, whereas the planters and their successors and later coloureds could access education overseas and later locally, slaves and their descendants had little access to education. According to reports of the Great Britain Board of Education (1901), there was no public elementary education in Jamaica before 1834. Any available education was for children of the free and privileged classes. W.J.

Gardner (1971, 203) reports in his history of Jamaica that "every man whose means would allow the expenditure sent his children to England for education". White and coloured children "of means" got classical education in England or in grammar schools established for whites in the colonies. Whatever education there was for black slaves was provided by churches. Missionaries provided instruction in pre-emancipation Jamaica in Sunday schools and night schools, following the pattern of Sunday school that had started in England for children who worked in factories but had Sundays free. These missionaries taught religion through memorization of hymns and biblical texts that they read aloud. Planters feared slave empowerment through literacy development, so the officials forbade the missionaries to teach blacks to read and write. The situation described by Frederick Douglass (quoted in Bizzell and Herzeberg 2001c, 1070) regarding slavery in the United States reflects Jamaica's: slave owners were not in favour even of religious instruction since they thought it would weaken their powers when slaves learned that all men are equal. A special report from the Great Britain Board of Education (1901, 577) records the planters' belief that "knowledge would entirely unfit the Negroes for the labour to which they were subjected".

Opportunities for literacy instruction for blacks seemed to increase, however, when the idea for a public system of education for all in the West Indies emerged in 1833 and was presented in the fifth resolution of the House of Commons. Shirley Gordon (1963) reports that at this same time in the nineteenth century, the government gave grants to schools in Britain to achieve universal elementary education, as happened in other European countries. Consistent with those developments, a Negro Education Grant was included in the Act of Emancipation for British Slaves that followed the fifth resolution. This grant was to provide moral and religious education for Negroes. It amounted to thirty thousand pounds per year initially, with allotment being dependent on the colony's number of ex-slaves. Jamaica got seventy-five hundred pounds of the total that was gradually increased each year but was discontinued in 1845. Thanks to this 1834 grant, elementary education was established in the nineteenth century for children of ex-slaves in all of the former British slave societies.

Although emancipation led to increased opportunities for literacy development for ex-slaves and their descendants, such development would only be partial because of the oral emphasis in teaching and the use of foreign instructional materials. As in other colonies, after the abolition of slavery, churches assumed responsibility for education in Jamaica. From the Negro Education Grant, the religious bodies received support to build schools, assist with teachers' salaries and train local teachers. However, as historian Carl Campbell (1970, 370) notes, the stress was on "moral formation and character formation as the primary business of the schools in the West Indies". Training for poor children was, therefore, to involve such Christian virtues as obedience, honesty, patience, and industry. Attendees would also be taught reading and arithmetic, but *writing would not be stressed*. Various researchers indicate that *writing was included at an extra cost* of one penny per week (see Drayton 1990, 201; Gordon 1968, 48). Gordon includes the following telling pronouncement that John Sterling submitted in an 1835 report that the British government had requested to help to determine the best agency to direct "Negro Education" after emancipation. Sterling wrote, "Writing is an accomplishment of little value to the very poor; and is less beneficial than almost any other branch of instructions in cultivating the faculties of the child" (quoted in Gordon 1968, 64). He, therefore, encouraged religious instruction to the exclusion of writing, recommending that anyone taught to write should pay for the instruction. Attaching a fee to writing on the basis that it would be of little benefit to the masses meant automatic exclusion of the very poor who would not have been able to pay for such instruction. This stipulation would have pleased the powers that be who, as Gordon writes, would have been more interested in keeping ex-slaves in low-paying jobs on the sugar estates than in having them in any literacy programme (11). This view which the Colonial Office's 1847 *Circular Despatch* supported suggests that even where writing was included it would not be treated as an avenue for social mobility for the poor. Governments were to "communicate such a knowledge of writing and arithmetic, and of their application to his wants and duties, as may enable a peasant to economise his means, and give the small farmer the power to enter into calculations and agreements" (quoted in Augier and Gordon 1962, 182). Such statements demonstrate that administrators' attitudes to the writing development of the children of ex-slaves were hardly different from those shown to slaves in earlier decades.

Also having an impact on children's literacy development in the postemancipation era were the teaching materials that would guarantee dissemination of Britain's superiority while developing students' grammatical knowledge. Teachers used the Bible and select readers and grammar books to ascertain students' grammatical knowledge of the English language. Among the available readers used were the *Irish National Readers* beginning in the mid-nineteenth century and *The Royal Reader Series* (which drew heavily on the content and format of the *Irish National Readers*) beginning in the 1870s. Drayton (1990) observes that the latter was in use in West Indian schools until 1954. E. Miller (1981, 373) notes that *Blackie's Readers* – a text published for Scottish children up to the 1930s – was also used in Jamaica up to the 1970s. It is not surprising that these materials that are experientially distant from the school child's Jamaican environment would have been coming out of the British Isles. As T. Miller (1997, 1, 165) indicates, it was in the British cultural provinces – Scotland and Ireland – that the first attempts were made to establish and formalize the conventions of English usage and taste so that these conventions could be taught to those desirous of moving from the margins into educated culture. In addition to those readers, Drayton (1990) identifies the following as the four main grammar books in use in the nineteenth century: Richard Hiley's *Grammar of the English Language with the Principles of Eloquence and Rhetoric* (1832), George Darnell's *An*

Introduction to English Grammar Consisting of a Graduated Series of Easy Lessons in Language (1846), Robert Sullivan's *An Attempt to Simplify English Grammar with the Observation and the Method of Teaching It* (1852) and George Currey's *English Grammar for the Use of Schools* (1858). Common to all of these grammar books is the presentation of English grammar based on Latin rules (Drayton 1990, 203).

The emphasis on grammar in the teaching materials means that English, itself, was not taught as a new language to students or as an integrated communication tool for public speakers and leaders. As in other colonies, it was taught, instead, as discrete subject areas including spelling, reading, handwriting, dictation, recitation, grammar and composition and writing at preuniversity levels. Emphasis in literacy instruction was placed on rote learning of vocabulary, definitions of parts of speech, and rules of grammar. Grammar learning was to be accomplished through synthesis, analysis and parsing. Parsing involved students' applying concepts regarding number, gender, case, person and tense to assign to each word in the sentence its part of speech (see Christie 2003, 11; Drayton 1990, 203). Rhetoric and eloquence were also taught. Drayton (1990) quotes Hiley's (1831) definition of these from his text, *Hiley's English Grammar Abridged with Questions for the Use of Young Pupils*. Hiley defines rhetoric as the "art which teaches us that choice and arrangement of words and phrases and that use of figurative language which shall convey our ideas in the most eloquent, impressive and persuasive manner", and eloquence as "the study of authors, the cultivation of memory and conversation by observation, reflection and the classics" (quoted in Drayton 1990, 204). These definitions emphasize arrangement and style, an emphasis that is consistent with teaching grammatical knowledge.

The emphasis on "eloquent" presentation of ideas in Hiley's (1831) definitions also points to the focus on the oral in teaching. In the nineteenth and early twentieth century, children did not engage in silent reading or *oral composition*. The emphasis then was on *pronunciation* and *intonation*, that is, on elocution – Thomas Sheridan's eighteenth-century (re)definition of rhetoric (see Bizzell and Herzeberg 2001b). Children, therefore, read aloud daily from reading books imported from Britain. Oral reading was also accompanied by "recitations" (oral rendering of a poem or gem that was memorized), dictations and transcriptions of portions of reading material. As T. Miller (1997, 138) notes, elocution always seemed to appeal to those who wished to speak like the English, that is, "those whose language it set out to eradicate". As well, this kind of preparation would not yield a local leader who could speak extemporaneously because elocution's focus was on *reading aloud* – "the art of oral interpretation" (139–40), where interpretation means *rendering* – and not spontaneous oral composition.

Still, it was expected that English language instruction in Jamaica would yield students who were competent or proficient in English. Their proficiency or communicative competence should be revealed in the situations for which instruction prepared them. These situations include final examinations, higher education at home or overseas, formal interactions in public, interactions with (other) native speakers of English, or interactions in other societies where English is the official medium of communication. A significant result of the language teaching techniques that imposed English on Creole speakers has, however, been high failure rates and underachievement (see, for example, Craig 1999, 227; UNESCO 1983, 74). Perhaps the most glaring accounts of such failure in students' language and literacy development appear in reports prepared by the English superintending inspector of schools and his mainly English assistants who executed and reported on school visits and examinations in the late nineteenth century until mid-twentieth century. In the ensuing sections, I quote extensively to demonstrate these inspectors' prescience and misconceptions regarding language development and to locate the roots of the myth of transience that university administrators propagated in the 1950s.

Towards the end of the nineteenth century – over sixty years after the introduction of universal elementary education in which English was the language of instruction, school inspectors observed no difference in language usage by the schooled and unschooled. Inspector C.E. Sterry would note in 1895 that "in the great majority of cases, children leave school from the highest standard no better equipped in the correct use of the English language than the people surrounding them who have in many instances never been to school at all" (quoted in *Governor's Report* 1896, 331). In 1914, one assistant inspector Bury observed that "English is one of the greatest stumbling blocks in Jamaica [sic] elementary schools" (quoted in Education Department 1915, 486). In 1920, another assistant inspector, Mr Mitchell wrote, "The correct use of the English language is perhaps the most difficult thing that the children have to learn. Predominant forms of speech in the home and on the street seem to overwhelm the results of teaching. Even the teachers in many cases resort to common and incorrect forms when teaching and questioning their classes" (quoted in Education Department 1921, 68).

Other assistant inspectors incorrectly considered English the native tongue and the only vehicle for expressing thought: Mr Mercier would write that "the urgent necessity of learning to express themselves properly in their native tongue should be impressed upon all scholars" (quoted in Education Department 1917, 344). Mr Mornan felt, "It would . . . be a great gain in the teaching of Writing and English if teachers would more generally begin early, not simply to teach writing but to teach it as the correct expression of thought" (quoted in Education Department 1917, 343). He wanted teachers to "realise the value of writing as a means of intellectual training, and also of the development of character" (ibid.). Mornan probably made the first statement in light of the fact that there was, as assistant inspector Lockett wrote, "a tendency to regard neat writing rather than the ability to express thought as the main object of this part of the curriculum" (quoted in Education Department 1918, 304). The conclusion was, in Lockett's words, "The force of habit is too strong to be counteracted by a limited acquaintance with correct English, and knowledge of the rules of Grammar seems to have little practical effect" (quoted in Education Department 1909, 451).

It appears, as Drayton (1999, 297) observes, that "English as a system of meanings was grasped by a small elite minority". Therefore, faced with the English linguistic system, most pupils applied the Creole rules that they knew intuitively – such as deleting final consonants and using an invariant verb form, a situation which led to inspectors expressing misconceptions about writing. Geo Hicks, one of the few assistant inspectors from the United States, mentioned as "frequently recurring errors" the following: "the omission and incorrect use of capitals, the omission and incorrect use of the apostrophe, the omission of final 's', the division of words in the middle of a syllable – (as trun-k, trium-ph, etc., somewhat frequent even in the papers of Pupil Teachers) – the substitution of 'on' for 'and', and the reverse, and of 'his' for 'is', and like errors" (quoted in *Governor's Report* 1894, 275). Hicks would also note that in composition, the "most prominent defect is the mistaken use of tenses and this defect is very general. Scholars in writing dictation very frequently omit the final 'd' or 'ed' of the past tense of verbs" (quoted in *Governor's Report* 1897, 385). When Hicks's proposed reasons for such occurrences are read with the benefit of hindsight, they seem hilarious. He wrote that "this omission might possibly be attributed to some lack of distinct enunciation on the part of the Inspector, were it not that it is so generally the habit of scholars in their written exercises to drop these terminations, sometimes putting them in, however, where they should not appear" (ibid.). However, the hilarity triggered by his consideration that students were in the "habit of making a wrong use of the present and past tense" (ibid.) also points to the persistence of the myth of transience with regard to language teaching in general in Jamaica. The myth emerges as early as Hicks's writing when he noted, "When this defect is removed, and scholars shall also have learned to recognize the completion of a sentence in their letters and essays, instead of running on with two, three, or four sentences without fullstop or capital, the common errors in composition will be lessened by fifty percent" (ibid.).

Other assistant inspectors' similar observations would reveal that although the problems were not going away, that fact remained unacknowledged. Among these inspectors, Mr Deer wrote, "children seem totally unable to write a grammatical sentence for even if the grosser forms of error are absent, the final 's' in both verbs and nouns presents a universal stumbling-block" (quoted in Education Department 1900, 375). He ignored the vernacular and the teachers' prescience, claiming instead that the "general excuse is that the children write the vernacular, but consistent and patient correction by the teachers must eradicate the worst faults" (ibid.). He would later remark, "Faults of speech and local idioms are faithfully reproduced, and even if correct otherwise, there is present an indefinable sense of a translation, sometimes literal, as though the child were not employing its native tongue, which, as a matter of fact it is not" (quoted in Education Department 1906, 53). By the early twentieth century, Mr Deer realized the reason "children seem unable to explain the simplest idea in idiomatic and grammatical English" is that "except during school hours, they never hear it spoken" (quoted in Education Department 1911, 395). He considered the writing so bad that he remarked "much of [English composition] still might be a rendering from another language by an indifferent translator so ungrammatical and lacking in idiom is the English and unusual the application of words and phrases" (quoted in Education Department 1912, 191). Mr Deer would later admit, "The speaking idiom must frequently crop up in written work in a country where people read in one language and talk in another" (quoted in Education Department 1916, 532). Another assistant inspector, Mr Nelson, would also write in 1915, "Children as well as others are more likely to write as they speak than to speak as they write" (quoted in Education Department 1916, 532). After all, as Mr Urquhart observed, "almost generally children do not look upon the school language as a means of self-expression at all" (ibid., 533).

These inspectors failed to realize what Urquhart hinted at: the students were being forced to code shift to (speak or write in) English alone, but they could not. In his observation, the students did not even practise code-switching between their vernacular and English, so shifting to English alone seemed a difficult, if not impossible, requirement. Because the students were more conversant with their "speaking" language, they conscientiously applied its rules to what was imposed in school. However, most teachers and inspectors did not recognize what Shaughnessy (1977, 11) would call "the intelligence of [students'] mistakes". The school inspectors, therefore, constantly recorded persistent problems in students' writing, and called the application of Creole rules *grammatical errors*.

Significantly, a few inspectors recognized that the problem did not lie with the students but rather with the methods. One assistant inspector, John Kerrick, made an observation in his 1898 report that characterized observations throughout much of the late nineteenth and early twentieth centuries: "In writing, composition remains, and appears likely to remain by far the weakest point. This is only to be expected, as very few of the scholars speak or hear anything approaching correct English, out of school at any rate" (quoted in Education Department 1899, 398). In that same year, assistant inspector R.B. Strickland wrote what I deduce is an unfortunate principle that has been prevalent in education in Jamaica: "I am not able to report much in favour of dictation and composition. I fear that too generally both subjects are left to *an assumed instinct* in the children aided by occasional practice" (ibid., 401; emphasis added). In the early twentieth century, another assistant inspector, McClaughlin, made similar observations in which he explicitly shifted the blame away from students. He noted that the "lamentable weakness is much more to be attributed to a want of proper tuition tha[n] any inherent want of capacity in the scholars" (quoted in Education Department 1918, 304). His observation that weaknesses in students' writing was not a reflection of their abilities was rare and so, consistent with the prevailing views of Creoles as bastardizations of standard languages, the general response was to eliminate weaknesses through the teaching strategy of correction.

Based on the school inspectors' observations and recommendations, teachers corrected – meaning *marked up* – student writing heavily and called it writing instruction. The annual reports from the Education Department at the turn of the twentieth century record that in their attempts to help teachers facilitate Creole speakers' acquisition of English, the inspectors recommended, as Mr John Kerrick advised in 1894, that teachers stop leaving students' original compositions unchecked. Feeling that the weakness in composition was due "partly to the want of a proper system of correction" (quoted in Education Department 1898, 432), Kerrick recommended,

> Everything written should be carefully corrected by the Teacher who should draw a line under every mistake in spelling, or piece of faulty construction or incorrect grammar. The child should then be required to re-write the exercise correcting each mistake to the best of his ability. The Teacher should then correct it again and in this second correction he should not only indicate the mistakes but tell the scholar what the right expression is, and make him write it out on his slate or in the Book ten or twenty times. (quoted in *Governor's Report* 1895, 222)

Kerrick felt that first "writing the corrections in full above the mistakes and giving them back to the scholar to look at . . . is almost as bad as not correcting them at all, for the average child will put the book away and pay no more attention to the matter" (ibid.). He was not aware, however, that the teachers' correction in the second round and multiple transcriptions would not necessarily have practical relevance for the pupils. Teachers actually followed the apodictic approach to correction that is implied in Kerrick's suggestions throughout much of the late nineteenth and twentieth centuries – and many still use it – even though it appears to be a futile exercise since students usually do not understand what has been corrected, the reason for the correction, or how to avoid repeating the error. The discourse of transparency is particularly evident in this area of correction and feedback for, as Connors and Lunsford (1988) as well as Lillis (1999) observe elsewhere, teachers often incorrectly assume that students understand their correction marks and symbols. In Jamaica, such assumptions abounded in the grammar schools, where students were usually from backgrounds in which English was widely spoken. However, as this chapter reveals, even those students experienced difficulties in passing qualifying examinations to attend the UCWI.

Besides the fact that students were to speak and write English based on what Strickland called "an assumed instinct", or through vague correction, at this early stage, language and writing development were often kept separate from content learning. This separation is evident in calls from inspectors for a kind of language across the curriculum programme. One assistant inspector, Mr Mercier, recommended that "greater practice in composition should be afforded by the other subjects in the curriculum" (quoted in Education Department 1919, 192). Another, Mr Kennedy, would assert in 1920 that "early success [in writing and English] will be attained if the subject is taught in correlation with the other subjects" (quoted in Education Department 1921, 68). Such advice was, however, ignored for more than a century, despite widespread failure.

The teaching focus was hardly different in the teacher training colleges that developed beginning with Mico College in the 1860s. These teacher training institutions played the role of secondary school for many aspiring Jamaicans from the elementary sector (as did the equivalent Normal Schools in the United States) until public secondary schools were established in 1879. Various historians report that there were elementary schools and teacher training colleges for blacks and poor coloureds, and preparatory school and local grammar/high school for coloureds and whites of "modest means", or preparatory school and British grammar school for whites and coloureds of "substantial means" (see Gardner 1971; Gordon, 1963). For over a hundred years, then, the highest levels of education available locally were provided by teachers' colleges (for students from low-income groups) and secondary-level schools (for students from middle to high income groups). These secondary schools were "fee paying private schools [that] grew from the need to educate the children of the upper and middle class who could not go "home", i.e., to Europe, to school" (UNESCO 1983, 45). Indeed, as Gordon (1968, 33) writes, "in Jamaica, secondary schools were not called middle class schools. But . . . they remained in practice what they did not claim to be in principle – the educational preserve of those who could afford it." The high schools in this secondary sector, with their academically oriented classics curriculum, became feeder institutions for the university. However, with later expansion in the secondary system, even these high schools changed – albeit slowly – to include students from elementary schools and Creole-speaking backgrounds.

When secondary schools increased in the late 1950s and onwards due to the government's attempts to increase access to education for the masses, language education continued to be based on the requirements of an English education. Students were taught English grammar, composition, literature, mathematics, scripture and English history, geography and physical sciences. In addition to English grammar that was taught as the first language of Jamaicans, Latin, Greek, and French language and literature were also taught in the grammar schools. Caribbean linguist Ian Robertson (1996, 113) asserts that Latin and Greek were thought to have "inherent goodness" and the power to "instil . . . academic rationalism" in users. Although Jamaica has millions of Spanish-speaking neighbours, their language was not considered. French was taught, not because of recognition of the West Indians in the nearby French islands, but to be consistent with the practice in English grammar schools. More important, the language policy in place in the early years of public education in Jamaica confirms that Jamaican Creole was neglected in favour of other languages and to the detriment of predominantly Creole-speaking children.

Unfortunately, what has been marked in the system is, as E. Miller (1981, 372) notes, "no compromise in bridging the gap between Creole and Standard English" for the Creole-speaking child who arrived at school where English was the medium of instruction. The result is that the failures in English, revealing lack of literacy development, continued into the late twentieth century and the new millennium. According to UNESCO's (1983, 12) report on Jamaica, "Private and public employers complain about the low levels of general literacy proficiency and trainability of secondary school leavers and are seriously worried about the continuing decline." This report also specifies that a factor that "weighs heavily in the primary schools is that of the language of instruction. Although English is the language of instruction and that of examinations, the majority of pupils enter school speaking Creole rather than English" (73). The report also mentions an estimation that "perhaps as many as 50% of the primary school leavers are functionally illiterate", to the extent that "the primary education system appears more as an economic and social liability than an asset" (74). Additionally, more than half of the candidates consistently failed the regional Caribbean Examinations Council (CXC) English language examination at the end of the fifth form (see Craig 1999, 227; Task Force 2004, 56–57; Taylor 2003, 1–2).[12] As was becoming evident in the 1950s in the UCWI, and as the next two chapters will establish, these students' experiences in written English usually influence their performance in higher education.

But why have these failures been so widespread and persistent? University personnel ignored the problematic foundations of the Jamaican school when they suggested that problems in the university be addressed in the school or through examinations, but what other specific contextual feature had they ignored? Indeed, what did the colonial and later university administrators not know or ignore when they contributed to institutionalizing linguistic prejudice?

Jamaica's Languages: Myths and Realities

It appears that colonial administrators and university personnel were mistaken in ignoring the vernacular spoken by the demographic majority. This language variety – Jamaican Creole – contributes to disagreement among Creole linguists regarding the specific linguistic model that obtains in the Jamaican language situation. Since the 1960s, some linguists at the UWI have been trying to convince academics and undergraduates, the Ministry of Education, and the society in general that two languages coexist in Jamaica: Standard Jamaican English, which is the country's *superimposed* official language, and Jamaican Creole, which is the *native* language of the majority (see Milson-Whyte 2014). With two languages present, the Jamaican context is described on the one hand as diglossic and on the other as a continuum. Jamaica's linguistic context can be described as diglossic if one recognizes that there are "two separate language varieties, each with its own specific functions within the society" (Devonish 1986, 9). Caribbean linguist Hubert Devonish (1986, 88) draws on the work of Charles Ferguson to explain that this is a "diglossia involving Creole as the language of everyday informal interaction for the mass of the population, and English as the written, public-formal, and official language". However, I. Robertson (1996, 113) maintains that the Creole and standard languages in the Caribbean are not really in a "complementary or diglossic relationship". Robertson draws this conclusion from his assessment of the variations in speech and the overlaps in use of the two languages, with Creole being used not only in informal settings such as the market, but also in formal venues such as the electronic media, church and parliament. Also, as Celia Brown (1991) observes, many Creole speakers who have gained social mobility continue to use the Creole rather than take on English patterns. Such speech behaviours that indicate Creole invasion in areas normally reserved for English erode the diglossia by undermining "the stability of the poles of English vis-à-vis Creole" (22).

In describing the Jamaican (and other Caribbean countries') language context, linguists also speak of a continuum ranging from basilectal Creole (varieties most removed from English) through to acrolectal English (varieties closest to the standard). Devonish (1986, 115) notes that "because of the similarity of the vocabulary of Creole and English, there has been a tendency . . . to develop a series of language varieties in between the most Creole varieties of language on the one hand, and the most standard varieties of English, on the other". The term "Creole continuum" is used to refer to the range of varieties between the Creole base and standard English. The use of the term *continuum* is, however, as problematic as the determination of the boundary between Creole and English. Craig (2006, 108) rightly notes that English Creole, varieties that constitute the mesolect (midway between Creole and English), and Standard English are "more distinguishable in theory than in reality". Some linguists such as Donald Winford (1993; 1997) continue to speak of a Creole continuum, whereas others such as Mervyn Alleyne use the term less readily, preferring instead a recognition of Creole as the *Jamaican* language with its own myriad variations (1988, 131; see also Alleyne 1994, 12).

Despite differences among these linguists regarding the Jamaican linguistic context, there is consensus that the Jamaican language is not slang, broken English, pidgin English, or a debased patois as some laypersons would believe. Although a continuum may be manifest in any one Jamaican's speech, studies show that Jamaican Creole is a fully developed linguistic system that can be distinguished from English and other languages based on its *morphology* (or grammar of word formation), *phonology* (or system of sounds), *syntax* (or organization of elements in a sentence), *lexicon* (or set of vocabulary items), and *semantics* (or meaning associated with lexical items) – features that qualify a language as such. Jamaican Creole is lexically related to English but the two languages differ with regard to the other features, especially phonology and syntax (see Alleyne 1980; Bailey 1966; Cassidy 1961; Cassidy and LePage 1980). Devonish (2001) highlighted these similarities and differences in a proposal for the inclusion of language rights in the draft charter of rights in the Jamaican constitution that he presented to a joint select committee of parliament in Jamaica. Devonish gave the following as "a rough estimate of the linguistic distance between Jamaican and English":

1. For the lexicon/vocabulary, about the distance between the lexicon of Spanish and Portuguese,
2. For phonology/pronunciation patterns, at least the same distance as that between the phonology of French and Spanish,
3. For morphology/word construction patterns, about the same distance as between the morphology of English and German,
4. For syntax/grammatical structure, ranging from about the distance between the syntax of French and Spanish to the distance between the syntax of English and German.

Items 2 to 4 are not dialectal differences: they indicate that the individual who is unfamiliar with Creole will not readily understand a Creole speaker, especially if (based on the continuum model) the latter is using basilectal Creole. However, because of the similarity in lexis (indicated in item 1), the English speaker who is unfamiliar with Creole will, after some exposure, be able to communicate – to some extent – with a monolingual Creole speaker, as a Spanish and a Portuguese speaker may be able to do. Where the Jamaican Creole speaker is concerned, the lexical similarity facilitates comprehension of English statements. This means that Jamaican Creole speakers' perceptive knowledge of English can appear to be high. However, the same is not usually true for production of oral or written English. Indeed, the lexical relation complicates matters. As Craig observes, "through high recognition, *the learner tends to get the illusion that he/she knows the lexifier already*" (1999, 6; emphasis in the original). The other unfortunate consequence of the close lexical relationship is the view that Jamaican Creole is broken English.

This similarity in lexis and the overlap in function of the two languages help explain why the sociolinguistic configuration and interaction in Jamaica defy facile descriptions. The presence of the two languages and the varieties along the English–Creole continuum facilitate code-switching but sometimes result in code-shifting and code-mixing – the kind of transculturation that occurs in contemporary multilingual societies. Code-switching (movement back and forth between two codes) is useful, especially in a diglossic situation. Code-shifting speaks to "the change into one language code and the continuous maintenance of the change", and is "a normal reaction of monolingual groups given tasks to perform in an inadequately acquired L2" (Craig 1999, 42). As I have written elsewhere (see Milson-Whyte 2013), code mixing is facilitated in Jamaica because of the close lexical relationship between Creole and English. As language educator Velma Pollard (1998, 10) says, "The close lexical relationship serves to camouflage the differences of phonology, grammar and idiom." Code-mixing is often confusing to the English speaker, but the "mixer" is usually unaware of the "mix" and unaware that the "mix" is not English. Hence we have such expressions as "Is English we speaking" (M. Morris 1999, 1) or "a hinglish mi a taak" (Pollard 1998, 10). Alleyne (1988, 138) observes, "Speech variation is very intense in Jamaica, and speakers command a series of levels of registers through which they shift without any necessarily apparent motivation." Difficulties arise, however, because speakers do feel that, as Morris and Pollard (above) have documented, they are always "speaking (in) English" (see Milson-Whyte 2013, 120–21). As linguist Pauline Christie (2003, 2) observes, few Jamaicans are "conscious of the extent to which their actual linguistic behaviour contrasts with the traditional ideal that they would very likely claim to uphold".

Despite the transcultural "varieties" in Jamaicans' speech, colonial administrators and later local leaders fostered the faulty assumption that since English was the official language, it was the first language or mother tongue of the majority of Jamaican students. This is the assumption that has been borne out in the methods and approaches employed in English language teaching at all levels of the Jamaican education system for a long time. English language teaching was seen as mere reinforcement of English – the language variety of the elite. In this approach, the Creole language was usually ignored or recognized only as a hindrance to mastery of English. With most teachers in the school system in the nineteenth century and at the UWI at its inception in the twentieth century being originally from Britain, teaching methods reflected those to which teachers had been exposed in Britain. Because the teachers were predominantly British, children were exposed to the variety of English that they spoke. Additionally, since those teachers were accustomed to instructing students who spoke dialects of English, they would not have known how to usefully include the Creole in teaching. Unfortunately, however, when local teachers began to be hired, they modelled their British teachers, avoiding and repressing the use of Jamaican Creole. Peter Maxwell, former president of Jamaica's National Association of Teachers of English, reports a local situation that may be painfully familiar to Spanish and American Indian students in the United States or to Creole speakers who are required to use a different standard language in schools in other Caribbean islands. P. Maxwell (2000–2001, 2) writes, "Traditionally, the school system has given recognition only to the official language, English, and there have even been schools which have fined pupils for using anything else on the school premises." Carrington (1978, 86) explains the reason for this penalty: "Within the framework of the education systems it is not until the 1970s that any official language syllabuses have discussed the existence of creoles and their educational implications with any degree of enlightenment." He summarizes the prevailing linguistic attitudes well: "Prior to this, the [Creole] languages have been variously proscribed, ignored or rejected as nuisances causing persistent errors in English which have to be eradicated by punishment and drastic language drills in English grammar (most of which have doubtful practical value)" (ibid.).

Increasingly, however, there is recognition that, as Peter Roberts (1988, 189) rightly says, "standard English for most West Indians is neither foreign nor native". This situation distinguishes the Jamaican experience from the colonial and early national periods in the United States, although similarities can be seen today given students called "Generation 1.5" for whom English is neither a foreign nor second language (see Mangelsdorf 2010, 114). Many children in Jamaica grow up hearing the English language, but just as many have difficulty producing it in speech or writing. Whereas many modern-day Jamaicans are simultaneous bilinguals, more are likely to be Creole monolinguals or Creole-dominant bilinguals. Therefore, English is perhaps better seen as a *second* language for many Jamaicans; however, even this categorization presents a challenge. As I have indicated elsewhere (see Milson-Whyte 2014), in the average classroom in a Jamaican public school, most pupils are monolingual Creole speakers, a few may be bilingual, some may speak English and Creole with varying degrees of facility, and very few may be monolingual English speakers. As various scholars recognize, this situation renders difficult adopting strategies directed exclusively to first language, second language or foreign language teaching (see Bryan 2004, 87; McCourtie 1998, 111).

In an attempt to right the wrongs of earlier administrators in Jamaica, various linguists have proposed ways to accommodate predominantly Creole speakers in education. Devonish (1986), for example, has been advocating for institutionalizing Creole as the major language of internal communication. In his view, this measure would allow Creole speakers to feel less disenfranchised than they do in the country, especially in legal matters where "Creole speakers are bound to be discriminated against on grounds of language" (89). However, as in the United States where discussions of non-standard dialects and languages other than English are sensitive matters, in Jamaica any suggestion about the use of Creole in hitherto English domains sparks much debate. Discussions of the legitimacy of Creole for educational purposes yields reactions such as those in the United States to the Conference on College Composition and Communication's *Students' Right to Their Own Language* (CCCC 1974) or to the Oakland School Board's 18 December 1996 resolution that acknowledged that Ebonics is the primary language of its African American students. As the third epigraph in this chapter from Carrington says, to speak of "language" in postcolonial situations is not merely to refer to verbal expression of thoughts and feelings or the creation of knowledge. It is, instead, an indication of entry into an ongoing debate on a very sensitive issue. This situation is captured well in Bakhtin's ([1934–35] 1981, 271) assertion that "we are taking language not as a system of abstract grammatical categories, but rather language conceived as ideologically saturated, language as a world view". This debate exceeds linguistic codes, with the concern being projecting a particular perspective or ideology. In the Jamaican weltanschauung, language usually means English. Whatever language can do or whatever can be done in or through language, that language is English because, as Pollard (1995) says, there is a "misconception that English is 'Language' rather than 'a language'". Thanks to the 1847 *Circular Despatch*, this erroneous association of English with *language* and not just *a language* is deeply ingrained in the Jamaican psyche, and significantly influences attitudes to writing and its development. As stated, the students who suffer the most because of this erroneous association constitute the majority – those who are monolingual Creole speakers or Creole-dominant bilinguals. Many of these children arrive at school already adept at code-switching and having other linguistic resources and principles of linguistic competence that could aid learning, but then find that their natural language abilities are ignored. The reality is that, rather than take an additive approach to language learning, the Jamaican school system has historically promoted what Nero (2010, 142–43) criticizes as "a linguistic trade-off" in which "acquisition or affirmation of one discourse comes at the expense of another". The result in Jamaica has been a form of silencing that has yielded the lack of personal and national development that is alluded to in previously mentioned reports (see Craig 1999, 227; Ministry of Education 2001, 3; Task Force 2004, 56–57; Taylor 2003, 1–2; and UNESCO 1983, 74). This situation has arisen because, as Lisa Delpit (2006, 94) writes regarding the experiences of many African American children who are required to express ideas while simultaneously applying new rules learned, "forcing speakers to monitor their language typically produces silence".

In recent times, linguists' persistence at promoting the realities of Jamaica's language context has begun to influence national language policies. In Jamaica's most explicit policy for language teaching to date, *Language Education Policy*, the Ministry of Education (2001, 3) described the Jamaican language situation as "bilingual with Standard Jamaican English (SJE) and Jamaican Creole (JC) being the two languages in operation". This document was prepared to address concerns about language use, inhibitions of learners, and unsatisfactory performance in English language examinations. The ministry's policy position "retains SJE as the official language and advocates the policy option which promotes oral use of the home language in schools while facilitating the development of skills in SJE". Importantly, there is recognition that "the fluid nature of language usage between these two languages, as well as the peculiar nature of the linguistic relationship they share, creates difficulty for the majority of Creole speakers learning English" (ibid.). Although the problem could very well be the approach taken in teaching rather than "the relationship" the languages share, this document pointed to a long-awaited recognition of the "real" linguistic context of the country and consideration of related teaching methods. This recognition is, however, limited to some representatives of the Jamaican Ministry of Education and other government officials since parliament did not approve the draft policy and it has not been disseminated widely in schools (see Nero 2014).

Changes in perception of the country's linguistic realities – though limited – also led to passing references to the "home language" in the curriculum guides for primary and secondary schools (such as the Primary Education Improvement Programme and the Reform of Secondary Education). For example, the *Revised Primary Curriculum* that was implemented in 1999 records the first objective in unit one of the first grade (grade 1) as "pupils will use home language to talk about themselves and their experiences" (Ministry of Education and Culture 1999, 298). This is in marked contrast to the largely implicit policies that were implemented up to and beyond the first half of the twentieth century to prepare students to *write* their way into the university. However, all of the statements really continue to support development in English only, ultimately maintaining its dominance and Creole's and Creole users' inferiority. As Carrington (1981, 131) writes, "One of the fundamental obstacles [to literacy development] has been the lack of reasoned relationship between the language of the learner and his community and the language of instruction." For a long time, Jamaica's education system ignored the "fundamental and long-standing principle of language teaching that a learner acquires the skills most readily when he is exposed to them in his own language in particular at the beginning of his exposure" (133). Continued high failure rates – as in those reported for secondary-level English language examinations or alluded to by university administrators (see Virtue 2013) – suggest that Carrington's (1981, 133) observation is still largely true in Jamaica: "Where [the principle] is finding its way into official thinking, its execution is poor and ineffective."

Conclusion

Because of the way in which English was imposed as the medium of instruction and because of the resultant failure evident in students' inability to demonstrate proficiency or communicative competence in English as required, I argue that educators in Jamaica have been sorely mistaken in expecting lower educational levels to prepare students to do disciplinary writing in English in the university. When students failed to write intrinsically in the first decade of the university's existence, administrators and educators perpetuated the myth of transience by locating the problem in the high school and in preparatory examinations. They suggested that the ills be remedied in the sixth form or that the institution consider different preparatory and entrance examinations. No one in this period suggested the need for writing instruction as an integral part of disciplinary learning; rather, administrators and academics seemed to perpetuate the faulty assumptions that locals used English based on an assumed instinct and that writing is an elementary skill that potential local leaders could unconsciously transfer to writing requirements in the university. These assumptions reflect the discourse of transparency, which becomes evident at the elementary level of education since the beginnings of public education in the country. In this system, excellence – as far as it could be associated with wealth and class – was valued over social equity. In other words, children of means could access educational opportunities in a system where provisions were not made for all children of school age to access the system and succeed. Simultaneously, English – the language variety of the elite – became the medium of instruction, thereby privileging those who already spoke that variety or could learn it quickly by virtue of exposure in the school. When administrators chose to use English as the medium of instruction in a land where the majority spoke Creole, and when teachers did not teach English but only taught *through* it, they conveyed the sense of transparency in language use. In other words, the belief was that students arrived at school prepared to use English and would therefore not need to be taught English. It is this same discourse of transparency that would emerge in the university setting: only that there the view was that after much *repetitive writing* and being educated, students did not require explicit instruction in producing disciplinary discourse.

These attitudes to the two languages are consistent with the rhetoric of transparency, specifically an attempt to promote those already in possession of the appropriate linguistic capital. The original British teachers and their later local successors maintained and perpetuated what Bourdieu (1991) termed the "habitus" – the habits, practices, and ideology – of a white elite. As M. Kazim Bacchus (1994, 2005) argues in his series on education in the ex-British Caribbean colonies, the policies and procedures implemented by the local elites and educational authorities served to (re)establish the legitimacy of the hegemony of the ruling class. Therefore, all children were taught literacy in English, often to the detriment of monolingual Creole speakers. Mastering written English is a Herculean task for many Jamaicans, and the result of marginalizing Jamaican Creole in the school system has been massive failure, though the connection is rarely made to the language of instruction.

In alerting Caribbean policymakers to the crucial link between personal development and the appropriateness of the language selected for literacy learning, I. Robertson (1996, 118) advises, "International currency may be sacrificed initially for a positive self-concept, or the other way around." In Jamaica, a positive self-concept and genuine language and writing development may have been sacrificed in the attempt to implement a deliberate English language policy and achieve international currency – an attempt that persistent failures confirm is largely frustrated. In the 1940s and 1950s, university administrators and many educators continued to focus on excellence and achieving international currency to the extent that they ignored various factors: the country's linguistic context, how many prospective local leaders would have learned English, and how writing in disciplines requires knowledge that extends beyond the linguistic code to codified writing conventions. The discussions surrounding a survey "Use of English" course that would be introduced in 1963 suggest that some administrators and faculty may have understood that writing enables and reveals learning, and, therefore, believed in tying writing instruction to disciplinary learning. However, the myths of transience and of the transparency of language in disciplines persisted largely because some academics associated explicit writing instruction in academe with remediation.

3 | Professionalizing the Aspirant Middle Class through Survey Writing after Independence, 1960s to the Mid-1980s

We considered that the orientation of our school programmes did not make West Indian students sufficiently aware of their unique cultural and historical background and failed to create the perception that would enable and inspire them to play a confident role in Caribbean and World Affairs. For these reasons we decided to introduce Survey Courses in the first years at University in such subjects as Caribbean History, the Development of Civilization and the Use of English. (UWI 1970, 3).

The assumptions of the discourse of transparency work to obscure the materiality of language and the operation of values in preferred rhetorical strategies, and so the "visibility" of language means that something is wrong, and the issue becomes one of remediation (Carys Jones, Joan Turner and Brian Street 1999b, 125).

Whereas at the start of the UCWI the concern was for preparing a small local elite to take over leadership of West Indian societies, by the 1960s, following in the wake of independence for many Caribbean territories, there were obvious expansions in the student body. National fervour was accompanied by desires for social mobility in students from modest homes. As governments facilitated these students' entry into higher levels beyond the elementary level of education, the university also responded to citizens' calls to make education relevant to preparing students who would enter the professional middle class. However, as in the 1940s and early 1950s when administrators and academics perpetuated the faulty assumption that writing is an elementary skill that potential local leaders could unconsciously transfer to writing requirements in the university, because of limited understandings of writing, administrators and faculty persisted in promoting the rhetoric of transparent disciplinarity and perpetuating the myth of transience in the 1960s to the mid-1980s. The rhetoric of transparent disciplinarity persisted especially regarding the institution's emphasis on excellence over social equity and faculty's association of writing instruction with remediation and view of writing as largely separate from disciplinary learning. In this period, administrators and faculty also persisted in stating that any problems in students' language use or writing should have been remedied in the high school, thereby perpetuating the myth of transience. These views emerged in the discussions surrounding the development and teaching in the "Use of English" survey course that was introduced in 1963 after the UCWI became the independent UWI.

The introduction of the "Use of English" survey course at the UWI was in an era that was marked by political independence for Jamaica and other Caribbean territories, upward social mobility through education for increasing numbers of students from less privileged backgrounds than those of the initial cohorts, and an impulse for relevance. Also significant in this period was the introduction of evening courses and nonresident students. This change suggested broadening access in an institution that is modelled on the elite English university and is, therefore, marked by concerns for excellence. Relying on information from past lecturers including Eric (David) King who was an undergraduate in the 1950s, "Use of English" tutor in the 1960s, and later course moderator in the institution, and through analysis of various course and course-related documents preserved by former course lecturers or available in the UWI (Mona) Archives, I explore the attitudes of administrators, content faculty, and "Use of English" staff to language instruction as it served to professionalize the aspirant middle class.

This largely documentary history will demonstrate that administrators and content faculty understood language and writing instruction as *remedial* instruction in English language and not necessarily as initiation into disciplinary rhetorical conventions. However, because "Use of English" faculty graded but did not teach grammar and because they eventually emphasized sociolinguistic content but not also disciplinary content, they too promoted formalist presuppositions. Academics, therefore, did not provide adequate opportunities for students to gain practical understanding of new content (including grammar) and to critically reflect on such new knowledge within disciplines. In essence, academics' incorrect assumptions about entering students led to a curriculum that appears to have been largely linguistically mistaken. Ultimately, the debate sparked over the conception, implementation and evolution of the "Use of English" course evidences the transparency conceptualization and, therefore, limited views of writing – beliefs that the focus of higher education ought to be excellence rather than equity; the academy is a single discourse community; writing is an intrinsic skill that is learned once and generalized to all other situations and is therefore not connected to disciplinary learning;

and any instruction in writing at the tertiary level serves the purpose of remediation rather than development in disciplines (see Russell 2002, 9–10). Hence, although it will appear that the rationale for introducing "Use of English" in Jamaica is different from that for introducing composition in the United States in the late nineteenth century to address issues of correctness in student writing, some attitudes expressed in the Jamaican situation are redolent of accounts (such as John Brereton 1995) of opposing attitudes to the need for composition in the United States in its early years.

Political Independence and the Impulse for Relevance

The emphasis on excellence at the UCWI was not immediately apparent at the beginning of the 1960s. Indeed, it appeared that the institution was shedding its English character that combined a University of London curriculum and an Oxbridge emphasis on elitism by expanding enrolment and providing access to hitherto excluded groups of students. These changes occurred after world-renowned economist, Professor (later Sir) W. Arthur Lewis, assumed duties as the first West Indian principal of the campus in April 1960. With his expansionist, egalitarian outlook, and probably in response to years of criticism of the elitist and conservative orientation of the UCWI, Lewis broadened the curriculum towards more instrumental ends and facilitated new campuses, eventually leading to the UCWI's independence from the University of London. Lewis expanded the student body from a solely upper- and middle-income group to include students from working classes and changed the campus from being predominantly residential to including evening students (see Sherlock and Nettleford 1990). The UWI's (2006–7, 1) *Official Statistics 2005/2006* records that whereas in 1959–60 only 695 students were registered at the UWI (Mona), by 1962–63 this number had risen to 1,486, with another 118 at Cave Hill and 583 at St Augustine.

While Principal W. Arthur Lewis is often credited with initiating this expansion in enrolment at the institution, changes in the UCWI's character also arose from tension between nationalism and regionalism. The 1960s was a decade in which many territories in the English-speaking Caribbean region shed their colonial status and became politically independent. Among these countries is Jamaica, which achieved independence in 1962. Several of these countries contributed financially to the regional university, leading Sherlock and Nettleford (1990, v) to highlight one of its peculiar features: "the British universities bargain with one government, we in the Caribbean negotiate with fourteen". This feature implies problems arising from having so many small-nation government contributors. Therefore, it is not surprising that, as various scholars imply and Vivienne Roberts (2003, 47) asserts, the UCWI/UWI has also been pulled between centrifugal forces of nationalism and centripetal forces of regionalism (see also Marshall 1998; Sherlock and Nettleford 1990). This tension has led to what Cobley (2000, 15) calls the "political and ideological struggle for the soul of the university in the region". Cobley associates this struggle with the Caribbean peoples' penchant for improvisation: the British established a regional university and encouraged the formation of a West Indian federation of islands that it could continue to dominate, but West Indian nationalists – notably Eric Williams, Oxford graduate, Howard University professor, and later premier of Trinidad – had other aspirations. These individuals saw in federation the route to independence from Britain. As the UCWI encouraged West Indian thought, the students and the islands from which they came experienced a sense of local identity – far greater than the collective identity that the institution was meant to promote (Cobley 2000, 14–15). Ironically, then, the attempted federation of West Indian islands and Guyana collapsed in the early 1960s as Caribbean islands gained independence from Britain. As individuals and islands asserted their identity, they also called for changes in the university to address the needs of students who aspired to join the professional middle class.

The pull of nationalism of the era extended to transformation through transculturation in the university, that is, through institutional and curricular changes that arose from appropriation rather than abrogation of materials from the University of London. The UCWI began as a ward of the University of London and a part of an imperial university system. Therefore, the UCWI's matriculation requirements, calendars, syllabuses, examinations, and degrees were the same as London's. However, as Nettleford (1986, 9) observes, the university's historical profile does not adequately reflect the long-standing tension between "a total Anglophile commitment" and a persistent attempt to provide education that is informed by "West Indian sensibility and historical experience". This attempt to be regionally relevant was partly inspired by public criticism of what Sherlock and Nettleford (1990, 126) call the institution's "limited access, inequality of educational opportunity and the wide gap between the content of education and the real world". Confronted with an external agenda, and with criticisms from many individuals in Jamaica and elsewhere about the relevance of a specialized English education, UCWI faculty and administrators began agitating for reform in the institution's early years. They began the process by selecting from the University of London's curriculum and reinventing it in the local context, although London had to approve the reinvention. Consequently, after operating as a college of the University of London, the UCWI received a new Royal Charter establishing it as an autonomous degree-granting institution in 1962.

The curricular and other changes that led to the UCWI's independence from the University of London also embodied the institution's attempts to respond to local demands for upward social mobility. In his address at the matriculation ceremony in October 1960, Lewis (1960) informed the gathering that the cost for each student at UCWI was £1,350 whereas a student could be sent overseas for £600 per year. He wished to reduce the costs at UCWI to £950 per year for each student. Lewis's premise for expanding the student population was, therefore, related to economics. However, the change he initiated would result in expansion in the middle class. Lewis seemed to reinforce the existing class structure when he informed the incoming students that they would be "among the leaders of West Indian society" and would have responsibility for "the mind, or the life or the work of other West Indians". In saying that they would have responsibility for shaping society, Lewis asserted that the students would be "the solid middle class of society". Most of the students whose social class Lewis confirmed would have been coming from sixth forms and would have been considered representatives of the meritocratic elite at the secondary level. However, based on LePage's (1955, 41–42) description of the UWI population in the 1950s, among the gathering there would have been students from the lower ranges of the middle class who were aspiring to increased social mobility. By 1963, there would also have been more students from this stratum in the university owing to the provision of evening classes and accommodation of nonresidential students beginning in 1963–64 (see UWI 1964, 120). Because of the political and social changes evident then, by the 1970s increasing numbers of students from lower-income homes would also have entered the institution. In this period, the then prime minister of Jamaica, Michael Manley, introduced "free education". This development followed explanations in the *New Deal for Education in Independent Jamaica* (1966, i) that the thrust in education would be based on the view that "opportunity for the best education that the country can afford must be open to every child, because all children are equally important". The democratization of education in this period of strong nationalist sentiment led to attempts to teach students who would not have got into high school and university in earlier years – not because of academic performance but on account of their social class and consequent financial means. The result was that more individuals than those in previous decades could use education as a route to enter and expand the existing middle class.

These changes are germane to my consideration of attitudes to writing instruction. Although faculty began to comment on problems in students' writing before the 1960s, large-scale instruction in language and writing did not appear until the 1960s. Indeed, large-scale language instruction was to surface almost simultaneously with the expansion in enrolment and curricular changes at the UWI in the 1960s. When the Mona campus began to accommodate nonresidential students in its second decade of existence, the university began to attract a large proportion of students from low-income groups, changing from a situation in which the majority of students were from middle-income groups that displayed facility in using English. The new cohorts of students, many of whom could not claim English as their first language, would be among the first to take "Use of English". This was one of three foundation (general education) courses introduced in the 1960s, when Caribbean conditions began to be increasingly emphasized in the curriculum over British courses that some critics such as Cobley (2000, 17) would later criticize as being "of doubtful utility" in the West Indies. Many of those first-generation university students were also first-language Creole speakers whose linguistic backgrounds are not irrelevant to discussions of writing instruction and personal, institutional and societal development. Analysis of the developments in and attitudes to that course confirms I. Maxwell's (1980, 378) observation that, despite the changes, the institution continued to emphasize excellence: this emphasis was to the extent that observers described the institution as one which ab initio "had been designed to be an institution of the highest academic standard and this ideal had been ardently preserved".

Ad Hoc Beginnings of "Use of English"

In the 1960s, the transparency conceptualization, specifically regarding emphasis on excellence over social equity, first becomes evident in the ad hoc beginnings of the "Use of English" course. Here, I am referring to how the course was introduced, which students were required to take it, what the course emphasis was, how teaching was to be conducted and faculty's subscription to the conduit metaphor. When this first *English language* course called "Use of English" was introduced at the UWI in 1963, it was offered to all students except those doing an honours degree and those in the social sciences. This interfaculty survey course, which did not stress writing, was modelled on a similar survey course that had been introduced in universities in England (Dyche 2006b). Parker (1978, 330) reports that survey and interdisciplinary courses were introduced in England to raise the prestige of general degrees, and familiarize students with their society's cultural, historical, political and scientific foundations. Therefore, in the early 1960s, following similar concerns in England that too many students there were taking special degrees, administrators encouraged students in Jamaica to do general rather than special degrees. The UCWI's achievement of full university status and the independence of various Caribbean countries would also have inspired reflection on the degree structures and their suitability to local needs. After officials from the three UWI campuses toured British universities, they made the announcement contained in the first epigraph to this chapter: general degrees and similar survey courses would be applicable to the developing West Indian society. These courses that were introduced in revised general degree programmes were to include English, the development of civilization (including a survey of the humanities and the development of science and technology), and the historical development of the Caribbean (UWI 1963a, 3). The British "Use of English" course had links to the study of rhetoric in terms of the different appeals people used and how to evaluate them. The focus at the UWI was also on language in use, with the tutors aiming to raise students' awareness about language in use in general and, by the 1970s, in the Caribbean in particular.

Towards mid-1963, after having decided to offer the survey courses, the upper administration appointed committees to define the content and instructional procedures for the new courses that would be included in revised degree programmes. The committee with responsibility for "Use of English" described it as "Practice of Oral and Written English. Different Kinds of Communication. Techniques of Argument. Critical Analysis of Commonplace English" (UWI 1963b, 1; UWI 1964, 171, 227). Senate Paper 18 (UWI 1963b) records that William Carr, a lecturer in the Department of English, would act as moderator for the course. Fifteen mixed classes, each with approximately thirty students from different faculties, would begin at Mona. Although earlier senate papers and minutes indicated plans for "Use of English" to be taught for two hours each week, Senate Paper 18 documents that there would be one-and-a-half hours for each class weekly – "a suitable time for which would be 5–6:30 p.m." (UWI 1963b, 1). Because there would have been about 250 day and evening students and limited accommodation in the Faculty of Arts, Carr (1963a, 3) recommended that some teaching would have to be done on Saturday mornings. Although evening and weekend classes may not seem unusual to contemporary readers, in the 1960s, a negative impression would probably have been created by the time and day when the course was to be taught. The large classes also suggest that students would probably not receive much individual attention. It appears, however, that because teaching was usually done in large lectures, thirty students in a "Use of English" class would have seemed like a small number.

Other faculty members also proposed how the course was to be taught. Among these were Figueroa, the dean of education, who had given the lectures in logic that are mentioned in chapter 2 and R.J. Owens the acting head of the Department of English. Based on their recommendations, in the first year, instruction in the "Use of English" course was given in weekly one-and-a-half-hour *seminars* and not in a large group lecture followed by a small group tutorial, as was the case in other courses. Teaching was (and still is) centralized, so all tutors and students used a common "Use of English" course content and course exercise syllabus that the course moderator prepared and distributed each term. The syllabus used in the first year was largely ill-defined because, according to Carr (1963a, 4), "Use of English" was "a course new both to teachers and students and development [could] only be created in the classroom not predicted in advance". For the second year of teaching in the course, Richard Allsopp (1964b), in his capacity as chief university moderator of the course, drew on Carr's (1963a, 1963b) and Owens's (1963) papers as well as suggestions from Jean Creary (1964) at Mona to "provide a more detailed programme for the guidance of tutors". This syllabus, "The 'Use of English Course'", contained a list of topics for teaching, class discussion and writing each week; an advance reading assignment (from a UC100 course textbook) as preparation for the class of the following week; and five in-course, out-of-class and essay assignments (including one review of a recently published book, magazine or issue of a journal to be done over the Christmas vacation). None of the books used in the course was written by a West Indian, which suggests that the university continued the tradition started at lower educational levels of using content materials that were usually foreign to West Indian sensibility – even though this lack could have been explained by a dearth of local materials.

Administrators solicited part-time help in order to offer the course, and this situation resulted in negative perceptions of "Use of English". Allsopp (1967) noted how attitudes to staffing served to undermine the status of the course and its teachers in academia. He reported that the problem with staffing intensified when medical, nursing, and theological students began to be required to take the course that was originally a requirement for students pursuing a general honours degree. Full-time staffing was not increased commensurate with increased numbers of students to be taught, so part-timers were continually sought – though usually not in sufficient numbers. More part-timers meant more scrutiny of marking, with moderation through reviewing of scripts "proving a heavy and exacting exercise" for Allsopp (5). Attitudes to the course and its facilitators were affected because, as Allsopp wrote, "it is impossible to avoid the impression among students, and . . . among staff, that a course which has to be largely carried by a number of 'outsiders' whose continuance in service cannot be guaranteed is not an important course" (3).

The vice chancellor attributed the problems in the first year to the short time in which administrators and faculty had to prepare for the course. The *Report to Council from the Vice Chancellor for the Year Ending 31st July 1965* (1965, 221) provides some explanation for the ad hoc feeling associated with the beginnings and structure of the course. It indicates that because the council decided only in June 1963 to offer the survey courses in October 1963, there was not enough time to "organize them completely satisfactorily" in terms of staff appointments and programme planning. The then vice chancellor explained that regular staff from other subject areas along with an abundance of part-timers taught in the course at Mona. He noted a situation that is reminiscent of literature faculty regarding composition in the United States: "the natural decision to give the 'Use of English' course in small groups made . . . a large demand on staffing far beyond the reach of the full-time staff in English literature, some of whom did not accept it as being within their domain". As well, with approximately four hundred students involved at Mona, and with inadequate arrangements for staffing, science students were not offered the course in the first year. The vice chancellor concluded that the survey courses had been heavily criticized because of those challenges and because "other students and staff not involved in the programme" considered the courses "an added burden" (ibid.; see also Allsopp 1965b).

Despite the vice chancellor's concessions, later course reports show that there were few changes in the course arrangements to improve perceptions of it. Allsopp's (1971) "Report on the Use of English Course" provides other reasons for which the course would be marginalized in Jamaica. While on the other campuses, the course was delivered two hours for each of twenty-five weeks for the year, an anomaly persisted at Mona where each session lasted only an hour and a half. Staffing problems also persisted: Allsopp observed that the university had "more than 800 students rising to more than 1,400 doing a compulsory Course, staffed by 2 to 4 full-time teachers aided by about 12 changing part-time teachers". He explained that on two of the campuses, those full-time teachers were "temporary replacements of the permanent appointees". Allsopp underscored that "the very high proportion of part-time staff at Mona in particular . . . [was] a factor undermining the effectiveness of the programme and general student attitude to the Course" (1971, 2). One result of large student numbers and limited staff was that the classes were too large, "making pursued discussion and effective approaches to *oral English* only notional" (3; emphasis in the original). In addition to increasing student numbers and to insufficient provision of teaching staff, there were also inadequate provision of secretarial help and lack of specified times for the course on some faculty timetables. Changes to the course that could have helped to increase staff and student perceptions of it were slow in coming. The seminar length changed to two hours in the late 1960s, and it was not until 1980–81 that the course was restructured at Mona to increase contact hours to three per week (King 1984, 1).

The course emphasis may also have affected how students and staff perceived the course. Allsopp (1964b, 1) recorded that the three initial aims of the course were to "train students to obtain maximum benefit" from lectures and printed materials, "acquaint students with the methods and purposes which can control the use of language", and "familiarize students with different languages of persuasion and to inculcate in the students a capacity for reasoned and coherent argument and discussion". Since the focus was on language use in the university, for the first eleven years, tutors emphasized

1. the development of thoughtful interpretation, clear thinking and critical judgement of all forms of communication in English,
2. intelligent statement of opinion in English, and
3. improved attitudes to types of language and a more enlightened use of "the Dictionary". (Allsopp 1974, 1)

Allsopp (1964b, 3) stressed that the course was meant to encourage students to develop their general knowledge in order to be able to present reasoned opinions. Increased knowledge was to be realized through "personal research", and students were to learn to evaluate sources, including dictionaries and reference works. However, administrators had originally conceived the course as a largely oral one. Discussion was central to teaching in the course, with the approach being one Eric King described as "more one of lecture-seminars than of lectures proper" in which the following topics were covered in the first year: "Attacking the power of print" in the first term, "communication and logic" in the second term and "critical approach to statistical information" in the third term. The seminar format confirms the recommended oral emphasis in the course. Students were forewarned that seminars were not lectures and that they were expected to participate actively for at least half of the time (unpublished data). According to King, in the late 1960s and onwards, the standard procedure was as follows. In the first fifteen minutes, the tutor reviewed very briefly the advance reading assignment and then invited students to ask the question(s) they had brought to class following their advance reading assignment. Other students in the class were then invited to supply their answer to the student's question, if they could. Finally, if no student could provide an answer with which the student who asked the question was satisfied, the class tutor intervened and hopefully supplied a satisfactory answer. In the next thirty minutes of the session, the tutor distributed a course-content-and-exercise handout and taught its content. The class then separated into small groups and completed the course exercise, each group doing a different one, in about thirty minutes. In the last forty-five minutes, the class reassembled for small groups to report back to the large group. These reports were usually followed by a culminating class discussion, with little if any requirement for individual students to write (unpublished data).

Consonant with the oral emphasis in the course was faculty's submission to the conduit metaphor, which reflects the discourse of transparency. With initial emphasis on study skills, extended writing seemed to be incidental. In the early years of the course, writing functioned as a demonstration of knowledge, especially in terms of note-taking in lectures and answers in examinations. What little writing was done in the course involved a two-stage linear process of "think" then "write", reflecting the conduit model of language discussed in chapter 1. Owens (1963, 2) had proposed that oral work be emphasized to develop "students' ability to listen, grasp and to reproduce" for two reasons: "People talk well before they write well" and "more work can be done, more quickly, and 'marking' is eliminated – though checking and correcting are not". The first reason epitomizes a myth that was prevalent then, and both reasons indicate what little stress was placed on actual writing development. Because Owens believed that in addition to the study skills that students would develop they should be taught "the rules of argument and the use of logic" (3), he recommended the use of what was then "the manual of rhetoric", Cleanth Brooks and Robert Penn Warren's *The Fundamentals of Good Writing* (1956). He believed this manual could introduce students to the modes of discourse and help students "realise that each type of discourse calls for a different use of English, and it calls for careful preparation and a clear plan of what is intended" (3). In all of these recommendations, Owens propagated the conduit model of language which is consistent with the rhetoric of transparency, for he believed "before any good writing of any kind can be done, the writer must think clearly" (3). In other words, in his view, writers did heuristic work in their mind, and writing merely served to record clear completed thought.

Carr (1963b, 3) would also support the conduit metaphor by stating explicitly the – not totally true – claim that "people speak well before they write well so the first term's work would be predominantly oral, getting students to shape and handle their own experience, to do justice in language, to what they themselves feel and think". Carr seemed convinced that it was thinking before speaking or writing that would allow for clear expression and prevent fraudulent language use in any discipline. He emphasized that the primary concern of faculty who would be involved in teaching the course, "the concern which ought properly to inform any university course, is the quality of the student's mind when he leaves the university" (4). Carr asserted that "a mind which can acquiesce to cliché, take the word for the deed, employ stale ingredients of language, permit words to shape thought rather than thought words is of manifest inutility to the society it lives in" (ibid.). In promoting thought as predeterminant of words, Carr unfortunately reinforced the conduit model of language – a sense that words are always and only in service of thought which precede them and are also transparent and neutral (see Lillis and Turner 2001, 62–63).

Although Allsopp (1964b, 2), unlike other early course moderators, encouraged a balance between oral and written work in the course, he also suggested that writing merely transcribes thought. His views emerge in a 16 January 1964 "Interview with Gladstone Holder", the government information officer in Barbados. This interview was to allow Allsopp (1964a, 1) to follow up on what Holder called "the question of whether or not this course could not be provided at Secondary level and so take some of the load off the University". In this interview, Allsopp advocated the view of language as transparent recording when, in defence of the course, he stated: "You must be able to express your thoughts clearly. *First think clearly then express them clearly* and analytically" (3). In this response, Allsopp expressed the conduit metaphor which separates thinking and inscription. In stressing the desire for honesty in communication, Allsopp asserted that a student has to be taught "to be clear about his own thinking, that his *clear thinking must precede expression* because the person should be clear on what he wants to say and learn the best way to say just that" (7). In these responses, Allsopp ignored the way in which expression/words can help to clarify thinking, that is, how through the process of writing the writer may discover what he or she really wants to say and how best to say it. Allsopp and others who perpetuated the conduit model of language encouraged people to believe that you demonstrate understanding through writing rather than also use writing as a means to gaining understanding. This emphasis on thinking before writing – although not expressed in such terms – probably helped to fuel later charges for the course to teach students to *write clearly*.

Excellence versus Equity: Assumed versus Real Linguistic and Writing Profiles of Students

Besides failing to exploit the usefulness of writing to learning and to developing thought, "Use of English" faculty as well as administrators attributed incorrect linguistic and writing profiles to some incoming students. Faculty's response to the realization that their assumptions were wrong also attests to emphasis on excellence rather than also social equity in the institution. Although there had to have been students from backgrounds in which they had limited contact with English, often only learning it in school, course materials continued to mention that the "Use of English" course was designed for students with high levels of proficiency in English. Donald Winford (1973a, 1), then-moderator at the St Augustine campus, explained that the course "presupposes familiarity with, and ability to use, Standard English". The course was concerned more with helping students develop the "capacity for reasoned and coherent argument and discussion" and the "ability to discern and comprehend nuances of meaning and precise language" rather than with learning "the conventions of standard written English" (ibid.). Winford (1977, 1) also explained that the course was structured "based on the premise that students [had] already acquired a basic command of these skills before entry into university". He admitted that "Use of English" faculty were "aware that certain language skills" besides those they addressed were "essential for University students, and that some students in fact lack[ed] certain of these skills". However, the "Use of English" staff were reluctant to make changes to the course to address written English conventions: "mechanics of Standard English (e.g., grammar, conventions of spelling and punctuation) as well as those involved in composition (coherence, paragraph structure, clarity of expression and the like)". This reluctance was because of staff's belief that the "Use of English" course "offer[ed] certain kinds of information, and address[ed] itself to certain more sophisticated types of language skill which . . . represent a vital ingredient in the academic programme of first year University students" (ibid.).

Mertel Thompson (1986), one of the "Use of English" tutors, shed light on the specific aspects of writing in which students did not demonstrate adequate levels of proficiency when she provided a description of freshman English students in Jamaica in a presentation at the Convention of the Conference on College Composition and Communication in New Orleans in 1986. Her exposé shows the extent to which the course as designed may not have met students' needs, and, instead, continued the tradition of the schools in using a curriculum that appeared to be linguistically mistaken. M. Thompson observed that some students "exhibit[ed] a lack of organizational skill, pa[id] scant attention to details and in general display[ed] very little control over their material". As regards "lower order concerns", she noted that "certain types of writing miscues [were] overwhelmingly present" (6). These often fell into three categories, indicating the influence of the oral Creole language, incomplete mastery of English – the medium of instruction, and lack of familiarity with the requirements of print. Facilitators concluded that "the language barrier engage[d] so much of [students'] attention that it inhibit[ed] progress both at the level of thought and surface correctness" (7). M. Thompson also observed that most of the students who "experience[d] greater problems" were those enrolled in the sciences (13). She explained this weakness based on the fact that – in that era – these students got little writing practice after the fourth form (grade 10) in high school when students were streamed into arts and sciences. She felt then that too much was being done in the one noncredit "Use of English" course that the university offered. The many components included "basic linguistic concepts, research skills, elementary principles of logic, the use of statistics in communication, the elements of style, and the use of emotive persuasion in advertising and political propaganda" (14). In her view, attempting to cover so much in twenty-two teaching weeks only led to "a highly structured, content-oriented approach to teaching and testing". Her recommendation was that, instead of attempts to include a reading and writing skills unit into the "Use of English" course, another course should be introduced "especially devoted to writing" because the "problem of adequate time preclude[d] successful teaching" (ibid.).

Students' writing challenges, especially as they relate to Jamaica's linguistic context, are also explained in Joyce Walker's "Some Comments on the Work Done by Students in Use of English" (1966). In this document, Walker presented excerpts from a science student's failing script to consider "the degree of his mastery of the conventions at the structural level of language" (1). With regard to spelling, she noted that many errors "illustrate the tendency to reconcile pronunciation with orthography" (3). She considered such confusion of "as" with "has" and "is" with "his" as reflecting how "pronounced speech habits work their way into the writing" although she did not mention that these were likely to be "Creole" speech habits. She felt that students could usually identify these errors in their and others' speech, but they persisted in writing. What is important is her notation that they were "all errors teachers ha[d] been pointing out for years", and they were not errors that "people [could] be reasoned out of". Still, she concluded that "perhaps these errors [were] not all that serious in that they d[id] not affect comprehensibility. They illustrate[d] however that it is worth insisting on some of the niceties in formal spoken English." Walker was careful to note that "the disregard of spelling conventions often develops into a dangerous habit. What is written on a page is misread" (ibid.). She felt that confusion of one letter with another could result in misinterpretation of an examination question. Walker also maintained that omission of inflections (such as – ed in the English past participle) "is often a matter of carelessness" and it is "possible to connect many of these faults in structure to looseness in thinking" (5). Interestingly, Walker did not include any consideration of the Creole lack of inflection in verb tenses that would be deeply entrenched in students' language habits and frequently transferred in English. As well, the problem could have been lack of revision and editing, for which time was clearly not provided in examinations, and which were not among the concerns of the course. Walker also suggested that there would need to be more writing in class without abandonment of discussion in order for students to be motivated to work on grammar. She noted, too, that "many students like[d] to feel that a close watch [was] being kept on their English and that as far as the conventions [were] concerned they [were] mastering new points" (11) – a telling statement about students' limited mastery of or comfort in English.

The problems that M. Thompson (1986) and Walker (1966) identified as being characteristic of young science students extended to other students. Walker's "Minutes of the Meeting of Lecturers in the Use of English at Cave Hill" (1972) includes the emphasis from Mona representatives that, as is established in chapter 1 based on Robotham's (2000) work, "it was not always the young N.1 [preliminary year] students fresh out of school that had problems with understanding and interpretation of material or even with organizing their work, but older students who had been occupying positions of authority for years" (5). It appears, however, that faculty ignored these students' needs when they adopted the "Use of English" course. Chapter 2 established that faculty had begun to complain about weaknesses in students' writing as early as the 1950s. However, when Allsopp (1964b) prepared the first detailed course syllabus, he seemed to ignore those problems and inadvertently encouraged a form of linguistic prejudice. As stated, unlike Owens (1963) and Carr (1963a, 1963b), Allsopp encouraged a balance between the written and oral in the course. He invoked Denys Thompson's *Reading and Discrimination* (1954) to stress the importance of written work – "only thus can it be ensured that every member of the group commits himself to an opinion" (Allsopp 1964b, 2). Allsopp noted that teachers should not insist on the essay form when an answer required listing points in complete sentences "since this is essentially a course in critical thinking, judgment and expression of constructed opinion". However, he added a questionable caution about grammar and spelling: "Although the course does not strictly concern itself with grammar and spelling students must clearly understand that (a) their work will be marked down for spelling and grammatical errors, and (b) inconsecutive or non-standard jottings will not be accepted as an 'answer in note form'" (ibid.). Allsopp's caution typifies a form of linguistic prejudice that is perpetuated in the university when graders deduct marks for aspects in which students seem to be weak but which a course does not teach expressly. In a system where many students are already made to feel uncomfortable in language at the primary and secondary levels, deducting marks for what is not taught explicitly demonstrates continued ignorance of the sheer trial that such students must endure in performing in English, and suggests that the university is the province of *only* students who are from an English-speaking/-supported background.

Allsopp's (1965b) treatment of the high failure rate in the course would also perpetuate the institution's emphasis on excellence and probably prevent students' special language needs from being addressed. Although every one of his reports mentioned a high failure rate, Allsopp insisted that the failures were not due to unacceptable English. His "Report on the Use of English Course 1964/65" reflects the transparency conceptualization with regard to evaluation, as defined in Lillis and Turner (2001, 58–60). In his report, Allsopp recognized as major faults students' lack of preparation for classes, unwillingness to share opinions in class, and written work that "too often showed a lack of common sense, and far too often was in shabby English or had bad grammar, which was always drawn to their attention in the marking" (1965b, 1). Allsopp noted that the part-time students often "seemed disillusioned" and rarely participated in discussions. In his view, afternoon fatigue alone could not account for their behaviour: "many [were] teachers and a failure or frequent low grade in what [was] still regarded as merely 'English' hurt . . . their pride without stimulating a thoughtful approach to the next project. In any event the Examination showed their English to be simply bad in many cases" (ibid.). Approximately two-thirds of the students failed the first final examination. One of the first faults that Allsopp noted that this test revealed was weaknesses in mechanics and grammar: "Punctuation was widely negligent or quite intolerable. There were a great many spelling errors in spite of the allowed use of a Dictionary in the Examination and the warning in the instructions to the paper. There was also a great number of faults of simple grammatical agreement, verbal and adverbial inflection, vocabulary, choice of word, and sentence structure." He added, "For most of these a mark was taken, for not only had there been plenty of warning during the year by [sic] the warning was repeated at the head of the paper." Here, Allsopp provided the background to the practice in which untaught aspects of writing are graded: "The course cannot treat such weaknesses, but where they occur, by the very nature of the course, they must be penalised" (2).

What Allsopp (1965b, 2) noted as weaknesses regarding the proper course concerns and the primary reason for failure typifies faulty assumptions about the transparency of evaluation terms. He asserted that there was "widespread failure to inspect a question properly and discern its actual requirements. . . . Indeed missing the point of a question was the greatest cause of failure." However, Allsopp did not acknowledge that teachers could have wrongly assumed that students would have been able to discern the "point of a question". After all, the syllabus/course outline had no section treating the metalanguage of evaluation. And this was a period when the "Use of English" course, like most content courses then and now, was concerned with only the product of the act of writing – when writing was involved. The high failure rate in the course, especially among evening (part-time) students, would be addressed in subsequent reports including Allsopp's "Report on the Use of English Course 1966/67". Here, Allsopp noted that many students failed because the examination "defies swotting up" (1967, 2), the practice of cramming in which students engaged for other courses. To address the continued high failure rate in the course, when Allsopp (1971, 3) gave his report on the Use of English course, he provided samples of student writing and his views about "the principal causes of failure and of the massive mediocrity of performance":

> The Course . . . pre-supposes that the student, having passed into the University through an "O" Level English Language entry requirement, comes with an operative command of English morphology and syntax and a reasonable disciplined sense of the structure and consecutiveness of recognizable sentences. Yet there is an indetermined number who . . . freely display English morphology that is unpermitted . . . or grossly undisciplined . . . and sentence structure that is also grossly undisciplined . . . or actually illiterate.

Because of the gravity of the identified weaknesses, Allsopp felt that "even if the U/E Course be heavily modified to pay substantial attention to remedial work, it is difficult to see how any one-year University Course could detect the roots of and then eradicate malpractices such as those displayed in [the samples]" (ibid.).

Despite the stated weakness, Allsopp (1971, 3) was not of the view that "the writing of unacceptable English account[ed] for a large part of the failures" in the course. What Allsopp would recognize in this report as the reasons for failure would also reflect the transparency paradigm regarding evaluation. Based on his experience, "the principal causes of failure and of the massive mediocrity of performance" were

(a) Widespread irrelevance due to misunderstanding (not misreading) of the core of a question, or the central claim in a statement.
(b) Unexpected ignorance of some middle-level educated vocabulary (although students are always invited to use a dictionary in the exam room).
(c) A very great lack of background reference, general knowledge and reading experience, and a persistence in unprepared, rather than informed, discussion.
(d) Certain difficulties attributable to Caribbean English. (Ibid.)

The last reason that suggests interference from "Caribbean English" is particularly interesting because it hints at views that prevailed then that the Creoles were forms of English as well as highlights the absence of explicit instruction in the metacognitive contrasts between the language required in the course and the varieties that students often used. Together, the factors that Allsopp identified as being responsible for students' failure suggest that there was need to increase writing and evaluation during the year. It is to be remembered that "Use of English" was a largely oral course with students completing only five (short) written pieces for the year. Increased formative evaluation could have allowed tutors to address "exam" techniques by discussing evaluation terms and the meanings of questions. However,

"Use of English" tutors seemed to omit such instruction that would have been considered "basic" for students who were presumed to have the requisite competencies in English for pursuing undergraduate studies.

Because the "Use of English" faculty attributed incorrect linguistic and writing profiles to some students, and probably because they did not carefully interpret examination results, they did not readily define and implement measures to address those students' special needs. Surely, they engaged in discussions about restructuring the course: by the close of the 1970s, the teachers at Mona had begun to depart from the original survey course to try to meet the language needs of new students. However, the various measures they employed to address the weaknesses of about 30 per cent of the institution's new and primarily first-generation university students were largely unstructured and unsuccessful. These measures included incorporating a six-week English proficiency component into the course and giving individual tutoring to students deemed weak in English language (Department of Linguistics and Use of English 1989, 1). A general recommendation was for the course to be offered on two levels to match the two general categories of students: UC100 – the regular course – and UC102 – a proficiency course. The proficiency course would address such topics as mechanics, structure, grammar, usage, and style (Use of English Staff 1980). However, these courses were not formally taught separately at Mona, probably because administrators' and faculty's lack of acknowledgement of the linguistic shifts in the academy continued to delay the development of the proficiency programme. Indeed, faculty's limited understanding of writing and its connection to learning in disciplines and outside of the academy resulted in neglect of many incoming students' special writing needs. Academics failed to follow through on suggested changes so that up to 1987, no course had been developed for students requiring a proficiency course although Mona had got approval to plan what its remedial course/programme would look like by the end of the 1970s (UWI 1979, 21).

"English": Academic Preserve or School Subject?

The increasing problems in students' writing would fuel a debate that signified that both "Use of English" faculty and content faculty ignored the role of writing in disciplinary learning and their role in students' writing development. This debate had actually started in the year the "Use of English" course was introduced when critics expressed opposition to teaching the course in the university. While upper administration considered new degree structures and the relevance of current degree programmes in 1963, various interest groups and individuals attempted to influence the decisions that would be taken regarding the survey courses through meetings or paper presentations. R.T. Smith (1963) reported the main points of one such meeting in his capacity as secretary of the West Indies Group of University Teachers. R.T. Smith's account suggests that the "Use of English" course was introduced in a climate in which deficiencies at the secondary level were being considered. R.T. Smith noted that among criticisms of the UWI's three-year general degree were views that "since most West Indian students come from . . . communities where reading and the fluent use of English is [sic] inadequate, all undergraduates should be introduced to the proper use of English and Logic" (2). Some critics called for such teaching to be done in the sixth form. Considering – as P. Roberts (1991, 1) points out – that the course came at a time of expanding education when the institution was shifting from elitist to mass orientation, critics could have considered the course as preuniversity. However, staunch advocates defended it vigorously. Among these was Figueroa (1963) who disagreed with transferring the teaching of the survey courses to the schools on the basis that the schools would experience much difficulty in offering some courses, with the English course posing special challenges if the focus is "Consequential Expression and Logic". He felt such difficulty would arise because the course "does not deal with matters that Sixth Forms manage too well, especially if we are to judge from the students who come from the schools, and who write such muddy and illogical prose in the scholarship exams" (1). Unlike what is conveyed in his description of the logic course in chapter 2, here, Figueroa demonstrates prescience regarding avoiding transfer of the responsibility for students' writing development to schools. Understanding that the survey courses could "encourage an awareness and an ability to think critically and imaginatively – to experiment and to judge" (ibid.), Figueroa cautioned that the UWI "should not slip out of its responsibility by asking the schools to do what it should be doing – encouraging its students to examine their environment, their history, their language, their values, themselves. . . . Even if the schools start, at their level, the kind of work envisaged by the general courses, we should expand and deepen this work, not give it up" (2–3).

Figueroa's (1963) insight before the "Use of English" course began was not necessarily acknowledged because course directors and other facilitators would also have to defend what they were teaching against outsiders' views that their subject could/should be taught in secondary schools. Among those who would defend the original "Use of English" course were R.J. Owens and William Carr, both of whom had been commissioned to assist with the development of the course in early 1963, and Allsopp, who became the first university moderator of the course. Part of the problem with the course lay in its title. The difficulty in naming the course is mentioned in "Information for 'Barbados College News'" from the College of Arts and Science, Barbados (1964). This document mentions that "both the names 'Survey Course' and 'Use of English' have caused much inquiry and both, indeed, are names used for want of better ones". However, the course was "intended to cover certain basic information which it is felt every Graduate should have, and which, heretofore, was not designedly provided by the University". Each survey course was meant to "lay the ground for a more critical and informed approach" by students in any discipline. Such names as "Uses of English", "Language and Logic", "Critical Thinking" and "Communication" were suggested for the "Use of English" course, with each providing clues about the course content. This content, the document emphasized, "ha[d] nothing to do with grammar and little to do with English language – précis and comprehension – such as is done in schools, or with literary criticism and appreciation which is a clearly defined aspect of English studies". Owens (1963) and Carr (1963b) had emphasized similar aspects of the course.

Cognizant of the difficulty in naming the course, Allsopp was careful to reject any association of the name with lack in the teaching of English. In his defence of the course against criticisms of its being *school English*, he *hinted* at content faculty's involvement in its teaching. In his "Interview with Gladstone Holder", Allsopp (1964a) emphasized that although he felt that secondary schools – specifically the sixth form sections – could offer a course resembling "Use of English", he did not feel that all aspects of the course could be addressed at that level. He emphasized that the course "was not really limited to English. It is the . . . discipline of thought and this of course is spread over all the studies, all the subjects" (2). In response to Holder's assertion that the course concerns about "the examination of thought, motive and feeling" should indeed be included in the English course at the secondary level, Allsopp made a statement that suggests he was aware of the importance of content faculty's being involved in instruction in thought and language. However, he made the point in a very cautionary way so that it was almost lost: Allsopp stated, "I feel that in the training of the teacher in communicating his subject . . . material to the student you can eventually get him to involve the training of thought even if he is teaching Geography." He added that the necessary discipline of thought "is the orientation of teaching generally; it can't be English alone" (3).

Content faculty did not necessarily share Allsopp's (1964a) views that they should be involved in "the training of thought". In fact, they would continue the debate about the course based on what they understood its purpose to be – as reflected in the course title. Therefore, by 1965, when "Use of English" staff members were faced with glaring grammatical and mechanical weaknesses in students' scripts but avoided making grammar a focus of teaching, other faculty seemed to be bent on making it an inevitable addition to the course. Some of these content faculty were unaware of the course's intended purpose but some were perhaps a little more conscious than some "Use of English" faculty of the needs of changing cohorts of students. This emerging "grammar" concern is evident in Allsopp's (1965a) "Report of a Conference on 'The Use of English' Course" held at the UWI at Mona. Conference participants discussed the widespread weaknesses that were appearing in students' written coursework and examination pieces on the three campuses in terms of written pieces containing logically unsound arguments, not answering the specific question set, and/or not answering the question clearly on account of faulty English grammar. They agreed to add a fourth aim to the course: "To improve the quality of the students' written expression" (2). This addition would necessitate "some remedial treatment of faulty grammar" in the course. Significantly, participants agreed that "the assumption that the students at this level should be able writers of grammatically correct English with good structuring was quite unrealistic" (3). When they *eventually* acknowledged that a faulty linguistic profile had been attributed to significant numbers of incoming students, participants decided that a test would be given in the first class each year to determine students' grammatical weaknesses. This decision meant that tutors would then use either a few classes or some minutes towards the end of each class to address the faults. As well, tutors would compile the common errors to inform future course planning regarding grammar.

Despite the decisions from the conference, neither "Use of English" nor content faculty really addressed students' problems based on any keen understanding of writing development or the region's linguistic realities. Content faculty associated visibility in language (that is, discussion of language challenges) with the need for remediation, and "Use of English" faculty avoided associating their course with remediation. However by doing this, "Use of English" faculty seemed not to address students' special language needs. They emphasized that the "Use of English" course was an *applied* English course, suggesting a reluctance to address issues of equity rather than excellence only.

The "Use of English" faculty's attitudes are probably explained by the theoretical underpinnings of the course and their training. According to King, at its inception, the development of the "Use of English" course and its teaching at the UWI were heavily influenced by research and new developments in the teaching of critical reading and writing in England at the time. Such research was being conducted by the Schools Council Programme in Linguistics and English Teaching, chaired by Peter Doughty; James Britton of the University of London Institute of Education and the Writing Research Unit Council; Basil Bernstein at the Institute of Education, London; and Randolph Quirk, Quain Professor of English Language and Literature, University of London. Work by Jean Piaget and Lev Vygotsky and ideas from the US based on grammar research that was being done at the Massachusetts Institute of Technology also influenced teaching and research interests but they were overshadowed by the English influence (King, unpublished data). W.E.K. Anderson's *The Written Word: Some Uses of English* (1963), which was used in the first half of the school year, gives a sense of what the focus of the course would have been: separate chapters address English in newspapers, advertisements, disguise, and arguments. This emphasis on the "range" of English usage speaks to issues of register and taste that were addressed in the course. The core text used when the course was introduced was Randolph Quirk's *The Use of English* (1962). That book, which was influenced by Quirk's observations in the Survey of English Usage at University College London, addresses "the nature, use, and range of English" (vi). It began as a series of talks commissioned by the BBC and aimed at stimulating "a mature and informed approach to our language, so that we can understand the nature of English, be encouraged to use it more intelligently, respond to it more sensitively, and acknowledge more fully the implications of its international use today" (ibid.).

According to King, in the eyes of the designers of the "Use of English" course at the UWI in the 1960s, "a mature and informed approach to our language", compared to the traditional English grammar approach to English teaching, which students in the Caribbean had been receiving in primary and secondary schools, constituted a new development in teaching. It implied, among other things, that course facilitators would help their students free themselves of the many misconceptions that they heard every day about language in general, and about English-based Creoles in the Caribbean and Caribbean English in particular. Indeed, the course was designed to challenge and, hopefully, remove what the course designers considered to be certain false notions about language that most students brought with them to the course. One misconception that was prevalent in the 1960s was that the Creole (popularly called "patois" in Jamaica) that the children of most poor black people spoke at home and when interacting informally among themselves was nothing but "broken English", and that it had "no grammar". Another misconception was that the language spoken in the newly independent Caribbean territories was simply "a regional dialect" of British English, just like the Yorkshire dialect was, and that proper standard English was the English that "people in England" spoke. In the context of these Caribbean countries' achieving political independence, the "Use of English" course was meant to foster more rational and informed thinking and writing among university graduates and the larger society about the nature of language and about how language functions, and also to remove misconceptions and change attitudes about Caribbean Creoles and Caribbean English within the society (unpublished data).

Based on the scholarship that informed the course, "Use of English" tutors defined language as "a system of arbitrary vocal symbols by means of which a social group cooperates" (Bloch and Trager 1942, 5). Working within the confines of the modes of discourse, these tutors adopted a theory of discourse that sought to analyse language behaviour in terms of the speaker's or writer's purpose, the intended audience's expectations, the function(s) the speech or writing was intended to serve, and the situation or context in which the act of communication was taking place. Such a discourse theory encouraged students to evaluate a speech or written text not in absolute terms of good or bad but in relation to how well it was likely to achieve its intended purpose, given the constraints imposed on it by the nature of the intended audience or readers and the communicating situation or context. The course was designed ultimately to sensitize students to the fact that communicative competence at university involved much more than writing correct, idiomatic, standard English – important as that is, and although grading in the course suggested otherwise. Students learned that communicative competence also involves a thorough knowledge of one's subject matter and a clear understanding of one's specific purpose in communicating. As well, it involves being conscious of, anticipating and satisfying, the expectations of one's intended audience, and overcoming the constraints imposed on the writer by the situation, or context, in which he or she was communicating (King, unpublished data). At first glance, the terms used may suggest that the "Use of English" tutors were concerned with how audiences, purposes, and contexts drive writing. However, the focus in the course involved not rhetorical theory in general – that the terms imply – but how students should prepare an expository versus a narrative essay, for example. In essence, then, this modes-driven approach was still somewhat limiting.

The academic disciplines in which the "Use of English" tutors had studied also influenced their attitudes to students' needs. "Use of English" tutors then had first degrees in English literature, linguistics, mass communication, or stylistics, but the overwhelming majority was in English literature. Most of the facilitators had been offered the part-time position of writing tutor in "Use of English" on the basis of their postgraduate training in the teaching of English, and on the basis of their experience, and proven success, in their full-time occupation – the teaching of English language and literature to tenth, eleventh, and twelfth graders preparing for their ordinary and advanced level examinations in high school. Consistent with the ideas of the staff who had degrees in literature, the emphasis in the course was on critical and stylistic analysis. Facilitators wanted students to understand style and focus on the purpose for writing. Rhetorical influence was limited to focus on the modes of writing and students' being able to differentiate among them (King, unpublished data). According to King, the emphasis was "more on analysis than on writing". As was the focus in the disciplines, what little writing there was in the course initially was focused almost exclusively on the product of the act of writing: the finished script. In this way, "Use of English" seems to fit the current traditional paradigm as defined by James Berlin and Robert Inkster (1980, 1): the informal essay and research paper were emphasized, with the focus being "the composed product rather than the composing process", and discourse was classified into (four) modes, with emphasis on exposition. Additionally, one of the representative current traditional texts, Brooks and Warren's *Fundamentals of Good Writing: A Handbook of Modern Rhetoric* (1956), was one of the fundamental readings in the "Use of English" course. And because the course did not really address how writing is relearned in new contexts but seemed instead to focus on applying skills learned in the past to note-taking in lectures, for example, it reflected what UK researchers describe as the study skills approach to academic writing (see Jones, Turner and Street 1999a; Lea and Street 1998). However, unlike the emphasis on usage in the current traditional model, the focus of instruction in the "Use of English" course was not grammar. Indeed, as stated, the "Use of English" staff tried to disassociate themselves from the teaching of grammar and tried to elevate the course. Bernstein (1971) and his ideas about elaborate and restricted codes with regard to roles ascribed to the speech of different classes helped the facilitators to justify having the course address misconceptions about language in the Caribbean.[13] Additionally, stress on functionalism in England in terms of allowing students to write naturally without emphasis on formal grammar (see Britton et al. 1975) was one of the weapons on which "Use of English" staff drew to justify exclusion of formal grammar instruction in the course – even though they penalized grammatical errors.

Not named but quite likely lurking in the shadows is the orality-literacy debate that scholars waged in the 1980s (see, for example, Bizzell 1988; Farrell 1983; Havelock 1982; Ong 1978, [1982] 1991, 1988; Street 1984). This debate continues to inform developments in teaching academic writing/composition/literacy in the United States and United Kingdom (see, for example, Daniell 1999; Horner 2013; M. Young 2013) with regard to the emphasis on helping students from largely oral cultures develop their reasoning and coherence in thinking (instead of focusing on grammar). Significant to the discussions is Walter Ong ([1981] 1991, 31–77) who proposed that members of oral and literate cultures have different ways of reading the world and organizing and expressing ideas – with the differences manifesting in behaviour, composition, speech and thought. In his view, literate cultures are more analytic than oral cultures because of the "consciousness-raising" (179) or restructuring of consciousness that literacy fosters. Ong ([1981] 1991, 106) drew on Bernstein's (1971) categorization of restricted (that is highly context-dependent) and elaborated (that is minimally/not context-dependent) linguistic codes, which he (Ong) says "could be relabelled 'oral-based' and 'text-based' codes respectively", to demonstrate how writing fosters development of codes that differ from oral codes. In Ong's ([1982] 1991, 26) view, teachers of writing need to be cognizant of these differences, especially when teaching students from oral or residual oral cultures, because "oral formulaic thought and expression ride deep in consciousness and the unconscious, and they do not vanish as soon as one used to them takes pen in hand".

With Ong's ([1982] 1991) proposals that "writing has transformed human consciousness" (78) and "writing is consciousness-raising" (179) and his and Havelock's (1982) work that linked literacy to personal cognitive development and to development of Western society, Ong and Havelock came to be associated with the view of literacy referred to as the theory of the great divide (between traditional cultures marked by orality and complex cultures so rendered by literacy) or great leap (in cognition because of individuals' and whole societies' associations with the Greek alphabet).[14] Coming at a time when cognitive theories of writing suggested that weaknesses in students' writing could be explained by weaknesses/faults in their minds (Flower and Hayes 1981), the Havelock-Ong theory seemed – like some people considered Bernstein's (1971) ideas before – useful for understanding difficulties some students experienced in writing in American colleges. However, some followers such as Farrell (1983) used the theory to defend the status quo, claiming deficiencies in some languages and consequent need for students who used them to learn standard English. These claims appear to have intensified criticisms of the Havelock-Ong narrative of literacy that seemed to associate literacy with academic literacy (see Bizzell 1988; Ong 1988).

Given how "Use of English" tutors seem to have used Bernstein's ideas, a statement such as the following would have resonated with them: "Our students from oral or residually oral cultures come not from an unorganized world, but from a world which is differently organized" (Ong 1978, 6). In a word, I am speculating that concepts from the Havelock-Ong narrative would have strengthened "Use of English" tutors' views that the largely oral Creole languages in the Caribbean are different from, but as legitimate as, standard languages. However, given the differences, emphasis would need to be placed on helping students organize their thoughts to reflect literate, informed thinking (see Allsopp 1988, 22–23). In their turn, other content faculty could have, like Farrell (1983), interpreted differences to mean weaknesses in, and occasioned by, Creole languages. In their view, addressing this state of affairs would require concentrating on teaching the grammar of the standard language – a position "Use of English" tutors were reluctant to adopt.

A Single Discourse Community: Visible Language Equals Remediation

This initial lack of emphasis on grammar instruction attracted criticisms of the course from those academics who associated any course in "English" with grammar instruction. Therefore, the "Use of English" course designers promoted the course as a way to facilitate students' language development with regard to critical or linguistic analysis and logical reasoning, whereas others emphasized writing instruction as remediation by calling for emphasis on grammar to address students' English language deficiencies. In this regard, although content faculty were highlighting the importance of addressing students' special language needs, they also expressed various faulty assumptions about writing. One of these was the view that if language is visible, its instruction ought to address the need for remediation. This is the myth that is implied in the second epigraph to this chapter: prior to discussions about problems in students' writing, language was largely invisible; however, when language became the subject of discussion, administrators and some content faculty immediately recommended that any instruction in language use had to serve the purpose of remediation and should in fact be addressed in the high school. In this way, they proved that, as Turner (1999, 150) writes about findings in the United Kingdom, "when language is working well, it is invisible. Conversely, however, when language becomes 'visible', it is an object of censure, marking a deficiency in the individual using it." The corresponding view was that the language/writing faculty should take responsibility for remediation – a view that would serve to marginalize such instruction in the academy.

The association of visibility of language and remediation is most evident in the actions of faculty from the Social Sciences and Natural Sciences. Eric King reports that social science students were not required to take the "Use of English" course on account of various factors: first, the Faculty of Social Sciences started much later than other faculties; second, the courses had the status of "honours courses" because courses such as economics were not taught in the high schools; third, the social science timetable was always full; and fourth – and most important – the faculty felt that "Use of English" was a sophisticated course because of its eventual focus on linguistics, Creole, and other language-related issues (personal interview, 16 July 2007). When faculty in Social Sciences were convinced that evening students exhibited limited writing abilities, they requested a special "remedial" course (see Academic Board 1985a). Hence, in 1986, "The Essentials of Good Writing" course was introduced for twenty-five students from Social Sciences (M. Thompson 1987). In this arrangement, there was no discussion about gearing a writing course to learning in the disciplines in Social Sciences; the concern was formalism.

Natural sciences faculty also associated visibility in language with the need for remediation; in fact, they were probably the most intent on calling for grammar emphasis, having called for changes to the course since the 1960s. Allsopp (quoted in Walker 1972, 2) reported that Natural Sciences faculty felt that students were "deriving little benefit from the Course". Later, in the first quarter of 1975, a Faculty of Natural Sciences committee considered the "Use of English" syllabus, reading list, and examination papers for June 1972 and June 1974 and the summary of recommendations from the "Use of English" conference held in January 1975 (E. Robertson et al. 1975). E. Robertson and the other committee members complained about what was being done in the course and about the "too long" weekly reading preparation, among other aspects. Most of their comments demonstrate their misunderstanding of the purpose of the "Use of English" course, the language situation in Jamaica, and the need for disciplinary writing instruction: They believed that "a Use of English course should remain a compulsory service for Science students, designed mainly to supplement their frequently inadequate background in English language proficiency". Committee members felt that "Use of English" tutors spent too little time on language proficiency and too much on "sophisticated topics for which many students [were] not yet ready" (1). Members emphasized that they understood "Use of English" staff's reluctance to address language proficiency, but they promoted the myth of transience in saying they understood that if the university were to change its admissions' policies that need would no longer be a concern. The committee members expressed ignorance of the course focus by stressing, "But until it does so, the need remains; surely that was why the Use of English course was created in the first place?" (2).

Perhaps because the Natural Sciences faculty misunderstood the course focus and the need for disciplinary writing instruction, in considering "Use of English" teachers' proposals to make the course a "First Year Course in all options", the members stated that their faculty would not consider "Use of English" as equivalent to a first-year course in Natural Sciences (E. Robertson et al. 1975, 2). They believed that a "basic Use of English course" should help *their* students:

(a) to understand the spoken language and to be able to take notes of salient points from lectures or discussions
(b) to read and comprehend standard English, to extract relevant information from books or papers, and to make useful notes or précis therefrom
(c) to understand the principles of logical argument and to recognize fallacies
(d) to appreciate that incorrect grammar and misuse of words frequently lead to unclearness or ambiguity
(e) to appreciate differences in meaning and to value the precision which they make possible
(f) to write reports and essays in as clear and as precise a manner as possible, without too much emphasis in the first place on the finer points of style. (Ibid.)

In expressing what they thought the "Use of English" course should be, the committee members were clearly trying to dictate the direction of the course without recognizing how *they* would probably be best suited to address most of the concerns that they expressed. They supported having two sections of "Use of English", but proposed that the first should have a remedial bent suitable for their students, and the other portion be only optional since it was "of less immediate concern of [theirs]". The members also suggested a curious kind of collaboration – that copies of examination papers, and a "complete set of the assignments" be sent to the vice dean of Natural Sciences for comment each year (3). Their idea of collaboration was not based on addressing disciplinary conventions, but rather emphasizing and ensuring that the basics of English grammar and mechanics be addressed. Thus, what Donald McQuade (quoted in Cheramie 2004, 145) wrote of composition studies in the United States would be true of writing/English language at the UWI: "It remains one of the few academic disciplines in which outsiders insist on naming and authorizing its activities, without accepting the intellectual responsibility – and the institutional consequences – for doing so."

By 1987 the "language" problem was so acute that some science faculty sought again to influence the course and to push for an emphasis on formalist concerns. This time, they blamed students' limited linguistic competence on research in the department of "Use of English and Linguistics" and on the course content, and ignored how students were learning their disciplines' content. In a 14 April memorandum, Ken E. Magnus (1987), then dean of Natural Sciences, brought to the Academic Board chairman's attention a 13 April 1987 newspaper article regarding the launching of Devonish's *Language and Liberation* (1986). Magnus was concerned that the book/launch seemed to promote development in Creole rather than in English because Devonish was arguing for instituting Creole as an official language in Jamaica. Magnus expressed concern because external examiners of undergraduates' papers in his faculty had been noting the following:

- "Language: The level of expression is generally low. The students are generally careless, not only with paragraph and sentence construction but with simple tense/number rubrics"
- "but *it is clear that the faculty members in the department are not placing enough emphasis on this aspect . . .* [sic] it is not enough to carry out a good study *you must also be able to present your results in a clear manner*". (1; emphasis added)

Ironically, the faculty in Natural Sciences seemed to miss the clear statement to *them* in the second comment, nudging *them* to address students' presentation of research. Had the faculty attended to the comment, they would have realized the need for addressing how doing, knowing, and writing are interconnected in learning in disciplines (see Carter 2007). Unfortunately, the response from the then head of Use of English and Linguistics, Pauline Christie, while being incisive, would reflect an opportunity missed to emphasize problems with language policy at lower educational levels and content faculty's contribution to students' writing development. Christie (1987) reminded the chairman of the academic board (and Magnus) that "Use of English" tutors are "not miracle workers. They cannot achieve in one year all that the schools have been unable to achieve in several years. Besides, the content of the "Use of English" course is not primarily remedial". Christie's response was accurate, but because she did not openly state why the schools may have failed, readers could have inferred that she implied – erroneously – that the real responsibility for language development lies with the secondary school.

A Single Discourse Community: Writing Content as Sociolinguistic Content

Ultimately, both "Use of English" and content faculty neglected to link writing development with learning in disciplines to really assist students. Essentially, they demonstrated limited understandings of the connection between content, writing, and learning. Importantly, the science faculty may have been moved to criticize what they believed Devonish (1986) was claiming because of the focus on Caribbean language in the course. Besides concerns about whether writing should be taught in the university or that the course should address proficiency matters, some content faculty were concerned that the course promoted the view that the stigmatized Caribbean Creoles were functional languages. In the 1970s, "Use of English" faculty had begun to address linguistic issues in the wider society, resulting in a shift from addressing general language issues to focusing on Caribbean language. This shift seemed to be consistent with movements and debates elsewhere. Significantly, at this same time, sociolinguists in the United States were advocating for recognition of non-standard dialects in the classroom. One result of their advocacy was the *Students' Right to Their Own Language* resolution that the Conference on College Composition and Communication adopted in 1974 (Smitherman 1999, 358). In his "A Brief Summary of the Aims and Contents of the Use of English Course", Winford (1973a, 1) emphasized the new aspects of the West Indian course which included "a detailed look at the roles of language varieties in their social context, the nature of Standard and Non-Standard languages, and the characteristics of Creole languages such as those used in the Caribbean area". "Use of English" staff considered such examinations important to the development of *informed persons* in the Caribbean where *prestige value* or stigma is attached to the different language varieties that serve different purposes.

By 1972, course readings reflected the changes, and the syllabus included Beryl Bailey's *Jamaican Creole Syntax* (1966) and Frederick Cassidy's *Jamaica Talk* (1961) (see "University Courses" 1972). The shift from a general focus on language to focus on Caribbean language issues in the 1970s is also evident in the record of course lectures that were given in the 1970s. The 1976 course manual indicates that five of nine lectures focused on language/linguistics, with such topics as "Communication and Language", "Some Contributions of Linguistics to the Use of English Course", "Linguistic Aspects of Communication in the West Indies", "Semantic Shift" and "Language and Ritual" (Cuthbert 1976). Kathryn Shields (1987a) explained that such topics constituted the "content component which [sought] to disabuse students' minds of the several misconceptions, shared by the wider community, about language, as well as about communication styles". Consequently, consistent with the prevailing national sentiments following independence, students learned that Jamaica had its own language, and that there were distinctions among British English, Standard Jamaican English, and Jamaican Creole. Shields argued that having that "content component" was important: "Especially at University level, the *importance of content to the production of appropriate language* cannot be overlooked" (emphasis added). This is a telling statement, begging the question of why the focus should have been *sociolinguistic* content and not also subject content to help students to write in their disciplines. The science faculty were not interested in the emphasis on linguistics, particularly the sociolinguistic content of the course. However, like Shields, they did not address how subject content could facilitate language production. They were merely interested in the remedial aspect of the course; hence, the reason they pointed to possible Creole interference in writing and requested that students receive assistance to eliminate the resultant errors and use *correct* English grammar.

A Plural Academy: Collaboration on *Problems* versus Disciplinary Writing *Requirements*?

It appears that neither content faculty nor "Use of English" faculty realized the extent to which they were promoting formalist presuppositions that would have limited students' critical reflection on and practical understanding of new content and how to convey it. Besides when content faculty tried to dictate what the course focus should be, and when "Use of English" faculty emphasized sociolinguistic content rather than also the content of students' disciplines, "Use of English" faculty also seemed to promote the erroneous view that writing is separate from disciplinary learning. This unfortunate promotion occurred when they, too, requested superficial forms of collaboration and suggested that disciplinary writing instruction should focus on *problems* rather than *requirements* in writing. These weaknesses were evident even before the "Use of English" course started in 1963.

Before the course started, Owens (1963, 2) suggested that there should be collaboration with lecturers in the other survey courses, but he did not make this suggestion based on disciplinary differences. He mentioned that a survey course lecturer could be present during discussion of a lecture that that individual had given. The discussion "would bring out practically the accuracy of recall, the accuracy of the notes taken, and give students a chance to talk over and to discuss what they had heard". Like Owens, Carr (1963a, 3) recommended collaboration with other faculty, but Carr's intention was to include a focus on disciplinary requirements. Carr felt that when the class had become "alert to questions of cogency and evidence", the tutor could present a badly constructed mini-lecture for students to critique and offer suggestions for improving it. As well, faculty in the History of Civilisation survey course could participate in a class to check students' note-taking skills. Carr recommended that a representative from history or science could present examples of good and bad historical or scientific writing and explain to students "his criteria of 'good' and 'bad'" (4). He also reminded his constituents that while the Department of English would "naturally cooperate in the teaching and [be] prepared to exercise supervisory control", it could not be "solely responsible for the teaching burden of the course" (5). In suggesting discussions for establishing the quality of the writing, Carr sought to address disciplinary requirements. He conveyed the sense that differences in academia were understood, even if only in a superficial way, in that he understood that there is a different way to *talk about*, not *create*, *knowledge* in each discipline. In talking about different kinds of communication with which students would come to terms, Carr (1963b, 3) noted "communicating information about a scientific experiment or explaining a scientific concept is clearly not the kind of communication which the poet or the novelist of [sic] the historian or the sociologist attempts". A one-page document, entitled "Use of English Course. Suggestions for Seminars 4–8" (1964) and attached to a two-page unsigned letter to a "Gordon" on 13 January 1964 also explicitly addresses differing disciplinary requirements. The sender (quite likely Carr since he was the then course moderator) asserted that "more extensive work is aimed at, with the hope of helping students to understand the stylistic problems they face in their different disciplines, as well as what they could expect to find in writing outside their own fields". The sender also noted that "some mention should be made of the difficulties of communication between disciplines which use the same words in different senses, as for example, medical 'motor', and mechanical 'motor', 'physic' and 'physics', mathematical and mechanical 'differential'" and so on.

Although the "Use of English" faculty seemed to consistently address disciplinary concerns, they tended to emphasize problems rather than general disciplinary requirements, and therefore emphasized formalist concerns although without specific considerations of the linguistic context. Consequently, they did not conceive of collaboration in broad terms that would have been beneficial to students' development in disciplines. When Allsopp (1968) presented the "Report on the Use of English Course 1967/68", he turned to content faculty for help with students' writing challenges. Allsopp mentioned that the many errors signalled a need for faculty to consider distributing a list of common errors that students should avoid in writing. He called for collaboration with faculty in other areas, but only in terms of grammatical/mechanical error identification: "We should get from other Departments written criticisms and perhaps samples of undergraduate English (in their experience) which might be of use in orienting some exercises in the course" (2). He made a similar request in 1972 after "Use of English" faculty considered a diagnostic test and/or a second course to address language deficiencies. Walker's (1972) "Minutes of the Meeting of Lecturers in the Use of English at Cave Hill" records that neither the matter of testing nor a second course was settled. Therefore, the meeting agreed that until a second course was considered again or designed, a workbook could be developed to help weak students to address the faults in their written work. In "A Use of English WORKBOOK", a letter sent in March 1972, Allsopp (1972) apprised colleagues of the "Use of English" tutors' decision to develop the workbook, and requested that faculty besides those involved in the course submit writing samples for inclusion in the workbook. Faculty's involvement would include "copying off complete sentences from students' written work in [their] subject as [they] mark it, containing examples of any of the following: faulty usage, regional or non-standard vocabulary, wrong choice of word, poor phrasing, faulty or weak grammatical structure, regular mis-spellings". Allsopp sent this request on the basis that "all persons marking . . . students' written work must come across striking examples of defective English which students bring with them to the University, and your special cooperation is respectfully sought in pooling these defects in an attempt to organise remedy". These categories would probably have been perceived as a sad commentary on the language policies implemented and the teaching methods employed at pre-university levels in Jamaica. Their presence at the tertiary level confirms the error in assuming that students could learn English instinctively, but they should also have awakened faculty's consciousness to the equally faulty assumption that students write intrinsically in any discipline. Unfamiliarity with new disciplinary discourse would have compounded such problems in the university setting, but neither the "Use of English" nor content faculty addressed that concern.

Winford (1973a) also considered disciplinary concerns but would also emphasize problems rather than disciplinary requirements, and he as well as Walker (1973) would experience the difficulty of having colleagues address differences in disciplinary requirements. In "A Brief Summary of the Aims and Contents of the Use of English Course", Winford pointed to the benefits of "familiarising students with the various purposes which language serves" (1973a, 1) to help students to become confident and to discriminate well when analysing other people's work and when they wrote (2). However, he recognized that although developing such abilities was useful for all students, notwithstanding their subject area, there was need for more work regarding disciplinary differences: "there is still a great deal of room for improvement in our attempts to orient the Use of English course towards the *problems peculiar to specific disciplines*" (ibid.; emphasis added). In this statement, Winford unfortunately suggested that disciplinary work is read in terms of *problems*, not *requirements*, to be addressed. However, Winford's (1973b) "Proposal for Development of Part of the Use of English Course" suggests ways in which recognition of disciplinary differences were frustrated. In this memorandum to heads of departments, deputy librarian, senior assistant librarians and assistant librarians, Winford called for modifications to the "study method" section of the course that included note-making, note-taking and organization of bibliographies. He indicated that treatment of this aspect of the course was "severely handicapped by not being followed up with practical experience geared toward the particular disciplines pursued by students" (1). He proposed that the various faculties cooperate and use the opportunity to make the course relevant to their students by "making suggestions about themes and topics in various disciplines which might be useful in providing practical experience in the use of the various devices of study method" (3). Communications from Walker also confirm that most attempts at soliciting campus-wide faculty assistance or at addressing disciplinary specifics – even if only in a limited way – were frustrated by administrative issues. In her "Letter to Mr Arthur Drayton, Vice-Dean, Faculty of Arts and General Studies", Walker (1973, 1) traced staffing problems and difficulties in addressing remediation. Walker's letter also showed a recognition of disciplinary differences, with Walker reminding the vice dean of having already mentioned to him "the need for the development of special emphases in the Course for students in different fields of specialization". She was concerned that such efforts were frustrated by lack of adequate numbers of staff members in their "many-faceted programme" (2).

Sometimes, the Arts faculty, and specifically "Use of English" faculty, blocked collaboration by rejecting proposals from within their ranks. Based on the perceived language problems in the course, Allsopp (1971, 4) offered some proposals that would include a call for collaboration and a reinforcement of the course's value. In his report on the Use of English course, he recommended that "with the agreement of other Faculties, appointments might be made of persons in those Faculties able to participate in teaching the F/GS U/E programme as a part of assigned duties. Such persons, bringing privileged information on the language material and possibly language difficulties encountered in their particular disciplines, might actually be a special advantage in orienting parts of the Course for their own Faculty students." Allsopp wished to address disciplinary differences through collaboration in teaching. The then pro-vice chancellor Leslie Robinson (1971b) would recognize the need to address such differences in his follow up "Letter to David King" regarding Allsopp's proposals. In Robinson's words, "The possibility of gearing parts of the course to the needs of particular groups of students should be further explored." However, the arts faculty did not support Allsopp's attempt to accommodate disciplinary difference in the course, and cast blame for students' deficiencies on the school. Minute 70 in the "Minutes of A Meeting of the Faculty of General Studies Committee, Mona . . ." (1971, 3) records their rejection of Allsopp's proposal to include content faculty in the course. In the committee's eyes, "it did not follow that such members of staff would necessarily be the best persons to take Use of English classes". The committee members refused to consider the disciplinary advantage because of concerns about content faculty's qualifications, workload and remuneration (ibid.).

King's (1971) "Some Proposed Modifications" also records rejection of Allsopp's (1971) proposal. In this three-page letter to the dean of the faculty of general studies in September 1971, King and Walker reported that the tutors at Mona did not favour disciplinary support in teaching in the course. They noted, "while we agree that the Use of English programmes would be benefited by the use of specialists in certain subject areas, we see the value of specialists to the programme largely in the planning stages, for consultation and in the preparation and development of proper course materials suited to the specific needs of the students" (2). The pro-vice chancellor would, however, continue to push for recognition of disciplinary difference even though his communication simultaneously seems to suggest he was probably unconsciously shifting the responsibility to "Use of English" facilitators as special groups demanded addressing concerns specific to their areas. In his one-page "Letter to Dr S.R.R. Allsopp", Pro-Vice Chancellor Robinson (1971a) wished to know if the "Use of English" course could accommodate an emphasis on "report writing" to facilitate the new programme in librarianship that would begin in October of that year. Robinson also reminded Allsopp that he (the pro-vice chancellor) had already mentioned that "the Nurses were anxious to have some work of this kind built into their Use of English programme". Robinson ended by suggesting that he was in favour of gearing the course to meet specific disciplinary groups: "I need not reiterate my own personal view that I can see no reason why the Use of English course has to be identical for all groups within the University." However, while Robinson promoted a course design that would be relevant to specific groups of students, he did not recommend that content faculty would need to contribute to that realization.

Writing: A Single, Generalizable Skill or Persistence of the Myth of Transience?

Perhaps, the kind of collaboration that Allsopp suggested did not materialize, and a proficiency programme to address students' special language needs was not immediately developed, because some academics held the same view as the public that neither the "Use of English" course nor a proficiency component belonged in the university. They promoted the myth of transience by suggesting the course would not have to be considered if the schools improved instruction or if the university changed its selection policy. Even when some faculty and administrators suggested the university had a responsibility to develop the region's human resources, their concern seemed to be less with helping students and more with *helping the university avoid blame for graduates' weaknesses*. In "Report on the Use of English Course 1968/69", then chief moderator Walker (1969, 1) noted observations that "the remedial aspects were becoming more pronounced". Added to those concerns, content faculty seemed to have misunderstood the aims of the course to the extent that some were requesting that their students who were exhibiting language deficiencies be provided special help. Walker explained that the challenge increased because "in an effort to teach more elementary aspects of usage and style, the proper concern of the Course might be set aside". Moreover, those involved in teaching in the course would offer remedial help where they could, but they felt that "this should not be part of the University's Use of English Course for which a student receives credit" (ibid.). Walker's (1972) "Minutes of the Meeting of Lecturers in the Use of English . . ." reports that attendees discussed a previous senate decision to institute a test to exempt students from the course and reduce numbers. By recommending that some students be exempt from the "Use of English" course while others took a remedial course, upper administrators demonstrated limited understanding of what it means to write or receive writing instruction in the university. Perhaps, in an unstated recognition of such limited understanding, attendees avoided the trap of passing the responsibility to secondary schools by pointing out that the course was "required and conceived to be a habit-forming system, whereas the examination was an almost marginal check of performance" (9). Attendees felt that "the University [could] not share the responsibility for teaching a full University credit course with the Secondary Schools, though this is in effect . . . what some proposals for exemption . . . made outside the meeting imply" (14).

Allsopp (1974), who had rejected the view that basic English problems accounted for most of the failures in the course, would be instrumental in laying the groundwork for addressing students' special language needs. In "UWI Use of English Course: Proposal for an Adjustment in Course Content", Allsopp acknowledged that the "Use of English" course served an important purpose in addressing the "undeveloped judgment and uncritical acceptance of written matter and lack of insight in interpreting almost any subtlety in mature English" that resulted in "massive mediocrity of examination results" in courses in the different faculties. However, he also felt that the "attention to performance" in the course had been "at the expense of attention to linguistic competence". The course had not been conceived to address "the grammatical conventions of morphological and syntactic structure, and verbal accuracy" (1). Allsopp noted that the very popular Cambridge GCE O-level English examination also focused on performance and did not test linguistic competence. He concluded that since neither of these forums addressed linguistic competence, tutors could only expect "the gross decay or increasing ignorance of the conventions of English spelling and structure which [were] commonplace with the older 'flogged' generation" (ibid.). Allsopp, informed readers that although – as he stressed before – he did not think the majority of students failed the course on account of grammatical or mechanical errors, he was aware that "the problem of substandard written English displayed in the U/E Course [was] too great to remain a peripheral objective, notwithstanding the merits" of the course. Therefore, he proposed a "compromise involving adjustment of content" (2) so that linguistic competence could receive "separate attention" (1).

The Faculty of Arts and General Studies' (1975) "Provisional Report of a Conference of Use of English Teachers" reveals that attendees disagreed with Allsopp's earlier proposals regarding remedial instruction, but "unanimously adopted the following motion" that reflects the persistence of the myth of transience even among the "Use of English" staff:

> The Use of English Conference recognizes that work in English Language proficiency is necessary and will continue to be necessary until the UWI changes its entry requirements; that such work in language proficiency should be provided either in remedial workshops or in individual schemes, and either using the workbook now

being prepared by Mr Allsopp or by other organized procedure; that the work in proficiency should proceed alongside the general Use of English course; and that where increased staffing is needed for the implementation of this proposal we emphasize the University's obligation to provide for this need or to eliminate the need for this provision, by the exclusion of students lacking in language proficiency by means of an appropriate English Language test as an entry requirement.

The academic committee would accept this "Use of English" teachers' January 1975 proposal and recommend that a Department of Linguistics and Use of English be created at Mona to include the then lecturer in linguistics, staff from the language laboratory, and the "Use of English" staff ("Matters" 1975). The creation of a department is significant because it meant that administrators were beginning to recognize the need for a stable unit to address writing requirements in the university – albeit only until they thought the problems had disappeared.

When the "Use of English" course was first offered in Jamaica, the rest of the university was not interested in talking about writing as a discipline. This situation was compounded when the university began to acknowledge weaknesses in students' writing and various segments called for the course to emphasize grammar. Content faculty considered the course as introduced to remedy the ill *until* the high schools began to do a better job of preparing students in English. King confirms that by 1967, the university had lost faith in the Cambridge GCE O-level results in English for Jamaicans and questioned the quality of students who were seeking admission to the university. Even students who had earned an "A" in the external examinations performed poorly in writing at the university. King recalls that when he started teaching in the course in the late 1960s, he heard terms such as "terminal" that suggested something "cancerous" was being associated with the course. At the same time, people in Barbados and Trinidad felt that the situation was particularly grave in Jamaica while their students were arriving at the UWI at Mona fully prepared. Barbadians and Trinidadians felt that funds were being used to teach grammar and other features that should have been taught in high school. The general view was that when the *Jamaican* government improved teaching in high schools, the course would disappear (King, personal interview, 16 July 2007). Therefore, far from approving of the critical and informed approach to the teaching of writing at the university level that the "Use of English" course had adopted, many academics and members of the public claimed that the teaching of "Use of English" did not properly belong at a university. By using the term "terminal" to emphasize that as soon as students improved the English survey course would not be needed, the UWI's administrators and even some writing specialists rejected the view that the work of literacy in higher education is not going away. Their attitudes suggested a belief in writing instruction as inoculation and prevented the development of both writing courses to address students' specific language needs and vital WAC programmes to allow students to learn both language conventions and content within disciplines.

Unlike most of the "Use of English" faculty who eventually supported addressing the problem internally, upper administration kept the focus on the schools' addressing linguistic competence. Minute number 367 of the Academic Board (1985b) minutes states, "Academic Board, Mona, heard from several of its members and expressed its concern that there appeared to be a great need for remedial English at the University and agreed to consider ways to improve the standard in conjunction with teachers in the Secondary Schools." Whereas in this case the suggestion was to *consider* the problem along with the schools, the schools would eventually be *blamed* for student performance. Minute number 686 of the University Academic Committee reflects academics' continued consideration for transferring the problem to schools: "UAC [University Academic Committee] noted the view expressed that the poor level of English of many UWI students had been a problem for a long time and that it was one for the schools to tackle. However, the committee also noted the view that the university needed to assist and that the Use of English Course which was probably not designed to deal with the problem should be modified" (UAC 1988a). Therefore, as in the months preceding the course and in the first few years after its introduction, interest groups were again faced with defending the "Use of English" course and addressing the university's responsibility to the students it was accepting but whose actual performance did not match the expectations held about their linguistic competence.

One of the groups to proffer views about the university's role in student's proficiency in English on all campuses is the Unit of Use of English and Linguistics (1987) at Cave Hill. The comments appear in the 1986/87 "Report on Proficiency of Third Year Students", the results of a rare study conducted to determine final year students' level of proficiency in English that is often considered "unacceptable". The report stresses, "It is thought that this deficiency reflects adversely on the University and that the University needs to take some action to rectify the problem. While the problem may be one inherited from the elementary and secondary levels of education, the reality is that UWI is at the end of the line and so gets and will continue to get the blame" (1). Like the UWI academics mentioned in chapter 1, those at Cave Hill were highlighting the serious situation in which the university would be blamed for the deficiencies in students' language usage. The recommendation was, therefore, for the university to get involved to *avoid blame* – not necessarily to *enable* students' development.

A similar recommendation that the university address the situation was also made in "Report on Faculty Review 1986/87" for the Faculty of Arts and General Studies, Cave Hill (1987). However, this document implies some academics' recognition of the need to cease perpetuating the myth of transience. Much of what is said in this document relates to the university in general, and what is said about

Cave Hill is also true for Mona. This report mentions that more than three-quarters of the incoming students did not have "genuine 'A' level qualifications" (2), and this number had been increasing steadily. As well, many new students were not coming directly from secondary schools, and more and more faculty members felt that the university was "not receiving the best products" from these schools (ibid.). Besides the weaknesses often noted in students' language use, the report mentions the generally poor quality of students' work exhibited in the quality of degrees awarded each year (4). The conclusion was for the university to play an active role in students' language development by *acknowledging* the problem and addressing it *in the university*. The writers insisted that administrators and faculty could not "sit back and blame the other levels of the educational system for the existence of the problem; all that does is to perpetuate the problem" (7). They considered potential restrictions on intake, but noted "any rigorous screening of applicants would cut intake by at least one-third" (ibid.) and the institution could not afford that loss of funds. The report recommended that the university strike a "pragmatic balance . . . between self-interest and commitment to acceptable standards" (8). The writers felt that the entrance examinations should be enlisted in this effort "primarily as diagnostic tools rather than as mechanisms to restrict intake" (ibid.). They were aware of the long-standing dilemma that the university has had to face: screen students to exclude those who cannot write, which means emphasizing excellence, or screen them to determine who may need extra help in writing in their disciplines – to achieve equity and maintain excellence.

The shrewdly discerning Allsopp (1988) would also express the view that the university should share the responsibility for students' language development. He recognized that the reason the secondary schools could not carry the burden alone was that the teaching methods were faulty. Nevertheless, he did not acknowledge that the problem was not only imported teaching methods but one also rooted in an imposed colonial policy yet to be dismantled. His comments appeared in "Report on the State of Written English at the UWI at Cave Hill, Barbados", a document prepared to give the background to the teaching of "Use of English" at the UWI, reasons for students' poor written English proficiency skills, approaches to teaching and changes needed. In preparing this document, Allsopp drew on his experience as university moderator until 1972, so his comments are applicable to Mona. Allsopp expressed that "consistently good written English is not automatically to be expected of the average student" (1988, 2). The situation being as it is, Allsopp recommended that "weak command of English must now be considered a fact of life at University level. Therefore blaming the school system (even if/when such blame is accepted and eliminated!) will not help present and immediate future students. About them UWI *must* do something, which *must* be remedial" (21; emphasis in the original). Allsopp explained that the school system may not represent the answer to the problem faced at the university because of imported teaching methods that not only were irrelevant to the region but also guaranteed failure. These arose from changes in Britain in the post-World War II era when schools stopped teaching Greek and Latin and consequently abandoned parsing – the process of identifying each component and its structural function in a sentence. Teachers abandoned "grammar fatigue" and replaced it with the "direct method" in foreign language teaching and "English at work" in teaching English to native speakers. The problem arose because, as Allsopp wrote,

> the Caribbean received and developed its share of these approaches without taking due account of the fact that in the massively <u>oral</u> cultures of the Caribbean the effective pragmatics of speech . . . made the parsing of <u>written</u> structures indispensable in a way that could hardly be argued in Britain. In our case it is perhaps the only available means of revealing to the Caribbean schoolchild that syntactic function is the vital factor in differentiating meaning in written language, and that therefore it must be scrupulously studied if educated international English is to be produced. (22–23; emphasis in the original)

Compounding the problem then, Allsopp asserted, was that teachers did not get formal training in English structure, with the result being that people often "take refuge in the argument that it is not necessary" (27).

Allsopp (1988, 15) also indicated that testing procedures did not contribute to students' development, and suggested shifts from emphasizing summative writing to exploiting formative writing. Allsopp advised that there is a sad error in not allowing students to see their corrected diagnostic test scripts:

> The only sure way to convince not only the failures but nearly the whole body of students that their command of English is faulty is to return the scripts to them as soon as possible after the test for organised corrective exercises question by question. By present departmental policy they never see these scripts again and . . . this is a serious error by which the most telling way of getting across urgent messages of deficiencies to the student is lost.

Nonuse of students' writing produced under examination conditions for developing proficiency and testing skills was consistent with the general emphasis on summative writing and little concern for students' language/writing development through formative writing in the university. The emphasis on *testing* writing was, unfortunately, consistent with the emphasis on testing *language* that students may not even have had as a first language.

Nonuse of students' scripts may also be associated with the original intentions of the course designers who were primarily concerned with oral discussions in the course. As stated, neither at its inception nor by the mid-1980s was the "Use of English" course concerned with knowledge creation through writing. Kathryn Shields's (1987a) defence of a five-year limit on the validity of a pass in the course confirms that the focus in "Use of English" in its early years was not writing, per se. Shields noted that up to 1983, the course focus included "the heightening of the students' awareness of language use in the society, and . . . the development of their higher-order reading skills". She mentioned that the lack of emphasis on extended writing was most evident in the final examination. There, students were allowed to answer up to 50 per cent of the questions in note form. It was not until 1984 that students were required to provide responses in continuous prose instead of short-answer note form. Such responses included reports, expository essays, commentaries, and analyses of argument and figures. It was only in 1985 that equal emphasis on writing and oral work was strengthened when a library skills component was introduced to formally expose students to research techniques and documentation.

The limited writing focus in "Use of English" before 1984 is also explained by the fact that the faculty were mainly from literature and promoted the emphasis on critical analysis of poetry. Such faculty were interested in a sophisticated awareness of language, and audience needs, which could easily be taught through reading. As well, there were no courses on writing theory. Faculty did not really have a concept of *writing* as a discipline then; they really just talked about "English". It was also easier to find passages for students to consider style, denotation, meaning, and so on, rather than to focus on teaching students to write, especially to prepare drafts. In a word, it was cheaper to teach reading rather than writing. Facilitators also assumed that students would transfer skills learned through reading to their own writing. There was also the belief in education that the initial focus should be on the oral; that is, students should learn to remove their errors in the oral first before there was any focus on writing (Eric King, unpublished data) – consistent with the conduit model of language expressed earlier. With no clear philosophy of writing as a discipline then, the belief persisted that writing was about regurgitating information. Consequently, writing largely occurred for examination purposes, and students did not get the practice to understand how writing helped with developing thought and learning.

Conclusion

Allsopp's reflection on the UWI's "Use of English" course recalls its focus: "in keeping with the course's intended stress on *using* English, its programme focus[ed] patently on *interpretative* and *operative* skills, declaring sentence structure to be not within its function" (1988, 3; emphasis in the original). As the chapter reveals, however, complaints arose from various segments of the university regarding students' level of English proficiency and the lack of teaching of aspects such as grammar and sentence structure in a course that seemed to be about "English". However, while content faculty were concerned about the quality of students' writing in the academy, they, like members of the public, were also confused by the nomenclature. As Allsopp, writes, "on all three campuses alarm [was] expressed and noted for some two decades over the structural faults of students' written English, which the Use of English course was not designed to remedy but which it [was] called upon to answer for largely because of its name" (9). Still, like some content faculty and administrators, "Use of English" staff had been operating on incorrect assumptions about incoming students. Consistent with the 1944 observation of the West Indian Committee of the Commission on Higher Education which suggested that the university would have a ready, "literate in English" set of candidates (Great Britain Commission 1945, 51), the course designers had assumed that virtually all students entering the university would have already achieved at least basic competence in standard English grammar and in the mechanics of writing. The designers had, therefore, made no provision, either in the allotment of teaching time or in the course syllabus, for tutors to help their students deal with their English proficiency problems in grammar, sentence structure and the mechanics of writing within the course. Allsopp (1988, 3) writes that "spelling and structure were, however, early and widely recognized as problems" so that as of the May 1965 examination students were allowed to bring in an English dictionary and, up to 1973, were "warned that a very serious view [would] be taken of faulty spelling, grammar and sentence structure". While acknowledging students' errors in English proficiency – through severe penalty, "Use of English" staff did not really teach to address those errors. What they attempted were informal inclusions of individualized instruction for the students concerned and superficial collaboration with other faculty members to address the *errors* in writing in different disciplines.

Besides those problems, in this period, while some academics acknowledged that the academy comprises several competing discourse communities, their acknowledgement never translated into the kind of meaningful collaboration to develop students' writing as rhetorical activity tied to specific disciplinary practices. In fact, content faculty, especially in Natural Sciences, considered writing instruction in the "Use of English" course as remediation of their students' language deficiencies – remediation that natural science faculty believed they should supervise superficially. Faculty's misconception that the necessity for discussion of, and explicit instruction in, writing meant a need for remediation rather than for consideration of language use beyond basic English in disciplines is perhaps the most glaring of those that appear in this period. Content faculty appeared to marginalize language development when, by insisting on what the course should teach, they transferred the responsibility for writing instruction to the "Use of English" staff. The result was reinforcement of the erroneous idea that academia is a single discourse community.

As well, statements from some "Use of English" staff, content faculty and administration suggested that the problems that were appearing regarding grammar and mechanics would disappear when the institution changed its matriculation requirements or when positive changes were realized in secondary schools. Such hope that writing instruction would continue in the university only until there were changes in the university's selection policy or there were changes at the secondary level signal the persistent myth of transience. The fact that that desire was not being realized helped to secure plans for restructuring the course to address remediation. By 1980 when content faculty's complaints persisted, the vice chancellor reported that "teachers on all campuses have accepted the need for supplemental teaching aimed at improving the language proficiency of students as early as possible in their academic career" (UWI 1980, 23). Students' English language proficiency would, therefore, become an enduring topic of discussion in the 1980s, and writing and language instruction would be increased in the course, but in response to the need for remediation. However, as indicated, the measures were ill-defined and unsuccessful.

Because the "Use of English" course maintained a limited focus on writing and was subsequently criticized, some of the important changes made to it in an attempt at achieving equity *in society* could have been overshadowed. Although the course may have begun as another English importation, by the 1970s it was already appropriated. One of its hallmarks was to be consciousness-raising with regard to students' awareness of language use in Caribbean societies. As Dyche (2006b) puts it, "by 1973, aspects of the educational and political agenda of Caribbean and other linguists had indeed found their way into the course". The unit offering "Use of English" was interested in disabusing students of the idea that the Caribbean Creoles are forms of broken English. This interest in the local languages, in the promotion of Caribbean Creoles as legitimate languages, was sparked in the wake of independence – at least for the linguists who were then employed to the university. These faculty members had to address the negative attitudes to Creole that manifested in negative labels attached to it. Their intention was to bring *language* to the fore of discussions about national identity and self-sufficiency by challenging university students to consider and act on those issues. However, other segments of the university were concerned that interest in Creole would not assist students in writing grammatically correct English, as critics of the *Students' Right to Their Own Language* in the United States believed about interest in non-standard dialects (see Sheils 1975). Hence, content faculty at the UWI vocalized their frustrations about the language deficiencies exhibited in students' writing, and called for the course whose focus was "English" to address such matters. Content faculty believed that instruction should address remediation by virtue of the fact that "language" was being taught. The "Use of English" faculty, however, rejected this deficit model of teaching for a long time. Even when course documents suggested a proficiency programme was being considered or developed, no formal programme was in place at Mona even after the mid-1980s.

That various individuals within the university had different views about the content and purpose of the "Use of English" course is not insignificant. As Dyche

(2006b) notes, "there were, from the beginning, two different, conflicting perspectives on the nature of the . . . course". Those involved with the course considered it as a *survey* course befitting inclusion in the academy, while other faculty and public figures considered it a *service* course to be taught in schools. To my mind, this attitude of the faculty and other individuals who were not involved in teaching the course is hegemonic in orientation. Seeing the course as having a corrective role, they perpetuated the belief of English as *language* rather than *a language*. Those in the survey camp were more interested in familiarizing students with broader sociolinguistic issues, yet they could not always be seen to be responding to student needs, especially those of increasing numbers of first-generation university students from Creole-speaking backgrounds who were aspiring to middle class status. And neither group seemed to consider how a focus on purposes and contexts would help students to critically reflect on disciplinary content and develop practical understanding of language use in disciplinary communities.

Tangible change to address primarily Creole-speaking students would not be evident at Mona until 1988. This change suggested that the university was shifting from an exclusive focus on excellence to – as I am arguing in this book – consider critical ways to achieve social equity and maintain excellence *in the institution*. This change came in the form of "Fundamentals of English" – a basic writing course developed to accommodate students deemed to demonstrate inadequate levels of proficiency in English. However, as I show in the next chapter, both supporters and opponents of this course continued to separate language development from learning in disciplines and outside the academy because they continued to shroud writing knowledge in formalism.

4 | Nurturing "Linguistic Orphans" with Basic Writing in the Post-National Era, Late 1980s to 2004+

Academic writing is never a student's mother tongue. (Sommers and Saltz 2004, 145)

Every time a student sits down to write for us, he has to invent the university for the occasion.... The student has to learn to speak our language, to speak as we do, to try on the peculiar ways of knowing, selecting, evaluating, reporting, concluding, and arguing that define ... the various discourses of our community. (Bartholomae 1985, 134)

[Basic writers] have been invited, and they are here. (Troyka 1987, 12)

Following the introduction of the "Use of English" survey course in 1963 after the UCWI became the independent UWI, content faculty associated writing instruction with remediation and suggested that development in writing is largely separate from disciplinary learning. Although the "Use of English" faculty rejected content faculty's emphasis on remediation, especially regarding formalist conventions, they did not associate writing with knowing in disciplines. In that period of the 1960s to mid-1980s, the two camps persisted in their views about whether the course should remain a survey or service course, and administrators and faculty also persisted in stating that any problems in students' language use or writing should have been remedied in the high school. By the end of the late 1980s, however, writing instruction began to evolve from a survey model to reflect "relevance" for the Caribbean context – the trajectory that this chapter addresses.

Beginning in the late 1980s, the UWI sought to *accommodate* those students who displayed limited mastery of English but who usually excelled in content areas. This accommodation started following persistent complaints by content faculty, "Use of English" faculty's eventual acknowledgement of many students' actual linguistic and writing profiles, and calls from groups within the institution to avoid an exclusionary policy and instead consider social equity to achieve regional development. It was also consistent with continuing expansions in enrolment in the post-national era. This was the late 1980s when nationalist sentiment was not as high as in the mid- to late 1960s in the Caribbean region and after Jamaica had changed hands from leaders who considered themselves democratic socialists to those deemed as capitalists.[15] The institution continued to realize expansions in enrolment in this period and a consequent increase in its number of Creole-speaking first-generation university students. The *Report of the Task Force on Tertiary Education* (1986, 41) reveals that increasing numbers of students had been from modest homes: "Within the UWI there has been steady growth in admission of students. These are from lower income homes." Many of these students, the report indicates, were admitted on the basis of their teacher training or nursing certificates. This report also referenced a study that showed that 45 per cent of the students enrolled then were actually from low-income groups (13). Such students would have been coming from backgrounds in which they had limited contact with English, often only learning it in school. A 30 per cent cess on tuition that was applied in 1986 did not stem the tide of students from Creole-speaking backgrounds in any significant way. In 1984–1985, enrolment on the Mona campus had increased by 166 to 5,345. In 1985–1986, when the government announced that students would have to pay 30 per cent of the economic cost of their education, enrolment decreased by 266 to 5,088. In the first year, when the cess was applied, enrolment decreased again to 4,979. However, by the next year, 1987–1988, enrolment increased by 256 to 5,235 students on the Mona campus (UWI 2006–2007, 2). In this same period, faculty continued to complain about students' language competencies, leading to evolution in the "Use of English" course.

The evolution of writing instruction at Mona involved introduction in 1988 of "Fundamentals of English" (the basic writing course that Chevannes 2005 invokes). Mona's administrators and faculty abandoned the faulty assumption that all students possessed the required English language competencies for writing in their disciplines. To address the problems demonstrated by many of those students, the Academic Board approved an entrance test and the elementary English course "Fundamentals of English" for students who received a borderline score on the test. This course served to "nurture" students who were, like those Irvine and Elsasser (1988, 314) observed in the US Virgin Islands, "linguistic orphans, expected to deny the existence of their first language [Creole] and read and write in a second one [English]" that they did not own. If they failed to give up the conventions of their first language, they often failed to demonstrate proficiency in English – a requirement for commencing university studies. For more than a decade, the university *accommodated* such students – displaying the egalitarian ethos that is consistent with democratization of education.

However, while the institution appeared to provide opportunities for all entrants to succeed, its emphasis was on *accommodating* those students only *temporarily*. Because administrators and faculty sought to *manage* rather than learn from students' language and writing challenges, they seemed to oscillate between the egalitarianism that is supposed to inform "the rhetoric of widening participation" (Lillis 1999, 66) and the elitist emphasis on excellence that is entrenched in the institution's foundations. By 2004, administrators and faculty seemed to be engaging in "new elitism", associated with institutions in the United States that were also facing tightened budgets and trying to abolish basic writing (see McNenny 2001; Soliday 2002). The university would divest itself of its basic writing course but would accommodate the duality of equity and excellence by "institutionalizing ambiguity" (Russell 2002, 27). This ambiguity is evident in the United States in the provision of general composition courses that were meant to prepare previously excluded students to write in the academy; however, they functioned as gatekeepers because they were associated with remediation or a liminal position. In Jamaica, ambiguity was institutionalized in a policy to accept students who did not get a clear pass on their entrance English proficiency test but not provide accommodations in the normal curriculum for those students to develop their writing before they were re-tested and could proceed to take their required first-year writing course(s), which they had to pass before being able to graduate. The result of this change was an unfortunate shift from "nurturing" to "testing" students, with the myth of transience yielding increasing marginalization of groups of students who did not display acceptable levels of mastery in written English.

Many academics who were in favour of this course wanted it to focus on formalist conventions; however, precisely because of that focus, those who countered it called for its teaching in secondary-level schools. Neither group realized the extent to which everyone was shrouding writing knowledge in formalism and continuing to separate language development from learning in disciplines and learning outside of the academy. This disconnect between writing and learning is evident in the introduction and development of the course, debates surrounding its development, and its eventual divestment from the university. I argue that the views about, and organization of, this course perhaps best demonstrate attitudes to the work of literacy, the persistence of the myth of transience at the UWI at Mona and the need for reconsiderations of the provisions (or lack thereof) for the students who arrive at the university with inadequate levels of proficiency in English. The development of "Fundamentals of English" marked a necessary response to changing cohorts and diverse abilities of students; however, its management – and that of the writing centre – suggest administrators and faculty may have ignored the country's distinctive social issues and the interconnectedness of writing and learning in the academy and language learning and use in society.

Students' Real Linguistic and Writing Profiles Acknowledged: Social Equity Considered

Because faculty and administrators attributed faulty linguistic and writing profiles to students, they did not immediately adapt the British model course that was introduced in 1963. However, they appeared to acknowledge students' varying language and writing abilities when, in the 1988–1989 academic year, the university finally began to offer a separate elementary English course for students who demonstrated low proficiency in understanding and producing written English. The university's chief moderator for "Use of English", Richard Allsopp, had first recommended in 1971 that a course be developed for such students on each campus, and content faculty had been calling for similar arrangements or for increased "remedial" focus in the "Use of English" course since the late 1960s. "Use of English" faculty made every attempt to disassociate the course and themselves from remedial instruction. However, when persistent complaints were received from various segments of the university in the mid-1980s to signal that the proficiency problem had become more acute, the "Use of English" faculty seriously considered a programme for the students concerned. These complaints had been lodged by faculty members in Social Sciences in 1985 and in Education in 1987 and by external examiners for the Faculty of Natural Sciences in 1986 and for the Caribbean Institute of Mass Communications in 1987 (see Dyche 2006b). The course developed in response to such complaints and to "Use of English" faculty's observations was "Fundamentals of English" (UC010).

I describe as "linguistic orphans" the students for whom this course was developed because these are students who, like those described by Irvine and Elsasser (1988, 314), found themselves without a language for written literacy. They had to abandon their oral Creole language in the schoolroom, but they never really developed mastery of the written English code. Although students from various territories could be found in this constituency in the UC010 course that was developed at Mona, most of the takers were Jamaicans. Dyche (1996b) confirmed this constituency in a letter to the editor of the then *Arts Newsletter* in which she attempted to correct inaccuracies about the English language courses and the university's responsibility in such teaching. Dyche pointed out that the percentage of non-Jamaican students from the English-speaking territories who took the UC010 course was "relatively insignificant, but there [were] at least ten in the course each year" (2). Given that there were two hundred to three hundred students in the course in each year in the 1980s and 1990s (Shields 1987b), if approximately ten were non-Jamaican, then over 95 per cent were Jamaican. As I have established, significant numbers of those Jamaican students were from Creole-speaking backgrounds.

The students who had to take this UC010 course can also be described as "basic writers". Shaughnessy (1977, 5), basic writing theorist and teacher whose work influenced the development of UC010 (see Dyche 1996a), concludes that basic writers are students who "write the way they do, not because they are slow or non-verbal . . . but because they are beginners and must like all beginners, learn by making mistakes. These they make aplenty." Basic writers in the Jamaican context are somewhat similar to those described by Shaughnessy, and their peculiarities can be inferred from the programme to which they are attached. Their course, UC010, was designed for students deemed to have demonstrated inadequate reading and writing skills in the English language proficiency test. Typically, students offered a place in UC010 received very low or failing scores in the reading comprehension, grammar, and analysis of numerical data sections, and wrote essays that – based on the mark scheme for the test – displayed a student's satisfactory, partial, or unsatisfactory competence in "giving focus/direction to the writing and in developing and organizing ideas". The writing was usually coherent and even if the student displayed unsatisfactory competence in giving focus, "the message [could] be generally understood". However, there usually was a significant problem at the level of expression: "recurrent – although not pervasive – errors of expression . . . detract[ed] from the overall quality of the writing" (Mark Scheme 2004). Trained and experienced markers and the academic advisers in the test unit usually determined that students offered UC010 could learn to correct many of the errors within a year.

The most concrete response to observations of and complaints about such students' limited English language proficiency came in Kathryn Shields's "Proposals for Upgrading Students' Proficiency in English" (1987b). In this document, Shields, who was then convenor of "Use of English", acknowledged students' linguistic and writing profiles by addressing the problem of having in the university many students who did not master basic English for reading and writing. She made recommendations similar to those from Allsopp (1971) for having students take a proficiency test on entry and an elementary English course if their test results confirmed limited English proficiency. She made such recommendations on the basis of observations that "Mona students who are granted UWI matriculation belong to two separate categories: those functionally literate in English [and] those who have limited ability to produce and understand coherent prose in English". Shields pointed out that the schools did not teach the skills of critical reading that were taught in the "Use of English" course, "basic tools as they are for maximum benefit to be derived from university education" (1987b, 1). She asserted that with increasing numbers of students being accepted into the university with limited proficiency in English, more was needed than the proficiency component that was added to the "Use of English" course five years earlier. Shields proposed that students sit a diagnostic test in the first week of the first term, and those failing to "demonstrate mastery of basic English skills" should take a noncredit course "Elementary English" before going on to "Use of English". This elementary course should be for two hours per week, with between eight and ten students in each group of a projected total of approximately three hundred students.

Administrators and faculty accepted Shields's (1987b) proposal, but not without objections. In the 1987–1988 *Departmental Reports* (1988, 9), the dean of the Faculty of Arts and General Studies mentions that "widespread concern at the low proficiency in English among many students led to approval of a Fundamentals of English course, compulsory for any new student registering for an undergraduate degree who failed a proficiency test on entry". Minute 905 of the minutes of Academic Board, Mona (1988b) confirms that the University Academic Committee (UAC 1988b) accepted Shields's two-pronged proposal for a diagnostic test and a related proficiency course to be offered beginning in October 1988, but not before the board noted that "the proficiency test should be taken and passed *before* a student was admitted to the UWI" and "for UWI to undertake basic English training was a misuse of its resources" (emphasis added). The appended course outline evidences the "basic English training" for which the course was criticized then and that would attract more criticism later. The topics to be covered over a twenty-three-week period would include format and style of essay/letter/report writing, reading comprehension skills, grammatical relation, and writing mechanics and sentence structure.

The *Departmental Reports* (1989) for 1988–1989 specified that whereas basic training began immediately following acceptance of the proposal, the test's gatekeeping function that the Academic Board sanctioned was not activated immediately. On first administration, the test "screened" new students "for competence in English" (46). However, it had not been administered to all new students (13–14). Shields's "Preliminary Report on UC010" (1989) confirmed that the first test was administered to only some entrants because of dislocation caused by Hurricane Gilbert in September 1988. This first test was two-and-a-half hours long and comprised an essay; a multiple choice section testing students' ability to distinguish between correct and incorrect grammatical structure, and identify basic grammatical concepts; and a comprehension exercise. According to Shields, the two hundred (of eight hundred) students who were offered UC010 were considered to be "unable to write grammatical English", "so lacking in organizational skills as to produce writing which is incoherent", "exhibiting a combination of the first two categories" and "unable to comprehend English at a basic level".

Convinced of what Shields (1989) called the "widespread and serious nature of the problem", the language department appointed a new full-time member of staff – Caroline Dyche – in December 1988. Dyche had responsibilities for developing and coordinating "Fundamentals of English", which began fully in the 1989–1990 academic year with students selected primarily based on their performance in the essay component of the proficiency test. Although the course had a full-time coordinator, the staffing problems that plagued the "Use of English" course would be magnified in UC010. The student–teacher ratio was twelve to one, but to achieve it, seventeen tutors were involved in the 1989–1990 programme – thirteen part-time and four full-time ("Report on UC010" 1989, 1). This staffing situation suggests how the institution perceived the course. On the one hand, it seemed to be accommodating the course, but on the other, it did not really make the necessary preparations for instruction.

Indeed, the weaknesses in Jamaican university students' language usage caught the attention of various stakeholders, but they did not really consider measures that would go beyond acknowledgement to meaningfully address the problem *within the institution*. Following the introduction of the course, Jamaica's National Association of Teachers of English recognized that the wishes expressed in the Colonial Office's 1847 Circular Despatch (described in chapter 2) had not been realized to date. The association observed that the test instituted at Mona showed that "many students with satisfactory grades in CXC English A and the [GCE] general paper did not write *grammatical English* at an acceptable level, and were not conversant with the organization and style appropriate to formal essay writing" ("General Paper" 1990, 27; emphasis added). Members of this primarily secondary-level association concluded, "The English A and General Paper examinations, it seemed, permitted other skills to compensate for weaknesses in *formal grammatical expression*" ("General Paper" 1990, 27; emphasis added). They recommended that secondary-level teachers would, therefore, need to do more in preparing students for university-level work.

Upper administration was also struck by the situation. However, what was even more striking was faculty's attitude to the problem along with the persistence of the myth of transience in the institution. So bad was the *language proficiency problem* perceived to be on all campuses that, as happened in the 1970s to early 1980s, it continued to merit inclusion in the university's *Vice Chancellor's Report to Council*. In 1989, the vice chancellor reported, "All three campuses continued to grapple with the problem of the *low level of competence in English Language exhibited by the majority of students*. This problem is exacerbated by limitations on staff caused by limited finances and an unwillingness by certain elements within the University to treat this as a University problem" (UWI 1989, 22; emphasis added). The inclusion in the report three years later was no more promising; indeed, it indicates a decline in the number of students who demonstrated an acceptable level of proficiency in English: "On all three campuses the Faculty continues to grapple with the problem of proficiency in the English Language. While programmes put in place are showing signs of success, the number of students who on entry to the UWI are proficient enough to reap the full benefit from university-level materials and teaching seems to be declining" (UWI 1992, 30).

These reports suggest that neither faculty nor administrators had adequately considered the complexity of the problem, especially regarding the country's linguistic context and development of public education. All of these reports highlighted the gravity of students' weaknesses; however, none addressed the problem in relation to the country's/region's linguistic context. No one seemed to suggest that teaching methods for Jamaicans would probably have to be different from those for Spanish or French speakers, for example, who may exhibit similar weaknesses but for different reasons when learning English. Although course materials included token sections on Creole, instruction was not consistently relevant to Jamaican students' linguistic backgrounds. Moreover, there is no documentation suggesting how instruction could have had practical relevance for such students if the course were designed to focus on real writing tasks in students' disciplines. This measure could have included grouping students based on their specific disciplines.

Oscillating between Egalitarianism and Elitism: Equity or Excellence?

Perhaps, because administrators and faculty did not consider the language problem in relation to larger social issues, and because they did not acknowledge how language and writing abilities develop, they often wavered between emphasizing excellence and striving for social equity. Chapters 2 and 3 highlight the ways in which academics at Mona emphasized excellence between the 1940s and early 1980s. The "Fundamentals of English" course signalled a concern for equity. However, beginning in the late 1980s, administrators' and faculty's attitudes to language and writing instruction were marked by oscillation between the two poles. This oscillation is almost expected, given that some faculty and laypersons opposed the teaching of "Use of English" – an *applied* English course – in the academy. After UC010 was planned and submitted for approval, some administrators and content faculty continued to "debate" the course's value. Minute 616 of the Academic Board, Mona (1988a) meeting records the contrary opinions that various attendees expressed with regard to Shields's (1987b) proposal:

> that a preliminary course would impose an additional burden on students; that (on the contrary) the course, by improving students' reading comprehension and basic writing skills, would assist them to follow other courses more easily; that a summer remedial programme would be inadequate in relation both to time allowed and the number of students able to enroll; that an extra (Preliminary) course would not extend the time spent at University for either part-time (Arts) students or preliminary (Natural Sciences) students; that many students had little motivation anyway for University courses, especially when so many examiners of Faculty courses marked for content and did not penalize poor expression, grammatical errors and illogical statements.

Minute 620 of Academic Board, Mona (1988a) bears the possible thoughts of contemporary readers regarding those continued concerns about whether the course is burdensome or beneficial, whether it should be done in the summer or during the first year, and whether students would be motivated to take it based on their content lecturers' grading practices. There, Professor Magnus reminded the meeting that "agreement had been reached about the need for such a course", so he was concerned that the Mona Academic Board "should still find it necessary, now that an actual proposal was finally submitted, to again debate about the need for such a course".

After the test was approved and the elementary English course was introduced, it appeared that the various segments of the university had accepted the need for what was then referred to as "remedial" instruction. Dyche (2006b) asserts that the shift from the single "Use of English" course for all students meant "an acknowledgement by the University of the wide-ranging language abilities and needs of its entrants, along with a glimmer of recognition of the diverse body of knowledge and learning being promulgated in the name of post-secondary English language studies". "Glimmer" is, however, the operative word because disagreements about offering the course reigned in the media and within the academy. The UWI vice chancellor reported in 1990 that "the introduction of a remedial Fundamentals of English Course at Mona sparked a public debate on language issues" (UWI 1990, 18). It is also not insignificant that the university labelled the noncredit bearing "Fundamentals of English" course as "preuniversity", indicating that its teaching belonged anywhere but in the academy.

As there were disagreements about offering a "remedial" course in the academy so was there concern about using the proficiency test for exclusion of students from the university. The Faculty of Arts and General Studies *Regulations and Syllabuses* (1989) for 1989–1990, which includes "Fundamentals of English" under its listing of university courses explains how both the test and course functioned as gatekeepers at different points in a student's university career. With the exception of students pursuing law, all first-year students had to take the proficiency test at the start of the academic year.[16] Students were advised that if they failed the test, they had to take UC010 and this "preliminary course [did] not count for credit towards the degree". If they passed the test or UC010, students proceeded to take "Use of English". However, until they passed UC010, they could not proceed in their degree programme: "No student failing UC010 [would] be allowed entry into any Second Year course in any Faculty." However, Minute 84 of the University Academic Committee (UAC 1988c) minutes includes a notation that the Faculty Consultative Committee, Arts and General Studies, felt that "the UWI had a commitment to develop the human resources of the region and that *it was not justifiable to institute an entrance test in English Language which would exclude from the university persons whose abilities in other areas would allow them to make a contribution to their societies and to the region*" (emphasis added). This view had been expressed earlier in the Faculty of Arts and General Studies' (1987) "Report on Faculty Review 1986/87" at Cave Hill.

In response to those concerns about the gatekeeping function of the course and test, and as happened with the "Use of English" course, the language department solicited content faculty's assistance in addressing the problem. In a draft response in 1993 to the dean of the Faculty of Arts and General Studies regarding questions about the especially high failure rates in the language courses, the then head, Mervyn Alleyne (1993), proposed to consolidate the regular programme. However, he noted that "other necessary measures will require the support and intervention of the university" (2). In pointing to the perception of content faculty's attitudes to language competence, Alleyne called for collaboration to bring about improvements in English language proficiency:

> Other Faculties will also have a role to play. They have to take up a clear position on the role of language in the education of their students and adjust accordingly the evaluation of their students. As it is now, there seems to be no overall policy, but the general tendency is for some Faculties or Departments or individual lecturers to ignore language competence in the grading of students or not to provide opportunities for students to display language skills in tests and examinations. (Ibid.)

Alleyne's request evidences a focus on formalism and concerns about who should attend to teaching students formalist conventions. Although such conventions represent only one aspect of writing that is often unfortunately taught separate from content, concern about who should teach them was only one reason for which faculty would waver in their support of the test and elementary English course.

Divergent opinions on the course would yield intermittent discussions about whose responsibility it was for financing it or about its place in the university. In the "Memo to Members" of the language department, Alleyne (1993, 3) indicated, "We shall also, in the course of the new calendar year, begin to examine proposals for phasing out UC010 or at least reducing its scope at UWI." Following recommendations by the department through the Faculty of Arts and General Studies board to phase out the course (*Departmental Reports* 1995, 38), Academic Board mandated a subcommittee to consider available reports and other relevant data on English language proficiency. The committee of Don Wilson, Joe Pereira and Caroline Dyche presented its findings in "Report on English Language Proficiency Requirements for UWI Mona Undergraduate Study" in January 1995. Wilson, Pereira and Dyche (1995) mentioned that among the significant problems that plagued the course was staffing: the facilitators were primarily part-time, there was high attrition and the complement reached the unwieldy number of twenty-two in 1995. However, "the Committee did NOT support the view that in principle remedial English instruction was not the province of the University". The committee members "felt that it was in the University's best interest to continue to offer a remedial course (within the regular academic year) *to those students who could be expected to have achieved the desired level of proficiency by the end of the course"* (10; emphasis in the original).

To support their recommendation, Wilson, Pereira and Dyche (1995) mentioned that the university could not ignore the high failure rate in CXC English language in Jamaica between 1984 and 1993. The mean failure rate, they report, was 67.369 per cent, with a high of 75.53 per cent in 1993 and a low of 56.42 per cent in 1984 (5). Therefore, the university needed to consider the attributes of the population from which it would select incoming students. The committee also referenced research that addressed "the international nature of the problem", specifically in "most American universities [that] routinely test the English proficiency of prospective students and offer remedial courses to those diagnosed as being weak" (6). Wilson, Pereira and Dyche, therefore, recommended that the university maintain the course and test, but make some changes to testing procedures. They recommended that some students be exempted from the test; however, like the academic committee did in 1988, they recommended that the test be a gatekeeper. The students exempted from the test would be those with CXC English Language Level 1, GCE English Language Grade A, or GCE A/O-level General Paper Grade A. "Conversely", they recommended, "those students required to take the entrance test who demonstrate marked incompetence in fundamental areas of written expression and/or reading comprehension should be excluded from the University until they have acquired the necessary skills and are able to pass the test" (11). If this controversial policy of exclusion were to have been enforced, the test would have had to be administered in March. That would have been in the semester before students started the UWI rather than at the beginning of the first semester when the diagnostic test used to be administered. The committee recommended the establishment of an English proficiency test unit (to begin in 1996–1997) to facilitate a first test from the unit in March 1998.

Although the committee's recommendations were accepted, some faculty members continued to voice their disagreement at the faculty board level. In the *Departmental Reports* (1996, 43) for 1995–1996, the head of Use of English and Linguistics outlined that the university had approved setting up an English proficiency test unit "to test all *applicants* to the university, with a view to excluding from entry to the university those who did not have the requisite English language competence. This would serve to contract the need for UC010, a pre-university-level course to be offered." The dean, in turn, emphasized the distance sought from remedial instruction by noting, "there was support in principle for decreasing our involvement in remedial English, largely divesting this to pre-university and summer school, focusing instead on a Proficiency Test on entry with the establishment of a Proficiency Test Unit in the Faculty" (16). At the same time that some faculty members and administrators were voicing disagreements about the course, Dyche (1996a) was writing to secondary-level teachers to outline the kinds of problems that were appearing in students' test scripts and the levels of success students experienced in the "Fundamentals of English" course. Dyche emphasized that despite the significant problems that students exhibited in syntax (in terms of sentence structure and idiom) and in other aspects of grammar (such as faulty subject verb agreement or incorrect use of singular or plural number or verb forms), "by the end of the year, the majority (approximately 70%) do succeed in attaining the standard required to pass the course and to produce in their other university courses a more acceptable level of essay writing than that displayed in the English Proficiency Entrance Test" (26). However, faculty and administrators did not seem to focus on the stated success in the course. The abbreviation of "Fundamentals of English" yields the acronym "FOE", and it seemed to represent some faculty's attitude to the course and some students' perception of it.

With the diagnostic proficiency test functioning as a gatekeeper – at least in the Faculty of Arts and General Studies – and thanks to the persistent myth of transience, plans to phase out UC010 increased in the late 1990s. The "Minutes of a Meeting of the DLLP held Thursday, October 2, 1997" states, "Once the Test Unit has become fully operational the UC010 programme will be offered on a reduced scale" (DLLP 1997, 3). In an April 2002 meeting of lecturers in the ELS and the head of the department who chaired the meeting, "The Chairman proposed that the Department consider moving the teaching of UC010 to Summer, commencing in the academic year 2003/2004. This would free up resources used for teaching UC010 to develop and teach third year English Language courses" (DLLP 2002b, 2). The explanation given about using available resources for upper-level courses is practical; however, that explanation ignored two significant implications of phasing out the course. One of these is the incorrect assumption that the problem that led to its introduction would be eradicated by the test; the other is the view that the institution seemed to be concerned more with students it perceived already wrote well than with basic writers, despite claims of increasing access to higher education – access that necessarily involved students who had not mastered English by the end of secondary schooling.

Institutionalizing Ambiguity: Neither Equity nor Excellence (?)

The "Fundamentals of English" course was still offered in the department in 2003–2004; however, by the 2004–2005 academic year, it was removed from the normal curriculum and campus budget, with less than satisfactory results for the institution's basic writing students. This is a change that, while being influenced by them, did not result from only the years of debate about remedial instruction in the academy and phasing out UC010. At the beginning of the 2003–2004 academic year, the university announced changes in the financial arrangements for courses. Among the changes was payment by credit. Since UC010 was equivalent to a six-credit course but was noncredit bearing, students protested having to pay for a course that did not count towards their degree. Following the protests and negotiations with representatives from the Guild of Students, the institution sanctioned changes to the course structure and administration. These changes that were likely to yield neither excellence nor social equity bespeak ambiguity on many levels: an institution that seemed to have relinquished control of its basic writing course to a unit in one of its departments, students deemed successful in content areas but weak in language and who were accepted without provisions for their writing development, and students who unknowingly strove to become complicit in their own marginalization.

Ambiguity is evident in the *Departmental Reports* (2005, 213) for 2004–2005 in which the dean of Humanities and Education explained, "The use of the English Proficiency Test (ELPT) . . . to identify potential matriculants who have deficiencies in writing English and to offer them a remedial writing course was taken a step further during the year. As a result of budgetary constraints, the remedial course UC010 is no longer offered as part of the normal curriculum for students needing to do the course." In those reports, the then head of the Department of Language, Linguistics and Philosophy explained that the course had been divested to the self-financing test unit *in the department*. With these new arrangements, the year-long course taught over fifty-two hours was reduced to an intensive one-semester course taught over thirty-nine hours. Based on those changes, the university gave students who failed the proficiency test various options for fulfilling their English language requirement. The head explained that "students identified as requiring remedial assistance were encouraged to sit and pass the course in the summer prior to their formal entry to UWI, or to seek alternative tuition during the summer, and re-sit the test at the end of that session" (54). By 2006–2007, the options were expanded: As one option, applicants who failed the test were encouraged to take the UC010 course during the summer prior to starting their first semester. Applicants could then retake the test in August. A second option allowed students to take the UC010 course during their first or second semester at the end of which they could retake the proficiency test. As a third option, students could choose to not take the UC010 course before retaking the proficiency test, but the test unit advised such students who intended to "challenge" the test to seek assistance with writing from sites outside of the university (Dyche 2007a).

In his explanation in 2005 for changes to UC010, the head of the Department of Language, Linguistics and Philosophy reported what I consider unsurprising low pass rates and concerns about writing that emerged following the changes:

> A UWI policy decision taken during the year at the request of the Guild of Students resulted in students not being compelled to take the divested UC010, but being allowed to take the end-of-course examination as a challenge. Students who sat the course did

significantly better than those who were registered for exams only, leading to more concern in the Department that those who continue to sit the examination without help in upgrading their skills will be severely handicapped and unable to sit their Level 1 Foundation courses. (*Departmental Reports* 2005, 54)

The low passes and concerns would persist while significant numbers of students continued to challenge the test. Indeed, Dyche (2006b) reports that following the implementation of the policy regarding UC010, the department witnessed "a high failure rate in the ELPT [English Language Proficiency Test], the resultant barring of students from pursuing their compulsory year 1 English language course (the Use of English replacement courses) and, ultimately, the delayed graduation of these students". The "Minutes of a Meeting of the DLLP held Monday, 27th February 2006" records attendees' concern about the high failure rates and "woefully poor writing skills of students" (DLLP 2006a, 5). Table 1 presents results that show a decline in enrolment and the corresponding dramatic and continuing decline in pass rate after the "Fundamentals of English" course was removed from the campus budget and reduced from fifty-two to thirty-nine hours of instruction.

The low pass rate reported following the change in arrangements for the course is in marked contrast to what obtained in the year-long course (see table 2). Table 2 presents figures showing a high pass rate in the six years preceding the policy change: over 80 per cent between 1998 and 2001, and over 75 per cent in the last two years. The exception in 2001–2002 when the pass rate was just over 60 per cent can probably be explained by students' significantly lower levels of proficiency in that year. The "Minutes of a Meeting of the DLLP held Thursday, 17th January 2002" includes complaints about "the quality of the cohort for the 2001–2002 academic year, whose performance, in the general view of the teaching staff, is the worst in the history of the [UC010] course's existence" (DLLP 2002a, 3). The increased numbers of students in the course in 2002–2004 (when this writer was the coordinator) has a twofold

Table 1. Results for the One-Semester UC010 Course for the Period Semester I 2004–2005 to Semester II 2006–2007

Semester	UC010 Enrolment	Pass Rate
I 2004–2005	309	63%
II 2004–2005	136	61%
I 2005–2006	142	35%
II 2005–2006	50	48.6%
I 2006–2007	106	36%
II 2006–2007	53	34.6%

Source: Data from Dyche 2007a.

Table 2. Results for the Year-long UC010 Course for the Period 1998 to 2004

Year	Number of Students Who Took UC010	Number (%) Passed
1998–1999	192	157 (82%)
1999–2000	240	approx. 85%
2000–2001	approx. 312	84%
2001–2002	304	60.5%
2002–2003	505	76%
2003–2004	538	77.3%

Source: Data drawn from the UWI, Mona's *Departmental Reports* (1999, 2000, 2001, 2002, 2003, 2004) for each corresponding academic year.

explanation: (1) in those years some individual faculties at Mona began to admit even students who had failed the proficiency test; and (2) joining the course were repeaters and other students who knew they had to take the course before doing their required standard writing course or before graduating, but who had delayed doing it as long as possible.

Not only was there a decrease in the pass rate in UC010 after the policy change, but the test unit also saw a decline in passes in the proficiency test. Dyche (2007a) reports, "With the declining enrolment in the UC010 course, one has seen a decline in the pass rate for the end-of-semester ELP tests taken by students". Table 3 confirms

Table 3. Results for the English Language Proficiency Test for the Period 1998–1999 to 2006–2007

YEAR	Number of Test Takers	Number (%) passed	010/Fail (1)	Fail (2)
1998–1999	3,468	2,676 (77.1%)	547 (15.8%)	245 (7.1%)
1999–2000	2,827	1,922 (68%)	605 (21.4%)	300 (10.6%)
2000–2001	2,654	1,882 (70.9%)	599 (22.6%)	173 (6.5%)
2001–2002	2,913	1,539 (52.8%)	685 (23.5%)	689 (23.7%)
2002–2003	2,553	1,423 (56%)	903 (36%)	207 (8%)
2003–2004	2,343	1,081 (46%)	1,150 (49%)	112 (5%)
2004–2005	4,163	2,362 (56.7%)	N/A	1,801 (43.3%)
2005–2006	4,541	2,186 (48%)	N/A	2,355 (52%)
2006–2007	4,140	1,867 (45%)	N/A	2,273 (55%)

Source: Data provided by English Language Proficiency Test Unit, Department of Language, Linguistics and Philosophy, UWI, Mona, Jamaica.

this declining pass rate (Donna Reid, personal communication, 5 November 2007). When the first proficiency test was administered prior to the start of the new academic year in 1998, 74 per cent of the 3,747 applicants passed (see UWI 1999, 46; *Departmental Reports* 1998). In the following year, 77.1 per cent of the applicants passed the test. With the exception of 2000–2001 when the pass rate was 70.9 per cent, the rates for the years following for applicants who did not possess the English language requirements to qualify for exemption from the test show a general decline in passes. This rate reached as low as 45 per cent in 2006–2007.

These results in table 3 are presented based on categories that Dyche (2007a) provides. Dyche explains that in 2006–2007 there were three possible result categories for the proficiency test: pass, fail (1) and fail (2). Applicants who passed the test could register for the appropriate level 1 course. Fail (1) meant that "with the remediation offered by the University, the applicant should be able to attain the necessary standard within the first year". Fail (2) indicated that the applicant "has an extremely low level of proficiency & is not recommended for admission". In this table, I combined the "genuine" UC010 total with a previous "borderline" category that used to be included for nursing and University of Technology applicants whose programmes did not require or allow them to take UC010. The "fail (2)" category reveals a failure rate that was on the incline since 2004–2005 when the UC010 policy change was implemented.

The decline in passes in the course and test is not unrelated to the fact that both students who took the new UC010 course and those who did not take it, along with new entrants, took the test. Additionally, as Dyche confirmed, many students were merely retaking the test without getting additional instruction (personal interview, 19 July 2007). Such students probably experienced stagnant or diminishing writing abilities in the semester or year(s) that they waited to take another test. The high failure rates also suggest the extent to which students were probably unaware that in succeeding in getting the institution to make taking the course optional, they would delay their own development and ultimately realize only a pyrrhic victory.

The declining pass rate may also be explained by other problems that were associated with the new UC010 course, one being differing objectives for the course and the test that students took. "Fundamentals of English" was a typical prerequisite model basic writing course. This model requires students to take and pass a prerequisite course, before registering for their regular first-year writing course(s) (Lalicker 1999, 6). Students who did not get a clear pass in the proficiency test were usually required to take and pass it before taking a standard first-year writing course. In the year-long programme in which students attended one two-hour weekly seminar, attention was given to developing their expository writing skills. In 2001–2002, a summary and a response essay were added to the course. Summary skills were included to ensure that students understood what they read and could express ideas in their own words in English. Since based on anecdotal evidence students' writing improved when they had the necessary content, the then coordinator added a response essay to allow students to have some content for their essay. Based on the course objectives given in the UC010 Course Outline (2003–2004) (that this writer as coordinator prepared), among the things students would have been able to do by the end of one academic year were:

- Write simple and complex sentence structures that comply with the grammatical and syntactic rules of the English language.
- Punctuate correctly.
- Write unified and coherent paragraphs.
- Plan, write, revise and edit essays and paragraphs as steps in the writing process.
- Read, analyse and evaluate paragraphs, articles and essays.

This 2003–2004 outline states that the "course seeks to improve the student's level of proficiency in English in an academic environment. The course is designed for students who need instruction in grammar, punctuation, sentence construction, paragraph development and essay writing" (1).

The one-semester course that was first offered in the first semester of 2004–2005 was guided by the same objectives. One crucial difference in instruction, however, was that students spent three hours per week in a two-hour tutorial and a one-hour workshop. In its new form, the course was taught each semester (including at Brown's Town, Knox and Moneague Community Colleges) at the end of which students took the proficiency test. The *English Language Proficiency Test Information Guide* (2007) explains that the test was "used to assess whether persons applying to pursue undergraduate degree programmes at the UWI Mona campus possess a satisfactory level of writing and reading proficiency in English for university academic purposes". Consistent with that description, up to the 2012–2013 academic year, the test included writing, reading and discrete grammar components. Candidates completed two writing tasks: a 300-word essay "on a topic of general interest", and a 250- to 300-word description of "numerical data contained in a table or in some form of graphical illustration". With regard to reading, candidates read one or more passages and provided answers to "alternative/multiple choice questions concerning any or all of the following: main idea/ secondary ideas; writer's attitude/tone/primary intention; literal and figurative meaning; explicit and implied meaning; organizational structure". Grammar was tested through "alternative/ multiple choice questions on any or all of the following : (a) Grammar of the Simple Sentence, (b) Grammar of Complex/Compound Sentences, (c) Idiomatic Usage (diction), (d) Idiomatic Usage (structures), and (e) Writing Mechanics & Spelling". The descriptions of the course and test demonstrate that whereas UC010 focused on essay writing and comprehension of prose texts, it did not (necessarily) address interpretation of numerical data that was included in the proficiency test. The equivalence of a UC010 examination with the proficiency test, therefore, represented an anomaly because UC010 did not necessarily prepare students for all of the components of the test. There may also have been problems related to the duration of the course. In her "Report UC010 Semester I, 2006–07", Eileen Scott (2007, 3), who coordinated the course for the stated period, noted that "tutors saw improvement in students' writing skills even among very weak students. However, there were calls for . . . a longer course." She concluded that "the students clearly benefitted although many need more time to consolidate gains" (4).

The differences in UC010 and the test and the high failure rates should have been cause for concern, for they suggested a need for re-examination of the arrangements for accommodating basic writers at Mona. The resultant low passes in the proficiency test taken by both those students who took the one-semester course and those who simply re-took the test without instruction suggested the need for more ethical actions from stakeholders regarding basic-writing Jamaican students at Mona. Chapter 2 established that in the Jamaican context a vernacular and an official language sharing the same vocabulary base coexist, posing myriad problems in English for learners. Because of the co-existence of these two lexically related languages and because of the way in which English is taught in many pretertiary level settings, many students often fail regional/ external examinations in English (Craig 1999, 227; Task Force 2004, 56–57) and the proficiency test. It, therefore, seems imprudent for administrators to have required that those students who failed the test but were accepted into the institution find the support to prepare them to enter the standard courses without mandating that the students did this before or during their first semester. Certainly, if students are consciously working on increasing their writing abilities, their writing and learning are likely to improve in their areas of specialization. The dean of Humanities and Education (2006, 1) writes that "the rationale of [the writing] courses is to provide students with what we identify as the essential skills that they need in order to pursue successfully their undergraduate studies". This means that by delaying in taking and passing UC010, students delayed in getting to the regular first-year courses that were meant to provide skills necessary for successful pursuit of the undergraduate degree. If the dean is right, when students delayed in taking and passing UC010, they not only took a long time to get their degree, since the latter was dependent on completing their mandatory writing course(s), but also benefited less than they could from their core courses.

Chevannes (2005) and others (see chapter 1 and Task Force 2004) recommend that instead of measures to address the problem in the institution, resources should be increased at lower levels of schooling to increase students' readiness for postsecondary level work. That recommendation is valid because there is great need for reconsideration of, and changes in, the current pedagogical practices in literacy teaching in the nation's schools. Communicative language teaching is widely practised and encouraged to the extent that children who need to are not developing metacognitive awareness of the contrasts between Jamaican Creole and English. Teacher training is still largely focused on teacher preparation for a situation in which English is the first language. There is yet to be serious preparation in contrastive analysis so that teachers in training will have a good sense of how to help the many Creole-speaking children that they will meet in schools. Further, with increasing acceptance of Creole as a language, there is increasing use of Creole in the media. There are, however, increasingly fewer English-speaking models for children from predominantly Creole-speaking backgrounds (see Shields-Brodber 1997). Resources are required to effectively address those deficiencies.

Although the recommendation is valid, and even if it were true that the language/writing problem would one day disappear, the needs of the present and immediate future cohorts of university students would still have to be addressed. As the *Report of the Task Force on Tertiary Education* (1986) confirms, some of those students are early childhood and primary school teachers with a very simple vocabulary, and some are teachers who barely scraped through their writing courses in training college and who will admit their weaknesses in written expression. Others are experienced workers who cannot remember the last time they wrote a personal letter or were able to give a complete oral report in formal English. In his recollection of the university's development in the text coauthored with Sherlock, Nettleford recognizes departures from an elitist model and recommends that administrators "open the doors of the University still more widely without sacrificing excellence" (Sherlock and Nettleford 1990, 303). Nettleford's statement typifies the genuine and reasonable concern about maintaining excellence that is usually expressed simultaneously with increased enrolment in the institution. However, whether administrators admit it or not, one of the attendant features of the democratization of education is the presence of students of low socioeconomic status, some of whom will not have mastered the language variety and registers appropriate for academic writing. Accepting such students requires appropriate measures to ensure that their entry into the university is, to borrow from Mary Muchiri et al. (1995, 178), "without intellectual brutality, loss of identity, and waste of talents".

Ambiguous "Writing Centre" Provisions

Like an institution's writing courses, its other writing resources can reflect how administrators and academics on the campus understand writing, and the UWI at Mona has also institutionalized ambiguity in its provision and management of its writing centre. This writing resource was started with the laudable "goal of improving communicative competence and empowering student writers ... of diverse backgrounds and experiences in writing, in a welcoming, supportive and collaborative environment" (Writing Centre 2007). Stephen North (1984) would probably have supported this mission given ideas expressed in his landmark essay on writing centres, such as writing centres are "one manifestation . . . of a dialogue about writing that is central to higher education" (440); writing centre personnel "talk to" student writers/visitors at any stage in the process of writing, with "variations on the kind of talk" including personnel and/or student writer reading, writing and questioning (443); and writing centre personnel "aim to make better writers, not necessarily – or immediately – better texts" (441). However, despite the mission, suggesting that the centre at the UWI at Mona was conceived and started as a place where students could go in for assistance with their writing, it departed from plans to provide maximum benefit to students taking the various writing courses in the department. As will be seen, discussions surrounding the centre and the provisions/lack of the requisite resources reflect local realities that North would probably describe as misconceptions and misrepresentations of writing centres as forms of the "grammar and drill center, the fix-it shop, the first aid station" (437) or "proofreading-shop-in-the-basement" (444), not falling in the category he envisioned – "centers of consciousness about writing on campuses" and grounded in the Socratic method of teaching (446).

The idea for Mona's writing centre[17] arose out of research that Monica Taylor was conducting regarding the concept of a self-access centre in 1996–1997 while she was teaching "Language: Exposition/Argument". She had received funding from the National Council of Teachers of English in the US to conduct a small project in her office that she was using as a resource centre. She had used the funding to buy books and other materials, and students would go to her office to consult or borrow the resources. From that project, Taylor saw the beginnings of what could be a full-fledged writing centre. Although she had read about writing centres and self-access centres in North America and Europe, when Taylor prepared the proposal for Mona's centre, she was considering a concept she had observed at Michigan Technological University, where graduate students were hired as writing consultants to meet with and hold sessions for other students (personal interview, 25 July 2007). Based on her proposal, the *Departmental Reports* (2000, 51) for 1999–2000 explains that a proposed "walk-in Writing Centre . . . would integrate computer-assisted learning and teaching with direct face-to-face help. This would be made available to anyone with English Language writing problems on the university campus." This early description already hinted at an unfortunate understanding of writing centres as, to borrow from Elizabeth Boquet and Neal Lerner (2008, 173), "triage stations in the battle against illiteracy".

Mona's writing centre was completed in July 2002 with the help of funding identified by the campus principal. It started operating in September 2002 and was formally opened in January 2003 (*Departmental Reports* 2003). However, in terms of physical structure, the layout did not reflect Taylor's proposal. Taylor had intended to have removable dividers (and not solid walls as were erected inside the building) so that large seminars could be held whenever necessary. She had also envisaged having booths instead of big counters and desks that were installed in the building. Some of those changes may be related to another significant change to the structure Taylor proposed – the designation of a section of the centre a linguistic laboratory (up to 2010–2011) for which the departmental administration contributed funds. In terms of offerings, services were free to students when the centre started, but that arrangement was changed, resulting in few students going there for consultation on their writing and writing specialists complaining about lack of assistance for students taking academic writing courses. This change occurred while Paulette Ramsay was coordinator of the writing centre.

Ramsay had added resources such as books for onsite use, and she started coaching sessions offered by graduate students who helped undergraduates with mechanical/grammatical problems. Two experienced writing tutors were also paid to offer one-to-one coaching, and then small group tutorial sessions for which undergraduates made reservations. There was to be a minimum of ten students in small group tutorial sessions, but some were cancelled because fewer than ten students registered for them. Decline in registration started in the second year of operations in the centre when students began to be required to pay to receive assistance. When concerns arose about funding for the centre towards the end of 2002–2003, Ramsay recommended that the department could ask students to pay J$100 (approximately US$2 at the time) once for the year. Although she knew paid service does not reflect the idea of a writing centre in general (see North 1984, 446) nor as Mona's was conceived, Ramsay had to suggest a desperate measure, because the immediate alternative was to cease operations. The result of introduction of the fee was a dramatic decline in consultations and reduction of assistance for basic and stronger writers to get help with language concerns in the context of essays that they were preparing (Ramsay, personal interview, 25 July 2007).

In 2006–2007 more concerns about funding arose and coaching ceased in the centre to be offered sporadically up to 2013–2014. After discussions in 2007 between the then head of department and writing faculty and reminders about the purpose of the centre, the department planned to request funding under a category such as "student welfare", since the university was not likely to provide funding for "paying a writing centre instructor" (Dyche, personal interview, 19 July 2007; Taylor, personal interview, 25 July 2007). This effort, like Ramsay's mentioned before and reflecting what North (1984, 446) calls "the trace of a survival instinct at work", is interesting because *student welfare* was, indeed, the central concern. However, because faculty had to avoid mentioning the real need of paying someone to ensure student welfare, one can only wonder at how much administrators really understand the critical nature of writing instruction and development and the linguistic paradigms within which they and writing specialists work. Interestingly, the centre's initial goal was probably not being realized on account of actions by both campus and department administrators. With the department successfully lobbying to house and administer the British Council's International English Language Testing System examination beginning in 2011–2012 in the section of the centre that had been used as a linguistics laboratory, the conditions for students using the centre for "writing" purposes became even more complex. At the same time, it was unclear whether funds would/could be allocated to the writing centre from profits derived from the International English Language Testing System.

Application of a fee in the centre can be understood in light of a straightened financial situation in the university in general. However, the ad hoc manner in which the change emerged, the continued lack of funding from the central budget (up to the 2013–2014 academic year), and questionable actions taken by different heads of department regarding use of the space suggest the need for more careful consideration of the centre's connection to the writing courses and the university and the role the centre could play in assisting all students, including those linguistically orphaned by the school system. Such considerations should have been undertaken when changes were made to the "Fundamentals of English" course and in light of the fact that students continued to be penalized for errors in grammar in the standard writing courses that did not necessarily include grammar teaching in their objectives.

Conclusion

The introduction of "Fundamentals of English" in 1988–1989 marked academics' acknowledgement of Creole-influenced students' varying language and writing abilities. However, because supporters and opponents of the course kept the focus on formalist concerns and continued to separate language development from learning in disciplines and learning outside of the academy, the course's position in the academy was tenuous. When the institution accepted basic writing students and offered them help, it supported egalitarianism – providing opportunities for all entrants to succeed. Changes in fee structure, leading to the removal of the course from the campus budget, suggest that the provisions were costly. "Who should bear the cost for instruction in 'Fundamentals of English'?" had to be, and probably will continue to be, a challenging question. Whatever the answer is, talk of dissolution of basic writing suggested elitism, aptly described by compositionist Edward White (2001, 19) as "the restriction of opportunities to the most 'deserving' – which often means to those from a relatively privileged home". Chapter 2 describes the extent to which such elitist approaches at the UWI were criticized because they are not consistent with expansions in education. However it seems that in order to escape the accusation of "new elitism", administrators at the UWI at Mona decided to accept the students but stop offering the basic writing course as one of its foundation courses.

Additionally, it was unclear if the institution was managing its writing centre so that it could be a valuable writing resource for all students who sought out-of-class assistance with their writing in all disciplines.

As professor of English at City College of CUNY Marilyn Sternglass (1999, 20) argues, basic writing students need the "requisite time" to develop, and, as the UC010 and English Language Proficiency Test results reveal, the developmental needs of basic writers may not be met by the replacement of extended time (one year) with intensive time (one semester). Worse yet, lack of engagement in any writing programme could only cause students' abilities to atrophy. Also, as indicated in the first epigraph in this chapter, no one can claim academic writing as his or her mother tongue. The reality is, however, that the student who is less than fluent in English and whose reading and writing abilities are underdeveloped will require extra time and help to master the formal variety of that language and later meet academic writing requirements within a discipline. Such a student who is accepted to study at Mona underscores Rose's (1985) challenge to the myth of transience and reminds educators that the work of literacy is here to stay, especially in a context where an imposed official language prevents students from first developing literacy in their first language. An immediate concern, then, was the importance of acting ethically and responsibly by ensuring support programmes for those whom basic writing specialist Gerri McNenny (2001, 11) calls "students occupying the borderlands of academe" but who were admitted to pursue undergraduate programmes at Mona. Indeed, the university had the responsibility to provide a model to ensure that the basic writing students it admitted were engaged with the act of writing, as were its other more fortunate and privileged students, so that all could learn to "invent the university", as David Bartholomae (1985) says in the second epigraph in this chapter.

In a presentation to the "Why English?" conference held at the University of Oxford in October 2006, Dyche (2006b), then coordinator of the ELS at the UWI at Mona mentioned that the UWI's English language courses had been accepted as "non-remedial bona fide tertiary level academic offerings" but plaguing further developments in the programme were "the University's straitened financial position" and ironic marginalization of students who demonstrate "poor mastery of standard English, the majority of whom originate from the lower social classes". This group of students, the basic writers, would continue to pose a significant challenge to writing programme and general administration as the university tried to fulfil its mission "to unlock West Indian potential" and simultaneously grapple with expanding enrolment to include them. As compositionist Lynn Quitman Troyka (1987, 12) writes, "Non-academics, as well as some academics, might assert: These students deserve no attention because they are not [university] material." However, the challenge to appropriately ensure their development in the academy deserved to be faced responsibly especially since, as Troyka reminds in the third epigraph in this chapter, basic writers usually come *by invitation*.

In referring to Jamaica's linguistic orphans in the academy as "basic writers", I wanted to acknowledge the influence of Shaughnessy's (1977) work on programmes developed outside the United States for such students (see Dyche 1996a). However, I also wanted to hint at the infiltration of developments in US composition in writing courses in the Caribbean. In the 1970s and onwards, the "Use of English" faculty had adapted the British survey course to give it an emphasis on Caribbean sociolinguistic issues. This emphasis meant introducing students to the various linguistic systems in the Caribbean and distinguishing among British English, Standard Jamaican English and Jamaican Creole. By the late 1990s and first few years of the new millennium, this emphasis was no longer apparent in the original "Use of English" course. Dyche argues that the sociolinguistic focus was changed because of changes in the high school curriculum, but the US influence provides a better explanation. After all, teaching the individual – presumably a monolingual English speaker – seems natural to the average US writing teacher. Indeed, the Conference on College Composition and Communication's resolutions such as *Students' Right to Their Own Language* (CCCC 1974) and *The National Language Policy* (CCCC [1988] 1992) have yielded no substantial change in the language of instruction and the target language in all written pieces in the average classroom. Additionally, many US universities have abolished or are considering abolishing their basic writing programmes and teaching only generic first-year writing courses where abolishing those is not also being considered. I suspect that because of the reduced emphasis on sociolinguistic content in the original "Use of English" course, facilitators in "Fundamentals of English" (this writer included) and the institution may not have sought persistently to *learn from* students' errors. The challenge that basic writing students presented was viewed as something to be managed rather than learned from in the way that Shaughnessy (1977) did with her students (including West Indians) in New York. However, if faculty and administrators gave due thought to Jamaica's linguistic context and the realities that examination results reveal, they would probably have considered how to provide for Jamaican Creole-influenced students on whose numbers they rely and who must function in a predominantly Creole-speaking region, notwithstanding their mastery of English or lack thereof. In the next chapter, I address the university's provisions for its stronger writers through valuable generic first-year writing courses which may have reflected as much ambiguity as the provisions or lack thereof for basic writers.

5 | Improving the Graduate's Profile via "Universalist" Writing at the Turn of the Century, 1990s to 2010+

The near universality of the first-year . . . writing requirement contains an implicit recognition that in higher education new levels of writing and expression are demanded. (Bazerman 2007, 2)

If we want to improve literacy in colleges and universities, we are going to have to give our students more practice and more feedback in a broader range of writing; we are going to have to introduce them to the discourse practices of a wider range of communities than can be offered in a [first-year writing course]; in a sense we are going to have to make writing instruction the responsibility of more than [writing] specialists and writing programs. (Smit 2004, 183)

Unless disciplines first understand the rhetorical nature of their own work and make conscious and visible what was transparent, the teaching of writing in the disciplines will continue to reinforce the myth of transience. . . . Writing in content courses will be seen merely as a further opportunity for evaluation or remediation, a means of introducing pedagogical variety . . . and not as a central part of disciplinary research or teaching. (Russell 2002, 300)

Although administrators and academics seemed to be divided regarding "Fundamentals of English" (UC010), the basic writing course that was meant to help the institution *accommodate* increasing numbers of students who displayed limited mastery of English but who passed examinations in content areas, by the turn of the twenty-first century administrators seemed to accept that standard (as opposed to "basic") writing instruction is important in the academy. This attitudinal change was important since there had been limited attention to *writing* in the "Use of English" course and many calls for teaching that course in secondary schools in the 1960s to mid-1980s. With this change, the institution enlisted writing, in terms of not only continuing to offer "Use of English" (under a new name), but also in mandating that all undergraduates take it or another standard first-year writing course before they could graduate from the institution. These developments signified administrators' and faculty's growing understanding of the importance of writing in the development of university students, confirming, as Bazerman (2007) says in the first epigraph in this chapter, "an implicit recognition" that higher education demands "new levels of writing and expression". However, because of limitations in resources and because course facilitators usually have to observe upper administration's stipulations in preparing course documents, course curricula included descriptions that focused on preparing students to write academic discourse for a general university-level educated audience and on addressing formalist concerns outside of disciplines.

One of the new courses, "English for Academic Purposes" (FD10A),[18] was introduced by upper administration in 1998 to be taught through the Department of Language, Linguistics and Philosophy. The introduction of FD10A at Mona helped to ensure that all students received instruction in academic writing since up to 1998 students in the Faculty of Social Sciences were not required to take "Use of English", even though faculty often complained about weaknesses in the students' writing (Dyche 2007b). However, FD10A focused exclusively on exposition, marking formalist concerns in the course. Exposition is the paradigmatic "universalist" genre because it is the mode that was central to current traditional rhetoric, which gave lip service to audience and situation and which treated writing as a decontextualized process (Berlin 1982; 1987, 7–9 and 36–38). Process, in this model, is informed by the conduit metaphor, which suggests that students complete heuristic work in their mind before they write. This two-stage process implies that the purpose of writing instruction is to help students to write clearly what they have thought about. Writing specialists in Jamaica, however, employed the four-stage process approach that is common in US composition teaching, and also attempted to adapt it based on the focus on summative evaluation in disciplines at Mona. Nevertheless, I will show that although process seems to have been adapted to cultural and disciplinary trends in Jamaica, it typified an emphasis on formalism. This focus is obvious in grading practices. As stated, the conduit metaphor implies a focus on writing clearly, that is, on grammar and usage. This focus may be considered good in the Jamaican context, although usage was *graded* strictly but was *not* necessarily *taught*.

The other course, "Writing in the Disciplines" (FD14A, later FOUN1401), which the Department of Language, Linguistics and Philosophy introduced in 2004, is an instantiation of the ELS members' attempts to address students' writing needs within disciplinary contexts. FD14A was meant to provide students who demonstrated high levels of mastery in English in qualifying examinations for university studies with an alternative to FD10A, some of whose content they would have covered in the sixth form. More important, FD14A was meant to distinguish between the needs of students from various disciplines who would be taught in discipline-specific workshops. Accordingly, the intention was to sensitize students to how people read and write in specific disciplines. However, plans such as teaching in discipline-specific workshops and content faculty's being involved in course delivery were not realized. Indeed, the arrangement of the classes and instruction in the course suggested artificiality. FD14A involved mixed groups of students from various disciplines and was taught solely by language specialists. The very general description, objectives and essay topics for this course and others suggest that these courses were probably not adequately grounded in the cultural context. In essence, administrators and faculty at Mona had enlisted writing in the form of what could be considered "universal" first-year writing in the United States and elsewhere; however, the various manifestations represent "universalist" models of writing that, I argue, prevented more than superficial consideration of Jamaica's linguistic context and distinctive social issues.

I argue that these courses were universalist because they were meant to ensure that *all* students received useful academic writing instruction when they started university, and the descriptions were usually very general – suggesting that they reflected norms that made them suitable to be taught elsewhere. In other words, the courses appeared to be universal. However, they were also universalist because, while appearing to have a universal reach, they simultaneously maintained a limited focus – on formalist concerns in the emphasis on exposition and in the ambiguous relationship to English grammar, which presented problems for many students and was graded but not necessarily taught. These emphases appear to have justified the marginalization of writing instruction because since they were so general, they could be addressed outside of disciplines, and, because of their broad reach, they overshadowed the need for attention to local and individual peculiarities. By emphasizing exposition and encouraging writing development in a general course outside of disciplines, faculty continued to keep disciplinary writing knowledge tacit. Because content faculty did not articulate writing knowledge, they managed to alienate learning from writing in disciplines. As well, faculty and administrators continued to unknowingly promote linguistic prejudice.

I am not exempt from some of these strictures. Having worked full-time in the writing programme from 2001 to 2004 and again beginning in 2008–2009, I am also cognizant of the challenges facilitators of advanced written literacy face in getting approval from administrators and other academics to effect positive changes in writing courses. And I know too well what it means to be stretched thin with the demands of coordinating and teaching large numbers of students while having limited resources and experiencing frustration in working effectively with colleagues who manage registration and other administrative tasks.

The institution seemed to have been moving beyond universalist writing courses when upper-level and graduate writing courses were introduced early in the new millennium. However, the provisions in these courses suggest that the institution's commitment to writing development was only partial; as well, the courses continued to emphasize form. The upper-level and graduate writing courses demonstrated continued separation of content from learning and marginalization of writing because content faculty transferred the responsibility for teaching graduate writing courses to writing specialists in the Department of Language, Linguistics and Philosophy. A master's in English language that the Jamaican Language Unit in the Department of Language, Linguistics and Philosophy introduced in 2005 appeared to offer good practical instruction in English courses. However, the focus on the code suggests that the course may have been limited regarding the treatment of writing instruction at the postsecondary level, how writing works, and how it works differently in different disciplines.

Formalism carried over into the latest development – a WAC pilot project that the Department of Language, Linguistics and Philosophy started in the Faculty of Pure and Applied Sciences in 2006–2007. The idea of "reinforcement" in terms of "support" with regard to writing *skills* recurred like a leitmotif in early project documents. Although this WAC initiative should have integrated writing and learning in disciplines, it highlighted academics' continuing limited understanding of the complexity of writing. Content faculty claimed that they wanted help with students' expression, and writing specialists were advocating a more "writing-intensive" undergraduate education to *improve the profile* of Mona's graduates. Writing faculty were therefore calling for content faculty to "support" writing facilitators and "reinforce" what students learned in writing classes. The reality was, however, an emphasis on form to the extent that everyone continued to shroud knowledge in formalism, and content faculty largely continued to keep writing knowledge tacit. I argue that either stance only served to alienate learning in the academy from learning language in disciplines and outside the academy. Although the WAC pilot project implied that academics had a deeper understanding of writing than they had had in earlier years, these developments were still not adequately incorporating the country's linguistic paradigms and reflecting the interconnectedness of writing and learning in disciplines. The general separation of writing from learning disciplinary content indicated a need for re-examining the universalist assumptions that informed developments in writing instruction at Mona at the turn of the century.

Enlisting Writing (Instruction): Universalist Models Foreshadowed

The formalist preoccupations of the turn-of-the-century writing courses were foreshadowed in changes to the original "Use of English" course name and focus. When the Department of Linguistics and Use of English began to offer "Fundamentals of English" (UC010) in 1988 to students who had not fulfilled entry requirements for placement in the standard "Use of English" course, the university was considering shifts from a year-long to a semester system. As was done with other courses, changes were made to the "Use of English" course to suit the semester system that started in 1990–1991 and came in fully, except in medicine, in 1991–1992. The department was mandated to develop semester versions of the course, so students could receive a grade at the end of each of two semesters. Based on the changes, "Use of English" (UC100) was taught for a brief period as "UC10A: Language: Style and Purpose" and "UC10B: Language: Argument" before the department reverted to offering the year-long course, with law students taking only the second semester portion. However, in recognition of the stigma attached to "Use of English" and to get away from misunderstanding associated with the course name, the department also changed the course to "UC120: Language: Exposition/Argument" (Eric King, unpublished data). The "120" designation marked the coding change, and the other portion the fact that the course presented exposition and argument in the context of language in general and language in the Caribbean in particular. In this same period, the department's name also changed. The *Departmental Reports* (1993, 42) for 1992–1993 mentions that in 1991–1992 the department had changed from *Linguistics and Use of English* to *Language and Linguistics* "to reflect the Department's broad perspectives on language competence".

The universalist models of writing that would be employed at Mona were foreshadowed in the changes made to "Use of English" (UC100) after it was renamed "Language: Exposition and Argument" (UC120). The course description from the *Faculty of Arts and General Studies Regulations* (1987, 82) for 1987–1988 informed students that the course "seeks to develop competence mainly in critical reading and in expository and analytical writing". Topics to be covered in the weekly lecture and tutorial/seminar which students had to attend embodied the emphases in the course since the 1970s:

1. The nature and functions of language in general and in the Caribbean in particular.
2. Kinds of writing, and techniques for achieving a given purpose.
3. Reasoning clearly and cogently in everyday language.
4. Advertising and propaganda as psychological persuasion.

5. The use and abuse of numbers/charts/tables in exposition and argument; or to effect psychological persuasion.
6. Library skills. (82–83)

Although "techniques for achieving a purpose" suggest a concern for rhetorical contexts, by 1992 the course description still emphasized modes/"kinds of writing", but only two – exposition and argument. This shift would mark what Sharon Crowley (1998, 212) calls the persistence of current traditionalism rather than real engagement with the situatedness of discourse production. In the Faculty of Arts and General Studies (Mona) *Regulations and Syllabuses* (1992, 38) for 1992–1993, the UC120 description is shortened to inform students that the aim is to teach them to "write expository and argumentative essays; and develop analytical and critical reading skills by identifying the characteristics of exposition and logical argument and distinguishing them from those of psychological persuasion". The *language* content was also emphasized in a statement that the course "uses as its content current information and ideas about the nature of language in general and its manifestation in the Caribbean in particular" (ibid.). This version of the course continued to be offered to students in all faculties except Social Sciences until 1998 when "English for Academic Purposes" (FD10A) was introduced. The *language* focus was, however, reduced as the UC120 course continued to evolve.

Dyche (2006b) asserts that between 1990 and 2006, "the hard fought for Caribbean sociolinguistic content was deemphasized, as due to the involvement of Caribbean linguists and English language educators on the regional examining bodies for secondary schools, this content was integrated into the upper secondary school curriculum, rendering the teaching of it at the tertiary level less necessary". I contend that while some of the changes in the course were made based on changes to the secondary school curriculum, some were made because of coordinators' concerns about the emphasis on language in the course. Such concerns were different from content faculty's complaints about the course focus in the 1970s and 1980s. As an example, although emphasis on writing had increased in the course in the mid- to late 1980s, new coordinators felt that students were still not writing enough in/for class meetings. In "Proposal for Restructuring of UC120", Vivienne Harding (2002, 1), in collaboration with Jasmin Lawrence, observed that insufficient time was being spent on writing in seminars and that the "number of lectures on language could be reduced and the information condensed". Other changes were made because of the influence from US writing research that was not necessarily appropriately adapted to the Caribbean region.

The topics on which students wrote their essays suggest a gradual shift from the course's primary focus on language, but they highlight the separation of writing in the course from writing in students' disciplines. The *general* focus is evident in expository essay topics such as "globalization" and "the role of language in the media coverage of the US/Iraq conflicts" and in moots for argumentative essays such as

"Caribbean males cannot restrict themselves to Standard English if they wish to be considered 'macho'" or "The death penalty is not a deterrent to murder" (UC120 Examination 2003). These topics, which the course coordinator usually determined, appear to test general knowledge or knowledge of current affairs, implying that the kinds of writing done in the course did not necessarily focus students on writing in any one discipline. This disconnect would become more pronounced when "UC120: Language: Exposition/Argument" was split into "UC10A: Language: Exposition" and "UC10B: Language: Argument" in the new millennium. That change was made largely in response to research findings about reading and writing. Based on transfer of knowledge research that showed that reading to write was a successful tool in teaching academic writing, the structure of UC120 was adjusted in 2002–2003 for facilitators to teach reading (instead of exposition) in the first semester and then writing (instead of argument) in the second semester. Facilitators felt that the concept of "reading to write" worked well in the UC10B portion of the course that was taught to law students, and the failure rate was insignificant. However, students in the year-long course found it difficult to make the connections between reading and writing because of the passage of time between one semester and the other. Therefore, after two years of experimentation, the UC120 team decided to maintain the "reading to write" concept but within each of the two genres of exposition and argument that would be taught separately. This experimentation contributed to decisions made in 2004–2005 regarding UC120. Consequently, in 2005–2006, the Department of Language, Linguistics and Philosophy reintroduced the split in "Language: Exposition/Argument", and the two *genres* were taught as two separate *courses* – UC10A and UC10B.

The very general emphasis that would mark later courses is pronounced in the descriptions of the separate versions of the course. With the exception of references to language in the Caribbean, the courses seemed appropriate for instruction elsewhere. According to the website, UC10A was

> designed to help students acquire the language skills they will need in order to successfully complete their academic programme; develop an understanding of the linguistic context in which they operate within the Caribbean region; and participate intelligently in discussions (both written and oral) regarding a variety of topics related to the disciplines within the Faculty of Humanities and Education. Classes provide instruction in reading and writing exposition. Students . . . work on individual as well as collaborative writing assignments in class, designed to develop communicative competence in a variety of discourse situations. (UC10A 2007)

The other portion, UC10B, addressed certain rhetorical considerations for argumentative discourse including such issues as the nature and types of argument, presenting a convincing argument with a claim and refuted counterclaims, structuring the argumentative essay and analysing arguments in everyday discourse. The course was designed to enable students to "respond critically to a variety of texts, identifying purpose, and central arguments; explain supporting evidence and analyse effectiveness and interrelationships", and "assess the needs of their audience in a variety of discourse situations and respond appropriately", among other things. The website advised students that "writing assignments allow for drafting and redrafting in keeping with the idea of writing being a recursive process" (UC10B 2007).

The weekly lecture topics in the UC10A Language: Exposition Syllabus (2007) indicated a general focus on language rather than also Caribbean language or disciplines in the humanities. These included functions of language, language and society, a light history of the English language, analysing expository writing and organizing the essay. Like those provided for UC120, the topics on which students wrote were also "general". However, students were advised to choose one and "formulate a question that is relevant to your research discipline". These topics on which students were to write an eight hundred word expository essay in the first semester of 2006–2007 included "Alternatives to Petroleum", "Child Abuse", "Cultural Icons in the Caribbean" and "The USA and World Politics". The course coordinator in 2006–2007, Janice Cools, acknowledged that helping students develop a question with relevance to specific disciplines was not a simple affair. She was not aware that facilitators in the course "actually str[o]ve to focus on different disciplines". She emphasized that students who took UC10A and UC10B were in the humanities, so although facilitators encouraged students to start out with a question that would be relevant to their discipline, their concerns were usually limited to literary or historical situations (personal interview, 19 July 2007). As in UC10A, the essay topics in UC10B no longer focused primarily on language. The topics from which students chose to write an 800–1000 word argumentative essay in the first semester of 2006–2007 included "the politics of response to natural disasters", "performance-based pay for teachers", "crime", "The Patriot Act" and "The benefits to be derived from an armed conflict between the United States of America and Iraq are not worth the costs". In the second semester of 2006–2007, they included "financing for political parties", "language rights", "developing countries hosting major international sporting events", "civil rights and religious practices" and "stem cell research". Clearly, while these topics were likely to keep students grounded in current regional and international events, they seemed somewhat limited in helping students consider very specific questions in disciplines that included literatures in English; history and archaeology; library and information studies; linguistics; media and communications; modern languages and literatures; and philosophy.

The influence of developments in US writing research is evident in two other significant changes that were made to UC120 in the 1990s and that were carried over into other courses. These were the introduction of a writing portfolio and adoption of a process approach to writing. Portfolios were introduced by Mertel Thompson who had received formal training in rhetoric when she completed her doctorate in the United States in the 1980s. Each portfolio contained answers to all assigned short-answer questions and practice exercises, two or more drafts of assigned essays and reports and weekly one-page reflections in which students explored and attempted to evaluate their learning/writing experiences in particular units or assignments. The pieces were prepared over time so the students could benefit from the drafting, rewriting, reflecting, refining and perfecting stages, which are components of the "universal" writing process. The process approach was adopted following various faculty members' exposure to developments in England and in US composition. The British influence came through the work of James Britton et al. (1975) on the development of writing abilities in children. Britton and his colleagues were dissatisfied with the shortcomings they perceived in the four traditional modes of discourse – narration, exposition, description and argument – because those categories addressed purpose or intention "only in terms of the intended effect upon the audience" (4). Britton and his colleagues were interested in "processes" involved in writing and therefore sought to "characterize all mature written utterances and then go on to trace the developmental steps that led to them" (6). Exposition was emphasized in teaching, and the process approach used was consistent with a lock-step system rather than the open, recursive nature of writing presented in the work of Britton et al. and emphasized by process theorists such as Janet Emig (1971), whose work paralleled Britton's (see Crowley 1998; Perl 1994; Tobin 1994).

Mona's writing specialists inflected the imported models with Jamaican cultural and disciplinary trends but only to a limited extent, especially with regard to the universal writing process. What process advocate Lad Tobin (1994, 8) calls "mechanistic process" stages that have attracted criticism in the United States were evident at Mona. Additionally, missing from the courses was process philosophy that opposed "traditional, product-driven, rules-based, correctness-obsessed writing instruction" (ibid., 5) – but which did not promote the view that the quality of the product was inconsequential. The process approach to writing that was adopted in Jamaica and was addressed in all of the courses consisted of the following four stages:

1. Prewriting: generating ideas through brainstorming, clustering and/or by some other strategy; planning, outlining, library and Internet research, and the preparation of citation cards.
2. Drafting: writing the essay first draft (focusing primarily on content and underlying essay structure), and including a page of cited references.
3. Revising: following peer and tutor review of the content and organization of the first draft based on a checklist provided for the course or by the instructor.
4. Editing and Proofreading: rereading the final essay draft for errors in sentence structure, grammar, style/idiom, and in the mechanics of writing.

As in other places, sometimes the syllabus requirements at Mona suggest that what was involved is what Crowley (1998, 211–13) and others consider process grafted onto current traditional rhetoric. The courses seemed to remain in the traditional vein because as Lester Faigley (1992, 14) says of composition studies in the United States, while such courses "professed to value process, it is not process for its own sake but rather the process of teleological development toward a product". At Mona, students could be told they had to prepare at least two drafts of their essays, and usually the first draft was written in class. The facilitator had to sign this draft (in some cases all pages) to ensure the draft was indeed written by the student. As well, the facilitator had to approve other changes that the student made to the first draft, and especially in the case of FD10A up to 2007–2008, the changes could not be extensive. As in other countries, the courses were so organized that they reflected the faulty assumption that there is a universal writing process: all students were expected to proceed in the same way, according to the pace of the course, with sources, outline and first draft required on specific days during the course. With few exceptions and later changes, typically students also wrote a timed final examination in the presence of proctors even though process writing informed the courses. That the "process" approach to writing was involved in the courses appears, then, to have been only notional, because when students wrote their first draft in class, it was not so much to allow students to employ varied/idiosyncratic composing processes, but more to check that the work was done by the student and signed off by the facilitator. Although, it is expected that in a system of limited resources, facilitators have to so organize time and other resources to ensure that all participants receive equivalent amounts of training and the disciplining schooling is meant to foster, the issue in the courses appeared to be one of questionable trust in students and superficial elements of process writing grafted onto a product-driven system.

Omission of process philosophy was most marked in the absence from course documents of what Faigley (1992, 49) calls process's "deemphasis of errors and its validation of students' experience rather than traditional authority". Grammar instruction was absent from the descriptions and syllabuses of the standard courses at Mona; however, the rubrics emphasized formalism. Additionally, grading could be quite rigid – an apparent residue from the days when the UWI had a special arrangement with the University of London: "in the anxiety to deliver good quality education, standards had been set at a punitive level" (Cobley 2000, 16). In those years when West Indian students took the same examinations but did not always cover the same amount of content as students in England, the pass mark was set at 40 per cent and West Indian students needed attain only 70 per cent to earn an "A". Those standards that remained in place up to 2013–2014 may seem to have been easily attainable, but they proved to be extremely difficult to achieve. In the language courses, the rubric used and special clauses for assessment epitomized a rigid emphasis on correctness. Up to 2008–2009, equal marks (of ten each) were allotted to the five categories on which students were graded – mechanics/grammar, organization, content, analysis and style (MOCAS). In FD10A, for example, up to 2005–2006, if students scored below the pass mark of four out of ten on any category in the coursework or in the exam, they failed the course. The rubric (called the MOCAS scheme) stated, "Papers submitted for grading must satisfy minimal requirements in all of the five features listed." Following were the descriptions provided in the rubric for the minimal passing score of four out of ten in each category. As expressed, students had to get that score or higher on every category in order to earn a passing grade on a paper:

- (M) Grammar & Mechanics: Exhibits some inconsistency in control of sentence boundaries and some lapses in usage but no more than 3 types of error occur or errors occur at an acceptable frequency.
- (O) Organization: Exhibits some level of organization but is deficient in TWO or more of the characteristics required.
- (C) Content: No misinformation present but there is some vagueness suggesting that the writer is not sufficiently well informed.
- (A) Analysis: Maintains a clear purpose most of the time BUT there is some evidence of lack of clarity or depth.
- (S) Style: Exhibits some clear lapses in register & tone. Uses unsophisticated vocabulary and limited sentence variety.

The emphasis on correctness and standard of taste, implied in the quantification of errors in mechanics and organization, was anomalous. Although grammar and mechanics were graded, those elements were not normally taught in the courses. Such attitudes to grammar typified academics' misrecognition of the country's linguistic paradigms and superficial understandings of writing. Worse, those attitudes continued to have serious consequences, the extent of which most academics seemed to be unaware. As in "Use of English" and its developments, one thing that remained constant in the courses was a concern expressed in previous decades about language deficiency. However, also constant were incidental measures to address the challenge. The "Minutes of a Meeting of the DLLP held Thursday, 17th January 2002", included complaints from two philosophy lecturers who "underscored the necessity of all students being exposed to FD10A to get much needed help to improve their essay writing skills" (DLLP 2002a, 5). In their view, "the quality of English used in writing, from first through to third year students, is astonishingly poor" (5). Schontal Moore (2006a, 2), in her capacity as coordinator, wrote in "FD10A Report . . . 2005/2006", "There continues to be great concern expressed by instructors over the low levels of grammatical and writing competencies exhibited by students. . . . As such instructors have had to dedicate more time to teacher-student consultation and expend more energy into grading assignments and devising creative methodologies to address problems evident in students' work." Unlike content faculty who normally transferred the responsibility for writing to the English language courses or to secondary schools, the facilitators in FD10A recommended addressing the grammar problem in the institution's writing centre. Moore wrote, "The consensus among FD10A staff is that some of these problems could have been addressed had The Writing Centre continued with the special seminars on improving writing skills that have helped so many other students in the past" (2). However, that kind of action would have required changes in the centre's administration. Moreover, this consideration still meant that academics were probably not consciously engaging with the country's linguistic realities and how they would have had to be addressed in teaching *in courses*. Cools had planned to address the problem *within* the courses by including grammar teaching for about ten minutes in each UC10A/UC10B seminar. Along with course facilitators, she had discussed the long-standing anomaly that saw students being told they would fail the coursework or final examination if they failed grammar, even though grammar teaching was not included in the syllabus. Cools was concerned that students were extremely weak in grammar, but besides the limited special workshops in the writing centre, students did not really get actual teaching in grammar. Like faculty in previous decades and later in FD10A, Cools felt the problem was acute (personal interview, 19 July 2007). Her attempt to address it *in the course* marked writing specialists' recognition of the challenging linguistic context in which they worked. However, even this recognition may have had its limits if the teaching of formalist conventions – as in an isolated ten-minute session – did not have practical relevance for students.

Institutional priorities explain how the process approach was employed at Mona. Mona's writing specialists recognized, as Sidney Dobrin (1997, 7) recommends, that "while theory helps inform pedagogy, pedagogy must be indigenous". The emphasis on correctness and standard of taste *in grading* was informed by continued association of prestige with English. As established above and as Dyche (1996c, 145) explains, this association "stems to a great extent from the sociopolitical role that English, and particularly written English, plays in what are predominantly oral Creole-speaking societies". Faculty at Mona desired that any approach employed yielded improvements in students' writing, particularly in terms of demonstration of mastery of the code. In the United States, process is criticized for not really improving writing because of the focus on passing through stages and on personal development (see, for example, Fulkerson 2005, 667). Also, some writing researchers critique the emphasis on recursiveness in general writing courses because that kind of reflective writing practice does not necessarily transfer to disciplinary courses where content faculty are not likely to require it, and students do not perceive its necessity for their success (see Foster 2006, 114–15). In Jamaica, a significant concern was improvement in writing, including instant writing as done in timed examinations. Timed "essay" examinations mean that in this system, as Russell and Foster (2002, 36) write of similar systems, "one-draft writing is king". In recognition of the fact that students were (and still are) largely evaluated through instant one-draft writing in final examinations, writing specialists gave students practice in *recursive thinking* for writing by requiring them to write at least one paper under test conditions. In UC10A and UC10B, for example, Cools appeared to respond to institutional priorities through evaluation in each course. Whereas there was 100 per cent coursework in UC120 since 1997, she reverted to pre-1997, when students had to complete coursework and a final examination that was supervised. Therefore, early in the new millennium, UC10A and UC10B students, returned to writing a final examination (worth 60 per cent) under test conditions. The topic on which students wrote was one that they would have been researching for the entire semester. This means they got a specific question on that research topic, and there was also a general question so that students would have been able to find a question on which to write (personal interview, 19 July 2007). Students wrote instant essays in final examinations for the courses in their discipline, so the requirement in UC10A/ UC10B and in the other courses was likely to give them practice in the art of writing such papers. The process stages were, therefore, applied at Mona only in so far as they were believed to improve writing. Still, what was missing in the courses was a sense of differences that may have obtained in different disciplines in the application of the various stages of any process.

The limited adaptations of US models in the Jamaican context can also be explained by the instructional materials used. Most of the readers, textbooks and handbooks used in the courses were procured from overseas; however, unlike in the 1960s when most were from England, most of those used at the turn of the twenty-first century were written by North American authors. Among these were Laurie Kirszner and Stephen Mandell's *The Brief [Holt] Handbook* (2004); Lynn Quitman Troyka and Douglas Hesse's *Simon & Schuster Handbook for Writers* (2005); Ann Raimes's *Keys for Writers: A Brief Handbook* (1999); Royce W. Adams and Becky Patterson's *Developing Reading Versatility* (2001); Sylvan Barnet and Hugo Bedau's *Critical Thinking, Reading and Writing* (1999); Barbara Harris Leonhard's *Discoveries in Academic Writing* (2002); Nancy Wood's *Perspectives on Argument* (2001); and Teresa Glazier's *The Least You Should Know About English* (2000). Caribbean texts that focus on writing were available but few. They included Barbara Lalla's *English for Academic Purposes Study Guide* (1998); Hazel Simmons-McDonald, Linda Fields and Peter Roberts's *Writing in English: A Course Book for Caribbean Students* (1997); and Merle Hodge's *The Knots in English* (1997). Wood's once heavily used textbook *Perspectives on Argument* was replaced in the first decade of the new millennium because facilitators were concerned that it was, in Cools's words, "steeped very heavily in American culture and controversies". Cools, and a team of faculty members, therefore, set out to produce a regional argument text that they hoped would reflect West Indian sensibility, with all selections written by Caribbean writers on the Caribbean (personal interview, 19 July 2007).[19]

The change to the UC10B textbook implied writing faculty's recognition of the importance of contextual assumptions and regional knowledge in the production and reception of discourse. However, most of the materials used indicated the infiltration of North American influence in the local courses – indeed, more North American than English or Caribbean influence. It may be argued that it was easier to import books from the United States than from England. However, the selections epitomized writing faculty's conscious engagement with developments in US composition teaching even though the emphasis at Mona was formal academic writing, rather than also personally expressive nonacademic discourse that is also taught in some US composition programmes. Indeed, writing faculty at Mona shared the general view held in the United States that, as Nancy Sommers and Laura Saltz (2004, 145) remind "academic writing is never a student's mother tongue". All of the Mona course objectives indicated a glaring similarity between the Jamaican situation and virtually all North American ones – the large aim of acculturation – of initiating new undergraduates into academic writing so they could "invent the university", as Bartholomae (1985, 334) puts it. According to Dyche, writing specialists were "trying to prepare students to write for the university, for academic purposes, making sure that they have certain skills in terms of critical thinking and analysis, that they know and can observe the different conventions such as citing sources [and] conducting research" (personal interview, 19 July 2007). The problem, however, was that most of the North American texts used promoted a universal writing process and the incorrect view that the academy is a single discourse community. This infiltration and adoption of faulty assumptions would become particularly evident when upper administration declared in the late 1990s that writing instruction was necessary for all students.

Academia as a Single Discourse Community: General Writing Instruction for/before Engagement in Disciplinary Work

After the mid-1990s, upper administration (including the principal and vice chancellor) proposed having a set of foundation courses in a preliminary year or semester concept (see Brandon 1996). This proposal signified US influence in terms of administrators' attempt to institute a foundation period similar to the year in which students take general education courses in US colleges. Faculty members did not accept the foundation year/semester concept; however, the Faculty of Arts and General Studies (Mona) *Regulations and Syllabuses* (1997, 44) for 1997/98 records that as of the 1998–1999 academic year the university would be "requiring *all* undergraduate students to complete nine credits of FOUNDATION COURSES over the period of their degree" (emphasis in the original). Specifically regarding language, the proposal meant that all students across the three fixed campuses would take a language/writing course. FD10A was proposed as the one-semester, three-credit English/communication skills course to be taught instead of UC120. All faculties had the option of doing this one-semester course, which Natural Sciences (later Pure and Applied Sciences), Medical Sciences and Education selected for their students. The Faculty of Social Sciences would also require this course of its students. Only the Faculty of Arts and General Studies kept the year-long "Language: Exposition/Argument" (UC120) course because it wanted its students to continue to take a six-credit course that involved "argument". In some senses, then, FD10A, with its very limited focus on language, may be seen as the triumph of those who had called for a less sophisticated linguistics-based course than "Use of English" in the 1970s and 1980s. Indeed, the course instantiates academics' ambivalent attitudes to writing development.

FD10A's introduction signalled administrators' belief in the importance of writing instruction in the academy. Changes in the provisions for teaching in the writing courses confirm this belief. The introduction of FD10A meant a move from the very unwieldy situation of having large numbers of part-time tutors to a manageable number of full-time instructors, indicating the value that the institution was placing on writing courses. In anticipation of the new FD10A course whose constituency would include the Faculty of Social Sciences, which had previously not required its students to take a language course, the Department of Language and Linguistics reduced staff numbers in UC010 and UC120 from approximately forty-four part-timers to thirteen full-time tutors (*Departmental Reports* 1997). By 1998, there were five full-time (tenured or tenure-track) lecturers in the Language Section and twelve full-time instructors on one-year contracts (*Departmental Reports* 1998).[20] "Instructor positions" were negotiated through the West Indies Group of University Teachers at Mona, with instructors expected to engage fully in teaching but not research. The reduction in the number of part-timers was also expected to address the long-standing concern from the 1960s about marking with the same standards since part-time tutors were not usually available for standardization or other training. While the proposal for this development indicates the institution was valuing writing instruction, it could also be seen to have marginalized writing instruction, because the course suggests that upper administration encouraged offering courses that would continue to lack a sense of initiation into disciplinary writing. FD10A, like its predecessor and successors, would be offered by language faculty and taught separate from disciplinary content. These arrangements suggested that the academy is singular, and general writing courses and their facilitators can provide all of students' required writing instruction. These limitations are evident in the emphasis on exposition, the corresponding emphasis on general topics directed at general university-level educated audiences, and the resultant superficial consideration of the rhetorical situation, among other features.

Courses designated English for Academic Purposes normally introduce students to the language and genres of writing in their disciplines such as the exact and social sciences (Benesch 2001, 4). However, although the FD10A course that was introduced through a top-down approach at the UWI bore the name "English for Academic Purposes", writing outside of a specific discipline and the expository essay dominated the course. This focus on exposition was consistent with the early years of English for Academic Purposes teaching and its practical rather than political stance in preparing students to adopt rather than also question disciplinary practices. Sarah Benesch (2001, 5) reports that the beginnings of English for Academic Purposes lay in attempts to "provide an alternative to English language teaching as humanities, preparing students to read literary texts". However, the course focus, at Mona, is to be understood in light of its origin. Since the course proposal arose from discussions at the upper administrative level, members of the Department of Language, Linguistics and Philosophy were not involved in the discussions to highlight the importance of other kinds of writing, especially argument. Those who proposed the foundation language course seem to have assumed that exposition is the typical mode of writing expected of university students in all areas except law. Administrators, therefore, enlisted writing but in a very limited way and with only a peripheral connection to the university.

While the focus on exposition bespeaks a narrow understanding of writing in the academy, the original course design was even more limited – a situation that the writing faculty at Mona tried to change. The course was designed to be offered by distance, with material given to students every other week; that is, the conception was that students would do most of the work by distance and have a face-to-face meeting with their tutor once every two weeks. That was the model held for the *foundation* courses by those who conceived them. Upper administration expected FD10A to be taught in the same way; however, members of the Department of Language, Linguistics and Philosophy lobbied to have the course taught face-to-face. Administrators' limited understanding of writing and how it develops is also evident in the time allotted to this course. Although the department had some success in changing the delivery mode, before the end of the first semester in which the course was introduced, staff began to complain about the course arrangements. The "Minutes of a Meeting of the DLLP held Thursday, October 29, 1998" includes complaints that "the time allotted for the course was not enough. The students were likely to leave with the same problems with which they entered" (DLLP 1998, 3). Ornette Blair, an instructor with extensive experience in the programme, confirms that when she started teaching FD10A in 2000, "the course focussed mainly on writing the research essay and summary writing. However, the syllabus included introduction of concepts such as 'Communicative Competence', 'Academic Writing', and 'Language Varieties in the Caribbean'. Therefore, it was always a race against time to complete all the planned tasks in the one-hour seminar" (unpublished data). Based on their understanding of writing development and in response to those complaints, the ELS faculty managed to lobby for a further increase to two hours per week in contact time by 2001.

Based on the input of writing specialists at Mona, the FD10A course developed from one in which the objectives were to enable students to develop essay-writing and English language skills to one the website described in 2007–2008 as being "designed to take students beyond basic competence in the comprehension and production of English prose, by building competence in the processing (reading) as well as production (writing) of the language of academic discourse" (FD10A 2007). Students were expected to develop competences in reading, writing and speaking, so that by the end of the thirteen-week semester they would be able to do the following, which could easily be required in a writing class outside of Jamaica:

(READING)
1. Distinguish academic writing from other kinds of writing
2. Identify a variety of styles appropriate to different academic audiences, contexts and purposes
3. Decode meaning in samples of academic writing
4. Critically analyse and evaluate written materials

(WRITING)
1. Manipulate a variety of styles appropriate to different academic audiences, contexts and purposes
2. Write competent summaries in paragraph form
3. Write short expository research essays (800 words)
4. Use approved citation and documentation techniques in written papers

(SPEAKING)
1. Orally present ideas individually and in groups
2. Discuss and comment on oral presentations done by peers
3. Critically evaluate and discuss written passages

(FD10A 2007)

What is intriguing in these objectives is the omission of objectives related to grammar instruction. While such instruction usually attests to an emphasis on form – as does exposition, its omission in Jamaica's linguistic context is questionable, bearing in mind that students were heavily penalized in this area that, based on end-of-semester course reports, accounted for the majority of the failures in the course. Given the apparent fears of association with remediation in the institution, FD10A coordinators probably felt that the course design would have compensated for the omission. In this thirteen-week, one-semester writing course, students were taught in two-hour seminars of twenty to twenty-five students. Students could supplement seminars with paid sessions in the writing centre (when those were available). An essay pretest was given in the first week of classes to diagnose potential weaknesses that could prevent students from passing the course, so students could seek help in eliminating those problems from their writing. Additionally, up to 2004, students were required to produce a writing portfolio, which included self-help exercises from Glazier's (2000) text and specified which weakness in the student's own writing was the target of each exercise, among other items. Such measures seemed insufficient, however, since – as outlined – coordinators continued to report language problems in significant numbers of students' written pieces.

Despite the very general nature of the course description and objectives, and the omission of substantive considerations of the linguistic context, students were given a sense of disciplinary difference in this course when they were taught about "academic English". They were taught that academic English is formal and objective, "may vary across disciplines" (in terms of format and jargon), is researched and documented, and is comprehensive (Lalla 1998, 91–98). There was at the same time, however, a negation of the persuasive element in writing. Lalla writes that objectivity is marked by honesty in collecting and selecting information and neutrality in conveying information. What Lalla's text, which was used in the course, did not convey was the sense that disciplinary writing differs in more ways than in format and jargon, that indeed the way meaning is made and what is understood as objective or neutral are contingent upon the disciplinary context. The somewhat superficial consideration of the rhetorical situation in the text carried over into the topics on which students wrote in the course.

Like those in UC120 and its derivatives, the essay topics that the FD10A coordinator determined before the course began each semester confirm the general nature of the course even though students from select faculties took it in specified semesters. Prior to the 2008–2009 academic year, these topics included the following taken from a combination of past examination papers:

- Responses to Domestic Violence
- Health Care in Developing Countries
- Ways in which the Personal Development of a University Student May Be Enhanced
- Road Fatalities in My Country and How These Can Be Reduced
- A Recent Scientific Innovation
- Communication across the Curriculum
- Popular Culture
- Healthy Lifestyles
- Science and Technology
- Heritage
- Education and National Development
- Man and the Environment
- Sustainable Economic Development
- Impact of the Arts
- Human Rights

- Language and Society
- The Road to National Development

Like the topics in UC120, many topics such as "Health Care in Developing Countries" or "A Recent Scientific Development" would have appealed to students in specific disciplines while others such as "The Road to National Development" and "Sustainable Economic Development" were likely to appeal to nearly all students (besides those from the Faculty of Social Sciences) in the course because the latter topics were concerned with communal success. However, like most of the topics, writing in the course was not fully linked to disciplines – and this remained true even after 2009–2010 when the coordinator (this writer) and other colleagues made conscious efforts to tailor the topics to the students' expected faculties each semester.[21]

Consistent with the conception of the FD10A course, students were expected to get content from their disciplines or general knowledge of current events to write on the topics. However, considerations of audience and purpose were problematic in the course. Because the topics tended to be about current global and national issues, they also focused on a general audience for whom students were to write their expository essay. The course seminar schedule instructed students that, when writing the expository essay on the topic chosen from the list provided in a given semester, they were to "be informative and write for English speakers with university level education" (FD10A 2007). This audience was usually considered as the facilitator or students. Although students from specific faculties enrolled in the course in a given semester, all students and the facilitator in a given seminar did not necessarily share specialization with the writer. This means that students had to omit or translate jargon and other discipline-specific features when they wrote course essays. Since the emphasis was on exposition, to inform or instruct, purpose was often not considered in terms of the topic itself or what students would want to do with the topic – in relation to a disciplinary audience. In other words, *the course did well in assisting students to write for a general academic audience*, but did not really address audience awareness in terms of having students write for, say, a science audience, using the relevant jargon and moves to achieve a specified purpose in that audience. Clearly, time would not have been available to accommodate all such requirements in a one-semester course for which students met only once for two hours each week. However, the view of writing that was likely to be conveyed was that the student was always writing for a general academic audience, and perhaps, unfortunately, what he/she needed to address were grammatical/mechanical writing concerns. Consequently, the course was not likely to meet its objective to provide students the opportunity to "manipulate a variety of styles appropriate to different academic audiences, contexts and purposes" (FD10A 2007).

The course emphasis on exposition was reinforced in February 2005 when a cross-campus gathering of language/writing specialists from the three fixed campuses recommended that "reading and writing exposition [would] continue to be the central focus of FOUN1001 (FD10A)" (WRITE Symposium II 2005, 4). However, changes that were probably as progressive as they were problematic were made to other aspects of the course at Mona. The *Departmental Reports* (2005, 51) for 2004–2005 mentions changes that included FD10A's being "revised to increase the tasks related to the development of the critical thinking skills of students". Other changes effected before 2008–2009 included de-emphasis of decontexualized summary writing, inclusion of two graded oral presentations, substitution of a writer's journal for the portfolio, grading of the research essay as the final examination, cumulative grading so that students no longer needed to pass coursework and the final examination separately in order to pass the course, and use of the APA instead of the MLA documentation style. These changes followed from suggestions given in cross-campus meetings and staff-student liaison meetings, and were meant to make the course "more relevant to students' needs, less burdensome to teach and more enjoyable for students and instructors" (Moore 2006a, 1). While most of these changes were positive, the last one may actually have perpetuated some misconceptions about writing.

One of the positive changes was that in the approach to summarizing in the course. Prior to the change, students read and summarized a passage under timed-test conditions. The better new approach required students to demonstrate summarizing skills in their annotated bibliography and other materials for their research paper. Another positive change related to evaluation in the course. Previously, some facilitators required oral presentations from students, but the presentations were not graded. Awarding marks for them encouraged students although some facilitators were concerned that longer presentations to be graded detracted from "writing" time. Also, although a process approach was employed in the course, previously students received marks only for the final research essay that they submitted. Up to 2008–2009, students kept a writer's journal, indicating facilitators' attempts to award marks to each student's process in conducting and writing up research over the semester. The portfolio that the writer's journal replaced included many items that were usually graded once they were submitted to the facilitator. It did not really serve to allow a student to work on one or just a few fixed pieces over several drafts and track his or her development as a writer.

Another positive change regarding evaluation was the shift to using a cumulative total in the course. Because the FD10A course was introduced on the other fixed campuses before it was first taught at Mona in 1998, writing specialists at Mona tried to observe the requirements on those campuses. One such requirement was a clause that students had to pass coursework and final examination separately. This clause meant that although the weighting was 50 per cent in-course test (coursework) and 50 per cent final examination and the institution's pass mark was 40 per cent, a student earning 40 per cent and above could fail the course if at least twenty marks had not been earned on each portion (that is on coursework and on exam). The amendment to this requirement is explained in "Report of Language Section Meeting Held Thursday, March 9, 2006". This report notes, "The section supported in principle OBUS [Office of the Board for Undergraduate Studies] 24/01/06 decision to change the assessment of FD10A to 40% in-course test and 60% final exam, and to add together both in-course test and final exam to determine the passing grade" (DLLP 2006b). Up to 2008–2009, the weighting was 40 per cent coursework/60 per cent examination, with students passing the course as long as they earned 40 per cent or more cumulatively. Some of the changes regarding the portfolio and writer's journal stemmed from this decision when the meeting "suggested that the in-course tests/assignments be revised to be more compatible with the new weighting and that these revisions take into account the cumulative weighting of both in-course test/assignments and final exam" (DLLP 2006b).

The change suggested more focus on the final examination – on instant/pressure writing – which contradicted "process". However, what students wrote under test conditions in the final examination was the final draft of the research essay that they would have been preparing over the semester rather than an instant essay on a general topic that they would have seen for the first time in the examination. Although students were still expected to produce effective writing in very limited time and with few materials, the change demonstrated writing faculty's attempts to recognize the developmental nature of writing, a feature that was hardly recognized in the previous scheme where students had to pass the in-course portion and the final instant examination separately in order to pass the course. Removing the final timed examination at that juncture would have been consistent with a flexible process approach; however, Moore believed that in the UWI context students would probably not have taken the course seriously if it did not include a final examination element (personal interview, 18 July 2007).

Besides those positive changes made prior to 2008–2009 was the potentially problematic change in the documentation style. During a lecture on documentation style, students were sensitized to various discipline-specific formats. Students saw examples of how sources were documented depending on the selected style, but the lecture focused primarily on APA. Students were, however, allowed to use a format required in their disciplines, but students needed to inform their facilitator about this beforehand. The fact that students had to inform their facilitator about using a style that was different from APA confirmed the emphasis on *one* style. One reason for focusing on one style in the course was that some content faculty did not always specify a particular style for students, seeming to accept the style used as long as the students used it consistently (Moore, personal interview, 18 July 2007). Clearly, the APA documentation style was more suitable than MLA for more students in the course, especially those from Education and Social Sciences. Moving away from MLA also marked a significant effort to avoid foisting "literary" requirements and practices on all students. However, the APA documentation style was probably problematic for students in the medical sciences and the Faculty of Pure and Applied Sciences. Additionally, if content faculty accepted any style a student used consistently, they may not have been helping students understand their disciplines' peculiar conventions.

The issue of documentation style in FD10A – as in other writing and content courses – was another instantiation of limited initiation of students into specific disciplines, in terms of a discipline's ways of knowing and writing that are often reflected in the documentation style used. The stipulation that students inform their facilitator about the style they would use underscored the emphasis on form rather than what was appropriate based on the rhetorical situation. In other words, the emphasis in the writing courses was still on mechanics – formalist conventions – in terms of basic requirements for in-text citation format and the reference list, rather than also on the way of knowing or outlook that was conveyed in the documentation style. Content and writing faculty's attention to these differences in disciplines would have demonstrated that they acknowledged the different needs of students from the Faculty of Pure and Applied Sciences, the Faculty of Social Sciences, the Faculty of Education and other constituencies. Of course, focusing on one documentation style represents organization of learning for ease of presentation and with the hope that students would develop the discipline required to manipulate other styles required of them in other courses. It also represents one way writing specialists survived in a system that often stretched writing course facilitators thin.

As the first decade of the new millennium drew to a close, writing specialists continued to try to make changes to the course based on a developing understanding of writing and concerns about the linguistic context; however, some changes had to be made based on departmental requirements. These latter, made by and in response to departmental administration, were significant and sometimes countered scholarship on writing. Beginning in the first semester of 2008–2009, the department merged the FD10A and UC10A courses and cohorts but kept the FD10A course name and code. This unofficial merger proved challenging for writing specialists and students because colleagues in charge of the online systems (registration, course containers and examinations) were unaware of the merger. Therefore, although the department treated the course as one, all systems in the university maintained two courses so that the coordinator's administrative duties – such as preparation of class lists and mark sheets, assisting students with registration questions and posting grades – meant moving back and forth between the separate course sites. The then coordinator (this writer, up to 2011–2012) faced the difficult task of trying to accommodate the instructions of departmental administrators, who wanted more readings and final examination tasks, and the requests of facilitators who were concerned about "reading challenges" of the students who usually took FD10A and about increased grading duties. Achieving a compromise meant devoting many hours to find appropriate readings and to help to remove glitches in the various named systems in 2008–2009. However, by the next academic year, reading assignments in the course were reduced in response to complaints from both students and other course facilitators. Colleagues also began to engage in discussions about "using language in context" – an objective added to the original three (reading, writing, speaking; see FD10A 2007) to incorporate the focus on language that used to be included in UC10A. These discussions led to suggestions for having short segments on grammar teaching in each seminar and for referring students to the writing centre for additional assistance, using referral forms that Taylor had created for use there. Discussions about including argumentative writing in the course proved futile because UC10B (by then FOUN1002), which focused on argument, was in place for the Humanities students and it was believed that, since only the then Faculty of Arts and General Studies had opted to keep the original year-long course in 1998, the heads of the other faculties would not consider providing additional time for their students to focus on argument.

Given those constraints and following on the changes that Moore had wrought up to 2007–2008, the FD10A team also attempted to strengthen the developmental approach to writing and improve assessment procedures in the course. Accordingly, a request was submitted and an approval received for assessment to change from the 50 per cent coursework/50 per cent examination weighting (to which facilitators had reverted in 2009–2010) to be, instead, by coursework only beginning in 2010–2011. With this 100 per cent coursework approval, other changes were made to the assignments and weighting, so that facilitators could engage in formative evaluation. Assignments required students to use the English language to present research essay proposals, critically analyse and evaluate materials, prepare essay outlines with some researched materials incorporated, orally present and critique those outlines, write a first draft of the documented essay, evaluate the first draft, critique one or more of their peers' drafts, offer and use revision suggestions on successive drafts of the documented essay and write a reflective essay that was meant to allow students to reflect on and demonstrate what they had acquired and/or honed in the course. Prepared under timed-test conditions, the reflective essay contradicted course facilitators' philosophy of teaching writing; however, it was kept because of emphasis from departmental administrators about having at least one assignment done under test conditions. Although full-time facilitators were available to teach writing courses at Mona, concerns remained about grading standards in instances when the courses were taught in other tertiary-level institutions. Therefore, rubrics were introduced and revised to standardize grading of the coursework pieces that students completed across the institutions and classes in which FD10A was offered, beginning in 2009–2010. These rubrics included a holistic essay rubric developed based on suggestions from writing faculty for use in all of the writing courses instead of the previously mentioned analytic MOCAS mark scheme.

Despite many challenges, FD10A facilitators tried to ensure that the course was serving a useful purpose in the institution and sites where it was offered. Although in staff-student liaison meetings, students often complained about the workload in the course, they also expressed appreciation for the skills-based developmental approach that helped them to learn valuable reading, thinking, researching and writing strategies that students considered crucial to their success at the UWI and beyond. Indeed, even though it focused largely on one mode of writing and one documentation style in a plural academy, FD10A functioned as a typical writing instruction course as described by the College of New Jersey (2004), with facilitators taking students through all the stages of the writing process and addressing global and local aspects of writing. Unfortunately, however, the arrangements suggested that the academy is singular and general writing courses and their facilitators can provide all of students' required writing instruction – and that this provision should be before disciplinary work begins.

A Plural Academy or Preparation and Prejudice?

The later course, "Writing in the Disciplines" (FD14A), would attempt to distinguish between the needs of students from various disciplines, but would be unsuccessful because of its eventual emphasis on social sorting and adoption of universalist paradigms regarding research and instruction. Beginning in September 2004, the Department of Language, Linguistics and Philosophy introduced FD14A as another first-year writing course for students who received upper range passes in the regional CAPE Communication Studies examination.[22] Dyche (2006a) explains that the course "was developed to meet the English Language needs of students with high levels of linguistic competence in English; for this reason, as of [the 2006–2007] academic year, it has been restricted to students with either a Grade 1 or 2 in the CAPE Communication Studies course". All Humanities (previously called Arts) and Law students took "Language: Argument" (UC10B) in the second semester, but Humanities students with the required CAPE passes in communication studies began to take FD14A instead of "Language: Exposition" (UC10A) in their first semester. Students from the other faculties took either FD14A or FD10A based on their pass ranges.

The conception of "Writing in the Disciplines" suggests academics' understanding of the importance of addressing writing in disciplines; however, it did not indicate involvement of content faculty in the course delivery. "Writing in the Disciplines" was a course that Paulette Ramsay and a team of other ELS lecturers had proposed; that is, this was not a course introduced by fiat from upper administration. The intention was for the course to be delivered in subject workshops so that students could focus on what was written in their disciplines, and how people read or wrote in those areas. However, that model of having disciplinary groups being guided in discipline-specific workshops was not adopted in the course. At best, students from specific faculties were expected to register for the course in designated semesters – as was the case in FD10A. Therefore, FD14A, Mona's version of writing in the disciplines, resembled a common WAC model about which Russell (2002, 310) cautions interest groups. Russell explains that teaching approaches involving "writing about the subjects disciplines study" and "learning to write in the ways disciplines do" were integrated in the 1970s and 1980s. However, beginning in the 1990s, distinctions could be observed in the references to the two approaches. Composition scholars referred to the first approach as WAC – "fundamentally 'writing to learn', developing cognitive performance in a field". The other approach was thought to be "fundamentally 'learning to write' professional discourse, the rhetorical marshalling of arguments in a field" (311) and called writing in the disciplines. The writing in the disciplines model that Russell cautions against is a mere revision of the more common general first-year writing course, involving facilitators whose specialization is literary analysis. Often, content faculty are not actively involved in the programme (297). Still, FD14A reflected writing specialists' awareness of gaps in addressing disciplinary writing requirements in the institution.

While the delivery of FD14A at Mona enacted faculty's deepening understanding of writing and its development than obtained with previous language/writing courses, various factors prevented accomplishment of disciplinary writing instruction. The course was beset by administrative problems in the first year, including glitches related to computerized registration, late arrival of texts, limited planning with the result being an overwhelming number of writing assignments, and a focus that was criticized as being very similar to FD10A. Taylor, who first coordinated "Writing in the Disciplines", considered the course a challenge. She felt the concept of teaching writing in particular disciplines was useful, but the kind of support material required had not been available, and one class per week was insufficient. She observed students' frustration as they grappled with insufficient time to reflect on and review all of the material that was being covered in one seminar. There was no time to focus on writing in each student's particular discipline. Adding to that frustration was the fact that each class was mixed. There was no class of Pure and Applied Sciences students, for example, so facilitators focused on writing in *all* disciplines in any one class. Despite the challenges, during her year as the first coordinator, Taylor followed up on suggestions from Ramsay to involve content faculty in the course. Ramsay's intention was for content faculty to give introductory lectures or participate in discussions at different points in the course. When Taylor communicated with lecturers from other faculties, her concerns were the kinds of tasks that students were expected to write in their disciplines. She had considered cross-modular/cross-faculty teaching in which students would be assigned a technical task that would require the content lecturer to examine segments of it. However, the collaborative element did not go beyond talking about usual required tasks (personal interview, 25 July 2007). Margaret Newman, who succeeded Taylor as coordinator in 2005–2006, tried to modify the course to reduce its many FD10A features. She also changed the texts used in the course. Initially, *Simon & Schuster Handbook for Writers* (7th ed.) by Troyka and Hess (2005) was used. Newman changed that text to Kennedy et al.'s *Writing in the Disciplines: A Reader for Writers* (5th ed., 2004) because she felt the latter "gave the students more guidance and teaching on writing from multiple sources" (Newman 2007). Christine Manion's *A Writer's Guide to Oral Presentations and Writing in the Disciplines* (2001) was also used in the course. Needless to say, these texts are external to the Caribbean reality, but were useful for a course that focused on general disciplinary writing.

Although the course texts appeared to provide disciplinary materials, other aspects of the course that Newman inherited in 2005 really focused little on disciplinary writing. The course description (which was different from what Ramsay proposed) hinted at limitations in the stated course objectives. The FD14A website informed students that the course would provide an alternative to FD10A or UC10A in which students would "acquire other essential writing skills, as well as an appreciation of the manner in which academic language reflects the thinking within each discipline" (FD14A 2007). The site also stated that the course had as objectives students' being able to

> demonstrate an awareness of the defining elements of academic discourse used in different disciplines; critically evaluate and discuss a variety of texts intended for specialist and general audiences; write competent summaries (descriptive, informative or evaluative) of texts in different disciplines; write in a variety of formats on discipline-related issues for specialist as well as general audiences; use approved citation and documentation techniques in written papers; and use writing to reflect their learning experiences. (Ibid.)

The course description suggested that students would consider different research methodologies, the thinking behind research, and writing conventions in different disciplines. However, realizing those objectives would probably have been limited because of the background of students and facilitators and the length of each seminar. Students were often from mixed groups, most of the facilitators in the course were not trained outside of literature, and a two-hour seminar hardly allowed time to consider materials from multiple disciplines. Given those constraints, students got very general – perhaps even stereotypical – introductions to "the defining elements of academic discourse used in different disciplines". Another description that was provided online (perhaps to clarify the objectives) and that students received as a handout in the second semester of 2006–2007 seemed even further removed from disciplinary writing, with wording that could fit any of the other courses. This handout stated that at the end of the course, students should be able to

1. analyse various discourse situations
2. critically evaluate and discuss a variety of texts
3. write competent summaries and paraphrases
4. use approved citation and documentation techniques in written papers
5. plan and write essays
6. revise, edit and proofread
7. conduct research

(FD14A 2007)

Other aspects of the course suggested that it involved more writing *of* the disciplines rather than writing *in* the disciplines. As preparation for their third week in the second semester of 2005–2006, students were to read from their texts "Subjects of Study in the Natural Sciences and Technology", "Humanities" and "Social Sciences", and note "two similarities and one difference". This reading assignment meant that this mixed group of students was being introduced to aspects of writing in various disciplines, which was useful exposure. As Merrill and Miller (2002, 210) opine, cross-disciplinary inquiries "make the rhetorical dynamics of academic discourses visible", thereby enabling students to "see knowledge making at work in different settings". However, given the assignments, students were probably not focusing specifically on how to write in their respective disciplines – the more immediately necessary and valuable skill.

Students' research projects also suggested work directed at only general academic audiences. For their research essay, students were told that they could choose their own topic. Those students who could not arrive at a topic were allowed to write on one of several that were covered in one of their textbooks. The only condition for all students was that they wrote on the topic "from [their] discipline's perspective". Writing on a broad topic from the discipline's perspective meant that students were to write on a topic that their discipline would deal with. For a topic such as "family", a student in a health-related discipline could write on "family health" or "community health" whereas one in social sciences could write on "family structure", "family functioning", "dysfunctional family", "changes in family structure", or "roles within families", among others. However, this approach proved difficult for students doing mathematics or physics, for example. Therefore, the instruction was changed to inform students that they could write on a topic in *another* discipline in which they were interested and with which they would like to challenge themselves. They should talk to their facilitator in such a case (Newman, personal interview, 30 July 2007). These instructions and the background of the students and facilitators suggest that students in this course, like those in FD10A, probably had to adapt their disciplinary relevant pieces to a general academic audience. While it would have been useful for students to be able to adapt disciplinary writing to the needs of diverse audiences, including the public, that kind of instruction was not the primary objective of the course.

Despite those limitations, the course represented a move to address disciplinary writing conventions, which, I argue, should inform writing instruction. However, the course embodied linguistic prejudice. Since only students with upper range passes in CAPE were allowed to take the course, initially facilitators did not complain as they did in the past about students' mastery of English. However, the rationale for offering the course to students who had the highest scores in CAPE seemed questionable; if it were such a good course, why were the students with more problems in writing not allowed to take it? Of the then first-year writing courses at Mona, FD14A most clearly addressed the need to assist students with recognizing and employing writing strategies in specific disciplines. However, this course also best reflected a contradictory emphasis on excellence over equity. In other words, this course evidenced some of the politics of literacy with which writing teachers usually engage: On the one hand, there is what Faigley (1992, 52) calls "the ideal of literacy as a means for achieving social equality" and, on the other, "a cynical acknowledgement of education as part of the machinery for sorting people into categories of winners and losers". The requirements suggest that the stronger (meaning *grammatically abler*) writers got the necessary exposure and those who really needed the exposure were excluded.

A kind of discriminatory social sorting was, therefore, implied in the prerequisites for the course. In fact, the UWI at Mona appeared to have explicitly offered differentiated educational opportunities based on the selection process for this course, but only for students with demonstrated high levels of mastery of English. The course could have empowered some students regarding disciplinary discourses, while other students would have been disenfranchised. Such arrangements highlighted the need to re-examine the assumptions on which this course and the other first-year writing courses were based. Having an alternative course for students with high levels of proficiency in English and from secondary institutions where they had already covered most of the sociolinguistic content of the other writing courses reflected commonsense. However, not wanting to copy CAPE or simply wanting to attend to students with upper range passes should not have been the reasons for offering instruction in writing in the disciplines. Additionally, if the course was meant to provide differentiated instruction, then it seems odd that in the very year that this "honours" course was introduced, the "basic" writing course (UC010) for less able (meaning *grammatically weaker*) writers was divested.

Re-examination of the assumptions on which FD14A was based was needed to lead to modifications that would indeed enable students to "write in a variety of formats on discipline-related issues for specialist as well as general audiences". *General audiences* seemed to be *adequately treated* in this course and the others. However, students would probably have grasped concepts better about writing for specialist audiences if content faculty were involved in instruction. The subject workshops that Ramsay recommended would have also proven useful in terms of grouping students who were specializing in the same area. However, a problem would have remained regarding facilitators who may not have shared the students' specialization. Professor of linguistics and language studies at Carleton University in Canada Aviva Freedman (1995, 140) highlights this problem in her critique of failed attempts at offering writing instruction *outside* of disciplinary discursive contexts: "It is very difficult for those who are not in fact immersed in these fields, who are not themselves disciplinary specialists, to be sensitive to and to articulate the complex nuanced understanding of what counts as evidence or appropriate warranting, or what can be accepted as shared knowledge." Freedman shows from her research that "simulations of disciplinary writing tasks . . . are just rhetorical complications of the task" that "carry with them the invidious possibility of causing inappropriate transfer when the student is confronted with the real thing" (ibid.).

Faculty could have reconsidered the kind of collaboration that Ramsay intended or that Taylor attempted to initiate in 2004–2005 in order to avoid the problems that could arise in what Freedman (1995, 140) calls "stand-alone WAC classes in which the writing teacher independently teaches one section on sociology, one section on literature, and one section on biology". FD14A could have actually included prompts from other disciplines, with the content faculty going to the writing class to discuss them – as used to be done in "Use of English" with faculty in the other survey courses. Such shared writing assignments and team teaching to link faculty courses and foundation writing courses would have been more useful than the end-of-semester panel presentations that a former FD10A instructor organized in 2001–2002 and in which a professor from the Faculty of Pure and Applied Sciences participated. This presentation seemed to reinforce writing for evaluation since the presentation was organized for content faculty and writing specialists to give students tips for writing just before the FD10A final examination in which students wrote an instant essay. While that kind of collaboration was useful, more was required to achieve transformation in attitudes to writing and in students' achievements in writing. Beginning in 2003–2004, panels of professionals from within the academy as well as from the private and public sectors were invited to address students taking (UC120 and later) UC10A/UC10B and lead discussions about the functions and processes of writing in their disciplines. Such changes reinforced the relevance of writing to students' development. However, they did not address the kind of actual instruction in disciplinary ways of knowing and writing that would have been beneficial to students. A well worked out programme would have involved writing-intensive courses beyond the first year to support writing-to-learn assignments used beginning in the first year.

Faculty's re-examination of FD14A would have also necessitated a re-examination of the other courses for various reasons. First, up to 2007–2008, students with lower range passes in CAPE took UC10A if they were in Humanities and FD10A if they were in other faculties, except Law. As I have explained, both FD10A and UC10A addressed exposition. Although it could have been argued that UC10A was an enriched course because it included a lecture and therefore three hours per week, it could also have been argued that resources were being stretched to have two different courses that addressed similar aspects of writing. It was also true that although the language emphasis in "Use of English" had been deemphasized in the then writing courses, UC10A still gave students more exposure to Caribbean language issues than did FD10A.[23] One may say such exposure was appropriate for students in the humanities, but based on the language prejudices identified in previous chapters, all students were likely to benefit from discussions about language and power that could have contributed to students' sense of identity and critical awareness. After all, although all of the courses perpetuated the hegemonic role of English, the accepted language of academe, UC10A lent itself to far more discussions on challenging linguistic imperialism and changing attitudes to language in the academy and in the society than did any other course. Second, the question, "What does following FD14A with UC10B mean for Humanities students?" should have been considered. If FD14A really did what it was supposed to do, a general "argument" course as its sequel would have been redundant. Alternatively, such a course could have acted like a test of what was learned in FD14A, but one would have needed to question the reason for having general language facilitators functioning as the examiners of specialist writing.

If administrators and faculty understood FD14A's potential, they would have considered different approaches to research and writing processes in all of the courses. One intriguing aspect of all of the courses was that, just as all students had to follow a lock-step writing process, all students had to find a specific number of sources as they researched to write their papers and then they were expected to use a specific minimum number of sources. In FD14A, students did not have to write their first draft in class as happened in FD10A, for example. The check in FD14A was the reference list, which could not be too different from the first one that students prepared. What was not taught, then, was the fact that even number of sources is contingent. The courses did, however, convey a sense that *writing begins before students actually think they are writing* because students usually have to do research and share findings. Unfortunately, however, because the moves in preparing a paper were not necessarily explained as writing steps, students may have actually left the courses thinking that writing was only the final paper they submitted. As compositionists Douglas Downs and Elizabeth Wardle (2007, 563) observe, "what students traditionally imagine as writing is actually only the final move in a much larger series of events". Content faculty also unconsciously passed on the erroneous idea when they did not explain to students that writing begins when they begin to plan and conduct their experiments and other studies that lead to reports or papers. Had students and faculty developed a new understanding of writing, they would have begun to understand what Carter (2007) describes as writing as knowing and doing in a discipline. This connection is evident even in the documentation style that is used; however, as in FD10A, the documentation style that students used in FD14A reflects convenience rather than substantial links to purpose and context. According to the 2007–2008 FD14A syllabus, each final draft had to be "correctly formatted according to the citation style preferred by [the student's] discipline". Students were advised that where their discipline had no stated policy, they were to use the APA documentation style. As expressed regarding FD10A, a clear connection was not made between documentation style and ways of knowing and doing in disciplines.

Much of the guidance that students received regarding documentation came in mixed-group sessions from librarians who tried to present various kinds of examples of sources, how to evaluate them, and how to document them in-text or at the end of a text. Unfortunately, many of the papers students presented suggested that they grasped neither the mechanics of documenting nor how to avoid accusations of plagiarism. The issues related to plagiarism could have stemmed from disciplinary misunderstanding, and those related to the mechanics of documentation from lack of disciplinary instruction. Instead of mixed-group sessions presented by librarians, students should have been assisted with such matters in the context of their own writing. Such assistance could have come from facilitators in the writing courses and from coaches in the writing centre. However, content faculty should also have been initiating students into the ways in which documentation styles characterize disciplinary epistemologies.

As happened in FD10A, as the end of the century approached, FD14A coordinators increased efforts to address shortcomings in the course. These included increased exercises to address English grammar because of persistent problems in students' written materials and facilitators' observations that students with high (I and II) passes in CAPE were not really writing better than students with lower range passes. To address complaints from both students and other facilitators regarding excessive numbers of assignments, these coordinators, especially Newman, attempted not only to reduce the number of assignments but also to make them relevant to students' disciplines. These efforts were, however, without direct/consistent involvement of other content faculty.

A Plural Academy: Beyond Universalist Models of First-Year Writing?

Other developments in the university suggest that the climate was right for consideration of content faculty's involvement in students' writing development. However, these developments also bring out in sharp relief ambiguities regarding the extent to which the university was indeed engaging in students' writing development. Other (nonfoundation) ELS courses taught to second and third year and graduate students and projects that arose early in the new millennium suggested academics' attempts to reach a wide cross-section of students and to address a variety of *English language* needs on the Mona campus. However, even when faculty attempted to move beyond the universalist model of first-year writing, they ignored the connection between writing and learning in disciplines. This omission was implied in content faculty's belief that writing specialists alone were responsible for students' – including graduates' – writing development. This omission seems to have persisted because of over-attention to the code – English language – that functioned to overshadow attention to other aspects of writing and the connection between writing and learning in disciplines.

The institution's partial engagement in students' language development and the disconnect between writing and learning in disciplines are evident in the provisions in upper-level and graduate writing courses. In 2004–2005, when FD14A was first offered, the Department of Language, Linguistics and Philosophy also offered "Language and Ethics" (LG20A, later LANG2001) for students in their second or third year and "The Art of Public Speaking" (LG30A – later LANG3001) for students in their third or final year. The *Departmental Reports* (2005) for 2004–2005 indicates that a member of the Language Section and a team of lecturers from Mass Communications delivered LG30A in the first semester. According to the LG30A website, the course focused on developing prospective graduates who could "deliver themselves confidently and competently" in public or professional contexts. Students learned to research, write and deliver a speech and then respond to an audience's questions about it. Naturally, the emphasis in the course was "delivery – that is, the choice and use of appropriate language, the proper use of the voice (including elocution, pronunciation, and voice projection) and the employment of visual aids". Although there was mention of enabling students to prepare "for various occasions", the emphasis was on language usage: the presentations for which they were being prepared would be "in a formal context, which often necessitates the use of English" (LG30A 2008). Clearly, this course helped to improve the profile of the institution's graduates by providing them with useful oral communication skills. However, it did not appear to address disciplinary learning. What it revealed most, however, was lack of understanding at the upper administrative level about language development because of the insistence on having the same minimum number of twenty students as in other courses on the campus. In the early years of the new millennium, the university mandated that the lowest number of students in any course was to be twenty. That decision can be understood in light of limited resources due to financial constraints; however, a "speaking" course in which individual speakers are graded usually requires small groups to be effective.

The other course, LG20A, which was designed for students in their second or third year, was first offered in the second semester of 2004–2005. Ramsay and a team of faculty from the philosophy section taught this course to students from the Faculty of Humanities and Education, specifically from the then departments of Mass Communications, Literatures in English, Linguistics and Library Studies. Based on the online course outline, students learned that "ethical issues are inherent in writing and speaking because what we write and say can influence users, either in a positive or negative way. Furthermore, how we express ideas affects people's perception of us and of our organization". By the end of the course, students were expected to develop "an understanding of the basis and justification of the ethical statements" and "an appreciation of the relationship between ethical questions and language usage" (LG20A 2007). Ramsay described the course as involving both reading and writing to help students to analyse other people's writing and to examine the ethical lapses, if any. As they read texts with a critical eye, students learned to determine the extent to which the writing was ethical, that is, adhering to ethical principles as they related to discourse modes. Ramsay felt that one of the emphases in the course that distinguished it from courses such as FD10A, UC10A and UC10B was treatment of the different ways in which people use language across cultures in writing and speaking. She understood that those courses tended to ground students in specific discourse types, which was only one aspect of LG20A. The purpose of having students examine other people's writing was that students would use the same principles to inform their own writing (Ramsay, personal interview, 25 July 2007).

Since this course involved much reading and analysis of other people's writing, it may have been skewed to reading rather than writing. More important, it appears to have been a very general "language" course that did not address ethics in relation to any discipline. In fact, the course appears to have addressed *universality in writing*: the topic covered in the sixth week was "increasing effectiveness by writing universally to include diversity of readers" (LG20A 2007). Certainly, "writing universally" would not have addressed the different purposes and audiences for which members may write in different/specific disciplines/contexts. There was no real treatment of disciplinary writing in the course, but because about three professional fields (journalism, library studies and linguistics) were represented, those students examined the code of ethics for those careers. The students critiqued the code of ethics and considered how they would breach the code of conduct if they were writing in those areas. The students who were not in a clear career area, such as those from literatures in English, considered the UWI students' code of ethics (Ramsay, personal interview, 25 July 2007).

Besides those courses, the ELS also started to offer business communication in the first semester of 2007–2008 to final year undergraduates who, according to the initial advertisement, "wish to master the art of communication in the professional business world" (UWI 2007a). This course was designed to help students "develop proposals, prepare reports, give effective oral presentations and communicate in a businesslike and professional manner". These descriptions suggest a course that was providing useful development for future graduates with respect to communicating beyond the academy rather than also in specific professional disciplines.

The Department of Language, Linguistics and Philosophy also prepared graduate-level "English Language" courses in this period; however, the focus on "English" seemed to promote the view that the responsibility for teaching graduate writing courses should be transferred to language facilitators. The *Departmental Reports* (2003, 56) for 2002–2003 mentions that in that academic year, the ELS "offered its first English Language graduate-level course, Advanced Academic English Language Skills to Social Science students". This is the course that Chevannes (2005) mentions in his article discussed in chapter 1. Chevannes reports that the Faculty of Social Sciences had requested this course, LG600 (later LANG6099), to assist graduate students, about 10 per cent of whom needed "a remedial course" to meet matriculation requirements. In mentioning that some critics may have considered the course "a waste of resources", Chevannes suggests that the course addressed only weaknesses in English grammar and mechanics (302). However, the Revised LG600 Outline (2003) syllabus specified a broader coverage. Most of the fourteen objectives addressed disciplinary writing considerations. Examples included students' being able to "identify the main uses of writing in their field", "employ the main features of writing in their field", "meet the expectations of readers in their field", and "practise appropriate documentation of their work". Only one objective mentioned mechanics, requiring students to be able to "control surface features such as syntax, grammar, punctuation, and spelling". Another graduate-level course that was developed and approved but not taught up to the 2013–2014 academic year was "Advanced Writing in English". This was a course in writing that the Modern Languages and Literatures department had requested to accompany their "Diploma in Translating". Taylor designed "Advanced Writing in English" to focus on professional writing and meeting the standards that would exist in students' professions. Based on this course description and the LG600 objectives, the course designers and some content faculty understood the extent of students' writing needs; that is, the courses suggested content faculty's acknowledgement of the multiple discourses in academia. However, they also instantiated content faculty's attempts to transfer the responsibility for writing development since there is no indication that the courses would have been taught collaboratively with writing and other content faculty. As well, the focus on "English" in a course for graduates in modern languages (where writing in other languages had to be considered) suggests how *writing* was *limited to English* in the university.

Another development in the Department of Language, Linguistics and Philosophy which was fulfilling an important need but probably keeping the focus too closely tied to "English" is the "MA in English Language" that was offered through the Jamaican Language Unit. The description indicates that this programme began in September 2005 and targeted "persons interested in English Language usage in Public Media, Editors, English Language Trainers and Teachers at the Post-secondary level (especially for courses such as CAPE Communication Studies, UWI courses such as UC010, UC120/FD10A/FD14A, and equivalent courses at Teachers' Colleges, and other universities and tertiary institutions)". Students were expected to develop "a sound technical knowledge of the structure and usage of English" and "gain a grasp of the social issues surrounding its use both within the Caribbean and around the world, and the competence to design and teach English language courses at the post-secondary level" ("MA in English Language" 2006). While the emphasis on English Language may have been useful for teachers in preuniversity institutions, it appears to have been limited for teachers who should have been doing more than helping students to write for general audiences. In other words, the programme did not seem to concentrate much on how English works and is worked in writing *within different disciplines* – a necessary concern for "English Language Trainers and Teachers at the Post-secondary level".

A Plural Academy or Collaboration as "Support" or "Reinforcement"?

Academics' attempts to address writing development beyond the foundation courses are also evident in the WAC pilot project that the Department of Language, Linguistics and Philosophy introduced at Mona in 2006–2007. WAC is an educational reform movement that dates back to the 1970s in the United States and that has roots in the language across the curriculum movement initiated by James Britton in British secondary schools. WAC is concerned with developing active learners of disciplinary content who also contribute to the production of disciplinary knowledge. This movement involves teaching approaches that focus on helping students (a) use writing to learn the content of specific disciplines, and (b) write for disciplinary audiences. The result of this distinction is that, as a pedagogy, WAC is often defined as having two significant components: writing to learn and learning to write (disciplinary discourse). The latter is also referred to as "writing in the disciplines" (Maimon et al. 1981) and "writing to communicate" (McLeod 2001).

The first component of WAC, "writing to learn", is consistent with moves towards student-centred learning and is *relatively* easy to adopt. Content faculty who employ this approach include low stakes writing in their teaching to help students engage with course content. The ungraded pieces that faculty assign involve exploratory writing that fosters active learning. Pieces such as the "minute paper", "quick write", "free write", or journal entry can break the monotony of a lecture by requiring students to respond to prompts that help students make sense of the course content. Although some low stakes writing pieces can be rigorous, the other component – "writing to communicate" – is pedagogically more complex because it is concerned mainly with learning to write in the discipline for disciplinary audiences. It requires that content faculty not only be concerned with content learning, but also initiate students into what Carter (2007) aptly terms the discipline's ways of knowing, doing and writing. Unlike in the first approach where content faculty and students tend to be in expert-novice relationships, "writing to communicate" presupposes an expert-apprentice relationship. This posture requires content faculty to subscribe to the popular view in composition studies that disciplines are discourse communities whose members share particular values and display ethnocentric tendencies. This component, "writing to communicate", is informed by a social view of knowledge and writing and overlaps with "writing to learn". However, the distinction between increasing learning through writing and increasing proficiency in writing matters at the UWI at Mona because of academics' stated desire for better writing from students and the moulding of graduates who are critical thinkers (UWI 2007b).

At Mona, the WAC initiative comes closer than the general writing courses to promoting the link between writing and learning and encouraging disciplinary writing instruction *in* disciplines. However, its first year (2006–2007) reflected limited considerations of content faculty's actual role in writing instruction and development, and did not adequately address the social construction of knowledge which informs "writing to communicate". The report on years two and three indicates attempts to address "writing (and speaking) to communicate" in disciplines (Altidor-Brooks 2008). However, this report acknowledges that these developments were on a very small scale, with less than 20 per cent of faculty participating in the Faculty of Pure and Applied Sciences and less than 30 per cent in the Faculty of Social Sciences. This limited participation in the project suggested a need for upper administration (and not just one department) to promote the centrality of writing to learning in disciplines and to endorse the project (as it did FD10A) to declare the UWI a WAC institution.

Mona's WAC initiative addressed the important need for academics to move beyond understanding writing as a generic skill and beyond seeing the responsibility for students' writing development as resting solely with language facilitators or a first-year writing course. In other words, the project suggests academics' deeper understandings of writing than were exhibited in earlier years. However, specific considerations of content faculty's involvement in explicit disciplinary writing instruction rather than in mere reinforcement of basic English language principles were not apparent in documents from the first year of the project. Although in the second year, the project team began to address directly the responsibility of content faculty for promoting writing as a learning and communication medium, the team's acknowledgement that some content faculty continued to equate writing with English grammar highlights the persistence of views about the transparency of language and writing (Alison Altidor-Brooks, personal interview, 19 November 2008). The result was that WAC was proving to be another universalist model of writing in its application at Mona.

The project's universalist orientation is evident in the development of WAC at Mona which indicates that some faculty's primary concern continued to be students' English language competence rather than actual writing development in disciplines. In the 2006–2007 academic year, the Department of Language, Linguistics and Philosophy began to pilot the project in the five departments in the Faculty of Pure and Applied Sciences (later Faculty of Science and Technology) – chemistry, life sciences, geography and geology, mathematics and computer sciences, and physics. The project was meant to help Pure and Applied Sciences faculty improve their pedagogy by integrating more writing into their courses so that students become more effective learners of their discipline. Project documents reveal that it arose out of a Writing Centre Day that was held in 2005, and was in part a response to a cross-campus meeting that the Office of the Board for Undergraduate Studies had organized for faculty and instructors in the English language writing courses and administrators in 2005 (WRITE Symposium II 2005). When the Writing Centre Day was held in 2005, the Harvard College (2003) film *Shaped by Writing* was shown and discussed by attendees and representatives from the ELS. The Pure and Applied Sciences faculty in attendance expressed concerns about students' writing and acknowledged that they needed help with students' written expression. Following such discussions, the Department of Language, Linguistics and Philosophy proposed the WAC project which began in earnest when compositionist Chris Anson (University Distinguished Professor of English at North Carolina State University) conducted the first workshop in January 2007. The project was to be evaluated at the end of two years to determine a model that could be used in other faculties.

The WRITE symposium that the Office of the Board for Undergraduate Studies organized also influenced the WAC project but did not realize much success in other ventures. This symposium involved a cross-campus collaboration of faculty in the foundation writing courses. These faculty members aimed to examine writing requirements for tertiary education and synchronize course content, delivery and evaluation. One agenda item at the meetings of the WRITE Symposium was the suggestion to increase the number of writing courses across the undergraduate degree in the Faculty of Humanities and Education. This suggestion is outlined in the *Departmental Reports* (2005, 23–24) for 2004–2005: "Recognizing the importance of writing for academic success, the Faculty with the approval of the Mona Academic Board and Board for Undergraduate Studies decided that as of the start of the 2005/06 academic year every student of the Faculty will be required to do a writing course at each of the three levels in order to fulfil requirements for the Bachelor's degree." Such plans were consistent with a new bachelor of arts degree in Liberal Studies "offering students a broad liberal education rather than narrow specializations at the undergraduate level" (24). This would have been a sensible direction to take to give students writing practice over all the years of their degree, but what was not mentioned was actual disciplinary engagement – which I am advocating. Also, there was no mention of what would obtain in the rest of the university – beyond the Faculty of Humanities and Education. The WRITE Symposium would consider and recommend some connections to disciplinary requirements; however, the main goals of this short-lived cross-campus initiative, including recommendations for writing courses at each level, were not fulfilled.

Despite the short-lived nature of this cross-campus initiative, the decisions and recommendations foreshadowed the way in which content faculty's involvement in students' writing development would be understood as *reinforcement* in terms of *support* rather than as *integral engagement* in instruction to *build on* and *expand* students' writing knowledge and abilities. This limited understanding of collaboration was evident when, in February 2005, members of the Office of the Board for Undergraduate Studies and representatives from the ELS on the three campuses considered the "university's thrust to improve the profile of its graduates and in doing so ensure that they were fully equipped to function and compete in a world in which ability to communicate is a crucial element of success" (WRITE Symposium IIa 2005, 2). These participants acknowledged that "competence in writing is addressed primarily if not only in the language foundation courses. However, writing and reading in the academy are complex processes that cannot be dealt with only at Level I of a three- or four-year academic programme, nor can they be addressed solely by those responsible for delivery of writing courses" (WRITE Symposium II 2005, 1). Attendees emphasized that "without *reinforcement* even the best undergraduate writer is unlikely to exhibit the levels of competence that are expected of a student upon graduation" (ibid.; emphasis added). In consideration of "disciplinary needs", attendees noted, "learning to write is a complex process, requiring continued practice and *reinforcement* over time" (2; emphasis added). With regard to practice, attendees acknowledged the limitations regarding financial and human resources with which the English language programme has had to contend over the years, and proposed solutions to "reposition [the] English language programmes within the context of international norms and regional needs and expectations" (1). In other words, attendees called for writing courses beyond the first year to facilitate more practice in writing: "the writing units on each campus will continue to develop Level II and III courses in the disciplines with input from faculty in those disciplines; all students should be encouraged to take these courses to ensure that they have achieved the level of competence in writing that is expected of a UWI graduate" (2). These recommendations marked an important step towards addressing writing instruction throughout the academy, but like other recent developments may not have acknowledged the complexity of writing development. For example, continued talk about "reinforcement" seemed to keep the concern at the level of the basics in English rather than move to considering actual development in disciplinary writing.

Also, although these suggestions evidenced academics' increased understanding of writing development, they still seemed to be "external" to the discipline. In other words, the suggestions did not address content faculty's full understanding of their role in students' development in writing *within their* discipline.

The WAC project that was introduced later would respond to the proposal for the "mandatory enrolment of every student in a writing-intensive course for each year of the undergraduate degree programme" (Moore 2006b, 4) but which had not been realized up to October 2006. However, documents from the first year of the project also emphasize content faculty's *support* of students' writing development. The background to the Department of Language, Linguistics and Philosophy's "Writing Centre Pilot Project Proposal" (DLLP 2006d) states that students' failure to "experience writing as an integral component of their university education in general, and their academic discipline in particular . . . is evidenced in the complaints by university staff and by employers about the weak writing skills of many students and graduates". In a letter sent to US WAC faculty to request a "kick-off" workshop, Moore, the then project coordinator, wrote "Currently, the general quality of students' writing at UWI is not what many lecturers would like it to be, and the feeling is that if students get more opportunities to write in their courses and are expected to achieve a certain standard in writing and English Language competence, then lecturers should begin to see a turn-a-round in students' writing. It's against this background that the WAC project is being implemented." These statements are indicative of content faculty's requests. Content faculty had expressed concerns that students' English language proficiency was affecting students' ability to communicate discipline-specific content (Moore, personal interview, 18 July 2007). Content faculty's concerns about improving students' communication of course content, therefore, determined aspects of the project's focus. Unfortunately, however, this focus appeared to be formalist conventions, addressed as "English Language competence", rather than disciplinarity/disciplinary writing.

This formalist preoccupation and omission of specific statements about how instruction in writing to communicate in disciplines would occur were evident in other project documents such as "UWI Mona Writing Centre Mission" (DLLP 2006c). This document stated that the facility was "a means of achieving the University's educational objective of producing students whose level of English Language communicative competence is consonant with success in their specialist and non-specialist academic courses as well as in their post-graduate studies and future occupations". It expressed that the facility's short-term objective was "to transform and enhance teaching/learning processes and to improve students writing by promoting & facilitating . . . institution-wide commitment to the incorporation of a WAC approach into the programmes of all departments so that students receive a writing-intensive education" (1). Moore (2006b, 3) would clarify that objective in the project proposal in which she justified the urgency for a WAC programme at the

UWI on the basis that "a majority of University students at both the undergraduate and post-graduate levels lack the communication skills required to function effectively at the tertiary level and in professional contexts". She explained that the WAC project had a twofold aim. On one level, the project was meant "to sensitize staff to the fact that writing is integral to students' education and should not be treated as a generic skill to be taught and mastered only in the English Language foundation courses". At another level, the project was "to train staff to effectively integrate WAC approaches into their courses' learning objectives and teaching methodologies to promote writing, critical thinking and communication skills" (ibid.). Moore also noted that one reason students did not continue to develop their writing abilities beyond the first-year language foundation courses was that "the requisite reading, writing and critical thinking skills introduced in these courses were not *reinforced* in other university-wide courses" (4; emphasis added). She, therefore, stressed the importance of collaboration to the success of the project. She drew on WAC research in the United States to assert, "Ultimately, the successes of the Writing Centre and the WAC pilot project will depend on the collaboration across disciplines and faculties to devise a WAC model that addresses the peculiar needs of students who come from primarily Creole-speaking environments, but who must 'use written language to develop and communicate knowledge in every discipline and across disciplines'" (5). While the explanations in the proposal suggest a more comprehensive understanding of writing and its value in education than other academics had expressed in earlier years, the explanations did not mention the necessary reflection on how writing varies in each discipline. They also did not address how actual instruction and students' development in disciplinary writing would be assured through a *writing-intensive* education. Surely, students could have received a writing-intensive education (as they did in the sixth form) without actual explicit instruction.

The centre's writing principles included statements that would suggest an understanding of differing writing practices in disciplines; however, these remained vague. They explained that students needed to "practise writing for different purposes & audiences using different modes" and "receive critical feedback from readers (peers & teachers) at all stages of their writing process" (DLLP 2006c, 1). Students also needed "instruction & help in overcoming their own writing/reading problems in the context of real writing/reading tasks" (2). The WAC principles identified in the document were, however, more explicit regarding disciplinary writing: "Writing is integral to a professional education in any discipline, and is not simply a generic skill easily mastered in one or two 'writing' courses and then transferred to all disciplines." Nevertheless, there is a sense that knowledge making and acquisition were separated from communication of knowledge, and the focus was on the student with no clear indication of how instruction would occur. The document emphasized, "Only by practising the conventions of an academic discipline will students begin to communicate effectively within that discipline" (ibid.).

Collaborative efforts in the academy, as Smit (2004) recommends in the second epigraph of this chapter and as Moore (2006b) recognized, would prove vital to revolutions in writing on the Mona campus. However, the kind of collaboration that would assure students' writing development – by promoting the importance of writing to learning and creation of disciplinary content and minimizing the focus on English language in courses – required academics' acknowledgement of the plural nature of the academy. Faculty were slow in acting in ways that are consistent with this acknowledgement. This lack of acknowledgement emerged in the varying attitudes displayed by content faculty as the WAC team endeavoured to include writing development in curricular reform. Content faculty in a small number of departments (Life Sciences and Chemistry in the Faculty of Pure and Applied Sciences and Economics in the Faculty of Social Sciences) were committed to engaging students in writing to communicate disciplinary content. However, the majority of departments in the institution did not participate in the project. Even in departments where administrators encouraged participation, some content faculty refused to participate or participated reluctantly (Alison Altidor-Brooks, personal interview, 19 November 2008). One reason was the traditional focus on English language. One of Altidor-Brooks's explanations that some faculty did not join the project on the basis that they felt students just needed more English grammar teaching suggests the extent of this focus. By focusing on English language, some faculty members continued to keep writing knowledge tacit and thereby managed to alienate learning from writing in disciplines. Another reason is that because WAC was not compulsory in the Faculty of Pure and Applied Sciences, it was very difficult to get content faculty to become involved with the project in the first year. However, more faculty joined the project after talking to others who were interested in trying the strategies (Moore, personal interview, 18 July 2007). These participants were beginning to understand or acknowledge that it is not true that students learn to write once and for all in high school.

Some content faculty's acceptance of the pilot suggests that they were beginning to accept their responsibility in teaching writing. What was important, however, was that content faculty also needed to realize the extent of that responsibility, which would have included *examining and making visible* their discipline's writing practices. The WAC team at Mona attempted to address this matter in year 2, with some participating faculty being asked to review and modify syllabuses. In one instance in economics, one faculty member was relieved of teaching duties so that she could read and respond to drafts that students submitted in various courses in economics. While this development was commendable, it also points to the then limited participation in the project. Certainly all faculty should have been reflecting on disciplinary practices. As Russell (2002, 300) cautions in the third epigraph in this chapter, if faculty members do not reflect on and explain their disciplines' discursive practices, they are likely to view writing in each course as "a means of introducing pedagogical variety" and an effort that will no longer be required after students' writing improves. However, the view of writing as a constant, "central part of disciplinary research and teaching" is crucial to improvements in WAC. Moreover, if content faculty do not have a conscious awareness of their discipline's rhetorical conventions, they may, as Russell writes, "mistake the inevitable struggles of students to acquire the rhetorical conventions of a discipline for poor writing or sheer ignorance" (18). The result is that content faculty are likely to continue to feel that a general first-year writing course or preuniversity preparation could and should provide all necessary skills for students to write within disciplines.

Faculty would, therefore, have had a better understanding of the kind of collaboration and instruction that would work if they understood that the myth of transience and the view of writing as transparent recording had militated against students' writing development in and across disciplines since the university's earliest years. Such an understanding was important to content faculty's involvement so that they would not consider their role as being to *support* writing specialists *until* the problematic situation improved. The more appropriate perspective was for faculty to be concerned with students' writing development *within* their discipline, and remember that learning to write is a lifelong endeavour. As well, if content faculty did not see writing as integral to disciplinary learning, they would see it as burdensome to disciplinary development. Russell (2002, 297) captures this situation well when, after examining many WAC programmes, he concluded that "even when WAC programs attempt to make writing part of every class, every discipline, the writing can be marginalized if it is perceived as an additional burden rather than as an intrinsic part of learning".

By the end of the two years of the pilot, the WAC team would begin to acknowledge significant challenges: the project did not have institution-wide support and regular official funding (McLaren et al. 2011, 260–62). Rather than relent, the team members tried to reinvent their plans. Drawing on the aims expressed in the institution's strategic plans and which included producing effective communicators, members shifted the focus from "writing" to "communication" across the curriculum. This means that, at Mona, WAC did not move from its "foundational" status to become "established" or "integrated" or "institutional change agent" as William Condon and Carol Rutz (2012, 362) describe the evolution of WAC programmes in the United States. It had, instead, morphed into communication across the curriculum with emphases in writing and speaking. Capitalizing on curriculum reform in the Faculty of Pure and Applied Sciences, and using her fellowship leave, team leader Ingrid McLaren launched the communication across the curriculum pilot project in that faculty in January 2010. This initiative involved infusing select levels 2 and 3 courses with writing and speech activities, so that those courses would be formally designated as writing intensive or speech intensive. As was the experience with WAC, beginnings were small: a few courses from life sciences and chemistry were so designated, with the team hoping that the other departments in that faculty and elsewhere on the campus would eventually be involved in the initiative (see McLaren 2010, 10, 14). This initiative, too, would require faculty to examine courses and strategies to make disciplinary practices visible.

Conclusion

Faculty's examining and making visible their discipline's writing conventions was crucial because of the persistence of universalist models of writing in the institution. These models enabled students to develop metacognitive awareness about writing as they wrote for general academic audiences but did not necessarily enable students to excel in disciplinary writing. Shortly after "Fundamentals of English" was introduced, the institution made other changes to the original "Use of English" course. Administrators and content faculty no longer linked writing instruction and remediation, but they still conveyed a sense that the academy is a single discourse community and that writing in disciplines is neutral and hardly influenced by persuasion. They did this by recommending that students' writing development take place outside of disciplines and by promoting emphasis on expository writing with training provided solely by writing specialists in the Department of Language, Linguistics and Philosophy. Therefore, although administrators seemed to enlist writing, they still marginalized its instruction. Indeed, the institution enlisted writing in the form of almost universal first-year writing, with its emphasis on the writing process and instruction before engagement in disciplinary work. However, just as administrators and linguists involved with "Use of English" had adapted British models to the cultural and social concerns of the Caribbean in the 1960s and 1970s, in the late 1980s and 1990s writing specialists at Mona attempted to inflect American models with Caribbean cultural and disciplinary trends. However, writing specialists' adaptations of the universalist model of the writing process and other aspects of writing from the United States to the linguistic paradigms and cultural contexts of the Caribbean remained superficial. Although process seems to have been adapted to cultural concerns and disciplinary trends, it really reflected emphasis on formalism. This emphasis was consistent with the focus on exposition that functioned as the paradigmatic universalist genre that kept process separate from disciplinary learning. The institutional context, involving many Creole-speaking first-generation students, was quite compelling. But linguistic prejudices were abundant and writing faculty had been stretched too thin and did not have the means and requisite support from upper administration to develop other models of writing that could engage with the linguistic richness and cultural distinctiveness of Jamaica and the Caribbean region.

Later developments such as FD14A, upper-level and graduate writing courses, proposals from the cross-campus collaboration of lecturers (WRITE symposium) and the WAC initiative suggest new and more comprehensive understandings of writing than those that obtained in discussions and delivery of UC100, UC120 and its derivatives and FD10A. However, such developments suggest that stakeholders had not gone far enough in transforming writing instruction to realize fully its potential and place in higher education. Past and current thinking about writing, in its emphasis on English language, had failed to develop a transformative model of writing and its instruction that took as its aim the development of students in disciplinary writing. The WAC project, for example, if fully implemented institution-wide could have yielded positive results because studies consistently show improvements in writing itself in new WAC/writing in the disciplines programmes (Haswell 2007, 341). However, some discussions surrounding the project at Mona did not reflect broadening to consider how content faculty understood writing and why they may have withheld instructional development. Early project documents did not convey a clear sense of content faculty's specific involvement in articulating their knowledge of writing in disciplines to build on students' knowledge of and in disciplinary writing. Because content faculty did not explicitly share their knowledge of disciplinary writing features and strategies, they conveyed a sense that learning and writing in disciplines are separate entities.

The collaborative effort needed to assure students' writing development would, therefore, have had to include content faculty's understanding of the importance of consciously including writing development in their goals for teaching and learning. Some economics course outlines at Mona were revised with such a view in mind (Altidor-Brooks 2008). However, as expressed, this revision was not done on a large-scale in the university. Far more faculty members needed to begin to shift their focus from concerns about eliminating grammatical problems in writing (so that students wrote better for content faculty to understand the "English" writing and for pass rates to increase) to concerns about instruction that could enable learning and assure students' success in the discipline during and after completion of studies. Some content faculty were yet to understand the extent to which writing makes learning visible. In the Jamaican context, this is learning of the code, codified writing conventions and content knowledge. If faculty understood the interconnection of writing and learning – in disciplines and outside the academy, they could have assisted students in using the code in meaningful ways to demonstrate both their knowledge in writing and knowledge of writing. In a country where mastery of the written code is a Herculean task for most Creole speakers, increasing numbers of whom were entering the academy, academics would have been well advised to consider how that mastery could have increased if students were not only graded on the conventions, but also taught them, and if students were allowed to focus on formalist requirements less in decontextualized situations and more in content areas whose practical relevance may have been immediately apparent to students.

Carrington's (1981) advice about language and teaching in the Caribbean is, therefore, applicable to writing and student development at the UWI at Mona. Carrington cautions that the "elimination of illiteracy in the English-speaking Caribbean must be undertaken as a positive act of public education linked to a conscious process of societal development. It must not be undertaken as an exercise in changing statistics for the vain improvement of national image" (200). Similarly, where university students' development is concerned, all involved should have considered writing instruction – disciplinary writing instruction – not merely as a way to eliminate problems to increase pass rates in any course or a way to improve the university's profile, but rather as a route to students' optimal development which would in turn impact institutional and national development. New attitudes to writing in the academy that departed from conventional yet largely inaccurate models of writing could have influenced attitudes at other educational levels and elsewhere in the society. Indeed, enlistment of rhetoric would have worked better than the attention to general university-level educated audiences or to formalist conventions. Such an engagement could have helped students see the connected ways of knowing, doing and writing in specific contexts to achieve specific purposes in specific audiences. In the next chapter, I indicate the very latest developments in Mona's writing courses and propose ways in which stakeholders at the UWI and in other institutions could engage "visible rhetoric" to foster learning, increase awareness about writing, and improve attitudes to writing and its development – for Creole-influenced millennial learners.

6 | Fashioning Versatile Creole-Influenced Writers through a Transcultural Rhetorical Perspective on Writing in the New Millennium, beyond 2010

Only when academia confronts its confusion of tongues and its myth of transience can the slow work of translation and transformation begin. (Russell 2002, 33)

One [question] is how the students who carry the cultural and linguistic marks of diversity can flourish in the classroom and benefit from knowing – and working with and across – two or more languages and rhetorical styles. (Rodriguez Connal 2000, 318).

Taking a rhetorical stance on writing can enable us to see writing "problems" as an opportunity for collaborative deliberations on shared needs. (Merrill and Miller 2002, 205)

We are interested in developing not only competent writers but also critical writers. Therefore, though we should make students sensitive to the dominant conventions in each rhetorical context, we must also teach them to critically engage with them. (Canagarajah 2010, 177)

The previous chapters demonstrate the ways in which the UWI at Mona developed from being a small university college conceived to select and educate a tiny elite to being an independent institution of higher education that would cater to developing large numbers of individuals from the Caribbean region. Important to this development was the institution's contribution to the advanced written literacy development of Creole-influenced students through various kinds of writing courses. Unfortunately, however, the provisions put in place for writing development suggest that for more than six decades, administrators and content faculty largely treated writing as separate from disciplinary learning. In other words, they seem to have understood writing as, to borrow from Merrill and Miller (2002, 207), "a prerequisite for professional knowledge that should have been mastered elsewhere". As a consequence, myths about writing prevailed in the institution. Subscribing to the myth of transience, stakeholders seemed to support the view that once better teaching is done preuniversity problems in university students' writing will disappear. Stakeholders also seemed to perpetuate the myth of the transparency of language (the rhetoric of transparent disciplinarity) in terms of seeing writing as a neutral, transparent medium for recording ideas; understanding writing instruction as remediation; providing opportunities for strong writers to develop their writing while marginalizing weaker writers; and promoting the academy as a single discourse community by expecting a general writing course and those teaching it to prepare all students to write in all disciplines.

Certainly, there was merit in the programmes that the university enlisted up to the turn of the twenty-first century to contribute to Creole-influenced students' advanced written literacy development. However, as expressed in the preceding chapters and as the first two epigraphs in this chapter imply, the assumptions on which the courses were based needed to be reexamined to yield genuine writing development. Various changes were made to the courses through official and unofficial undertakings of individual coordinators and instructors; however, elaborate re-examination, sanctioned by upper administration, would follow the ELS's first quality assurance review that was done in 2009. The reviewers would support ELS members' assertions that writing development does not occur through inoculation of the type done in a one-semester or one-year writing course. Working with the momentum generated by the response to the quality assurance review report, the ELS continued to re-examine the existent courses. The result was a proposal for five new courses. Four of these courses would be geared to students who satisfied entry requirements regarding English language proficiency in specific faculties; the fifth course would be the "stretch" version of one of the previously offered foundation courses and geared towards students who fail to satisfy minimal entry requirements in English language. Given that this course would be taught in two semesters, it could be seen as a return to teaching a modified version of "Fundamentals of English" – although this detail was not stated in the proposal. As reported in "Bloody English", the Board for Undergraduate Studies approved the proposal in January 2013 for the programme to begin in the 2013–2014 academic year (Virtue 2013).

Given the history outlined in the preceding chapters and summarized below, four faculty-specific[24] writing courses and *reinstitution* of a basic writing course represent quite an achievement on the part of writing specialists and in the institution. As stated, the previous courses tended to promote writing for a general educated audience, yet the well-rounded graduate is expected to be able to write for general, public audiences as well as disciplinary and professional audiences – and this is especially true in this digital age when "writing" seems to be more popular than reading, and people who write aim to publicize both their personal and public writing in very public electronic forums. Is it then to be taken that the new courses will assist the institution's Creole-influenced students to realize this goal? The answer is a resounding "Yes!" – as was the case for the general writing courses before them. All of these kinds of writing courses can assist students with writing; the question is what the focus is in each type. And, how can an institution, such as the UWI at Mona, assist Creole-influenced students in enhancing their writing abilities to realize the complementary goals of writing for multiple audiences? What are some factors that an institution should consider to truly enable the advanced written literacy development of Creole-influenced students in this millennium – students that, as the second epigraph in this chapter reminds, are acquainted with "two or more languages and rhetorical styles" (Rodriguez Connal 2000, 318) and that facilitators would like to be, as the fourth epigraph in this chapter expresses, "not only competent writers but also critical writers" (Canagarajah 2010, 177)?

The historical antecedents and current and changing circumstances – including expansions in higher education, widening participation of diverse groups of students, and increased demands and platforms for writing – suggest that Creole-influenced students are likely to benefit from a transcultural rhetorical perspective on writing. This stance involves the institution's moving beyond merely enlisting writing or continuing to promote the myths of transience and of transparency of language in disciplines. Arguably, the UWI has begun the shift. However, a full turn is dependent on a progressive way to view (1) the reach of transculturation, especially as concerns how Creole-influenced students *do language*; (2) writing in disciplines as visible rhetoric; (3) writing instruction in the academy as developmental and necessary across the years of a student's degree programme; (4) the academy as plural, having multiple tongues in its many disciplines, but which Creole-influenced students – by their very linguistic/cultural experiences – are advantageously poised to manipulate; and (5) the goal of writing development as social equity in an atmosphere of excellence.

Summary of Misconceptions about Teaching Academic Writing to Creole-Influenced Students

Incorrect views that language and writing are transparent mediums and that all of students' writing needs can/should be addressed before disciplinary work begins were evident in various ways at the UWI at Mona. First, there was the absence of writing instruction in most of the institution's first decade of existence because of academics' beliefs that students had developed sufficient mastery of English and learned to write sufficiently in disciplines while preparing to enter the university. Administrators and faculty also perpetuated the faulty assumption, evident at the elementary level, that students speak English and write in that language based on an assumed instinct. Second, when the "Use of English" course was first introduced in the early 1960s, course administrators used the conduit metaphor in relation to language, incorrectly emphasizing that writers do heuristic work in their mind before writing. By emphasizing that writers think before they write well, course administrators ignored the power of writing in developing thought and achieving clarity. Third, by the late 1960s and 1970s, course administrators expressed incorrect assumptions about the transparency of evaluation terms in their attempts to address high failure rates. Fourth, although it was evident that course administrators and tutors had attributed incorrect linguistic and writing profiles to students, formal developmental programmes were not implemented to address students' special language needs. This lack was due partly to content faculty's misunderstanding about the visibility of language, and partly to "Use of English" faculty's attempts to avoid associating the course with "remediation". Once writing became visible (that is, a subject of discussion), content faculty declared the aim of writing instruction to be remediation. They also promoted the view that writing development was to be in the language course and that writing could be sufficiently developed in one year or one semester. "Use of English" facilitators resisted the association of the course and, by extension, themselves with remediation. Fifth, some "Use of English" faculty believed that the challenges posed by students' unsatisfactory writing could be addressed through collaboration; however, their understanding of collaboration seemed limited. Sometimes when "Use of English" faculty highlighted disciplinary differences in the academy, they did so in ways that addressed *problems* in writing in disciplines rather than disciplinary writing *requirements*. Therefore, the arts faculty, and specifically "Use of English" facilitators, did not support the chief moderator's recommendation for collaboration in teaching in the course. Sixth, when "Use of English" faculty mentioned the importance of content to written language production, they did so in relation to Caribbean language, which was the stated content of the "Use of English" course, and not (also) in relation to the content of students' disciplines. Seventh, persistent debates about whether language/writing instruction belonged in the university suggested – incorrectly – that students learned to write before engaging with new content and contexts. The result was that content faculty subscribed to the myth of transience. Eighth, when various segments of the university recommended that the institution become involved in students' language and writing development, their recommendations seemed to be based on attempts to help the institution avoid blame for problems in students' writing rather than for the institution to enable learning and realize student development. This involvement and attendant attitudes were evident in the institution's basic and standard writing courses.

When academics eventually acknowledged students' linguistic and writing profiles in virtue of the language problems many students were believed to exhibit, the institution introduced a basic writing course for students who failed an entrance diagnostic test. Some academics consistently challenged this egalitarian approach largely because of their concerns about associating the university with remediation and bearing the responsibility for the financial costs. By the early years of the new millennium, that "Fundamentals of English" course was removed from the campus budget and normal curriculum – although some faculties continued to accept students who failed the proficiency test. Such actions evoke questions about the responsibility for the writing development of primarily Creole-speaking first-generation university students. Since such students could not take their standard first-year writing course that administrators believed taught skills essential to success in students' academic disciplines, the institution was conveying a negative message by accepting students but not providing equal opportunities for their success. Lack of adequate provisions for such students' development suggests that the students were invited and then marginalized. This lack also suggests stagnation at the UWI, arising, as T. Miller (1997, 21) says of English universities, "when . . . received traditions are not assessed against the changing needs of students". The standard first-year writing courses suggest some consideration – albeit insufficient – to provide for new populations of students, with such courses functioning, as T. Miller describes the teaching of English, "as an area where the conventions of academic discourse and the learned culture still come into contact with those who have not been taught to respect them" (29). However, general failure to make adequate provisions for basic writers could only lead to widespread problems. As continued complaints about students' writing in the standard writing courses were revealing, the work of literacy will always come back – and in frightening ways if it is continually ignored.

Beginning in the late 1990s, administrators accepted that standard (as opposed to "basic") writing instruction is important in the academy. With this change, the institution enlisted writing, in terms of not only continuing to offer "Use of English" (under a new name) but also in mandating that all undergraduates take it or the foundation communication course, "English for Academic Purposes" (FD10A), to teach students exposition. This FD10A course and others developed after it signify administrators' and content faculty's growing understanding of the importance of writing in the development of university students and attest to academics' recognition that higher education requires new forms and levels of writing into which students have to be initiated in the academy. However, the focus on exposition evidenced attention to form – with form determining a limited purpose and general audience. That focus – on exposition and not (also) on argument – also indicated administrators' incorrect assumption that writing in the academy is not largely dependent on presenting convincing claims, that is, that writing is not dependent on rhetorical persuasion. The later standard writing course, "Writing in the Disciplines"

(FD14A), that the ELS developed was meant to address students' writing needs in disciplinary groupings. Although it revealed prejudices regarding sorting of students into strong and weak writers, it had the potential to be a bridge course. This course could have helped students to shuttle between general and disciplinary writing, and helped faculty in the ELS and in other disciplines to collaborate in the interest of students' writing development. The WAC pilot project that was introduced in 2006–2007 came closest to promoting writing instruction within disciplines. However, it reflected limited considerations of content faculty's actual role in writing instruction and development, and it did not enjoy campus-wide support.

Confronting Misconceptions about Teaching Academic Writing to Creole-Influenced Students

In the first semester of the 2009–2010 academic year the first quality assurance review of the ELS was undertaken, arising from discontent inside and outside of the ELS and from attendant requests from ELS insiders and outsiders – although a formal review of established disciplines had become standard practice in the institution in the late 1990s (see Dyche et al. 2010, 110–13; OBUS 2009, 1). The report derived from this review would support much of what course facilitators knew about the development of academic literacies as well as propose new pathways to benefit students and foster staff development. Among these, the reviewers noted unrealistic expectations in the institution that "the foundation courses ought to, and can, guarantee that students who pass a single one of the Language Foundation courses will always be able to produce error-free prose" (OBUS 2009, 9). Because of the misconception that writing is a generic skill, one-semester courses in academic writing had been the norm in the institution. To address that misconception, the reviewers reminded of current scholarship on writing development of which course facilitators were well aware:

> Writing is not a single set of practices, hence students' ability to produce a certain kind of writing with ease is not indicative of their ability to produce other kinds of writing: fluency in writing is instead contingent on a host of factors, including degree of cognitive challenge, familiarity with genre, time constraints, affective conditions. This means that errors students make in their syntax or use of notational conventions may be a sign not that they lack "basics" but that they are undertaking more challenging work instead of remaining in the preserve of attempting what they already know how to do. (10)

The reviewers also noted that because of the designation of the courses as foundation and because of factors over which course facilitators had no control, the language programme "appears to remain caught in its actual offerings within a more generic view of writing" (OBUS 2009, 10). In other words, it seemed that the courses "offer students generic and fixed sets of forms and processes for writing; and the lack of a full programme of courses that the Section staff would like to offer gives the false impression to students that writing practices are uniform rather than diverse and changing" (10-11). Reminding that "a language curriculum that treats writing as a uniform, generic set of forms and skills will *not* prepare students for their continuing education and development as writers" (10), the reviewers proposed that the ELS rename the foundation courses as "Critical Writing or Critical Language Skills courses to more accurately reflect what they can and cannot accomplish" (13); require students to take at least two such courses, one of which could be the course in argument (UC10B); and develop a more varied programme to address the diverse needs of students, reflect the variability in writing in different disciplines, and be true to current scholarship in the discipline of rhetoric and composition or academic literacies.

In response to the recommendations, senior members of the ELS decided to redesign FD10A (and FD14A) as Critical Academic Literacies I (CAL I) and UC10B as Critical Academic Literacies II (CAL II). The latter (CAL II) was to focus on argument and critical thinking and the former (CAL I) would comprise four faculty-specific prongs involving critical reading and writing in the various faculties – with each refined based on consultation with colleagues in each faculty. Preliminary responses from colleagues in Pure and Applied Sciences and Social Sciences suggested that faculties outside of Humanities and Education would not be able to accommodate UC10B – another nondisciplinary offering – in their programmes. ELS members, therefore, focused on using comments and suggestions from colleagues in other faculties to refine CAL I, yielding Critical Reading and Writing in Education; Critical Reading and Writing in the Social Sciences; Critical Reading and Writing in Pure and Applied Sciences and Medical Sciences (later Science and Technology and Medical Sciences); and Critical Reading and Expository Writing in the Humanities. Although Humanities and Education are in one merged faculty, they were separated and the (unfortunate) emphasis on "exposition" in the Humanities' course was meant to account for the fact that those students – unlike all others – would benefit from the course in argument (UC10B) in the second semester of their first year. The ELS also developed a year-long course called Critical Reading and Writing in the Disciplines for students who would normally be recommended to take "Fundamentals of English". This development regarding "Fundamentals of English" was – partly – in keeping with the reviewers' suggestion that "to give those who need the course more incentive to take it, this course might be stretched to take place over two semesters in reduced size classes, with those completing the one-year version fulfilling the equivalent work for FD10A and therefore earning equivalent credit" (OBUS 2009, 5).[25] Although many members of the ELS were not able to contribute to the courses or the discussion surrounding them, some senior members of the ELS and departmental administration proceeded to seek approval of the "new" courses. Following approval of the courses by the Mona faculty boards and Academic Board, the Board for Undergraduate Studies approved them in January 2013, leading to the aforementioned "Bloody English" news article.

This new slate of courses would present commonplace challenges in terms of time to take root and be evaluated. Based on evaluations of the first few years of offering this new slate of courses, ELS members would be expected to effect changes as much as would be allowed in the aspects of courses that they can control. However, readers can imagine that with the shift – in the main – from one thirteen-week one-semester general writing course to another thirteen-week one-semester faculty-specific writing course, the quality assurance reviewers' observations would probably still be applicable: "The current arrangement of all students except Humanities being required to take only one Level 1 one-semester English Language Foundation course puts undue pressure on these individual courses and the students enrolled by failing to give sufficient time for the course to accomplish what is needed" (OBUS 2009, 13). The reality is that what remain in question are *one-semester courses* in which facilitators have a greater task of addressing general writing requirements and discipline-specific strategies in faculty-specific courses in one semester of thirteen weeks. If the dynamics are not carefully planned, these faculty-specific courses could, therefore, prove even more burdensome than their (more) general predecessors for both facilitators and students. Again what the reviewers noted in 2009 could still hold true in later years when "faculty-specific" is substituted for "foundation": "What other universities attempt to accomplish in an array of courses over several semesters the Foundation courses are charged with accomplishing in a single course in a single semester" (11).

Recommendations for Abandoning Misconceptions about Teaching Academic Writing to Creole-Influenced Students

How, then, can this situation be avoided? More generally, how can content faculty and writing specialists help to foster increased numbers of Creole-influenced students who master content knowledge but are also engaged in advancing the discipline through creating knowledge that they can communicate to disciplinary and other audiences?

Changing Terms for Discussing Writing

The history of writing instruction at the UWI, revealing continued separation of writing and learning and inadequate attention to the country's linguistic realities, suggests that faculty need to change the terms in which writing is discussed and develop a shared vocabulary and better articulation of writing. If the "writing"/"English" problem that faculty often mention is to be addressed in the high school as Chevannes (2005) and others say, what will content faculty at the UWI do to help high school teachers? Sometimes, academics' saying that the high school should prepare students could well be the problem. Some schools may be trying to complete the UWI curriculum instead of teaching students the aspects of the English language – the language of instruction – that they need to know based on the extent of the influence of Creole in their lives. Further, what makes the Jamaican situation interesting is not only that the rhetoric of transparent disciplinarity and the myth of transience are perpetuated in higher education, but also that when academics transfer the responsibility for students' writing development to teachers at the secondary level, they are transferring their challenge into an already knotty situation.

Language (instruction) was for a very long time rather ill-defined and consistent with colonial policies that have yielded little success in terms of students' acquisition or mastery of English. Predominantly Creole speakers at the secondary level continue to fail at alarming (though really *unsurprising*) rates in English examinations, academic writing course reports continue to highlight grammar as being one of the main reasons for students' failure, and employers and other members of the public do not judge such students' language abilities favourably. Thanks to the democratization of education after the 1970s, far more students than before from heavily Creole-influenced backgrounds have accessed postelementary education. However, the reality is, as Brown (1991) and Drayton (1990, 1999) propose, that monolingual Creole-speaking students who got the opportunity to access secondary and postsecondary education have probably transformed the school system more than it has transformed their language usage. Taylor (2003) confirmed this suspicion in her report of a study of the verbal encounters in a range of schools from grade 2 at the primary level to the university level. Taylor discovered "widespread and unselfconscious use of Creole and concomitant absence of English" (235). The classrooms she observed were "in various stages of surrender or accommodation to the dissolution of the hegemony of English" (238). This situation parallels what school inspectors observed in late nineteenth and early twentieth century Jamaica, and what has happened in the wider society where Creole is openly and increasingly used in public places that were once considered formal and reserved for English.

Academics cannot afford to ignore these social realities when planning for student development in higher education. Indeed, it seems unwise to ignore the consequences of implementing monolingual education policies in a society that is not monolingual and where the language imposed in education is not that of the demographic majority. Whether academics like it or not, in an age when educators are encountering increasing numbers of students from groups/communities traditionally underrepresented in higher education, a key concern has to be how to address grammar – the grammar of the language of writing and instruction – while not keeping students' focus on formalist concerns – a focus that can prevent development in thinking, knowledge acquisition and communication through writing.

Other questions related to "terms" that may be useful for academics to consider include the following: What do we mean by *being prepared before* university? What do students learn before coming to the university? Should we be thinking about what each student may need, based on discipline/field and future employment/profession? What will the student entering engineering or computer science need as opposed to one going into history or linguistics? The responses to these questions should inform plans for what students will learn in the academy. However, the institution has also to engage with what students will do with their learning in professions after they graduate. As Devonish (1998, 2) emphasizes in a paper presented to the Board for Undergraduate Studies regarding developments in testing and language courses, what will graduates need in their professional fields? What should "the exit level [writing] competences of UWI graduates . . . be?" To adequately address these questions, writing specialists and other faculty throughout the university need to develop a shared vocabulary for talking about writing – a vocabulary that goes beyond basic/minor *skills* to discussion of writing *abilities* and disciplinary ways of knowing, doing and writing. Ultimately, better articulation of writing instruction may be needed throughout the education system to coordinate what students learn in preuniversity settings, what they should learn in the academy, and what they are likely to do with that learning beyond the academy.

Adopting a Rhetorical Stance

Because of the weaknesses outlined in the ways in which Mona's administrators and faculty seem to have understood writing and how students learn to produce it in the multiple disciplines that constitute the academy, I propose a transcultural rhetorical perspective on writing that goes beyond superficial considerations of purpose in a predetermined genre in both general first-year courses and WAC and beyond faculty-specific courses, and that attends to Creole-influenced students' transcultural sensibilities. A rhetorical approach rests on the view that disciplines are rhetorically constructed through writing and on the knowledge that writing makes learning visible to students and facilitators. It also requires all stakeholders' awareness that Creole-influenced students' writing development is ongoing, necessary for achieving social equity, and a shared responsibility. By attending to writing, Creole-influenced Jamaican students can begin to reflect upon their own learning processes, and by attending to writing, Mona's faculty can discover strategic junctures in students' learning processes where intervention and collaboration can be most effective. By attending to writing, content faculty at Mona are challenged to address how knowledge is composed in their respective disciplines and the processes that students go through to acquire and convey that knowledge as well as contribute to knowledge making. By attending to writing, the UWI at Mona is also challenged to attend to students' learning processes, including what students learn before coming to the institution, what they will learn in the institution, and what they will do with that learning after they leave. As writing faculty usually experience in the classroom, attending to writing can enable the institution to discover strategic sites in the learning process where interventions and collaborations can help Creole-influenced students. General first-year writing is one of those sites, WAC is another and faculty-specific writing is but another. As Merrill and Miller (2002) assert in the third epigraph in this chapter, rhetoric provides useful categories for such interventions because its attention to purpose, audience and situation provides facilitators and students with metacognitive categories that can be used to help students in transferring learning from prior occasions to novel situations and problems.

Rhetoric can also help foster the connection between writing and what anthropologists Carlos Vélez-Ibáñez and James Greenberg (2005) call "funds of knowledge". These are the "strategic and cultural resources that households contain" (47). Other educators use this concept in their work to refer to the interpretive strategies, cultural assumptions and collaborative networks that students bring to the academy (see González, Moll and Amanti 2005). Rhetoric can foster the connection between students' "funds of knowledge" and academic writing requirements if faculty break out of formalistic modes such as exposition and work from the language, experience and engagements that Creole-influenced Jamaican students bring to the classroom. A rhetorical stance on writing focuses not on formal conventions but on interpretive and problem-solving strategies that can be used in varied situations. It enables understanding that writing, as Canagarajah (2010, 176) expresses, is not "a narrowly defined process of text construction" but is instead "rhetorical negotiation for achieving social meanings and functions". As I have argued in this book, keeping disciplinary writing knowledge tacit or shrouding it in formalism works to alienate learning in the academy from learning and language outside the academy. A better approach is for all faculty to provide students with connected ways of knowing, doing and writing; and rhetoric's aides for metacognitive analyses can help with that challenge. As "an ability, in each . . . case, to see the available means of persuasion" (Aristotle 1991, 37), and with its attention to situation, purpose and audience, *rhetoric* may help faculty and students make the connections in writing between disciplines' different ways of reading and re-making the world and their own varied ways of responding to such re-readings.

Drawing on Creole-Influenced Students' Transcultural Sensibilities: Intersections with Code-Meshing and Translingualism

Jamaican students' ways of reading the world are necessarily transcultural. Jamaican Creole epitomizes transculturation. Confirming this ongoing process of selection and reinvention that takes place when cultures/languages come in contact are Hazel Simmons-McDonald and Ian Robertson's (2006) observations that a few Creole varieties are becoming anglicized or decreolized, and therefore sharing more similarities with English than those at the other end of the Creole-English continuum. Bearing in mind this natural process that occurs in interactions in society, educators should consider how we may usefully employ it in classrooms to help bridge divides between Creole and English, between students' ways of knowing and doing and the institution's requirements. In a word, we should consider adopting *transcultural* rhetoric that, as Louise Rodriguez Connal (2000, 321) writes, "expresses the sensibilities of people whose cultures are hybridized – people who affiliate with two or more cultures, languages, or dialects". A transcultural approach will include educators' acknowledgement of the different varieties of language that obtain in the society, students' varied relationships with and uses of these varieties and the different discourse communities that constitute educational institutions. In higher education, a transcultural rhetoric of writing involves crossing and bridging divides to include the diversity that necessarily attends expansions in education.

Jamaicans are influenced by Creole in varying ways and display a range of linguistic postures including being English-only speakers who understand Creole, English-dominant bilinguals, Creole-dominant bilinguals, equally bilingual in Creole and English, or Creole-only speakers who may or may not understand English. Because of their experiences with two different language varieties – including more than ten years of schooling in which the language of instruction is English, Creole-influenced students in a university are not likely to be "Creole-only speakers who do not understand English". Many Jamaican university students (who display forms of bilingualism) are adept at code-switching in speech and code-shifting in writing. However, as in supposedly monolingual situations where there is variable language competence, some Jamaican students experience difficulty in switching between English and Creole or in shifting to English when required. These latter students may lack metalinguistic awareness of their different languages and tend to produce mixtures of both languages in which meaning is not immediately accessible to an English-speaking audience. All Creole-influenced Jamaican university students, however, have what Craig (1994, 130) describes as "a diglossic capacity" for switching between their two languages. For Craig, "this is the root of their special problem" which manifests in difficulties with reading, vocabulary and comprehension (ibid.). I recognize the real challenges that attend many Creole-influenced individuals' ability to code-switch, and encourage the need for measures to address the same where they appear in higher education.[26] Though switching and shifting can reflect difficulties in manipulating linguistic codes (see Buell 2004; Craig, 1999, 42), they can reflect attention to one's situation, purpose and, even more so, audience. And audience is a pervasive notion with which individuals grapple in a university. From interacting broadly with administrators versus academics and specifically with facilitators and peers in individual departments and units, students have to consider who the recipient of their oral and written presentations is. After all, the audience will determine the content and discourse features that attend such.

Making shifts based on audience is virtually second nature for the average Creole-influenced Jamaican – and this is an ability that content faculty can draw on to enable students to transcreate knowledge and experiences. Transcreation is a term that I am borrowing from advertising. Used with reference to cross-cultural endeavours in advertising or marketing, transcreation is a highly audience-aware strategy, the aim being to tailor advertisements or products (such as websites or posters) originally designed for other audiences to suit new ones through evoking in the new audience(s) the same reactions triggered in the original audience. Making material originally designed for a source audience resonate with a new audience requires intimate knowledge of the target language and other cultural elements: transcreation involves much word-play to balance fidelity to the impact of the original message, idiomatic accuracy and respect of cultural nuances in the target audience. Therefore, as with translation, while the transcreator needs to be creative and have knowledge of the languages and nuances of both source and target cultures, the target audience's language is usually (one of) the transcreator's native language(s). As expressed, Creole-influenced students – in the main – are influenced by at least two language varieties. By virtue of their experiences, these students are prime candidates for engagement in transcreation as they move from one language to another, one discipline to another, one domain to another, from academy to society and so on – but with some *assistance*. The Creole-influenced speaker knows something very well – to make audience accommodations. Drawing on this fund of knowledge, faculty can assist Creole-influenced students in addressing the question, "How do you write to respect the expectations of the audience?"

Since, as Craig (1999, 6) writes, many Jamaicans' receptive knowledge of English is higher than their productive competence in the language, students may tend to transcreate material into their preferred language after hearing that material in another language. In the case of students for whom Creole is dominant, new/understood material that needs to be reflected to an English audience undergoes multistage processing: besides the initial transcreation (from English to Creole), the students have to consider requirements of the audience, translate and recreate from the source (what they as Creole-dominant speakers know) to suit the audience, and be constantly aware of and resisting the eternal presence of their diglossic potential, whose influence will vary for different individuals. Given these variations, some students will be able to transcreate knowledge fairly quickly and effectively while others will need assistance to do the same. Creole-students' transcultural nature – their acquaintance with more than one language and rhetorical style – calls for careful scaffolding from more experienced faculty so students can, to borrow from Canagarajah (2010, 175), "carve out a space for themselves within conflicting discourses".

But a transcultural perspective can also help facilitators understand deliberate mixes that some Creole-influenced students may produce as they attempt to meet various audiences' expectations. Besides those who comfortably or uncomfortably shift to think in one language when required, many Creole-influenced individuals are like those Latinos Juan Flores (1993, 219) describes in his use of the concept of transcreation with reference to Latino linguistic inventiveness – "interlingual innovation". Flores's description helps with understanding this aspect of Creole-influenced student writers' linguistic development: "Even for the most monolingual of Latinos, the 'other' language looms constantly as a potential resource, and the option to vary according to different speech contexts is used far more often than not" (219–20). This situation is quite similar to the diglossic nature of Creole-influenced students, most of whom have at their disposal two language varieties – elements of which they use in combination depending on their abilities. Indeed, the situation of Latinos and Creole-influenced students is typical of multilinguals. As Flores asserts, "'Trans-creation', understood in this sense of intercultural variability and transferability, is the hallmark of border language practice" (220). The creative linguistic practices involved in transcreation hint at a kind of freedom and a focus on genuine communication:

> The irreverence implicit in trans-creative expression need not be deliberately defiant in motive; it reflects rather a largely unspoken disregard for conventionally bounded usages insofar as such circumscription obstructs the need for optimal specificity of communicative and cultural context. The guiding impulse, articulated or not, is one of play, freedom and even empowerment in the sense that access to individual and collective referentiality cannot ultimately be blocked. (Flores 1993, 220)

This perspective on writing accepts linguistic inventiveness as enabling communication even while ignoring traditional usages.

In adopting this posture – accepting linguistic inventiveness that might not reflect conventional usage but that enables communication, faculty would not be alone. Indeed, some readers may have recognized that the transcultural rhetorical perspective that I suggest with regard to Creole-influenced Jamaican students intersects with other proposals of educator-researchers in the United States for engaging with the various languages that multilingual students use. These proposals are linked to the increasing numbers of nontraditional students who present varied linguistics resources (and challenges) in higher education. They include the strategy of code-meshing – incorporating non-standard dialects and other Englishes in standard language materials (Canagarajah 2006; V.A. Young 2007, 2009) – and the philosophy of translingualism, whose proponents value difference in language and encourage negotiation, rather than reliance on fixed rules and forms, for production of meaning in interactions (Horner et al. 2011). These proposals arise from beliefs about similarities in dialects of English (V.A. Young 2007, 134), about the languages of multilinguals constituting a continuous – rather than discrete – repertoire on which they draw in each instance of communication (Canagarajah 2009, 19–23), and about academic underachievement arising from code-switching pedagogies (V.A. Young 2007, 106; 2009) that enforce what Horner and Trimbur (2002, 594) call "a tacit policy of unidirectional English monolingualism". Proposals in Jamaica for including the home language in elementary levels of education would be considered an attempt to *accommodate* linguistic difference in education. Code-meshing goes beyond this kind of accommodation to *incorporate* differences: "code-meshing promotes linguistic democracy, as students are not called to choose but rather allowed to blend language and identities" (V.A. Young, Martinez and Naviaux 2011, xxiv). Advocates of translingualism, in their turn, propose new perspectives on error, calling for educators to engage with expressions that appear unidiomatic but convey a range of valuable meanings when plumbed (see Lu 1994, 2004, 2010; Canagarajah 2010, 175–76) and for *all* language users – and not just the previously minoritized – to engage in conscious meaning-making work (Canagarajah 2010, 177; Horner et al. 2011, 307).

Blending codes or dialects or styles (code-meshing) and determining meaning in each given interaction (translingualism) are standard features of the lived reality of many bi/multilinguals, including Creole-influenced students, so I can envisage the intertwined pedagogical, psychological and sociopolitical benefits that code-meshing and translingualism promise. Indeed, as a conscious code-mesher and as an educator who can testify to the sheer trials and failures of many Creole-influenced language users in their attempts to function in English only, I endorse these pedagogical initiatives. However, for those same reasons and more, I am careful to indicate how application of these initiatives could be problematic for Creole-influenced students – many of whom have been disenfranchised by a system that ignores the need for differentiated instruction. As I have written elsewhere, in applying these strategies, educators of Creole-influenced students are likely to encounter challenges based on factors such as some language users' inability to code-switch effectively, the way Creole languages are stigmatized and the value communities attach to the various languages they use so that some ardent code-switchers and code-shifters would reject Creole inclusion in any form in a classroom (see Milson-Whyte 2011, 2013, 2014). In a word, while I deem it useful to include natural practices in classroom settings, I also consider important the value communities attach to the various languages they use, because this valuing is a critical inhibitory factor to needed radical changes in education.

These important considerations are linked to the treatment of linguistic differences. In promoting code-meshing as a pedagogical strategy, V.A. Young (2007, 134) argues that what he calls Black English Vernacular and White English Vernacular are not very different, and students blend them in their everyday interactions (106). In their turn, Horner et al. (2011, 307) propose that "in endorsing a translingual approach, we seek to move beyond an additive notion of multilingualism. We call for working to achieve fluency across language differences in our reading and writing, speaking and listening, so that we become adept at processes of making and conveying meaning." Both camps are less concerned with differences in individual languages and more concerned with what can be achieved through cross-languaging. This perspective is good, but, perhaps, not immediately useful for the current Jamaican context where many Creole-influenced students have been disenfranchised because of tacit assumptions about similarities in Creole and English – even while Creole was being stigmatized – and resultant neglect to help students develop metacognitive awareness of the differences in the language varieties they use. Significant pedagogical changes are needed for many Jamaican students to be able to distinguish Jamaican Creole from standard English for circumstances that continue to require production in English and to be able to appreciate when they are consciously code-meshing – in terms of actually blending two *different* varieties for specific outcomes – as circumstances allow. And this kind of engagement is likely to be supported by legitimizing the Creole language – a move that would involve establishing linguistic boundaries and which would counter recent discussions about blurred linguistics boundaries promoted by code-meshing and about developing fluency across languages promoted by advocates of translingualism. Additionally, proposals for translingual work tend to be based on the view that students are not only bi-/multilingual but also bi/multiliterate (Bawarshi 2010; Canagarajah 2010) – a situation that does not hold true for most Jamaicans who are literate in English but not also in Creole.[27] Given Jamaican peculiarities and considering the range of coverage of this book to include facilitators in not only general writing courses but also specific disciplinary courses, I consider it useful for educators to begin with a transcultural approach to include transcreation because, as presented, it could advance efforts at legitimizing Creole varieties (whether these are separate Creoles in the Caribbean or the various dialects of Jamaican Creole), help Creole-influenced students develop metacognitive awareness of their linguistic resources, and encourage educators to engage in the attendant reflective teaching for these students' academic writing development.

Ultimately, as Wilson, Pereira and Dyche (1995) suggest, the university needs to consider the attributes of the population from which it selects incoming students to determine resources and opportunities needed for students' advanced writing development. Additionally, faculty may need to adjust how they read what is traditionally viewed as errors in students' writing in English. Attempting to learn from, rather than manage, errors in students' writing may teach much about not only students' linguistic inventiveness but also their development with regard to English and disciplinary content. Drawing on Creole-influenced students' penchant for varying language to suit audience needs or for engaging in linguistic inventiveness can contribute to educators' endeavours to help students shift into and become comfortable in different discursive and disciplinary domains as they learn to adopt and adapt the features of these domains for optimal communication.

Making Rhetoric Visible in the Plural Academy to Contribute to Social Equity

Faculty can also help assure Creole-influenced Jamaican students' development by ceasing to promote separation between knowledge creation and acquisition, writing and learning and by acknowledging the plural nature of the academy. Crucial to their endeavours is engagement of a twofold rhetorical perspective on writing: acknowledgement of the suasive nature of writing in disciplines and attention to rhetoric's aides – purpose, context and audience – to determine appropriateness of modes of writing. Important, too, is content faculty's understanding that their engagement will determine the extent of students' writing development and achievement of both social equity and disciplinary excellence. In other words, there is need for students' writing development to become the acknowledged responsibility of every faculty member – a better understanding of writing instruction than the misconception at the secondary level that *anybody can teach English*.

Acceptance of the proposal at Mona to teach four *faculty-specific* writing courses indicates content faculty's acknowledgement of the plural nature of the academy. However, given that each faculty is made up of several individual departments/disciplines, students are still likely to get *very good*, general exposure to writing in different areas in a specific faculty. As the quality assurance reviewers noted, "Insofar as writing affects knowing, students writing in specific disciplines and reflecting on differences in the writing practices of diverse disciplines could come to learn not just diverse ways of writing, but the differences that these ways of writing make in what is known" (OBUS 2009, 13–14). Such learning occurs when courses are "taught in a way engaging students in researching and contesting such differences" (14). The reality is that such opportunities require time that – as has already been stated – is limited in a thirteen-week one-semester offering. Given the differences in writing in individual disciplines, content faculty cannot expect the "faculty" umbrella to cover the discourse features of all disciplines. Faculty-specific courses are but "bridge" courses, involving writing "in"/"from" many disciplines in a faculty and preparing students for writing "inside" specific disciplines. Content faculty will, therefore, need to *build on* the experiences and skills students gain in their one-semester writing course. This expansion should include discussions about specific requirements in a specific discipline that are likely to be different from those in other disciplines – so that content faculty reveal their understanding that plurality in the academy extends beyond different faculties (schools, colleges, or departments) to individual disciplines. Creole-influenced students, by their very linguistic and cultural experiences with audience awareness, are advantageously poised to manipulate such differences as they take courses from different disciplines.

To successfully assist in Creole-influenced students' initiation into their disciplines and development in writing, content faculty will have to break out of "the habit of disciplines to make their rhetoric invisible in the service of epistemic authority" (Bazerman 1995, 259). Often faculty do not articulate their disciplinary conventions because of the gradual way in which they learn them, because there is little reward for engaging in such articulation, and because if disciplinary conventions remain tacit, disciplines and their adherents remain competitive in the academy. It seems commonsensical, however, that students will more readily or effectively learn a discipline's discursive practices if faculty make them visible to students. After all, the reality is that if fewer students are conscious of effective disciplinary writing practices, fewer students will succeed in the discipline and even fewer in the larger professional community. Only the few who are succeeding are likely to be in the community's inner circle and lauded for their accomplishments. Russell (2002, 306) identifies the dilemma elsewhere when he writes,

> If the educational system teaches greater numbers of students to enter academic discourse communities, and through them, coveted professional roles, there may be increased competition, economic dislocation and political conflict. If, however, the system frankly acknowledges that it is excluding students from professional communities on the basis of their language rather than committing its resources to teaching the linguistic forms of those communities to those students, the results might also be painful.

Content faculty should also avoid denying the rhetorical and persuasive aspects of their disciplinary writing practices because they wish to distance themselves from rhetoric's association with the probable – that which is like truth – rather than with Truth. Content faculty often claim to be doing disinterested, objective writing, but such a claim is challenged by the very fact that they aim to publish what they write, which means attempting to convince readers to accept the way that faculty recount their experiences in writing. Additionally, since all texts aim to influence, that is, persuade readers to adjust their feelings, attitudes, beliefs, or actions, all texts may be said to be *suasive*. In other words, all texts reflect persuasion, what Carolyn Miller and Davida Charney (2007, 594) rightly call "the underlying essence of human communicative language use". Even if content faculty were to disagree that all writing is informed by rhetoric and its attention to context, audience and purpose, that is, if they were to believe that there are nonpersuasive types of writing – as narrative, descriptive and expository writing are thought to be – students would still need help with producing such writing *within/inside* specific disciplines.

If content faculty acknowledge the suasive nature of writing, they can help students become aware of the extent to which disciplines are language communities whose approaches and practices are shaped by language. General first-year writing courses and faculty-specific courses may introduce students to forms of writing and thinking found in many disciplines, but not to the actual writing and thinking within a specific discipline. The reality is that often what is taught in a first-year writing course in institutions will reflect where the writing programme is based. Very often the focus is literary or linguistic analysis because the programme is located in the humanities, and specifically in an English or linguistics department. Because writing is context-bound, "a collaborative process of negotiating situational exigencies" (Merrill and Miller 2002, 24), teaching it only in a general writing course can pose problems for facilitators and students. Content faculty's involvement in writing instruction can help students understand the concept that effective writing is suitable for its purpose, context and audience. Whereas the facilitator in a general writing course may not fully appreciate an effective piece of writing directed to physicists, for example, because that appreciation is dependent on certain shared facts, procedures and interpretative practices, other content faculty can help students understand the context-bound nature of "good" writing. Faculty-specific courses, in their turn, are likely to focus on writing found in the various disciplines in a faculty, and facilitators can help students identify metacognitive aspects of such writing. However, to successfully join their respective disciplines, students need expert initiation into their discipline's language practices. Moreover, for students to develop in the disciplinary community, content faculty have to *build on*, to *expand*, what students glean from facilitators in introductory writing courses.

Besides acknowledging the contingency involved in writing in all disciplines, content faculty should appreciate writing's power in making learning visible. As Merrill and Miller (2002, 205) remind writing programme administrators, "writing can make learning visible" in ways that can disorient content faculty because when students present their writing, faculty realize "they can no longer assume that what they teach is what students learn". That writing makes learning visible leads to unease among faculty when writing reveals that the students learned neither the content nor the discourse features for conveying the content. For content faculty to meaningfully address this situation, they have to "recognize that courses are co-authored with students" (ibid.). Such coauthoring yields success when newcomers are appropriately initiated into a discipline's rhetorical perspectives, that is, how the discipline works. Unfortunately, however, faculty often persist in critiquing the student learning (or lack thereof) that is made visible through writing, rather than begin to exploit writing's potential beyond demonstrating learning. In other words, they continue to consider writing, as Merrill and Miller say, as "an isolated skill" rather than as "a means of negotiating situational constraints to achieve shared purposes" (206). However, if faculty acknowledge that writing is more than a way to demonstrate or test learning, faculty can help students understand writing as a way to learn, to think and to construct new knowledge.

If content faculty emphasize *processes* in developing writing, they can help students to appreciate both summative and formative writing, rather than just the former with which students and faculty are accustomed and whose revelatory nature can be discomfiting. Unfortunately, however, content faculty often resist a "process" approach to writing. Although they may acknowledge the processes for themselves, content faculty do not always guide students through them. This assumption can be made on the basis that the focus is usually on the written product that is graded and returned to students or kept as university property for a specified period and then discarded. The various process stages such as planning, drafting, peer editing, and revising are not usually built into content syllabuses. Of course, the suggestion here is not that content courses should begin to look like introductory writing courses, but rather that content faculty should consider how they, too, will enable Creole-influenced students' writing development by drawing on some aspects of process writing. In year 2 of the WAC project at Mona, students were required to produce at least two drafts of essays in a few courses in life sciences and economics (Altidor-Brooks 2008). One drawback, however, was that the reader of early drafts was not always the faculty member who taught the course but an assistant (graduate student) or another faculty member who got leave of absence from teaching to respond to drafts. Where it is difficult to include multidrafting, content faculty can help students increase their proficiency in writing by "includ[ing] a series of smaller writing assignments that are designed to structure students' learning sequentially" (College of New Jersey 2004). By emphasizing processes in developing writing, content faculty can help students appreciate that writing is both a learning technology and an epistemic activity that is complex: "Learning to write is a complex process, both individual and social, that takes place over time with continued practice and informed guidance" (Council [2000] 2008). It is a lifelong practice that shapes thinking, learning and knowledge creation and distribution.

Omission of the process stages or sequentially arranged writing assignments from many syllabuses may be because content faculty often consider stages in writing preparation as transparent. As Russell and Foster (2002, 33) remind, "Because writing is so deeply embedded in modern education in the form of lecture notes, exams, reports, journals, research papers and countless others, it tends to be transparent, an element that in many systems cannot be separated from the larger work of learning. It often disappears, becomes unavailable as an object of discussion, as do discussions of its teaching." However, as Mary Jane Curry and Theresa Lillis (2003, 3) highlight, even if content faculty could assume that disciplinary rules and conventions were a part of students' "'common sense' knowledge" when the higher education system was "small and predominantly homogenous", that assumption is "no longer justified within current contexts where significant changes are affecting all aspects of teaching and learning, including student academic writing". Given the changes in student intake at Mona, and as Lillis (1999) observes in UK universities, content faculty cannot continue to view the writing conventions of their disciplines as "common sense" because many first-generation university students are often not familiar with those conventions. These students may have, as Bizzell ([1982] 2003, 401) observed in students elsewhere, "such limited experience outside their native discourse communities that they are unaware that there is such a thing as a discourse community with conventions to be mastered. What is underdeveloped is their knowledge of the ways experience is constituted and interpreted in the academic discourse community and of the fact that all discourse communities constitute and interpret experience." Lillis (1999, 127) asserts that the confusion such students experience in higher education indicates "an institutional practice of mystery" that is so "ideologically inscribed that it works against those least familiar with the conventions surrounding academic writing". In the Jamaican context, faculty have to remember that the concern is increasing numbers of not only first-generation university students, but also Creole-influenced students with varying levels of mastery in English. Addressing the diversity of such student populations implies, as Lillis and Turner (2001, 66) write,

> a need to cloud the discourse of transparency, to reflexively critique the assumptions and expectations that have their roots in a socio-culturally different historical period and look to the formation of new pedagogies that better engage with students, who are welcomed into the academy by the rhetoric of widening participation, but at the same time denied an adequate participation by taken-for-granted assumptions about academic conventions.

If faculty expect Creole-influenced students to enter and meaningfully contribute to the conversations in their discipline during or after studies, faculty cannot continue to rely on tacit assumptions that may be embedded in disciplinary reading and writing requirements. Faculty will have to teach students explicitly to transform their discipline in the same way that faculty attempt to do through their research and writing. Lillis (1999, 144) recommends that for first-generation university students to succeed in academia, content faculty should consider more contact with them regarding writing, that is, more discussion of writing tasks and disciplinary writing conventions. What she advises in the United Kingdom is applicable elsewhere:

"Although this may be considered difficult, if not impossible to organize within the constraints of current resources, it is a price that has to be paid if widening access to higher education is our aim." The reality is that the social cost of past policies in Jamaica is so great that although differentiated instruction – as in a basic writing course, standard writing courses inflected to suit specific kinds of Creole-influenced students, or in extra consultation sessions with students in disciplines – may be costly, it may very well be useful if it is informed by what students' writing teaches about the needs of current Creole-influenced students. Teaching in "Writing in the Disciplines" (FD14A) suggested an attempt to provide differentiated instruction since that course was arguably similar to honours courses in the United States. However, that course seemed to have grouped too many different kinds of Creole-influenced learners having wide-ranging associations with and mastery of English language. The course also lacked its equivalent at the lower end – a course for writers with far less developed abilities in reading and writing in English. Reinstituting one kind of basic writing in the stretch course, "Critical Reading and Writing in the Disciplines", means that the needs of students with known or immediately obvious weaknesses in writing in English will be addressed. But what of students with high or average passes in qualifying examinations but who write in ways that lead to questions about their passes? Given the diglossic capacity that can lead to problems for Creole-influenced students, what opportunities are available for continued development of students' metalinguistic awareness of contrasts in Creole and English? Since administrators at the UWI at Mona are no longer educating a tiny elite but have opened up the institution to more students, they have to consider how to consistently provide writing instruction for a *range* of Creole-influenced students.

As the UWI at Mona faces undeniable expansion in enrolment, content faculty can aid more students in realizing their academic, intellectual and professional potential by explicitly initiating students into disciplinary writing practices. If content faculty do not provide explicit disciplinary writing instruction to address the issues of access and exclusion, the institution is not likely to realize the equality that is implied in the democratization of education in Jamaica and in the Caribbean region. Additionally, administrators cannot expect excellence when they admit Creole-influenced students with less than the required writing competences in English but neglect to provide appropriate writing resources for them. As Russell (2002, 331) writes, "Our lives are linked by the written word in ways so pervasive and mundane that we forget sometimes how powerful writing is." Writing is, indeed, "powerful, even when it seems transparent – and . . . the problems of learning to write in new ways are not transient but a permanent condition of (post)modern life" (ibid.). Faculty ought, therefore, to desist from associating weaknesses revealed in writing with any lack in students – what Merrill and Miller (2002, 207) reject as some "personal inability to learn a natural skill" – when the issue may well be "the discipline's failure to articulate its work" to neophytes so that they can become familiar with its genres and conventions or faculty's failure to learn from students' attempts to critically engage with disciplinary discourses.

Facilitating Students' Necessary, Ongoing Writing Development

Content faculty may be concerned about *what* they would teach were they to become integrally involved in writing instruction. The suggestions in the Council for Writing Program Administrators' ([2000] 2008) *Outcomes Statement for First-Year Composition* may be a good place for content and writing faculty to begin to plan a sequenced writing programme. This statement proposes five major outcomes for writing instruction: rhetorical knowledge; critical thinking, reading and writing; processes; knowledge of conventions; and composing in electronic environments. To help students develop "rhetorical knowledge", faculty would help students learn the main features and uses of writing as well as readers' expectations in their fields. With regard to "critical thinking, reading, and writing", faculty could help students to learn the "uses of writing as a critical thinking method", the "interactions among critical thinking, reading, and writing" and the "relationships among language, knowledge, and power in their fields". To help students understand "processes", faculty could help students learn "to build final results in stages", "review work-in-progress in collaborative peer groups for purposes other than editing", "save extensive editing for later parts of the writing process" and "apply the technologies commonly used to research and communicate within their fields". Students can develop their "knowledge of conventions" if faculty help them learn the "conventions of usage, specialized vocabulary, format, and documentation in their fields" as well as "strategies through which better control of conventions can be achieved". Despite variations in use, digital technologies are involved in writing in all disciplines in the twenty-first century. Students can hone their skills in using these technologies with content faculty's guidance on "how to engage in the electronic research and composing processes common in their fields" and "how to disseminate texts in both print and electronic forms in their fields".

There are also the few examples of courses in the institution that suggest content faculty's attempts at contributing to students' writing development – even though they may not be part of a sequenced programme.[28] One of these is "LITS1007 (E10G) – Reading and Writing about Literature" – which was introduced in 2000 in the Department of Literatures in English. This course represents an attempt at disciplinary writing instruction and conveys pitfalls that can be expected. Its website informs students that "guidance and practice are provided in . . . how to read the literary genres of prose fiction, drama and autobiography; how to write literary essays using basic principles of argumentation and paragraph organisation; and how to evaluate the critics and use them discriminately. . . . Guidance is also provided in the general management of learning and study activities" (LITS1007 [E10G]: Reading and Writing about Literature 2007). This course developed out of a series of essay-writing workshops that one lecturer, Curdella Forbes, used to hold for students taking a course in Shakespeare in the late 1990s. Forbes started the workshops because students "seemed to have no idea how to read a literary work" and demonstrated weaknesses in organizational and analytical skills in writing. She addressed those issues and focused on *"basic things* like the necessity of analyzing an essay question to ensure what it required [and] what . . . words such as 'discuss', 'evaluate', [and] 'comment on' mean" (emphasis added). She developed the course after promptings from the students, many of whom, she reports, "improved quite significantly". Forbes was hoping to have her faculty colleagues team teach in the course; however, that vision was not realized due to "the stigma of remediality" that faculty attached to the course. Forbes recalls that her colleagues felt the course involved "teaching remedial English". They "decided" that the course would be useful for students who had not taken the A levels even though Forbes pointed out that students with A and O levels were producing "horrifically bad essays" and both groups were benefiting from the workshops. Consequently, the course was not compulsory (Curdella Forbes, personal communication, 16 December 2007). As well, initially only part-timers taught in it. When full-time faculty taught in the course, it remained the purview of one individual – not a team.

Evaluation terms and comprehension of essay questions are not "basic things" for first-generation Creole-influenced university students: this is one of the main points that this book makes. The opposing view evokes questions about the assumptions on which this laudable course was developed. Still, if, indeed, this course works to make visible to students literary writing practices, it may well serve as a model that other disciplines could adopt. Like Forbes (and the other individual lecturers who have taught in the course), researchers in various disciplines in other countries have begun to study and document the writing practices and discourse features of their discipline. Bazerman and Rogers (2007, 171), for example, give a synopsis of findings in anthropology, economics and history elsewhere. The challenge and excitement for the UWI faculty is to study their writing practices and regional influences that they may have introduced into international publications. This challenge for content faculty in helping students understand disciplinary writing practices – from a rhetorical stance – extends to electronic environments that may facilitate and require different strategies and features for texts than do print modes. Faculty's metacognitive awareness of disciplinary discursive features and practices (especially those that they may have transcreated) can only aid student's acquisition, creation and communication of disciplinary knowledge.

For content faculty to engage fully in helping students write to learn and communicate disciplinary knowledge, faculty development has to be emphasized in the institution, and faculty development programmes have to be ongoing. The WAC team at Mona coordinated a few workshops in conjunction with the Instructional Development Unit,[29] provided resources for interested faculty, and organized focus groups by disciplines and encouraged them to participate in online discussions (on Mona's virtual learning website); however, far more measures are needed to target all faculty in the institution. Faculty development programmes can be included during the annual new staff orientation in the summer and in sessions during and between semesters. Informal face-to-face sessions can also be arranged for the exchange of ideas about writing. Continued faculty development is important because of the unfortunate association of grammar teaching with writing instruction. As White (1989, 149) notes, content faculty often feel that "the teaching of writing means only endless red-marking of student writing products, with an emphasis on mechanics". Some faculty members who studied in preprocess times will probably expect one-draft writing from students although a little reflection would remind them of the kinds of revision in which they engage before publishing their own writing. For content faculty to effectively participate in a writing programme that is engaged in more than grammar/mechanics and one-draft writing, they may require introduction to the basic elements of current writing theory and research in general and to the language to talk about rhetorical strategies in particular.

Because what writing specialists teach are the metacognitive aspects of writing, particularly the processes and choices involved in writing, content faculty may argue for transfer of knowledge from first-year writing or faculty-specific writing to writing within disciplines. However, as Downs and Wardle (2007, 557) argue, although transfer of knowledge is almost a given in education, transfer is not necessarily explicitly taught in a general writing course. At Mona, the volume of work that was often covered in first-year writing prevented explicit teaching of transfer. In Jamaica and elsewhere, first-year writing courses are typically overburdened. One UWI, Mona, dean asserts that the courses "provide students with what we identify as the essential skills that they need in order to pursue successfully their undergraduate studies" (Dean of Humanities and Education 2006, 1). Course descriptions indicate that these "essential skills" are many: thinking critically, thinking about rhetorical contexts, varying writing, improving grammar, preparing and delivering oral presentations, understanding and using specific documentation styles, working in teams, and observing deadlines inter alia. What John Trimbur (1999, 11) says of the US composition course is also true of first-year writing at Mona: "The first-year course is, without doubt, . . . the performative space where we enact our imagined orientations toward literacy." The result is oversaturation of the course. As Trimbur sees it, "the required first-year course has acquired a surplus of meanings and purposes". It has been "charged to do everything from ensuring students' academic success to fostering their personal development as individuals to guaranteeing they will get a job when they graduate" (14). Also, as Foster (2006, 11) writes of US composition teachers, teachers of general writing courses, "juggle two pedagogical goals:

they must teach writing as specific mastery in [writing courses] while recognizing that students must learn to write as knowledge-makers in specific fields beyond [the writing course]". Accomplishing such mammoth tasks presupposes a shared responsibility for students' writing development, but institutional provisions contradict this view.

One reason so much responsibility is put on writing teachers is that English/writing remains an interdisciplinary discipline. It informs teaching and learning; it is central to evaluation; and it draws on theory from other disciplines. However, more may be realized if that responsibility is shared. The general writing course or faculty-specific course should enable students to be mindful of, and respond to, the exigency that calls forth a writing task. However, as Smit (2004) reminds readers in his study of the developments in composition regarding its core mission of teaching writing, it would be foolish to believe that students are going to learn to write for the academy in a matter of one or two semesters. As Smit writes, "People learn to write by being immersed in various discourse communities, and they learn the discourse practices of those communities by a process of assimilation, which can be aided by appropriate scaffolding, forms of overt instruction that make them self-consciously aware of the genre conventions used in the discourse of the community and the social practice those conventions embody and codify" (206). Content faculty should, therefore, help neophytes to study discourse practices and features, write the community's genres, and also critique them for personal development and development of the discourse community throughout the duration of students' studies.

Re-enlisting General First-Year Writing in Sequential Writing to Enable Students' Development of Cross-curricular Aptitudes

Identifying the burden on first-year writing courses and calling for the involvement of content faculty is not an indication that I believe in abolishing general first-year writing courses. On the contrary, my view is that such courses are useful as the *first stage* in a *sequenced programme* for writing development. What I proposed above are ways for content faculty to become involved in students' development in disciplinary writing in ways that do not appear to be mere interference in the discipline of writing – as was the case in the 1970s and 1980s. In this section, I wish to emphasize the value of general writing courses and programmes, propose ways to modify them and argue for sequential writing. Should a writing studies programme be developed, writing specialists could focus on teaching about writing and their other content areas. With writing specialists passing on disciplinary expertise as they teach about writing, the foundation programme could more obviously reflect writing as a field of scholarly inquiry as other faculty courses do.

My proposal is, therefore, different from Russell's for Russell argues against general writing courses and for writing in the disciplines. Russell is sometimes associated with some postprocess views about writing. For example, Russell's stress that writing is not generalizable is a key strand in postprocess theory. Postprocess scholars have been influenced by postmodernist perspectives, specifically the rejection of universal theories and master narratives and the foregrounding of situatedness – the emphasis on the importance of context to appreciation of writing. Postprocess advocates take issue with the writing process because it presents a grand narrative about writing. They also question the view that writing can actually be taught, suggesting, as Lynn Bloom (2003, 37) observes, that it is "an unteachable algorithm". One of the leading postprocess advocates, Thomas Kent (1999), argues against discourse production or analysis as systemic or codifiable or generalizable processes. His antiprocess stance would mean abandoning writing pedagogy. Joseph Petraglia (1995, xi), another postprocess advocate who also opposes general writing courses, writes that such courses constitute "general writing skills instruction (GWSI)". He explains that this framework of writing instruction is informed by the "idea that writing is a set of rhetorical skills that can be mastered through formal instruction. These skills include the general ability to develop and organize ideas, use techniques for inventing topics worthy of investigation, adapt one's purpose to an audience, and anticipate reader response" (ibid.). Petraglia offers rather simplistic critiques of GWSI and calls for its revision because he feels it erroneously "sets for itself the objective of teaching students 'to write', to give them the skills that transcend any particular content and context" (xii).

In his turn, Russell (1999) believes that there is no one universal writing process, but instead plural writing processes that are associated with each "activity system". An activity system, Russell writes, refers to "collectives (often organizations) of people who, over an indefinite period of time, share common purposes (objects and motives) and certain tools used in certain ways" (81). I agree with Russell that facilitators should study, classify and commodify the writing processes associated with these systems and "involve students with (teach) them in a curriculum that is sequenced" (88) to help students understand how such processes work in actual systems. However, while I do agree with teaching writing as plural processes, I do believe that some aspects of writing are generalizable while others are specific to each discipline. I believe that the sequence to which Russell refers should begin with general first-year writing courses because there facilitators can teach transferable aspects of writing as well as help students realize how disciplines differ and begin to develop metacognitive awareness to function in different discourse domains.

Russell's (1995) critique of first-year writing turns on its separation of writing and learning in disciplines. Russell acknowledges that a general writing course "can and often does provide a curricular space for welcoming students to higher education and thus, potentially, for broadening rather than restricting access to those social roles colleges and universities prepare and credential students to enter" (51). However, he questions GWSI's aims of "improving students' writing and teaching students a general academic or public discourse" (56). He indicates that GWSI courses are believed to "teach students to write or to write better what is thought of as a universal educated discourse, a general kind of discourse that all educated (or truly educated) persons in a culture share" (60). He calls this the "hypothetical universal educated discourse (UED)" that is often referred to as "academic discourse" or "public discourse". He notes, however, that writing is a "protean tool" that different disciplines and discourse domains appropriate and transform (ibid.). He, therefore, proposes that in order to "teach students to write academic discourse one must engage them in a specific activity system – and therefore specific genres – where academic work goes on" (63). He opposes "the myth of UED" that he believes is propagated in courses that purport to teach "an overarching discourse, which other activity systems (disciplines or professions) ought to use instead of their own 'jargon'" (63–64). In his view, GWSI courses "mask the differences in disciplinary discourses" (67) because they involve attempts to "teach writing without teaching the activities that give writing meaning and motive" because they separate writing from disciplinary learning (65). As well, GWSI functions to absolve disciplines and content faculty of the responsibility to make explicit their ways of thinking, knowing and writing to students needing such instruction: "The existence of separate and general writing courses encourages disciplines to mistakenly assume that they do not teach 'writing' but only 'content'" (67).

I agree and disagree with Russell's (1995, 1999) compelling assertions: I agree, as indicated earlier, that there is no one academic discourse and students learn to write a discipline's discourse through active engagement within the discipline. However, I agree with Merrill and Miller's (2002, 214) reminder to writing programme administrators that "although there may be no generic academic discourse that can be taught in formulaic form, the rhetorical strategies involved in mediating genres of discourse can be learned, formally as well as experientially", in a general writing course (or faculty-specific course). I, therefore, support both writing instruction within disciplines and general writing courses for Creole-influenced learners.

To counter the weaknesses that he perceives in GWSI, Russell (1995, 73) proposes "a general introductory course *about* writing" of the sort that I recommend below. He writes,

> Such a course would not have as its object teaching students to write or improving their writing per se, any more than an introductory psychology course claims to make students better adjusted or a course in music appreciation claims to make its students better singers (although that might be one effect of the course). Rather its object would be to teach students what has been learned about writing in those activity systems that make the role of writing in society the object of their study. (Ibid.)

In other words, such a course would teach the findings of the research traditions that study writing and could "help to remove the remedial stigma from writing and its teaching in academia" (74).

While ultimately I, too, argue for a general writing course about writing that leads to writing instruction *within* disciplines, I do so in the awareness that disciplinary writing instruction can appear to be dogmatic, and some disciplines are beginning to intersect, thereby blurring disciplinary boundaries. Among compositionists who argue against discipline-specific writing instruction, Kurt Spellmeyer (1989, 269) values finding authentic voice and manifesting "essayistic introspection and digression". Spellmeyer believes that discipline-specific writing instruction that focuses on "objectivity of academic discourse" (273) through suppression of beliefs, feelings and values "encourages an attitude of calculating alienation" (267). In other words, through the "effacement of subjectivity" (265), discipline-specific instruction results in "a pervasive absence of commitment" (271) in student writers. This happens because instead of teaching students how to "enter a discipline by finding their own voices" (275), it "encourages both conformity and submission" (266) to the conventions of discourse. He feels that often students have "nothing of [their] own to say" because their primary focus is to abide by the discipline's "rules and fulfill its expectations" (271).

Here, I believe that Spellmeyer (1989) is actually arguing against exactly what happens or can happen when rhetoric is not made visible in each discipline. If, in each discipline or in some English for Academic Purposes courses for second language English speakers, professors suggest that writing is neutral, then there is no need for students to find a voice or to attempt to say anything new. Students would be expected, instead, to present neutrally old information that would be presented using what Freire (1972, 45–51) calls the "banking concept" of teaching and learning. However, what I believe to be Russell's (1995, 1999) concern, and certainly what I am emphasizing, is involvement of content faculty in discipline-specific instruction, which does the very opposite by making clear to students disciplinary conventions and the extent to which those are guided by personal attempts to be rhetorically persuasive. As Spellmeyer writes in his defence of "the exploratory, contravening essay" (263) à la Montaigne, "it is both dishonest and disabling to pretend that writing no matter how formal or abstract, is not created by persons from within the contexts – historical, social, intellectual, institutional – of their lived experience" (269). Appropriate instruction would, therefore, be transformative rather than transmissive, thereby foregrounding the socially and contextually constructed nature of disciplinary writing and promoting writing development.

Another claim against disciplinary writing instruction comes from Michael Carter (2007, 410) when he reminds readers that "disciplinary boundaries themselves are porous and in flux; the disciplines are not fixed containers at all". Carter highlights an interesting movement in the academy in which the separate divisions of declarative knowledge are being challenged by cross and interdisciplinary studies and by mergers occasioned by straitened financial situations. To my mind, these developments may actually bring into sharp relief some Creole-influenced students' difficulty in navigating disciplinary requirements. Therefore, although I agree that disciplinary boundaries are being blurred, precisely because of the potential confusion that can arise from such blurring, I believe that there is merit in recognizing and teaching the separate ways of knowing, doing and writing that seem to keep some students from excelling in some specific disciplines. Hence, my recommendation for administrators, writing specialists and other content faculty to bridge the divides between general writing instruction, faculty-specific instruction and actual instruction in writing within disciplines for Creole-influenced students.

My proposal is also different from Downs and Wardle's (2007), for the two compositionists also seem to argue against a general course that teaches writing and instead promote only a course that teaches *about* writing. While I agree with them that general writing courses can foster misconceptions about writing, I am also emphasizing the ways in which a truly rhetorically driven course can help to eliminate the misconceptions that I highlight. My proposal is also different from the suggestions made in the WRITE symposium (II 2005; IIa 2005) discussed in chapter 5. Those recommendations suggest a disparate set of courses taught at each level of the undergraduate programme. They also speak to content faculty's support of, rather than explicit engagement in, writing instruction to *build on* students' knowledge and strategies. I promote sequenced writing courses because my stated concern is not so much with actual improvements in writing which are very often concerned with formalism; rather, my concern is more with attitudes to writing and how it works. If academics' attitudes change in regard to disciplinary writing instruction, general writing instruction and introduction to what one of Downs and Wardle's critics calls "what we now know of the nature of writing" (Kutney 2007, 279), institutions are likely to implement measures that reflect changed attitudes and *eventually* yield improvements in writing.

One benefit of general first-year writing courses, then, is they can help avoid the risk of oversaturation in courses geared to specific faculties or disciplines. General first-year writing courses are especially useful to newcomers to the academy. It is in first-year writing courses that such students have the opportunity to reflect on the changes that they are experiencing, how their university experiences may be affecting their identity, how they can participate in professional discourses, and how their university experience is likely to shape their future. As Bazerman (1995, 256) says in his response to individuals who advocate abolishing first-year composition in the United States, the "first-year writing course has often served as precisely a place that introduces students to the critical reflective discourse that provides the medium for the undergraduate experience". It is in this course that, as he says, "students reflect on themselves as students in the language of students, as they engage with disciplines in the role of students". In this way, the course is "precisely an introduction into the literacy practices of being a university student" (254). Whereas in the United States, such courses allow for students' transition into professional discourses, in Jamaica they served the same function primarily for those students who did not have the experience of exposure to some form of disciplinary writing in the sixth form. For past sixth formers, the writing courses served as a pause for students to reflect on the expectations of high school writing versus those of university writing. For all students, the general first-year writing courses were the most likely places in the institution where they could be *introduced* to writing for a variety of purposes and audiences, including personal, public and academic or professional. All students bring with them "funds of knowledge" (Vélez-Ibáñez and Greenberg 2005, 47) – their interpretive strategies, cultural assumptions and collaborative networks – that first-year writing courses can connect with in ways that writing in their disciplines may not. First-year writing courses provide spaces where, as cross-cultural writing researcher Anne-Marie Hall (2007, 463) writes, "students develop both the craft to represent themselves and their ideas in language and also the reflective ability and the vocabulary to talk and think about writing". What is important is that in addition to acknowledging and exploiting students' funds of knowledge, facilitators of first-year writing courses usually introduce students to a range of literate activities that are found in the university. At Mona, facilitators tried to avoid foisting one set of discursive strategies on to students, for to have done otherwise would have only incorrectly suggested that what obtains in one discipline is appropriate in all others. In other words, writing teachers tried to avoid what Bazerman (1995, 257) calls the "discursive chauvinism" that some faculty and students exhibit in academia. Writing specialists tried, instead, to "make visible and real over the period of a student's evaluation a variety of discourses, so that the students [could] reorient to and evaluate new discourses as they bec[a]me visible and relevant" (ibid.). In this way, students were encouraged to appreciate their own strategies as well as begin to exploit strategies that are indispensable in new or unfamiliar rhetorical situations. Faculty-specific courses would require removal of some of the introductory/initiatory aspects and more emphasis on writing in many disciplines in specific faculties. If the elements were to be kept along with the new focuses, the faculty-specific courses could be burdensome to both students and facilitators.

To avoid the temptation to oversaturate faculty-specific courses (or other general first-year writing courses), writing specialists, like content faculty, could benefit from adopting a rhetorical approach to writing instruction. This posture requires moving beyond the concern in the WAC project at the UWI that writing is not a generic skill and instead revealing to students writing's place in negotiating generic disciplinary conventions. Instead of teaching some mythical universal academic writing for specific faculties because of the false assumption/promotion that the academy consists of one coherent discourse, faculty will need to continue to promote the academy as well as faculties as polyglot (Harris 1997, 106) and lobby for provisions to enable them to teach writing as always already rhetorical. By abandoning a formalist perspective and employing a rhetorical one in teaching writing, writing specialists may better assist students in developing writing abilities. With provisions for students to receive differentiated writing instruction (albeit inadequately differentiated), a rhetorical stance could ultimately enable writers of varying abilities to be introduced to the ways in which knowledge is made, re-made, and conveyed in different domains.

As for content faculty, the *WPA Outcomes Statement* may provide a useful starting point for facilitators in first-year writing courses, especially when the stated outcomes are used in combination with standards set by specific institutions or specific groups of institutions, as the Council ([2000] 2008) recommends. First, with regard to "rhetorical knowledge", the courses should focus on rhetorical situations to enable students to address issues of purpose and audience and conventions of format and structure, voice, tone, level of formality and genres – as appropriate for those situations. This perspective means *working from purpose and audience to determine genre*, rather than having genre (almost always exposition) determine other writing moves that tend to descend into formalism. Given no named genre in the "new" courses (except for the one for the humanities), and despite the risk of oversaturation, facilitators should be able to include sessions on "argument". Second, if the courses are to foster development of students' "critical thinking, reading, and writing" in readiness for application in their disciplines – that is for writing *within* disciplines – then the courses should provide opportunities for students to "use writing and reading for inquiry, learning, thinking, and communicating". This development should involve opportunities for students to take writing assignments through a series of tasks that include researching, evaluating and synthesizing sources, as well as integrating their views and their sources' – *after* their identified purpose leads them to a specific genre for writing. Such instruction should also help students "understand the relationships among language, knowledge, and power" – issues that are particularly important in Caribbean societies where there is an oversupply of linguistic stigmata. Third, the courses should continue to introduce students to "processes" of writing by engaging them with multiple drafts that are usually a precondition for producing successful texts. Instruction should, however, help students "develop flexible strategies" for, and understand the recursive features of, considering, creating, developing and polishing a text – rather than limit students to pages signed, or reference limits stipulated, by facilitators. Increased opportunities for students to engage in balanced self- and peer-evaluation and address different audiences using varied technologies may enable them to understand the "collaborative and social aspects of writing processes". Fourth, to help students acquire "knowledge of conventions", the first-year courses should include *substantial* teaching sessions to allow students to "learn common formats for different kinds of texts", "develop knowledge of genre conventions, ranging from structure and paragraphing to tone and mechanics", "practice appropriate means of documenting their work" and "control such surface features as syntax, grammar, punctuation, and spelling".

Based on faculty's continued complaints about language problems in writing, facilitators cannot continue to practise the policy that was evident since the 1960s, when students were heavily penalized for surface errors that were not addressed in the "Use of English" course. What is required is almost a paradox: recognition of the language situation and a reflection of it in teaching – not the usual focus on English as a requirement without adequately effective means of addressing it. The required instruction to keep students self-consciously aware of metacognitive contrasts in English and the oral Creole that many use should take place in the context of real writing that students are producing in either the first-year writing classroom or their discipline. Finally, to help students with "composing in electronic environments" in the digital age, first-year writing courses should expose students to using formal and informal electronic environments in all aspects of conceiving, developing and sharing texts, as well as helping students "understand and exploit the differences in the rhetorical strategies and in the affordances available for both print and electronic composing processes and texts" (Council).

Providing explicit, deliberate writing instruction within the disciplines and employing a rhetorical approach to writing are not the only moves that may be worthwhile in a writing programme for Creole-influenced students. Teaching writing studies may also be useful. Since writing instruction in a general or faculty-specific (one-semester) first-year course only can convey the sense of writing as inoculation, should a *sequence of courses* be developed and approved to include disciplinary writing instruction and engaged rhetoric, facilitators could see a change in the incorrect view that writing courses are meant to inoculate students with grammar and punctuation of supposedly university-level strength. One of the reasons content faculty (and students) may feel that writing courses are merely about mechanics, grammar and syntax could be that these courses involve a wide range of topics about which writing facilitators sometimes have only general knowledge. This situation can lead to the misconception that writing has no content. Downs and Wardle (2007, 553) rightly assert that "our field reinforces cultural misconceptions of writing" such as "writing is not a real subject [and] writing courses do not require expert facilitators" because "we continue to pursue the goal of teaching students 'how to write in college' in one or two semesters – despite the fact that our field calls this possibility into question". Downs and Wardle consider first-year writing "the very course where misconceptions are born and/or reinforced" and propose that writing facilitators shift "from acting as if writing is a basic, universal skill to acting as if writing studies is a discipline with content knowledge to which students should be introduced, thereby changing their understandings about writing and thus changing the ways they write" (ibid.). Given the history at Mona, this change could influence content faculty's and the public's perspective of postsecondary writing instruction.

Teaching writing studies at Mona would mean having first-year writing courses functioning as introduction to writing studies or as introduction to writing within disciplines in a vertical curriculum. Either approach would be worthwhile because each course at other levels could have a different, though connected, focus and increase the visibility of rhetoric in writing. In other words, first-year courses could continue to address the generalizable aspects of writing – what Downs and Wardle (2007, 578) call the "transferable conceptions" – while recognizing that writing is not a generic skill. A sequence of courses that would include modified versions of the upper-level and graduate courses discussed in chapter 5 as well as new courses would counter the universalist nature of one writing course that can generate students' success in academia. Additionally, the first-year courses could address the persuasive, subjective aspect of all writing; make visible the contingent/context-bound/specialized nature of writing; and emphasize the interconnectedness of reading, research and writing. Because the courses in this sequence would use writing research and not only language or general topics as the course content, they would reveal writing as a field of scholarly inquiry and improve views about writing instruction and writing specialists. Such a programme could help to disentangle academic "writing" from subject "English" – a consideration that seems crucial in the Creole-influenced Jamaican environment, where students who are less than confident in English may feel equally diffident in knowledge acquisition and creation and its conveyance in writing. Teaching a sequence of writing courses in which students learn about language, oral and written literacy and rhetoric, in the Creole-influenced context may recover some of the ground lost in teaching Creole-speaking students in English before they became literate in the Creole.

In an introductory course in the sequence, teachers could teach writing's disciplinary ways of knowing to better enable students to appreciate *other* disciplinary ways of knowing. Students could begin or continue to learn the various cognitive and composing processes, rules, conventions and rhetorical practices of other discursive worlds, so that they develop necessary cross-curricular aptitudes to succeed as they shuttle across disciplinary discourse communities. Such aptitudes could include understanding "how shared expectations and experiences become codified in the conventions that constitute domains of inquiry" (Merrill and Miller 2002, 206). After all, students need more than a one-shot-inoculation-type first-year course to enable them generally to succeed in understanding and producing written academic discourses and specifically to enter the professional discourse of their field. An introductory course to a curriculum in writing would also be a good way to avoid overlaps with CAPE and instead focus on theories, discoveries, trends and controversies in writing. Such a course could lead to disciplinary writing courses as well as courses that focus on writing for the public such as "Science/Geography/

Economics for the Public". There could also be more co-teaching in certain subjects as happened in "Language and Ethics" with participants from philosophy and language. Whatever the approach taken, all faculty have to remember, as the *WPA Outcomes Statement* reminds, that as students progress through their studies their writing "abilities not only diversify along disciplinary and professional lines but also move into whole new levels where expected outcomes expand, multiply, and diverge" (Council [2000] 2008).

If Mona's writing programme were reconceived (with support from upper administration) to include an introductory course to writing within disciplines (or even a writing major), more realistic conceptions of writing would be possible rather than the mere consideration of writing as being without content. Such a course could be seen as some other introductory courses in the academy. It could point out the shared features of writing which include taking a stance; developing paragraphs; using jargon, citation and documentation; research writing as advancing disciplinary conversation; writing moves in different parts of a piece of writing; and writing to be rhetorically effective based on purpose, situation and audience. It would, however, emphasize that these concepts are best understood in specific disciplinary contexts because disciplines understand these common features in different ways. As stated, "writing is neither basic nor universal but content- and context-contingent and irreducibly complex" (Downs and Wardle 2007, 558). This course would enable students to explore such questions, as Downs and Wardle ask, "How does writing work? How do people use writing? What are the problems related to writing and reading and how can they be solved?" Such a course would promote writing as "a subject of scholarly inquiry" and "a researchable activity rather than a mysterious talent" (560). This introductory writing course could, as John Trimbur (1999, 12) proposes, "name names, identify contributions, chart trends, describe controversies, and otherwise introduce students to the intellectual life" of the field of writing. Additionally, the upper-level courses would build on each other by reinforcing concepts addressed in earlier courses as well as introduce new ones. Since all courses in the sequence would be rhetorically oriented, they would not need to be separated in terms of genres – an unfortunate arrangement that means many students, including top level leaders of government, have graduated from Mona without formal exposure to techniques for analysing and producing argument. Overall, a sequence would make first-year writing courses less oversaturated than they have been or risk being. This would help first-year writing courses shed, what Trimbur calls, their "ambiguous identity on the border between [high] school and [university]" (17).

The rhetorically informed introductory writing course in a sequenced programme could also teach students to develop and maintain an inquiring stance on language, research and writing and contribute to developing writers who know conventions but are also able to critically engage with them, as the fourth epigraph in this chapter suggests. Based on their research, Downs and Wardle

(2007, 577) conclude, "Teaching students what we know about writing and asking them to research their own writing and the writing of others encourages . . . self-reflection and mindfulness, thereby improving the possibility that students will maintain a stance of inquiry toward writing as they write in other disciplinary systems." A course encouraging this posture of inquiry is likely to help students see, as Canagarajah (2010, 176) recommends, that "texts are not simply context-bound or context-sensitive; they are context-transforming". In the Jamaican context, such a course may also help Creole-influenced students to engage critically with issues of language, knowledge and power. It could help them to engage critically with language and the way it positions Jamaicans in social classes as well as with the values and practices of the various disciplinary discourses to which they will be introduced in the academy. Since, increasingly, students will shuttle between and across various discourse communities, it is important that they are not only assisted in learning (about) new discourse domains but also taught how to shuttle between these domains. As Russell and Foster (2002, 42–43) say in their cross-national study of writing, "because the epistemologies of various disciplines are often radically different, students must develop a chameleon rhetorical capacity to move from one to another, to converse differently in different networks of people through their written response to specialist reading and talk". Teaching a sequence of writing courses in which students learn about language, oral and written literacy, knowledge and power in the Jamaican context may help Creole-influenced students to understand the different interpretive strategies and codified conventions that obtain – and can be challenged – in different discourse domains.

Coda: How Writing Works

I have proposed that by attending to writing from a transcultural rhetorical perspective, students, faculty and institutions can better reflect on and address writing challenges. More important, it will help critics understand *how writing works*. As I have established, critics have complained about student writing in higher education in Jamaica in every decade since the establishment of the UCWI. While a few of these complaints address weaknesses in logic and reasoning, most of them have stressed errors in English grammar and mechanics. When critics complain about quantifiable errors in writing, they usually highlight weaknesses in lower levels of education. Consequently, they tend to suggest that when problems in those sectors are remedied, higher education will not have to contend with them. In essence, the complaints and accompanying suggestions often reflect the myth of transience. More recent critics, particularly journalists, tend to present the problems as if they are new. The first groups of students at UCWI shared similarities in social background and academic preparation, but early documents suggest that it is time for commentators to recognize that they cannot really speak of any lost halcyon day of good writing in the university. Additionally the country's history of education suggests that locating remedies for problems in higher education requires careful reflection. Such reflection should mobilize academics, administrators and the concerned public to consider that writing is central to learning and to most forms of evaluation and think about how students make sense of a discipline's concepts through writing – and writing in a language situation in which many are largely orphaned.

Bearing in mind the persistence of the complaints about student writing and the inherent weaknesses in some suggestions to address the problem, I recalled the country's colonial history of education and the imposition of "grammatical English" on a largely Creole-speaking population to demonstrate the following points. First, the imposition of English as the medium of instruction was informed by the view that learners (at the elementary level) use language in speaking and writing based on an assumed instinct. Second, the problems that emerged at the elementary level as a consequence of that language policy have largely been ignored since mention of high failure rates has not been followed by significant changes in pedagogy. Third, the same myth about writing instinctively abounded in the university in its first decade and later in the promotion of knowledge acquisition and creation without initiation of students into disciplinary writing practices and conventions. In other words, the separation of students from their first language and the separation of language and learning since the beginnings of public education in Jamaica would be evident in higher education. Fourth, the problems inspiring the complaints are a signal that commentators should not assume that learning to write in one context will necessarily transfer to writing in other genres in other contexts. In other words, writing is not learned once and for all, but is learned and relearned in new contexts. Writing is, indeed, as Chevannes (2005, 306) describes education, a marathon and not a sprint event. Hence, although the stated focus of this book is writing and its instruction and development in postsecondary education, it also embraces the interconnections of language use in the society, language teaching in schools and writing in higher education in Jamaica. It establishes the importance of paying attention to schools, but not in the naïve way of suggesting that when they prepare students better the academy can abandon writing programmes. Rather, the development of schools in Jamaica and students' linguistic and cultural experiences suggest a need to address schools to help faculty to determine what funds of knowledge Creole-influenced students bring to university writing classrooms.

The continued complaints about student writing also suggest that some people continue to focus on English grammar and mechanics – the conventions of the code, which constitute only one element of writing. Exclusive focus on the code means that other aspects of the writing process may be being ignored. However, writing instruction has to be understood as more than enforcement of standards of grammatical and mechanical correctness. Jamaica tends to be error obsessed where writing is concerned. The correlate is error avoidance and fear on the part of students. I am not suggesting that the academy should ignore what Geneva Smitherman (2000, 130) refers to in the United States as the national "mania for correctness", but I am suggesting that writing specialists and other content faculty should avoid being defined by it, and instead attempt to consider – as advocates of translingualism propose – what students have to say rather than reduce evaluation and discussions of writing to a grammatical/mechanical error hunt. As H.G. Widdowson (1994) asserted in his plenary address at the TESOL Convention in 1993, custodians of language are often disturbed by deviances in spelling and grammar because such deviances signal that outsiders are entering a previously excluded domain – "the community". As explained in chapter 1, and as Widdowson asserted, "It is not that [spelling] greatly interferes with communication: It is usually not difficult to identify words through their unorthodox appearance. What seems to be more crucial is that good spelling represents conformity to convention and so serves to maintain institutional stability" (380). Of grammar, Widdowson notes, "Because language has built-in redundancy, grammatical conformity is actually not particularly crucial for many kinds of communicative transaction. . . . If the reason for insisting on standard English is because it guarantees effective communication, then the emphasis should logically be on vocabulary rather than grammar" (380–81). In sum, he indicated, "it tends to be the communal rather than the communicative features of Standard English that are most jealously protected: its grammar and spelling" (381). While it is important for those wishing to gain access and be respected in academic communities to realize that deviations can lead to exclusion from them, those within ought also to be aware that they send contradictory messages when on the one hand they speak of increasing access but on the other refuse to initiate neophytes into both the identitarian (communal) and interactive (communicative) aspects of the discipline. Additionally, educators lose opportunities to learn from Creole-influenced students' linguistic innovations by attempting to manage apparent errors. Standing in the way of this learning and some Creole-influenced students' progress may be what Lu (2010, 51) refers to as "our learned distaste for non-idiomatic English lexicons and grammar – our learned inclination to view them as either exotic or downright stupid, nonsensical, incorrect". Managing this "learned inclination" – rather than perceived errors – may prove fruitful on many levels.

I am also not ignoring the fact that many content faculty seem to have been focusing on *content* for a long time, that is, they have been grading on content only. Such content faculty demonstrate hypocrisy when they complain in meetings about students' writing deficiencies but award very high grades to such writing. Often, they excuse that contradiction by saying that they are not writing teachers and the English/writing teacher or high schools should provide the required instruction for students. The result is that some aspects of writing are still ignored. What I am calling for is a balanced, responsible approach to writing development so that content faculty may realize that they are the ones who will best indicate to students how errors of whatever kind can affect a writer's ethos and how other aspects of writing that writing specialists emphasize should also be addressed.

Critics' focus on skills is also informed by the view that there is a uniform standard English that has been isolated and reduced to teachable rules. However, rather than reify writing, academics should acknowledge its protean, heterogeneous nature – a competence and a medium that will be redefined in different disciplines. As Rose (1985, 358) recommends, "If the skills designation proves to be resistant to change, then we must insist that writing is a very unique skill, not really a tool but an ability fundamental to academic inquiry, an ability whose development is not fixed but ongoing". Faculty have, too, to recognize that academic discourse is, as Crowley (1998, 233) observes, "a mythical genre". This persistent myth has unfortunately fostered and supported the belief that universal standards of literacy exist. However, it is time for academics to acknowledge, and the concerned public to understand, a social perspective on writing: As Russell (2002, 12) reminds, "As a social activity, writing is inevitably embedded in and conditioned by a community. By its very nature it is local, context specific, dependent on a community for its existence and meaning. *Literacy* is thus a function of the specific community in which certain kinds of reading and writing activities take place." Understanding the complexity of writing may help critics avoid using alarmist rhetoric in relation to students' writing and instead channel energies into identifying ways to enhance the writing development of all Creole-influenced students. This is especially important for Creole-speaking first-generation university students who are most likely to be disenfranchised, torn as they are between two languages, having to disregard their first language and learn to write in English – a language that has not really become their own.

Ultimately, my recommendation regarding Creole-influenced students' writing in higher education is that faculty move away from colonial conceptions that focused on *grammatical English* to invoke rhetoric and accept the way English becomes diffracted in different disciplines, and that faculty assist students in learning, and critically engaging with, those disciplines' ways of knowing, doing and writing rather than merely transmit some archaic view of English culture and values and formalist conventions. Faculty's focus should be not so much on teaching "English" with all the monolingual monolithic monopoly that the term implies but more on empowering students through instruction in writing for both general and disciplinary purposes to understand how they can transcreate knowledge and language as they "go native" (Kuhn 1970, 204) in specific disciplines. Faculty can achieve this shift in focus if they take a rhetorical stance on writing, which focuses on interpretive and problem-solving strategies that everyone can use in varied situations. As Merrill and Miller (2002, 215) remind regarding writing and language, "task forces and ad hoc committees [often] make institutional changes without bothering to do the sort of research that is required in any other form of scholarly activity". Instead of relying on such structures, Mona's writing specialists must endeavour to reveal their awareness that "helping students demonstrate appropriate writing outcomes requires expert understanding of how students actually learn to write" (Council [2000] 2008). Writing specialists may increase their contribution to students' development by helping other academics and the concerned public to understand that writing is a lifelong practice and that it simultaneously makes learning visible and reveals and aids acquisition and expansion of disciplinary practices.

Content faculty should also recognize that the errors that journalists and academics often identify speak to language difficulties of Creole-influenced students, whose problems are compounded by the academy's requirements. Indeed, there is a need for recognition of probable weaknesses in students' English language acquisition without faculty's abdication of their responsibilities for students' holistic writing development, especially as regards helping students to navigate the situational contingencies that are inherent in writing in different disciplines. If our concern is widening participation, then we have to be prepared to use the linguistic and other discursive resources that those invited bring to the learning situation. If we desire knowledge production (rather than merely reproduction), and by extension personal, institutional and national development, then all stakeholders have to be integrally involved in students' writing development. The *institution* has to recognize writing as visible rhetoric rather than as transparent recording of reality affected only by one's ability to master English grammar and mechanics. *Content faculty* have to acknowledge the rhetorical nature of their work and assist students in understanding how knowledge is rhetorically constructed. Content faculty have also to remember the various discourses that exist in the academy and assist in initiating neophytes into their respective disciplinary conventions. *Writing specialists* need, too, to remain aware of such varied discourse communities and engage rhetoric's aides to emphasize such differences in teaching so that *students* will learn to transfer strategies, learn new ones as situations demand, and learn to critically engage with conventions as they strive for personal, disciplinary and other forms of development. A transcultural rhetorical perspective on writing – in general writing courses, faculty-specific courses, courses about writing and courses within other disciplines – is important to reducing the alarmist rhetoric that some academics and lay practitioners associate with problems in writing because of inadequate attention to the need for differentiated instruction for Creole-influenced learners and because of their lack of acknowledgement or unawareness of how writing works.

Notes

1. Although complaints about student writing often follow expansion plans in higher education (see, for example, Brereton 1995; Rose 1985; and Russell 2002 regarding the United States; and Ivanič and Lea 2006; Jones, Turner and Street 1999a; Lea and Street 1998; Lillis 1999, 2001; and Lillis and Turner 2001 in the United Kingdom), Chevannes (2005) was the only conference contributor who explicitly referenced the UWI's writing programme.
2. I invoke Russell's (2002) and Rose's (1985) theories and recent research from the United Kingdom not because I am proposing a (neo-)colonial imitation or adoption of US or UK models. However, I recognize that the US college established a writing tradition in the nineteenth century that has allowed for focused research on writing. This tradition is a useful reference point for English and European higher education institutions that have recently begun to offer academic writing instruction and to study the discipline. More important, US writing research and UK research into language use have been influencing developments in some of the UWI's writing courses since the 1960s – especially in terms of the texts used in courses. As well, recent recommendations from the UWI's English language foundation programme include the intention "to reposition [its] English language programmes within the context of international norms and regional needs and expectations" (WRITE Symposium II 2005, 1).

    Additionally, although I rely on Russell's (2002) work as I examine the history of academic writing instruction in Jamaican higher education and highlight the need for new attitudes to writing and its instruction at the UWI at Mona, I disagree with some of his proposals and some views he supports because of my experience in teaching academic writing and because of perceived needs of Creole-influenced students. These areas of divergence will become clear in the concluding chapter.
3. This idea was expressed much earlier in the United States by Bizzell ([1982] 2003, 401–2) in her promotion of the idea of "discourse community": "Academics are, perhaps, too ready to assume that such operations as 'describe' or 'analyze' are self-evident, when in fact they have meanings specific to the academic discourse community and specific to disciplines within that community."
4. ELS colleagues (and documents) referred to these as "discipline-specific" but as the discussion will reveal, the courses were aligned to faculties, each of which includes various disciplines.

5. Although I am guided by the author-date system of the *Chicago Manual of Style* in this book, when I cite sources from the archives at the UWI at Mona I use a different format to pay deference to the archives' documentation format requirements.
6. See, for example, Canagarajah 2006, 2009, 2013; Horner, Lu and Matsuda 2010; Horner et al. 2011; V.A. Young 2007, 2009; and V.A. Young and Martinez 2011.
7. Based on the documentation of these various scholars, only four pre-UWI tertiary institutions operated in the West Indies. The first – the Caribbean's only tertiary institution with roots before the twentieth century – is Codrington College, which was established in 1710 in Barbados. It awarded degrees in theology and, beginning in 1878, in secular subjects through an arrangement with the University of Durham in England. The second, Queen's College in Spanish Town, Jamaica, was opened in 1873 but shut down within a year due to lack of funds. The third, a university college founded in affiliation with Jamaica High School in 1890, closed by 1912. The fourth institution is the Imperial College of Tropical Agriculture that was established in Trinidad in 1921–22 and was incorporated into the UWI as the Faculty of Agriculture in 1960.
8. The implied biases in such terms may not resonate well with contemporary linguists or advocates of World Englishes, but I retain them for what they convey about university students of the day.
9. See, for example, the French Surrealist André Breton's (1947, 80) panegyric to Aimé Césaire in which Breton described the famous Martinican poet and statesman as a "Black man who handles the French language better than any living White (French) man could" (my translation).
10. The first set of thirty-three students was admitted to the single Faculty of Medicine in 1948. The other faculties were added later: Natural Sciences in 1949, Arts in 1950, Education in 1953, and Economics and Political Science in 1958.
11. "Man" is used deliberately here because, although female students numbered among all entering cohorts at the UCWI, the majority of the "leaders" were, in fact, men.
12. The Caribbean Examinations Council (CXC) was established in 1972 in response to calls for examinations that were regionally relevant but would also be recognized internationally. The first examinations were administered in 1979.
13. Basil Bernstein's description of restricted codes led to interpretations related to deficiency in speakers' cognition and/or expression and not related to restrictions based on class relations (see Bernstein 1971, 18–19; Atkinson, Davies and Delamont 1995, x;). However, unlike many scholars in the United States and elsewhere, "Use of English" faculty at Mona did not seem to believe that Bernstein was promoting a linguistic deficit position; rather, it appears that they used Bernstein's descriptions of restrictions on languages based on the roles ascribed to languages (see Hymes 1995, 6–7) to help to argue for the legitimacy of all language varieties. Of course, content faculty at Mona seemed to consider the Creole as being "restricted" and thus "limited" for communication purposes.
14. Among those who would criticize this polarized literacy-orality theory is Brian Street (1984) who has called it the autonomous model of literacy because it purported to be ideologically neutral, uninfluenced by social and cultural contexts or power structures.
15. The leaders included "democratic" in describing their orientation to distance themselves from a communist ideology.

16. Beginning in the Faculty of Arts and General Studies (Mona) *Regulations and Syllabuses* (1993) for 1993–94, the course description was revised to indicate exemption from the test for law students with A-level passes in both English language and English literature.
17. I had coined this term before I became familiar with North's (1984) essay. I would like to thank the reviewer who brought the work to my attention.
18. This code was changed to FOUN1001 in 2008–2009 based on a new online registration system. Here onwards, I indicate the new codes for courses, but use the older/more popular ones to refer to the courses.
19. This initiative led to the publication of Ramsay et al.'s Caribbean reader *Blooming with the Pouis: Critical Thinking, Reading and Writing across the Curriculum* (2009).
20. These were later upgraded to two-year contracts.
21. For Humanities and Social Science students, these topics included Aid and Dependency; Changing Trends in _____; Children's Rights; The Gaming Industry; The Green Revolution; Human Rights; The Humanities and the Caribbean; Management of Resources; Politics in the Caribbean; Recession and _____; Sports and Development. For students from Pure and Applied Sciences, Medical Sciences and Education, these topics included Crime and Forensics; Cultural Icons and Media; Education in the Twenty-First Century; Ethics in Sports; The Fast Food Industry; The Haitian Crisis; National Development and Individual Responsibility; Practical Applications of _____ (a theory in your discipline); Science and Ageing; Science and Body Image; Social Values and the Digital Era; Taxation and Development; Technology and _____; Tertiary Education and Marketability; Vocational Education and Career Opportunities; War and Youth. When a blank was not followed by a parenthetical guide, students could fill in whatever they wished to complete the topic.
22. CAPE is somewhat similar to advanced placement (AP) in the United States. CAPE and Cambridge advanced level courses are really postsecondary level programmes that are offered in the sixth form in the Caribbean. They are the general matriculation/entry requirements for students' acceptance at university to do the three-year first degree, a significant difference from the United States where students complete the first degree in four years after displaying arguably less rigorous and less fixed secondary level passes.
23. Students at Mona who would not have taken CAPE would not have covered some topics on language. As an example, CAPE Communication Studies focused much on the language varieties in the Caribbean whereas FD10A normally sensitized students to the subject through one class discussion held after students did a reading on language varieties. CAPE also addressed discourse types (the modes) whereas FD10A focused on exposition only (see CXC 1998, 1). Moore introduced a few lectures in FD10A to try to give students the exposure they would have missed because they had not taken CAPE. By 2009–2010, the number of lectures was increased to one for nearly every week of the semester to address language and all of the other topics covered in FD10A.
24. Although ELS colleagues (and documents) referred to these courses as "discipline-specific", each was aligned to a specific faculty comprising multiple disciplines.
25. The reviewers suggested a year-long course bearing three credits; however, students received three credits for each of the two semesters of Critical Reading and Writing in the Disciplines that they completed successfully.

26. See Milson-Whyte (2013, 2014).
27. Thanks to exposure to foreign languages in the school system, some Jamaicans are literate in languages besides English. My concern here, however, is with English and Jamaican Creole which would be applicable to the majority of Jamaicans.
28. As indicated in chapter 1, I focused mainly on courses and programmes offered through the ELS in the Department of Language, Linguistics and Philosophy at the UWI at Mona. (I am also concerned with promoting an understanding of writing as revelatory of learning and as enabling learning when considered from a rhetorical rather than formalist perspective.) I have, therefore, not treated a course such as "SY69C – Technical Writing" which graduate students in the social sciences were taught in the summer beginning in 2005, and which was then offered during the regular academic year after 2007–2008. The Department of Sociology, Psychology and Social Work introduced this course that addresses such writing concerns as plagiarism, citation, summarizing, and paraphrasing to "help students to minimize and even eliminate continuing problems in writing at the graduate level" (Paul Martin, personal communication, 17 December 2007). Before summer 2007, the course was taught in the "advanced stages" of the programmes of students pursuing a master's degree in psychology, sociology, demography and anthropology; however, a change was made to teach it "earlier so that the effects of the training [could] be more evident during their programmes" (ibid.). I have also not treated the social writing that is taught in media and communications as well as the voices of other content faculty who may treat academic writing instruction in one way or another in their disciplines.
29. This unit was renamed the Centre for Excellence in Teaching and Learning in 2013.

References

Academic Board, Mona. 1985a. 11 April 1985. UWI Archives, Item No. 122, Syllabuses and Regulations. Survey Courses. File No. 83-9, Part No. 2. File Start Date 1979.
———. 1985b. 13 June 1985. UWI Archives, Item No. 125, Syllabuses and Regulations. Survey Courses. File No. 83-9, Part No. 2. File Start Date 1979.
———. 1988a. 9 June 1988. UWI Archives, Item No. 170c, Syllabuses and Regulations. Survey Courses. File No. 83-9, Part No. 2. File Start Date 1979.
———. 1988b. 7 July 1988. UWI Archives, Item No. 175A, Syllabuses and Regulations. Survey Courses. File No. 83-9, Part No. 2. File Start Date 1979.
Adams, Royce W., and Becky Patterson. 2001. *Developing Reading Versatility*. 8th ed. Fort Worth: Harcourt.
Alexander, Robin J. 2000. *Culture and Pedagogy: International Comparisons in Primary Education*. Oxford: Blackwell.
Alleyne, Mervyn. 1980. *Comparative Afro-American: An Historical-Comparative Study of English-Based Afro-American Dialects of the New World*. Ann Arbor: Karoma.
———. 1988. *Roots of Jamaican Culture*. London: Plato.
———. 1993. "Memo to Members of the Department". Department of Language and Linguistics. UWI, Mona, Jamaica. 21 December.
———. 1994. "Problems of Standardization of Creole Languages". In *Language and the Social Construction of Identity in Creole Situation*, edited by Marcyliena Morgan, 7–18. Los Angeles: Centre for Afro-American Studies, UCLA.
Allsopp, Richard. 1964a. Interview with Gladstone Holder, government information officer, Barbados. Bridgetown, Barbados. [16 January].
———. 1964b. "The 'Use of English Course'". College of Arts and Science, UWI, Barbados. October. UWI Archives, Item No. 26, Syllabuses and Regulations. Survey Courses. File No. 83-9, Part 1, 1964–1979.
———. 1965a. "Report of a Conference on 'The Use of English' Course Held . . . on Friday August 6, 1965". UWI, Mona, Jamaica. [October].
———. 1965b. "Report on the Use of English Course 1964/65". College of Arts and Science, UWI, Cave Hill, Barbados. [25 June].
———. 1967. "Report on the Use of English Course 1966/67". College of Arts and Science, UWI, Cave Hill, Barbados. [6 July].
———. 1968. "Report on the Use of English Course 1967/68". College of Arts and Science, UWI, Cave Hill, Barbados. [August].

References

———. 1971. "Report on the Use of English Course". College of Arts and Science, UWI, Cave Hill, Barbados. [16 March]. UWI Archives, Item No. 77, Syllabuses and Regulations. Survey Courses. File No. 83-9, Part 1, 1964–1979.

———. 1972. "A Use of English WORKBOOK". Letter to All Teaching Colleagues. UWI, Cave Hill, Barbados. [16 March].

———. 1974. "UWI Use of English Course: Proposal for an Adjustment in Course Content". College of Arts and Science, UWI, Cave Hill, Barbados. [30 December].

———. 1988. "Report on the State of Written English at the UWI at Cave Hill, Barbados". Unit of Use of English and Linguistics, UWI, Cave Hill, Barbados. [July].

Altidor-Brooks, Alison. 2008. "WAC Report: Writing across the Curriculum (WAC) Programme/Project. September 2007–December 2008". Kingston: UWI.

Anderson, Benedict. 2006. *Imagined Communities: Reflections on the Origin and Spread of Nationalism*. Rev. ed. London: Verso.

Anderson, W.E.K. 1963. *The Written Word: Some Uses of English*. London: Oxford University Press.

Aristotle. 1991. *On Rhetoric: A Theory of Civic Discourse*. Translated by George A. Kennedy. New York: Oxford University Press.

Atkinson, Paul, Brian Davies and Sara Delamont. 1995. Introduction to *Discourse and Reproduction: Essays in Honor of Basil Bernstein*, edited by Paul Atkinson, Brian Davies and Sara Delamont, vii–xiv. Cresskill, NJ: Hampton Press.

Augier, F. Roy, and Shirley C. Gordon. 1962. *Sources of West Indian History*. London: Longman.

Bacchus, M. Kazim. 1994. *Education as and for Legitimacy: Developments in West Indian Education between 1846 and 1895*. Waterloo, ON: Wilfrid Laurier University Press.

———. 2005. *Education for Economic and Political Development in the British Caribbean Colonies from 1896 to 1945*. London, ON: Althouse.

Bailey, Beryl. 1966. *Jamaican Creole Syntax: A Transformational Approach*. Cambridge: Cambridge University Press.

Bakhtin, Mikhail M. [1934–35] 1981. "Discourse in the Novel". In *The Dialogic Imagination: Four Essays by M.M. Bakhtin*, edited by Michael Holquist, translated by Caryl Emerson and Michael Holquist, 259–422. Austin: University of Texas Press.

Barnet, Sylvan, and Hugo Bedau. 1999. *Critical Thinking, Reading and Writing: A Brief Guide to Argument*, 3rd ed. Boston: Bedford/St Martin's.

Bartholomae, David. 1985. "Inventing the University". In *When a Writer Can't Write: Studies in Writer's Block and Other Composing Process Problems*, edited by Mike Rose, 134–65. New York: Guildford Press.

Bawarshi, Anis. 2010. "The Challenges and Possibilities of Taking Up Multiple Discursive Resources in U.S. College Composition". In Horner, Lu and Matsuda 2010, 196–203.

Bazerman, Charles. 1988. *Shaping Written Knowledge: The Genre and Activity of the Experimental Article in Science*. Madison: University of Wisconsin Press.

———. 1995. "Response: Curricular Responsibilities and Professional Definition". In *Reconceiving Writing, Rethinking Writing Instruction*, edited by Joseph Petraglia, 249–59. Mahwah, NJ: Lawrence Erlbaum.

———. 2007. Introduction to *Handbook of Research on Writing: History, Society, School, Individual, Text*, edited by Charles Bazerman, 1–4. New York: Lawrence Erlbaum.

Bazerman, Charles, and Paul Rogers. 2007. "Writing and Secular Knowledge within Modern European Institutions". In *Handbook of Research on Writing: History, Society, School, Individual, Text*, edited by Charles Bazerman, 157–75. New York: Lawrence Erlbaum.

Benesch, Sarah. 2001. *Critical English for Academic Purposes: Theory, Politics, and Practice*. Mahwah, NJ: Lawrence Erlbaum.

Berlin, James A. 1982. "Contemporary Composition: The Major Pedagogical Theories". *College English* 44 (8): 765–77.

———. 1987. *Rhetoric and Reality: Writing Instruction in American Colleges, 1900–1985*. Carbondale: Southern Illinois University Press.

Berlin, James A., and Robert P. Inkster. 1980. "Current-Traditional Rhetoric: Paradigm and Practice". *Freshman English News* 8 (3): 1–4, 13–14.

Bernstein, Basil. 1971. *Class, Codes, and Control: Theoretical Studies towards a Sociology of Language*. London: Routledge and Kegan Paul.

Bizzell, Patricia. (1982) 2003. "Cognition, Convention, and Certainty: What We Need to Know about Writing". In *Cross-Talk in Comp Theory: A Reader*, 2nd ed., edited by Victor Villanueva, 387–411. Urbana, IL: National Council of Teachers of English.

———. 1988. "Arguing about Literacy". *College English* 50 (2): 141–53.

Bizzell, Patricia, and Bruce Herzeberg, eds. 2001a. "From *Institutes of Oratory*". In *The Rhetorical Tradition: Readings from Classical Times to the Present*, 2nd ed., 364–428. Boston: Bedford/St Martin's.

———, eds. 2001b. "A Course of Lectures on Elocution". In *The Rhetorical Tradition: Readings from Classical Times to the Present*, 2nd ed., 881–97. Boston: Bedford/St Martin's.

———, eds. 2001c. "From *Narrative of the Life of Frederick Douglass*". In *The Rhetorical Tradition: Readings from Classical Times to the Present*, 2nd ed., 1070–75. Boston: Bedford/St Martin's.

Blair, Hugh. (1783) 1965. *Lectures on Rhetoric and Belles Lettres*, edited by Harold F. Harding. Carbondale: Southern Illinois University Press.

Bloch, Bernard, and George L. Trager. 1942. *Outline of Linguistic Analysis*. Baltimore: Waverly Press.

Bloom, Lynn Z. 2003. "The Great Paradigm Shift and Its Legacy for the Twenty-First Century". In *Composition Studies in the New Millennium: Rereading the Past, Rewriting the Future*, edited by Lynn Z. Bloom, Donald A. Daiker and Edward M. White, 31–47. Carbondale: Southern Illinois University Press.

Boquet, Elizabeth H., and Neal Lerner. 2008. "After 'The Idea of a Writing Center'". *College English* 71 (2): 170–89.

Bourdieu, Pierre. 1991. *Language and Symbolic Power*, edited by John B. Thompson, translated by Gino Raymond and Matthew Adamson. Cambridge, MA: Harvard University Press.

Brandon, Ed. 1996. "Foundation Semester". Facsimile memo to Dr Marlene Hamilton. 8 July. UWI Archives, Item No. 7, Syllabuses and Regulations. Survey Courses. File No. 83-22, Part No. 1. File Start Date 1997.

Brereton, John C., ed. 1995. *The Origins of Composition Studies in the American College, 1875–1925: A Documentary History*. Pittsburgh: University of Pittsburgh Press.

Breton, André. (1947) 1983. "Un Grand Poète Noir". In *Cahier d'un Retour au Pays Natal* by Aimé Césaire, 77–87. Paris: Présence Africaine.

Britton, James, Tony Burgess, Nancy Martin, Alex McCleod and Harold Rosen. 1975. *The Development of Writing Abilities (11–18)*. London: Macmillan.
Brooks, Cleanth, and Robert Penn Warren. 1956. *Fundamentals of Good Writing: A Handbook of Modern Rhetoric*. London: Dennis Dobson.
Brown, Celia. 1991. "Language Situation and Sociopolitical Structure in Jamaica". MA thesis. UWI, Mona.
Bryan, Beverley. 1998. "The Story so Far", introduction to "Language Learning and Teaching in a Creole-Speaking Environment", special issue, *Caribbean Journal of Education* 20 (1): 1–8.
——. 2004. "Language and Literacy in a Creole-speaking Environment: A Study of Primary Schools in Jamaica". *Language, Culture and Curriculum* 17 (2): 87–96. http://dx.doi.org/10.1080/07908310408666685
——. 2010. *Between Two Grammars: Research and Practice for Language Learning and Teaching in a Creole-Speaking Environment*. Kingston: Ian Randle.
Buell, Marcia Z. 2004. "Code-Switching and Second Language Writing: How Multiple Codes Are Combined in a Text". In *What Writing Does and How It Does It: An Introduction to Analyzing Texts and Textual Practices*, edited by Charles Bazerman and Paul Prior, 97–122. Mahwah, NJ: Lawrence Erlbaum.
Campbell, Carl C. 1970. *Towards an Imperial Policy for the Education of Negroes in the West Indies after Emancipation*. Kingston: UWI Press.
Canagarajah, A. Suresh. 2006. "The Place of World Englishes in Composition: Pluralization Continued". *College Composition and Communication* 57 (4): 586–619.
——. 2009. "Multilingual Strategies of Negotiating English: From Conversation to Writing". *JAC: A Journal of Composition Theory* 29 (1–2): 17–48.
——. 2010. "A Rhetoric of Shuttling between Languages". In Horner, Lu and Matsuda 2010, 158–79.
——, ed. 2013. *Literacy as Translingual Practice: Between Communities and Classrooms*. New York and London: Routledge.
Carr, William. 1963a. "The Use of English". Paper Presented at the meeting of the Subcommittee on the Use of English, UWI, 7 August 1963. UWI, Mona, Jamaica.
——. 1963b. "Uses of English at the University of the West Indies". Paper presented in a Series, "New Trends in University Education". No. 2. University Radio Service. JBC Sundays 2:00 p.m., Saturdays 7:45 p.m. August.
Carrington, Lawrence D. 1978. *Education and Development in the English-Speaking Caribbean: A Contemporary Study*. Buenos Aires: UNESCO/ECLA/UNDP Project on Development and Education in Latin America and the Caribbean.
——. 1981. *Literacy in the English-Speaking Caribbean*. Paris: UNESCO.
Carter, Michael. 2007. "Ways of Knowing, Doing, and Writing in the Disciplines". *College Composition and Communication* 58 (3): 385–418.
Cassidy, Frederic G. 1961. *Jamaica Talk: Three Hundred Years of the English Language in Jamaica*. London: Macmillan.
Cassidy, Frederic G., and Robert LePage. 1980. *Dictionary of Jamaican English*. 2nd ed. Cambridge: Cambridge University Press, 1980.
CCCC (Conference on College Composition and Communication). 1974. *Students' Right to Their Own Language*. Special issue, *College Composition and Communication* 25 (Fall): 1–32.

———. (1988) 1992. *The National Language Policy*. Accessed 28 January 2006. http://www.ncte.org/about/over/positions/category/div/107643.htm

Cheramie, Deany M. 2004. "Sifting Through Fifty Years of Change: Writing Program Administration at an Historically Black University". In *Historical Studies of Writing Program Administration: Individuals, Communities, and the Formation of a Discipline*, edited by Barbara L'Eplattenier and Lisa Mastrangelo, 145–65. West Lafayette, IN: Parlor Press.

Chevannes, Barry. 2005. "Sprinting Over the Long Distance: Education at a Crossroad". In Holding and Burke 2005, 297–306.

Christie, Pauline. 1987. "Comments from the Dean, Faculty of Natural Sciences, concerning the Department". Memorandum to PVC Augier, chairman, Academic Board, Mona. UWI, Mona, Jamaica. 7 May. UWI Archives, Item No. 141, Syllabuses and Regulations. Survey Courses. File No. 83-9, Part No. 2. File Start Date 1979.

———. 2003. *Language in Jamaica*. Kingston: Arawak.

Clark, Burton. 1983. *The Higher Education System: Academic Organization in Cross-National Perspective*. Berkeley: University of California Press.

Cobley, Alan G. 2000. "The Historical Development of Higher Education in the Anglophone Caribbean". In *Higher Education in the Caribbean: Past, Present and Future Directions*, edited by Glenford D. Howe, 1–23. Kingston: UWI Press.

Coffin, Caroline, and Ann Hewings. 2003. "Writing for Different Disciplines". In Coffin et al. 2003, 45–72.

Coffin, Caroline, Mary Jane Curry, Sharon Goodman, Ann Hewings, Theresa Lillis and Joan Swann. 2003. *Teaching Academic Writing: A Toolkit for Higher Education*. London: Routledge.

College of Arts and Science, Barbados. 1964. "Information for 'Barbados College News'". Bridgetown, Barbados. 6 July.

College of New Jersey. 2004. Writing Intensive Course Guidelines. Accessed 14 October 2008. http://www.tcnj.edu/~writing/faculty/intensiveguide.html

Condon, William, and Carol Rutz. 2012. "A Taxonomy of Writing across the Curriculum Programs: Evolving to Serve Broader Agendas". *College Composition and Communication* 64 (2): 357–82.

Connors, Robert J., and Andrea A. Lunsford. 1988. "Frequency of Formal Errors in Current College Writing, or Ma and Pa Kettle Do Research". *College Composition and Communication* 39 (4): 395–409.

Council for Writing Program Administrators. (2000) 2008. *WPA Outcomes Statement for First-Year Composition*. Accessed (9 June 2006) 19 April 2013. http://wpacouncil.org/positions/outcomes.html

Craig, Dennis. 1994. "The University in its Sociolinguistic Context". In *People and the Environment: Preserving the Balance*, Report of the Proceedings of the 15th Congress of the Universities of the Commonwealth, edited by Eileen A. Archer, 127–32. London: Association of Commonwealth Universities.

———. 1999. *Teaching Language and Literacy: Policies and Procedures for Vernacular Situations*. Georgetown, Guyana: Education and Development Services.

———. 2006. "The Use of the Vernacular in West Indian Education". In *Exploring the Boundaries of Caribbean Creole Languages*, edited by Hazel Simmons-McDonald and Ian Robertson, 99–117. Kingston: UWI Press.

Creary, Jean. 1964. "Outline Syllabus for the Use of English Course". UWI, Mona, Jamaica.
Crowley, Sharon. 1998. *Composition in the University: Historical and Polemical Essays*. Pittsburgh: University of Pittsburgh Press.
Currey, George. 1858. *English Grammar for the Use of Schools*. SPCK.
Curry, Mary Jane, and Theresa Lillis. 2003. "Issues in Academic Writing in Higher Education". In Coffin et al. 2003, 1–18.
Cuthbert, Marlene, ed. 1976. *Language and Communication*. Bridgetown, Barbados: The Cedar Press.
CXC (Caribbean Examinations Council). 1998. *The Caribbean Advanced Proficiency Examination (CAPE) Communication Studies Syllabus*. St Michael, Barbados: CXC.
Daniell, Beth. 1999. "Narratives of Literacy: Connecting Composition to Culture". *College Composition and Communication* 50 (3): 393–410.
Darnell, George. 1846. *An Introduction to English Grammar Consisting of a Graduated Series of Easy Lessons in Language*. SPCK.
Dean of Humanities and Education. 2006. Memorandum from the dean to Ingrid McLaren, "Schedule of Delivery of Language Foundation Courses 2006/07". Faculty of Humanities and Education, UWI, Mona, Jamaica.
Delpit, Lisa. 2006. "What Should Teachers Do? Ebonics and Culturally Responsive Instruction". In Nero 2006, 93–101.
Department of Linguistics and Use of English. 1989. "Report on UC010, 1988/89". UWI, Mona, Jamaica.
Departmental Reports. Mona. 1988. 1987–1988. UWI, Mona, Jamaica.
———. 1989. 1988–1989. UWI, Mona, Jamaica.
———. 1993. 1992–1993. UWI, Mona, Jamaica.
———. 1995. 1994–1995. Vol 1. UWI, Mona, Jamaica.
———. 1996. 1995–1996. UWI, Mona, Jamaica.
———. 1997. 1996–1997. UWI, Mona, Jamaica.
———. 1998. 1997–1998. UWI, Mona, Jamaica.
———. 1999. 1998–1999. UWI, Mona, Jamaica.
———. 2000. 1999–2000. UWI, Mona, Jamaica.
———. 2001. 2000–2001. UWI, Mona. 2001. Accessed 2 May 2005. http://www.mona.uwi.edu/reports/report00_01/artsed.pdf
———. 2002. 2001–2002. UWI, Mona. 2002. Accessed 2 May 2005. http://www.mona.uwi.edu/reports/reports02/Arts%20and%20Education.pdf
———. 2003. 2002–2003. UWI, Mona. 2003. Accessed 2 May 2005. http://www.mona.uwi.edu/reports/reports03/facultyofartsandeducation.pdf
———. 2004. 2003–2004. UWI, Mona. 2004. Accessed 2 May 2005. http://www.mona.uwi.edu/reports/reports04/facultyofhumanitiesandeducation2.pdf
———. 2005. 2004–2005. UWI, Mona. 2005. Accessed 10 July 2007. http://www.mona.uwi.edu/reports/0405/humed.htm
Devonish, Hubert. 1986. *Language and Liberation: Creole Language Politics in the Caribbean*. London: Karia Press.
———. 1998. "The English Language Proficiency Test". Department of Language and Linguistics, UWI, Mona, Jamaica. [10 October].

———. 2001. "Language Rights in the Draft Charter of Rights in the Jamaican Constitution". Department of Language, Linguistics and Philosophy, UWI, Mona, Jamaica. [May].
DLLP (Department of Language, Linguistics and Philosophy). 1997. Minutes of a Meeting of the DLLP held Thursday, October 2, 1997. Faculty of Humanities and Education, UWI, Mona, Jamaica.
———. 1998. "Minutes of a Meeting of the DLLP held Thursday, October 29, 1998". Faculty of Humanities and Education, UWI, Mona, Jamaica.
———. 2002a. "Minutes of a Meeting of the DLLP held Thursday, 17th January 2002". Faculty of Humanities and Education, UWI, Mona, Jamaica.
———. 2002b. "Minutes of English Language Section, DLLP. April 2002". Faculty of Humanities and Education, UWI, Mona, Jamaica.
———. 2004. "UC010 Report for 2003-4". DLLP, UWI, Mona, Jamaica.
———. 2006a. "Minutes of a Meeting of the DLLP held Monday, 27th February 2006". Faculty of Humanities and Education, UWI, Mona, Jamaica.
———. 2006b. "Report of Language Section Meeting Held Thursday, March 9, 2006". DLLP, UWI, Mona, Jamaica.
———. 2006c. "UWI Mona Writing Centre Mission". English Language Unit, UWI, Mona, Jamaica.
———. 2006d. "Writing Centre Pilot Project Proposal". English Language Unit, UWI, Mona, Jamaica.
Dobrin, Sidney I. 1997. *Constructing Knowledges: The Politics of Theory-Building and Pedagogy in Composition*. Albany: SUNY Press.
Downs, Douglas, and Elizabeth Wardle. 2007. "Teaching about Writing, Righting Misconceptions: (re)Envisioning 'First-Year Composition' as 'Introduction to Writing Studies'". *College Composition and Communication* 58 (4): 552–84.
Drayton, Kathleen. 1990. "'The Most Important Agent of Civilisation': Teaching English in the West Indies, 1838-1986". In *Teaching and Learning English Worldwide*, edited by James Britton, Robert E. Shafer and Ken Watson, 200–225. Clevedon, Avon: Multilingual Matters.
———. 1999. "Ideology and Culture in the Caribbean: Transmissions through Language Policy in the Education System". In *Gender in Caribbean Development: Papers Presented at the Inaugural Seminar of the University of the West Indies, Women and Development Studies Project*, 2nd ed., edited by Patricia Mohammed and Catherine Shepherd, 290–99. Kingston: Canoe.
Dyche, Caroline. 1996a. "Characteristic Errors of Students Who Fail the UWI Mona English Proficiency Entrance Test". *Journal of English Teaching* 23: 20–26.
———. 1996b. Letter to Mr Wint, editor, *Arts Newsletter*. Department of Language and Linguistics, UWI, Mona, Jamaica. [26 February].
———. 1996c. "Writing Proficiency in English and Academic Performance: The University of the West Indies, Mona". In *Caribbean Language Issues: Old and New – Papers in Honour of Mervyn Alleyne on the Occasion of his Sixtieth Birthday*, edited by Pauline Christie, 143–59. Kingston: UWI Press.
———. 2006a. "Equivalence of FD14A to FD10A for Purpose of Satisfying Faculty of Social Sciences Course Prerequisites". Memorandum to the dean, Faculty of Social Sciences. DLLP, UWI, Mona, Jamaica. 5 September.

———. 2006b. "English Language Education Policy-Making in a Multilayered Reality: A University of the West Indies Case Study". Paper presented at the "Why English?" Conference, University of Oxford, England. 26–28 October.

———. 2007a. "Excerpt of Report on English Language Proficiency Issues at UWI Mona (for presentation at Faculty of Humanities and Education Retreat, May 17, 2007)". ELS, Language, Linguistics and Philosophy, UWI, Mona, Jamaica. [May 2007].

———. 2007b. "English Language Education Policy and Divergent Realities: A University of the West Indies Case Study". *Caribbean Journal of Education* 29 (2): 359–82.

Dyche, Caroline, Alison Brooks, Ingrid McLaren and Hubert Devonish. 2010. "Legitimizing the Illegitimate: The Quality Assurance Review Process". *UWI Quality Education Forum* 16: 110–23.

Education Department. 1898. "Report on the Education Department for the Year Ended 31st March 1897". In *Departmental Reports for 1896–1897*, 419–39. Kingston: Government Printing Establishment.

———. 1899. "Report on the Education Department for the Year Ended 31st March 1898". In *Departmental Reports for 1897–1898*, 387–406. Kingston: Government Printing Establishment.

———. 1900. "Report on the Education Department for the Year Ended 31st March 1899". In *Departmental Reports for 1898–1899*, 367–80. Kingston: Government Printing Establishment.

———. 1906. "Report for the Year Ended 31st March 1905". In *Departmental Reports for the Year 1904–05*, 49–58. Kingston: Government Printing Establishment.

———. 1909. "Report for the Year Ended 31st March 1908". In *Departmental Reports for the Year 1907–08*, 446–54. Kingston: Government Printing Establishment.

———. 1911. "Report for the Year Ended 31st March 1910". In *Departmental Reports for the Year 1909–10*, 387–403. Kingston: Government Printing Establishment.

———. 1912. "Report for the Year Ended 31st March 1911". In *Departmental Reports for the Year 1910–11*, 185–95. Kingston: Government Printing Establishment.

———. 1915. "Report for the Year Ended 31st March 1914". In *Departmental Reports for the Year 1913–14*, 473–500. Kingston: Government Printing Establishment.

———. 1916. "Report for the Year Ended 31st March 1915". In *Departmental Reports for the Year 1914–15*, 521–41. Kingston: Government Printing Establishment.

———. 1917. "Report for the Year Ended 31st March 1916". In *Departmental Reports for the Year 1915–16*, 331–50. Kingston: Government Printing Establishment.

———. 1918. "Report for the Year Ended 31st March 1917". In *Departmental Reports for the Year 1916–17*, 293–307. Kingston: Government Printing Establishment.

———. 1919. "Report for the Year Ended 31st March 1918". In *Departmental Reports for the Year 1917–18*, 183–92. Kingston: Government Printing Establishment.

———. 1921. "Report for the Year Ended 31st December 1920". In *Departmental Reports for the Year 1920–21*, 61–71. Kingston: Government Printing Establishment.

Emig, Janet. 1971. *The Composing Processes of Twelfth Graders*. Urbana, IL: National Council of Teachers of English.

English Language Proficiency Test Information Guide. 2007. Kingston: English Language Proficiency Test Unit, UWI. Accessed 16 July 2007. http://www.mona.uwi.edu/dllp/language/elptu/index.htm

Faculty of Arts and General Studies. 1975. "Provisional Report of a Conference of Use of English Teachers Held in the Council Room, Mona, on January 3 & 4, 1975". UWI, Mona, Jamaica.
Faculty of Arts and General Studies, Cave Hill. 1987. "Report on Faculty Review1986/87". University of the West Indies, Cave Hill, Barbados.
Faculty of Arts and General Studies (Mona). 1987. *Regulations and Syllabuses*. Academic Year 1987/88. Kingston: UWI.
———. 1989. *Regulations and Syllabuses*. Academic Year 1989/90. Kingston: UWI.
———. 1992. *Regulations and Syllabuses*. Academic Year 1992/93. Kingston: UWI.
———. 1993. *Regulations and Syllabuses*. Academic Year 1993/94. Kingston: UWI.
———. 1997. *Regulations and Syllabuses*. Academic Year 1997/98. Kingston: UWI.
Faigley, Lester. 1992. *Fragments of Rationality: Postmodernity and the Subject of Composition*. Pittsburgh: University of Pittsburgh Press.
Fanon, Frantz. 1952. *Peau Noire, Masques Blancs*. Paris: Editions du Seuil.
Farrell, Thomas J. 1983. "IQ and Standard English". *College Composition and Communication* 34 (4): 470–84.
FD10A: English for Academic Purposes. 2007. Accessed November 3. http://www.mona.uwi.edu/dllp/courses/fd10a/index.htm
FD14A: Writing in the Disciplines. 2007. Accessed June 27. http://www.mona.uwi.edu/dllp/courses/fd14a/index.htm
Fergus, Howard A. 1998. "Jubilee Assessment: Some Achievements of the University of the West Indies in the Non-Campus Countries at Fifty". In *Celebrating the Past . . . Charting the Future . . . A View from Within: Proceedings of the 50th Anniversary Symposium*, 21–33. Kingston: UWI.
Figueroa, John J. 1957. "Paper for Faculty of Arts". UWI, Mona. 12 December, 1957. UWI Archives, RG 1, Box. No. 23, Item No. 99, Faculty of Arts Papers, 1957–March 1959, Part. 1.
———. 1963. "General Survey Courses and the Secondary Schools". (Paper for Appraisals Committee) Department of Education, UWI. 21 June 1963. UWI Archives, MA 96.2, Paper No. 31, Council, UWI Appraisal Committee – 1963 First Report and Papers Submitted.
———. 1971. *Society, Schools and Progress in the West Indies*. Oxford: Pergamon Press.
Flores, Juan. 1993. *Divided Borders: Essays on Puerto Rican Identity*. Houston, TX: Arté Público Press.
Flower, Linda, and John R. Hayes. 1981. "A Cognitive Process Theory of Writing". *College Composition and Communication* 32 (4): 365–87.
Foster, David. 2006. *Writing with Authority: Students' Roles as Writers in Cross-National Perspective*. Carbondale: Southern Illinois University Press.
Foster, David, and David R. Russell. 2002. Conclusion to *Writing and Learning in Cross-National Perspective: Transitions from Secondary to Higher Education*, edited by David Foster and David R. Russell, 319–39. Mahwah, NJ: Lawrence Erlbaum.
Freedman, Aviva. 1995. "The What, Where, When, Why, and How of Classroom Genres". In *Reconceiving Writing, Rethinking Writing Instruction*, edited by Joseph Petraglia, 121–44. Mahwah, NJ: Lawrence Erlbaum.
Freire, Paulo. 1972. *Pedagogy of the Oppressed*. Translated by Myra Bergman Ramos. Harmondsworth, Middlesex: Penguin.

Fulkerson, Richard. 2005. "Composition at the Turn of the Twenty-First Century". *College Composition and Communication* 56 (4): 654–87.
Ganobcsik-Williams, Lisa. 2006. "General Introduction: Responding to the Call for Academic Writing Theory and Pedagogy". In *Teaching Academic Writing in UK Higher Education: Theories, Practices, and Models*, edited by Lisa Ganobcsik-Williams, xxi–xxvi. Houndmills, England: Palgrave Macmillan.
Gardner, W.J. 1971. *A History of Jamaica: From Its Discovery by Christopher Columbus to the Year 1872, including an Account of Its Trade and Agriculture; Sketches of the Manners, Habits, and Customs of all Classes of Its Inhabitants; and a Narrative of the Progress of Religion and Education in the Island*. London: F. Cass.
"The General Paper: A Report on the NATE Workshop Held at UWI". 1990. *Journal of English Teaching* 17: 27–31.
Glazier, Teresa F. 2000. *The Least You Should Know About English*. 7th ed. Fort Worth: Harcourt Brace.
González, Norma, Luis C. Moll and Cathy Amanti. 2005. "Introduction: Theorizing Practices". In *Funds of Knowledge: Theorizing Practices in Households, Communities, and Classrooms*, edited by Norma González, Luis C. Moll and Cathy Amanti, 1–24. Mahwah, NJ: Lawrence Erlbaum.
Gordon, Shirley. 1963. *A Century of West Indian Education: A Sourcebook*. London: Longman.
———. 1968. *Reports and Repercussions in West Indian Education*. London: Ginn.
Governor's Report on the Blue Book and Departmental Reports 1892–1893. 1894. Kingston: Government Printing Establishment.
Governor's Report on the Blue Book and Departmental Reports 1893–1894. 1895. Kingston: Government Printing Establishment.
Governor's Report on the Blue Book and Departmental Reports 1894–1895. 1896. Kingston: Government Printing Establishment.
Governor's Report on the Blue Book and Departmental Reports 1895–1896. 1897. Kingston: Government Printing Establishment.
Great Britain. Board of Education. 1901. *The Educational Systems of the Chief Colonies of the British Empire. Special Reports on Educational Subjects*. Vol. 4. London: Wyman and Sons.
———. Commission on Higher Education in the Colonies. 1945. *Report of the West Indies Committee of the Commission on Higher Education in the Colonies*. London: His Majesty's Stationery Office.
Gunner, Jeanne. 2004. "Doomed to Repeat It? A Needed Space for Critique in Historical Recovery". In *Historical Studies of Writing Program Administration: Individuals, Communities, and the Formation of a Discipline*, edited by Barbara L'Eplattenier and Lisa Mastrangelo, 263–78. West Lafayette, IN: Parlor Press.
Hall, Anne-Marie. 2007. "Review Essay: *Writing with Authority; Students' Roles as Writers in Cross-National Perspective*, by David Foster". *Rhetoric Review* 26 (4): 462–67.
Harding, Vivienne A. 2002. "Proposal for Restructuring of UC120". Kingston: Department of Language, Linguistics and Philosophy, UWI, Mona, Jamaica. [14 June].
Harris, Joseph. 1997. *A Teaching Subject: Composition since 1966*. Upper Saddle River, NJ: Prentice Hall.
Harvard College. 2003. *Shaped by Writing: The Undergraduate Experience/Across the Drafts; Students and Teachers Talk About Feedback*. DVD. Dir. Nancy Sommers.

Haswell, Richard. 2007. "Teaching of Writing in Higher Education". In *Handbook of Research on Writing: History, Society, School, Individual, Text*, edited by Charles Bazerman, 331–46. New York: Lawrence Erlbaum.

Havelock, Eric. 1982. *The Literate Revolution in Greece and its Cultural Consequences*. Princeton: Princeton University Press.

Hiley, Richard. 1831. *Hiley's English Grammar Abridged with Questions for the Use of Young Pupils*. London: Simpkin & Marshall.

———. 1832. *Grammar of the English Language with the Principles of Eloquence and Rhetoric*. London: Simpkin & Marshall.

Hodge, Merle. 1997. *The Knots in English*. Wellesley, MA: Calaloux.

Holding, Rheima, and Olivene Burke, eds. 2005. *Revisiting Tertiary Education Policy in Jamaica: Towards Personal Gain or Public Good*. Kingston: Ian Randle.

Horner, Bruce. 2013. "Ideologies of Literacy, 'Academic Literacies', and Composition Studies". *Literacy in Composition Studies* 1 (1): 1–9.

Horner, Bruce, and John Trimbur. 2002. "English Only and U.S. College Composition". *College Composition and Communication* 53 (4): 594–630.

Horner, Bruce, Min-Zhan Lu and Paul Kei Matsuda, eds. 2010. *Cross-Language Relations in Composition*. Carbondale: Southern Illinois University Press.

Horner, Bruce, Min-Zhan Lu, Jacqueline Jones Royster and John Trimbur. 2011. "Language Difference in Writing: Toward a Translingual Approach". *College English* 73 (3): 303–21.

Hunte, Christopher Norman. 1978. *The Development of Higher Education in the West Indies*. Sherman Oaks, CA: Banner Books.

Hymes, Dell. 1972. Introduction to *Functions of Language in the Classroom*, edited by Courtney B. Cazden, Vera P. John and Dell Hymes, xi–lvii. New York: Teachers College Press.

———. 1995. "Bernstein and Poetics". In *Discourse and Reproduction: Essays in Honor of Basil Bernstein*, edited by Paul Atkinson, Brian Davies and Sara Delamont, 1–24. Cresskill, NJ: Hampton Press.

Irvine, Patricia, and Nan Elsasser. 1988. "The Ecology of Literacy: Negotiating Writing Standards in a Caribbean Setting". In *The Social Construction of Written Communication*, edited by Bennet A. Rafoth and Donald L. Rubin, 304–20. Norwood, NJ: Ablex.

Ivanič, Roz, and Mary R. Lea. 2006. "New Contexts, New Challenges: The Teaching of Writing in UK Higher Education". In *Teaching Academic Writing in UK Higher Education: Theories, Practices, and Models*, edited by Lisa Ganobcsik-Williams, 6–15. Houndmills, England: Palgrave Macmillan.

Jones, Carys, Joan Turner and Brian Street. 1999a. Introduction to *Students Writing in the University: Cultural and Epistemological Issues*, edited by Carys Jones, Joan Turner and Brian Street, xv–xxiv. Amsterdam: John Benjamins.

———. 1999b. "Mystery and Transparency in Academic Literacies". In *Students Writing in the University: Cultural and Epistemological Issues*, edited by Carys Jones, Joan Turner and Brian Street, 125–26. Amsterdam: John Benjamins.

Kennedy, Mary Lynch, William J. Kennedy and Hadley M. Smith. 2004. *Writing in the Disciplines: A Reader for Writers*. Upper Saddle River, NJ: Prentice Hall.

Kent, Thomas. 1999. Introduction to *Post-Process Theory: Beyond the Writing Process Paradigm*, edited by Thomas Kent, 1–6. Carbondale: Southern Illinois University Press.

King, David. 1971. "Some Proposed Modifications to the Chief Moderator's 1970/71 Report on the Use of English Course FGSP 8, 1970/71 as It Affects the Mona Campus". Letter to the dean, Faculty of General Studies, UWI, Mona. 15 September 1971. UWI Archives, Item No. 79, Syllabuses and Regulations. Survey Courses. File No. 83/9, Part 1, 1964–1979.

———. 1984. "Projection". Department of Linguistics and Use of English, UWI, Mona, Jamaica.

Kirszner, Laurie, and Stephen Mandell. 2004. *The Brief [Holt] Handbook*, 4th ed. Fort Worth, TX: Harcourt Brace.

Kuhn, Thomas. 1970. *The Structure of Scientific Revolutions*. Chicago: University of Chicago Press.

Kutney, Joshua P. 2007. "Will Writing Awareness Transfer to Writing Performance? Response to Douglas Downs and Elizabeth Wardle, 'Teaching about Writing, Righting Misconceptions'". *College Composition and Communication* 59 (2): 276–79.

Lalicker, William B. 1999. "A Basic Introduction to Basic Writing Program Structures: A Baseline and Five Alternatives". *BWe: Basic Writing e-Journal* 1 (2). Accessed 2 May 2005. http://www.asu.edu/class/english/composition/cbw/bwe_fall_1999.htm

Lalla, Barbara. 1998. *English for Academic Purposes Study Guide*. St Augustine, Trinidad: UWIDEC.

Lea, Mary R., and Barry Stierer, eds. 2000. *Student Writing in Higher Education: New Contexts*. Buckingham: Open University Press.

Lea, Mary, and Brian Street. 1998. "Student Writing in Higher Education: An Academic Literacies Approach". *Studies in Higher Education*. 23 (2): 157–72. doi: 10.1080/03075079812331380364

Leonhard, Barbara Harris. 2002. *Discoveries in Academic Writing*. Boston: Heinle & Heinle.

LePage, R.B. 1955. "The Language Problem in the British Caribbean". *Caribbean Quarterly* 4 (1): 40–49.

———. 1959. Memorandum to the dean, Faculty of Arts. 24 February 1959. UWI Archives, RG 1, MA 92.1, Box 21, Item No. 97, Faculty of Arts, General, 1956, Pt. 4.

Lewis, W. Arthur. 1960. *Address by the Principal, Dr W.A. Lewis on the Occasion of the Matriculation of New Students at Mona on 7 October 1960*. Kingston: University College of the West Indies.

LG20A: Language and Ethics. 2007. Accessed June 25. http://www.mona.uwi.edu/dllp/courses/LG20A

LG30A: The Art of Public Speaking. 2008. Accessed January 3. http://www.mona.uwi.edu/dllp/courses/LG30A/

Lillis, Theresa. 1999. "Whose 'Common Sense'? Essayist Literacy and the Institutional Practice of Mystery". In *Students Writing in the University: Cultural and Epistemological Issues*, edited by Carys Jones, Joan Turner and Brian Street, 127–47. Amsterdam: John Benjamins.

———. 2001. *Student Writing: Access, Regulation, Desire*. Florence, KY: Routledge.

———. 2006. "Moving Towards an 'Academic Literacies' Pedagogy: Dialogues of Participation". In *Teaching Academic Writing in UK Higher Education: Theories, Practices, and Models*, edited by Lisa Ganobcsik-Williams, 30–45. Houndmills, England: Palgrave Macmillan.

Lillis, Theresa, and Joan Turner. 2001. "Student Writing in Higher Education: Contemporary Confusion, Traditional Concerns". *Teaching in Higher Education* 6 (1): 57-68. doi: 10.1080/13562510020029608

LITS1007 (E10G): Reading and Writing about Literature. 2007. Accessed December 8. http://www.mona.uwi.edu/liteng/E10G.htm

Locke, John. (1689) 1695. *An Essay Concerning Humane Understanding*, 3rd ed. London: Black Swan.

Lu, Min-Zhan. 1994. "Professing Multiculturalism: The Politics of Style in the Contact Zone". *College Composition and Communication* 45 (4): 442-58.

———. 2004. "An Essay on the Work of Composition: Composing English against the Order of Fast Capitalism". *College Composition and Communication* 56 (1): 16-50.

———. (2010). "Living-English Work". In Horner, Lu and Matsuda 2010, 42-56.

MA in English Language. 2006. Accessed September 20. http://www.mona.uwi.edu/dllp/jlu/masters/index.htm

Magnus, Ken E. 1987. "Use of English". Memorandum to the chairman, Academic Board. UWI, Mona. 14 April 1987. UWI Archives, Item No. 139, Syllabuses and Regulations. Survey Courses. File No. 83-9, Part No. 2. File Start Date 1979.

Maimon, Elaine. 2002. Foreword to *Writing in the Academic Disciplines: A Curricular History*, 2nd ed., by David R. Russell, ix-xi. Carbondale: Southern Illinois University Press.

Maimon, Elaine, et al. 1981. *Writing in the Arts and Sciences*. Cambridge, MA: Winthrop.

Mangelsdorf, Kate. 2010. "Spanglish as Alternative Discourse: Working against Language Demarcation". In Horner, Lu and Matsuda 2010, 113-26.

Manion, Christine. 2001. *A Writer's Guide to Oral Presentations and Writing in the Disciplines*. Upper Saddle River, NJ: Prentice Hall.

Manley, Michael. 1974. *The Politics of Change: A Jamaica Testament*. London: André Deutsch.

Mark Scheme for Writing Tasks. 2004. Kingston: Test Unit, Department of Language, Linguistics and Philosophy, UWI.

Marshall, Woodville K. 1998. "Celebrating the UWI's Survival". In *Celebrating the Past . . . Charting the Future. . . . A View from Within: Proceedings of the 50th Anniversary Symposium*, 9–12. Kingston: UWI.

"Matters to a Meeting of the Faculty of Arts and General Studies Committee of October 30, 1975, from a Meeting of Academic Committee of 3rd July 1975". 1975. The Registry, UWI, Mona, Jamaica. 28 October.

Maxwell, I.C.M. 1980. *Universities in Partnership: The Inter-University Council and the Growth of Higher Education in Developing Countries 1946–70*. Edinburgh: Scottish Academic Press.

Maxwell, Peter. 2000–2001. "A New Language Education Policy for Jamaica". *Journal of English Teaching* 28: 2.

McCourtie, Lena. 1998. "The Politics of Creole Language Education in Jamaica: 1891–1921 and the 1990s". *Journal of Multilingual and Multicultural Development* 19 (2): 108–27. doi: 10.1080/01434639808666346

McLaren, Ingrid. 2010. "Another Country Not My Own: Crossing Disciplinary Borders, Forging Alliances within the Framework of a (Communication across the Curriculum) CAC Initiative in the Sciences". *International Journal of English and Literature* 1 (2): 10–15. http://www.academicjournals.org/ijel/PDF/Pdf2010/November/McLaren.pdf

McLaren, Ingrid A.M., Caroline A. Dyche, Alison Altidor-Brooks and Hubert Devonish. 2011. "Survival or Natural Death? Issues Related to the Sustainability of Writing across the Curriculum Programmes". *Journal of Academic Writing* 1 (1): 254–66. http://e-learning.coventry.ac.uk/ojs/index.php/joaw/article/view/12/68

McLeod, Susan. 2001. "The Pedagogy of Writing across the Curriculum". In *A Guide to Composition Pedagogies*, edited by Gary Tate, Amy Rupiper and Kurt Schick, 149–64. New York: Oxford University Press.

McNenny, Gerri. 2001. "Writing Instruction and the Post-Remedial Writing University: Setting the Scene for the Mainstreaming Debate in Basic Writing". In *Mainstreaming Basic Writers: Politics and Pedagogies of Access*, edited by Gerri McNenny and Sallyanne H. Fitzgerald, 1–15. Mahwah, NJ: Lawrence Erlbaum.

Merrill, Yvonne, and Thomas P. Miller. 2002. "Making Learning Visible: A Rhetorical Stance on General Education". In *The Writing Program Administrator's Resource: A Guide to Reflective Institutional Practice*, edited by Stuart Brown and Theresa Enos, 203–17. Mahwah, NJ: Lawrence Erlbaum.

Miller, Carolyn R., and Davida Charney. 2007. "Persuasion, Audience, and Argument". In *Handbook of Research on Writing: History, Society, School, Individual, Text*, edited by Charles Bazerman, 583–98. New York: Lawrence Erlbaum.

Miller, Errol. 1981. "From Research to Action: Language Policy in Jamaica". *Prospects: Quarterly Review of Education* 11 (3): 372–80.

Miller, Susan. 1989. *Rescuing the Subject: A Critical Introduction to Rhetoric and the Writer*. Carbondale: Southern Illinois University Press.

Miller, Thomas P. 1997. *The Formation of College English: Rhetoric and Belles Lettres in the British Cultural Provinces*. Pittsburgh: Pittsburgh University Press.

Milson-Whyte, Vivette. 2011. "Dialogism in Gina Valdés' 'English con Salsa': A Poetic Address on Accommodating Linguistic Diversity through Code Meshing". In *Code Meshing as World English: Policy, Pedagogy, Performance*, edited by Vershawn Ashanti Young and Aja Martinez, 143–67. Urbana, IL: National Council of Teachers of English.

———. 2013. "Pedagogical and Socio-Political Implications of Code-Meshing in Classrooms: Some Considerations for a Translingual Orientation to Writing". In *Literacy as Translingual Practice: Between Communities and Classrooms*, edited by A. Suresh Canagarajah, 115–27. New York: Routledge.

———. 2014. "Working English through Code-Meshing: Implications for Denigrated Language Varieties and Their Users". In *Working English in Rhetoric and Composition: Language, Locations, Interventions*, edited by Bruce Horner and Karen Kopelson, 103–15. Carbondale: Southern Illinois University Press.

Ministry of Education and Culture. 1999. *Revised Primary Curriculum*. Primary Education Improvement Programme GOJ/IDB II (PEIP II). Kingston: Ministry of Education and Culture.

Ministry of Education, Youth and Culture. 2001. *Language Education Policy*. Kingston: Ministry of Education, Youth and Culture.

"Minutes of a Meeting of the Faculty of General Studies Committee, Mona, Held on Friday, 23rd April, 1971". 1971. UWI, Mona, Jamaica.

Moore, Schontal. 2006a. "FD10A Report/Statistics for Semester One 2005/2006". Department of Language, Linguistics and Philosophy, UWI, Mona, Jamaica

———. 2006b. "A Proposal for Writing across the Curriculum Project (A Writing Centre/English Language Section Research Initiative)". Department of Language, Linguistics and Philosophy, Faculty of Humanities, UWI, Mona.

Morris, Mervyn. 1999. *Is English We Speaking and Other Essays*. Kingston: Ian Randle.

Muchiri, Mary N., Nshindi G. Mulamba, Deoscorus B. Ndoloi and Greg Myers. 1995. "Importing Composition: Teaching and Researching Academic Writing Beyond North America". *College Composition and Communication* 46 (2): 175–98.

NCTE (National Council of Teachers of English). 2007. *Adolescent Literacy: A Policy Research Brief*. Accessed 21 September 2007. http://www.ncte.org/about/over/positions/category/literacy/127676.htm

Nero, Shondel J., ed. 2006. *Dialects, Englishes, Creoles, and Education*. Mahwah, NJ: Lawrence Erlbaum.

———. 2010. "Discourse Tensions, Englishes, and the Composition Classroom". In Horner, Lu and Matsuda 2010, 142–57.

———. 2014. "De Facto Language Education Policy Through Teachers' Attitudes and Practices: A Critical Ethnographic Study in Three Jamaican Schools". *Language Policy* 13: 221–42. doi: 10.1007/s10993-013-9311-x

Nettleford, Rex. 1986. *The University of the West Indies as a Regional University in the English-Speaking Caribbean: Past, Present and Future Trends in Academic, Administrative and Organizational Aspects, with Special Emphasis on Future Implications on the Restructured UWI*. Caracas, Venezuela: Regional Centre for Higher Education in Latin America and the Caribbean (CRESALC).

New Deal for Education in Independent Jamaica. 1966. Kingston: Ministry of Education.

Newman, Margaret. 2007. "FD14A Coordinator's (Draft) Report 2005/6 and 2006/7". Department of Language, Linguistics and Philosophy, UWI, Mona, Jamaica.

North, Stephen. 1984. "The Idea of Writing Centre". *College English* 46 (5): 433–46.

OBUS (Office of the Board for Undergraduate Studies). 2009. *Review of the English Language Section*. Kingston: OBUS, UWI.

Ong, Walter J. 1978. "Literacy and Orality in Our Times". *ADE Bulletin* 58: 1–7.

———. (1982) 1991. *Orality and Literacy: The Technologizing of the Word*. London and New York: Routledge.

———. 1988. "A Comment on 'Arguing about Literacy'". *College English* 50 (6): 700–701.

Owens, R.J. 1963. "Use of English Survey Course". 22 July 1963. Registry, UWI, Mona. 9 Aug. 1963.

Parker, Paul C. 1978. "Change and Challenge in Caribbean Higher Education: The Development of the University of the West Indies and the University of Puerto Rico". PhD diss., Florida State University, 1972.

Perl, Sondra. 1994. "Writing Process: A Shining Moment". Introduction. In *Landmark Essays on Writing Process*, edited by Sondra Perl, xi–xx. Davis, CA: Hermagoras.

Petraglia, Joseph. 1995. "Introduction: General Writing Skills Instruction and Its Discontents". In *Reconceiving Writing, Rethinking Writing Instruction*, edited by Joseph Petraglia, xi–xvii. Mahwah, NJ: Lawrence Erlbaum.

Pollard, Velma. 1995. "A Language or Languages for Jamaica". *Vistas* 2 (4).

———. 1998. "Code Switching and Code Mixing: Language in the Jamaican Classroom". *Caribbean Journal of Education* 20 (1): 9–20.

Pratt, Mary Louise. 1991. "Arts of the Contact Zone". *Profession* 91: 33–40.
Quirk, Randolph. 1962. *The Use of English*. London: Longman.
Raimes, Ann. 1999. *Keys for Writers: A Brief Handbook*. 2nd ed. Boston: Houghton Mifflin.
Ramsay, Paulette, Vivienne Harding, Janice Cools and Ingrid McLaren. 2009. *Blooming with the Pouis: Critical Thinking, Reading and Writing across the Curriculum*. Kingston: Ian Randle.
Report of the Task Force on Tertiary Education. 1986. Kingston: Ministry of Education.
"Report on UC010, 1988/89". 1989. Department of Linguistics and Use of English, UWI, Mona, Jamaica.
Report to Council from the Vice-Chancellor for the Year Ending 31st July 1965. 1965. UWI. UWI Archives, MA96.2.
Revised LG600 Outline (for Sociology). 2003. Department of Language, Linguistics and Philosophy, Faculty of Humanities and Education, UWI, Mona, Jamaica.
Roberts, Peter. 1988. *West Indians and Their Language*. New York: Cambridge University Press.
———. 1991. "Proposal to Make Available to Sixth Forms and Tertiary Level Institutions a Two-Year Equivalent of UC100/UC10A + UC10B to Replace the Cambridge General Paper". Memorandum to the head of Department of Linguistics and Use of English Mona and the head, Department of Language and Linguistics, St Augustine. UWI, Cave Hill, Barbados.
Roberts, Vivienne. 2003. *The Shaping of Tertiary Education in the Anglophone Caribbean: Forces, Forms and Functions*. London: Commonwealth Secretariat.
Roberston, E., et al. 1975. "Sub-committee to Consider the Use of English Course". Faculty of Natural Sciences, UWI, Mona. 4 March 1975. UWI Archives, Item No. 122, Syllabuses and Regulations. Survey Courses. File No. 83/9, Part 1, 1964–1979.
Robertson, Ian. 1996. "Language Education Policy (1): Towards a Rational Approach for Caribbean States". In *Caribbean Language Issues: Old and New – Papers in Honour of Mervyn Alleyne on the Occasion of his Sixtieth Birthday*, edited by Pauline Christie, 112–19. Kingston: UWI Press.
Robinson, Leslie R.B. 1971a. Letter to Dr S.R.R. Allsopp. UWI, Mona, Jamaica. 10 May 1971. UWI Archives, Item No. 71, Syllabuses and Regulations. Survey Courses. File No. 83/9, Part 1, 1964–1979.
———. 1971b. Letter to David King. UWI, Mona, Jamaica. 29 March.
Robotham, Don. 2000. "Changing a University: Reconciling Quantity with Quality – The Case of the University of the West Indies". In *Higher Education in the Caribbean: Past, Present and Future Directions*, edited by Glenford D. Howe, 237–50. Kingston: UWI Press.
Rodriguez Connal, Louise. 2000. "Transcultural Rhetorics for Cultural Survival". In *Language Ideologies: Critical Perspectives on the Official English Movement*, Vol 1, edited by Roseann Dueñas González, 318–31. Urbana, IL: National Council of Teachers of English.
Rose, Mike. 1985. "The Language of Exclusion: Writing Instruction at the University". *College English* 47 (4): 341–59.
Russell, David. 1995. "Activity Theory and Its Implications for Writing Instruction". In *Reconceiving Writing, Rethinking Writing Instruction*, edited by Joseph Petraglia, 51–77. Mahwah, NJ: Lawrence Erlbaum.

———. 1999. "Activity Theory and Process Approaches: Writing (Power) in School and Society". In *Post-Process Theory: Beyond the Writing-Process Paradigm*, edited by Thomas Kent, 80–95. Carbondale: Southern Illinois University Press.

———. 2002. *Writing in the Academic Disciplines: A Curricular History*. 2nd ed. Carbondale: Southern Illinois University Press. First published 1991.

Russell, David, and David Foster. 2002. "Rearticulating Articulation". Introduction. *Writing and Learning in Cross-National Perspective: Transitions from Secondary to Higher Education*, edited by David Foster and David R. Russell, 1–47. Mahwah, NJ: Lawrence Erlbaum.

Scott, Eileen. 2007. "Report UC010 Semester I, 2006–07". Department of Language, Linguistics and Philosophy, UWI, Mona, Jamaica.

Shaughnessy, Mina P. 1977. *Errors and Expectations: A Guide for the Teachers of Basic Writing*. New York: Oxford University Press.

Sheils, Merril. 1975. "Why Johnny Can't Write". *Newsweek*, December 8, 58.

Sherlock, Philip Manderson, and Rex M. Nettleford. 1990. *The University of the West Indies: A Caribbean Response to the Challenge of Change*. London: Macmillan Caribbean.

Shields, Kathryn. 1987a. "Justification for the Re-imposition of a Five-year Time Limit for *Use of English*". 1987. UWI Archives, Item No. 159, Syllabuses and Regulations. Survey Courses. File No. 83-9, Part No. 2. File Start Date 1979.

———. 1987b. "Proposals for Upgrading Students' Proficiency in English". Department of Linguistics and Use of English, UWI, Mona. 1987. UWI Archives, Item No. 153A, Syllabuses and Regulations. Survey Courses. File No. 83-9, Part No. 2. File Start Date 1979.

———. 1989. "Preliminary Report on UC010". Department of Linguistics and Use of English, UWI, Mona. 10 January.

Shields-Brodber, Kathryn. 1997. "Requiem for English in an 'English-Speaking' Community". In *Englishes Around the World*, vol. 2, *Caribbean, Africa, Asia, Australasia: Studies in Honour of Manfred Görlach*, edited by Edgar W. Schneider, 57–67. Philadelphia: John Benjamins.

Simmons-McDonald, Hazel, and Ian Robertson. 2006. Introduction to *Exploring the Boundaries of Caribbean Creole Languages*, edited by Hazel Simmons-McDonald and Ian Robertson, xiv–xvi. Kingston: UWI Press.

Simmons-McDonald, Hazel, Linda Fields and Peter Roberts. 1997. *Writing in English: A Course Book for Caribbean Students*. Kingston: Ian Randle.

Smit, David W. 2004. *The End of Composition Studies*. Carbondale: Southern Illinois University Press.

Smith, R.T. 1963. "General Degree Structure: Report of an Open Meeting Co-sponsored by the Senior Common Room and the West Indies Group of University Teachers Held on May 22nd, 1963 at Mona". UWI Archives, MA 96.2, Council, UWI Appraisal Committee – 1963 First Report and Papers Submitted.

Smitherman, Geneva. 1999. "CCCC's Role in the Struggle for Language Rights". *College Composition and Communication* 50 (3): 349–76.

———. 2000. *Talkin that Talk: Language, Culture, and Education in African America*. London: Routledge.

Soliday, Mary. 2002. *The Politics of Remediation: Institutional and Student Needs in Higher Education*. Pittsburgh: University of Pittsburgh Press.

Sommers, Nancy, and Laura Saltz. 2004. "The Novice as Expert: Writing the Freshman Year". *College Composition and Communication* 56 (1): 124–49.

Spellmeyer, Kurt. 1989. "A Common Ground: The Essay in the Academy". *College English* 51 (3): 262–76.

Sternglass, Marilyn S. 1999. "Students Deserve Enough Time to Prove They Can Succeed". *Journal of Basic Writing* 18 (1): 3–20.

Stone, Carl. 1988. "The Threat of Mediocrity". *Daily Gleaner*. 6 July, 8A.

Street, Brian. 1984. *Literacy in Theory and Practice*. New York: Cambridge University Press.

Sullivan, Robert. 1852. *An Attempt to Simplify English Grammar with the Observation and the Method of Teaching It*. Dublin.

Task Force on Educational Reform, Jamaica. 2004. *A Transformed Education System*. Kingston: Ministry of Education, Youth and Culture.

Taylor, Monica. 2003. "Towards a Model of Verbal Interaction in Jamaican English Language Classrooms". PhD diss., UWI, Mona.

Thompson, Denys. 1954. *Reading and Discrimination*. Rev. ed. London: Chatto & Windus.

Thompson, Mertel E. 1986. "Literacy in a Creole Context: Teaching Freshman English in Jamaica". Paper Presented at the 37th Annual Meeting of the Conference on College Composition and Communication, New Orleans, LA, 13–15 March 1986. ERIC Document No. ED 276 054.

———. 1987. "Report on the Essentials of Good Writing Course 1986/87". Memorandum to Dr Pauline Christie, head, Department of Linguistics and Use of English. UWI, Mona. 29 June.

Tobin, Lad. 1994. "Introduction: How the Writing Process Was Born and Other Conversion Narratives". In *Taking Stock: The Writing Process Movement in the '90s*, edited by Lad Tobin and Thomas Newkirk, 1–14. Portsmouth, NH: Boynton/Cook.

Trimbur, John. 1999. "The Problem of Freshman English (Only): Toward Programs of Study in Writing". *WPA: Writing Program Administration* 22 (3): 9–30.

Troyka, Lynn Quitman. 1987. "Defining Basic Writing in Context". In *A Sourcebook for Basic Writing Teachers*, edited by Theresa Enos, 2–15. New York: Random House.

Troyka, Lynn Quitman, and Douglas Hesse. 2005. *Simon & Schuster Handbook for Writers*. 7th ed. New Jersey: Prentice Hall.

Turner, Joan. 1999. "Academic Literacy and the Discourse of Transparency". In *Students Writing in the University: Cultural and Epistemological Issues*, edited by Carys Jones, Joan Turner and Brian Street, 149–60. Amsterdam: John Benjamins.

UAC (University Academic Committee). 1988a. Minutes. UWI Archives, Item No. 166, Syllabuses and Regulations. Survey Courses. File No. 83–89, Part No. 2. File Start Date 1979. 24 March

———. 1988b. UWI Archives, Item No. 175A, Syllabuses and Regulations. Survey Courses. File No. 83-9, Part No. 2. File Start Date 1979. 7 July.

———. 1988c. UWI Archives, Item No. 184, Syllabuses and Regulations. Survey Courses. File No. 83-9, Part No. 2. File Start Date 1979. 25 November.

UC010 Course Outline. 2003-2004. Department of Language, Linguistics and Philosophy. UWI, Mona, Jamaica. Accessed 2 May 2005. http://www.mona.uwi.edu/dllp/courses/uc010/course.htm

UC10A: Language: Exposition. 2007. Accessed June 27. http://www.mona.uwi.edu/dllp/courses/uc10a/index.htm
UC10A: Language: Exposition Syllabus. 2007. Accessed June 27. http://www.mona.uwi.edu/dllp/courses/uc10a/syllabus.htm
UC10B: Language: Argument. 2007. Accessed June 27. http://www.mona.uwi.edu/dllp/courses/uc10b/index.htm
UC120 Examination. 2003. Department of Language, Linguistics and Philosophy, UWI, Mona, Jamaica.
UCWI (University College of the West Indies). 1954. *Memorandum for Applicants for Entry as Undergraduates in October 1954*. Kingston: UCWI.
———. 1959. *Calendar 1959-60*. UWI Archives, MA 96.2.
UNESCO (United Nations Educational, Scientific and Cultural Organization). 1983. *Jamaica: Development of Secondary Education*. Paris: UNESCO.
Unit of Use of English and Linguistics. 1987. "Report on Proficiency of Third Year Students, 1986/87". UWI, Cave Hill, Barbados.
"University Courses: Use of English Syllabus 1972-73". 1972. UWI.
"Use of English Course. Suggestions for Seminars 4-8". 1964. UWI, Mona, Jamaica. 13 January.
Use of English Staff, Mona. 1980. "Proposal for Restructuring of Use of English Course". UWI, Mona, Jamaica. 27 February.
UWI (University of the West Indies). 1963a. "First Report of the Appraisals Committee of Council, Submitted to the Council of the University for Consideration at its Meeting on 25 June 1963". 11 June 1963. UWI Archives, MA 96.2, Council, UWI Appraisal Committee – 1963 First Report and Papers Submitted.
———. 1963b. Senate Paper 18. "Report of the Committee of Deans and Co-opted Members Appointed by Senate to Work Out Details of the General Degree Introductory Courses". 2 October. UWI Archives, MA 96.2, *Senate Papers 1963-64*.
———. 1964. *Calendar 1964-65*. UWI Archives, MA 96.2.
———. 1970. *Vice Chancellor's Report 1970*. UWI Archives, MA 96.2.
———. 1979. *Vice Chancellor's Report 1979*. UWI Archives, MA 02.3.
———. 1980. *Vice Chancellor's Report 1980*. UWI Archives, MA 02.3.
———. 1989. *Vice Chancellor's Report 1989*. UWI Archives, MA 02.3.
———. 1990. *Vice Chancellor's Report 1990*. UWI Archives, MA 02.3.
———. 1992. *Vice Chancellor's Report 1992*. UWI Archives, MA 96.2.
———. 1999. *Vice Chancellor's Report 1999*. UWI Archives, MA 96.2.
———. 2006-2007. *Official Statistics 2005/2006*. Kingston: Office of Planning and Institutional Research, UWI.
———. 2007a. "Business Communication". Accessed 8 February 2013. http://myspot.mona.uwi.edu/proffice/uwinotebook/entry/1003
———. 2007b. *Draft Strategic Plan 2007-2012*. Kingston: Office of Planning and Development, UWI. Accessed 25 July 2007. http://www.mona.uwi.edu/opair/strategic-plan/draft-strategic-plan-2007-2012.pdf
———. 2012. *Strategic Plan 2012-2017*. Kingston: Office of Planning and Development, UWI. Accessed 18 February 2013. http://www.mona.uwi.edu/opair/strategic-plan/UWI+Strategic+Plan+2012-2017+(Final).pdf

Vélez-Ibáñez, Carlos, and James Greenberg. (1992) 2005. "Formation and Transformation of Funds of Knowledge". In *Funds of Knowledge: Theorizing Practices in Households, Communities, and Classrooms*, edited by Norma González, Luis C. Moll and Cathy Amanti, 47–69. Mahwah, NJ: Lawrence Erlbaum.

Villanueva, Victor. 1993. *Bootstraps: From an American Academic of Color*. Urbana, IL: National Council of Teachers of English.

Virtue, Erica. 2013. "Bloody English! UWI, UTech Students Struggle with the Language". *Sunday Gleaner*, January 27, A4.

Waldo, Mark. 1996. "Inquiry as a Non-Invasive Approach to Cross-Curricular Writing Consultancy". *Language and Learning across the Disciplines* 1 (3): 6–22.

Walker, Joyce. 1966. "Some Comments on the Work Done by Students in Use of English". UWI, Mona. 12 December.

———. 1969. "Report on the Use of English Course 1968/69". UWI, Mona, 1969.

———. 1972. "Minutes of the Meeting of Lecturers in the Use of English at Cave Hill 28th to 29th January, 1972". UWI, Mona.

———. 1973. Letter to Mr Arthur Drayton, vice dean, Faculty of Arts and General Studies. UWI, Mona.

White, Edward M. 1989. *Developing Successful College Writing Programs*. San Francisco: Jossey-Bass.

———. 2001. "Revisiting the Importance of Placement and Basic Studies: Evidence of Success". In *Mainstreaming Basic Writers: Politics and Pedagogies of Access*, edited by Gerri McNenny and Sallyanne H. Fitzgerald, 19–28. Mahwah, NJ: Lawrence Erlbaum.

Whyte, Millicent. 1977. *A Short History of Education in Jamaica*. London: Hodder and Stoughton.

Widdowson, H.G. 1994. "The Ownership of English". *TESOL Quarterly* 28 (2): 377–89.

Wignall, Mark. 2007. "How Did He Enter UWI, Mona?". *Jamaica Observer*, 6 May, 2A.

Williams, Eric. (1950) 1994. *Education in the British West Indies*. New York: A&B Books.

Wilson, Don, Joe Pereira and Caroline Dyche. 1995. "Report on English Language Proficiency Requirements for UWI Mona Undergraduate Study". UWI, Mona.

Winch, Christopher, and Peter Wells. 1995. "The Quality of Student Writing in Higher Education: A Case for Concern?". *British Journal of Educational Studies* 43 (1): 75–87.

Winford, Donald. 1973a. "A Brief Summary of the Aims and Contents of the Use of English Course". UWI, St Augustine, Trinidad. February.

———. 1973b. "Proposal for Development of Part of the Use of English Course". Memorandum to heads of department, deputy librarian, senior assistant librarians, assistant librarians. UWI, St Augustine, Trinidad. 6 June.

———. 1977. "Revision of U/E Course". Memorandum to vice dean, Faculty of Arts and General Studies. UWI, St Augustine, Trinidad. 25 November.

———. 1993. *Predication in Caribbean English Creoles*. Amsterdam: John Benjamins.

———. 1997. "Re-examining Caribbean English Creole Continua". *World Englishes* 16 (2): 233–79.

Wood, Nancy. 2001. *Perspectives on Argument*. New Jersey: Prentice Hall.

WRITE Symposium II. 2005. "Recommendations from the English Language Foundation Programme Review Meeting Mona, 18th February 2005". Faculty of Humanities and Education, UWI. February.

WRITE Symposium IIa. 2005. "Position Paper in Response to Feedback Given to the WRITE Symposium Proposal for Language Foundation Courses". Faculty of Humanities and Education, UWI. 3 June.

Writing Centre. 2007. Mission Statement. Accessed November 3. http://www.mona.uwi.edu/dllp/language/writers/writing.htm

Wynter, Hector. 1959. "Letter to R. Eustace". 16 March. UWI Archives, RG 1, Box 22, Item No. 97, Faculty of Arts, General, January–June 1959.

Young, Morris. 2013. "Sponsoring Literacy Studies". *Literacy in Composition Studies* 1 (1): 10–14.

Young, Vershawn Ashanti. 2007. *Your Average Nigga: Performing Race, Literacy, and Masculinity*. Detroit: Wayne State University Press.

———. 2009. "'Nah, We Straight': An Argument against Code Switching". *JAC: A Journal of Composition Theory* 29 (1–2): 49–76.

Young, Vershawn Ashanti, and Aja Y. Martinez, eds. 2011. *Code-Meshing as World English: Pedagogy, Policy, Performance*. Urbana, IL: National Council of Teachers of English.

Young, Vershawn Ashanti, Aja Y. Martinez and Julie Anne Naviaux. 2011. "Code-Meshing as World English". Introduction. In *Code Meshing as World English: Policy, Pedagogy, Performance*, edited by Vershawn Ashanti Young and Aja Martinez, xix–xxxi. Urbana, IL: National Council of Teachers of English.

Index

A

academic discourse, 216; as mythical genre, 227; plurality of, 8–9, 22

academic English, qualities of, 160

academic literacies, 8, 23, 31, 195

academic literacy: as foundation of eloquence, 8–9; international currency of, 75–76; transcultural rhetorical approach to writing, 37–38; UNESCO report on, 68; writing as assumed instinct, 34, 35, 45, 58, 65, 66–67, 74–75, 192, 225

academic literacy courses: "Advanced Academic English Language Skills" (LG600/LANG6099), 176; "Advanced Writing in English", 176; business communication course, 175–76; "Critical Academic Literacies I" (CAL I), 195; "Critical Academic Literacies II" (CAL II), 195; Critical Reading and Expository Writing in the Humanities, 2, 195; Critical Reading and Writing in Education, 2, 195; Critical Reading and Writing in Science and Technology and Medical Sciences, 2, 195; Critical Reading and Writing in the Disciplines, 2, 195, 210, 231n25; Critical Reading and Writing in the Social Sciences, 195; Critical Reading in the Social Sciences, 2; discipline-specific courses, 30, 229n4; "Elementary English", 124; "English for Academic Purposes" (FD10A), 156–66, 193; "Essentials of Good Writing", 101; evolution of at Mona, 120–22; foundation courses, 8, 156–66, 166–73, 195; "Fundamentals of English" (UC010), 14, 36, 118, 120, 147, 185, 193; graduate writing courses, 146, 173–74, 176; "Language and Ethics" (LG20A/LANG2001), 174–75; "Language: Argument" (UC10B), 147; "Language: Exposition and Argument" (UC120), 147–49; "Language: Style and Purpose" (UC10A), 147; "MA in English Language", 176–77; postgraduate programme, 41; "Reading and Writing about Literature" (LITS1007), 211–12; "Use of English", 3, 36, 37, 77–79, 82–118, 144, 147, 185, 192; WAC pilot project, 194; "Writing in the Disciplines" (FD14A), 145, 166–73, 193–94, 210

academic literacy crises: media reports of, 1–2, 3, 10–13, 19; student intake and quality/quantity controversy, 7, 11–13, 110–13; in United States, 2–3

academic rationalism, 67

academic writing, 14, 18, 63; conflicts in acquisition of writing, 22–23; and critical thinking, 8, 90, 95, 162, 211, 220; as generalizable skill, 10, 24, 27, 109–15, 117, 215; linguistic initiation, 28–29, 34; misconceptions of, 10, 191–94; perpetuation of misconceptions, 13–16; plurality of, 8–9, 22; recommendations

academic writing (*continued*)
for teaching, 196–204; relationship with inquiry, 37; role of in knowledge creation, 7, 27, 143; socialization model, 23; study skills approach, 23, 98–99; use of logic in, 56–57; as visible rhetoric, 23, 37–38, 205–11. *See also* myth of transience; myth of transparency; transparent disciplinarity; writing instruction
accommodation, 120, 143–44
Act of Emancipation for British Slaves, Negro Education Grant, 60
Adams, Royce, W., *Developing Reading Versatility*, 155
administrators, and problems of language and writing, 58–59
"Advanced Academic English Language Skills" (LG600/LANG6099), 176
"Advanced Writing in English", 176
Alexander, Robin, 35, 44
Alleyne, Mervyn, 69, 128
Allsopp, Richard, 83, 87, 94–95, 101, 108–9, 116, 122; "A Use of English WORKBOOK", 106–7; "Report of a Conference on 'The Use of English' Course", 95–96; "Report on the Use of English Course", 84–85, 106–7; testing procedures, 114–15, 123; on "Use of English" course, 90–93, 110, 113–14, 115–16
Altidor-Brooks, Alison, 183
ambiguity, institutionalizing of, 130–37
Anderson, Benedict, 41
Anderson, W.E.K., *The Written Word*, 96
Anson, Chris, 179
apodictic approach to corrections, 66–67
argumentative essays, 148–49
Asquith Commission, 47, 48
An Attempt to Simplify English Grammar with the Observation and the Method of Teaching It (Sullivan), 62
assumed instinct, writing as, 34, 35, 45, 58, 65, 66–67, 74–75, 192, 225

audience expectations, 97–98, 161, 201–2
authorship, compromising of, 16
autonomous model of literacy, 99, 230n14

B
Bacchus, M. Kazim, 47, 75
Bahamas, School of Tourism, 6
Bailey, Beryl, *Jamaican Creole Syntax*, 104
Bakhtin, Mikhail, 9, 73
banking concept of teaching, 217
Barbados, University of the West Indies regional campus, 6
Barnet, Sylvan, *Critical Thinking, Reading and Writing*, 155
Bartholomae, David, 141, 156
basic writers, 140, 193; described, 123; developmental needs of, 141; as linguistic orphans, 142
Bazerman, Charles, 9, 27, 143, 144, 212, 218–19
Bedau, Hugo, *Critical Thinking, Reading and Writing*, 155
Benesch, Sarah, 158
Berlin, James, 44, 98
Bernstein, Basil, 96; elaborate and restricted codes, 99, 230n13
Bizzell, Patricia, 209, 229n3
Blackie's Readers, 61
Blair, Hugh, 57
Blair, Ornette, 158
"Bloody English!" (*Sunday Gleaner*), 1–2, 39, 190, 196
Bloom, Lynn, 215
Blooming with the Pouis (Ramsay, Cools), 155, 231n19
Boquet, Elizabeth, 138
Bourdieu, Pierre, 45, 75
The Brief [Holt] Handbook (Kirszner, Mandell), 155
Brereton, John, 79
Britain. *See* United Kingdom
British colonial policy: British instructional materials, 60–62; colonies as post-war liabilities, 48; Commission on Higher

Education in the Colonies (Asquith Commission), 48; island scholarships, 47–48; and linguistic imperialism, 43, 45–46, 227; Negro Education Grant, 60; philosophy of education, 47–49, 59–60, 230n7; white planter class, views on education, 5, 47
British Council: International English Language Testing System examination, 140
Britton, James, 96, 151, 177
Brooks, Cleanth, 86, 98
Brown, Celia, 69, 197
Bryan, Beverley, 43, 46, 72; *Between Two Grammars*, 39
Burke, Olivene, *Revisiting Tertiary Education Policy in Jamaica*, 13
business communication course, 175–76

C
Cambridge GCE O-level examinations, 110, 111
Cambridge School Certificate (Ordinary level) examination, 51
Campbell, Carl, 60
Canagarajah, A. Suresh, 199, 202, 224
Caribbean Advanced Proficiency Examination (CAPE), 21–22, 222; Communication Studies examination, 166, 170, 171, 231n22, 231n23
Caribbean Examinations Council (CXC): English language examinations, 68, 125, 230n12
Caribbean region, as archetypal contact zone, 4
Carr, William, 83, 87, 90, 94–95, 105–6
Carrington, Lawrence, 9, 72, 74, 187
Carter, Michael, 29–30, 217–18; writing, as knowing and doing, 172–73, 178
Cassidy, Frederick, *Jamaica Talk*, 104
Charney, Davida, 207
Chevannes, Barry, 197, 225; discipline-specific courses, 30, 176, 229n4; and myth of transience, 20; role of tertiary education in Jamaica, 13–16, 229n1; "Sprinting Over the Long Distance", 13–16
Christie, Pauline, 71, 103
Clarke, Burton, 32
Cobley, Alan, 47, 48, 49, 80, 81–82
code-meshing, 38, 200–205
code-mixing, 70–71
code-shifting, 70–71, 200–201
code-switching, 200–201; lexical relationship of English and Creole, 70–71; school language vs vernacular idiom, 64–66, 73
collaboration, 102, 116; of faculty for language competence, 128, 192; *problems* vs *requirements*, 105–9; team teaching, 171; in WAC pilot project, 180, 182, 183–84, 186
Commission on Higher Education in the Colonies (Asquith Commission), 48
communication across the curriculum pilot project, 184–85
communicative language teaching, 136–37
composition, courses, 3, 8, 33, 38, 79, 102; and amibiguity 121; and literature faculty, 84; and oversaturation, 213; and personal writing, 156; and process approach to writing, 144, 151, 152. *See also* academic literacy courses
comprehension, of disciplinary discourse, 15–16
conceptual knowledge vs process knowledge, 29–30
Condon, William, 184
conduit model of language, 25–27, 82, 86–87, 115, 144, 192
Conference on College Composition and Communication: *Students' Right to Their Own Language*, 11, 72, 104, 142
Connors, Robert J., 66
contact zones, 4
content faculty, 9; involvement in writing instruction, 207–8; *Outcomes Statement for First-Year Composition* (Council

content faculty (*continued*)
for Writing Program Administrators), 220–21; perceptions of disciplines, 29–30; provision of student feedback, 16
contextual variability, 31
Convention of the Conference on College Composition and Communication: writing miscues, categories of, 88–89, 90
Cools, Janice, 150, 154, 155; *Blooming with the Pouis*, 155, 231n19
corrections, apodictic approach to, 66–67
Council for Writing Program Administrators, *Outcomes Statement for First-Year Composition*, 211
Craig, Dennis, 58, 69, 70, 200, 201; *Teaching Language and Literacy*, 39–40
Creary, Jean, 83
Creole continuum, 69–70
Creole-influenced students: and academic literacy crisis, 1–2, 3; academic writing, misconceptions about teaching, 194–96; academic writing, recommendations for teaching, 126, 186–87, 196–204; acceptance in academic community, 39, 189; accommodation of, 120, 143–44; assumed linguistic profiles of, 88–93; definition, 3, 6; diglossic capacity of, 200–201; English language proficiency test, 2, 14, 121; failure rates, 12–13, 58, 63, 128; "Generation 1.5", 72; *Language Education Policy*, 73–74; lexical relationship of English and Creole, 5–6, 69–71; linguistic innovations, 226; as linguistic orphans, 36, 120–21, 122–23; problems of language and writing, 58–59, 63–66, 140; school language vs vernacular idiom, 64–66, 73; summary of misconceptions, 191–94; weakness of in English language, 1–2, 38
Creole language: basilectal Creole, 69, 70; effect on proficiency test, 136; English Creole, 69; Haitian Creole, 15; interconnections of in society, 225; Jamaican Creole (JC), 73; as Jamaican native language, 68–69; as legitimate language, 69–70, 117; lexical relationship to English, 5–6, 69–71; as linguistic transculturation, 5–6, 37, 69–71, 200–205; marginalization of, 75–76; misconceptions about, 97; neglect of in public education, 68, 71–72, 73; orality-literacy debate, 99–100, 122–23, 230n13, 230n14; recommendations for literacy teaching at lower levels, 136–37; stigmatization of, 5, 17
"Creolese English", 50, 230n8
"Critical Academic Literacies I" (CAL I), 195
"Critical Academic Literacies II" (CAL II), 195
critical reading, 8, 96–98, 115, 211, 220
"Critical Reading and Expository Writing in the Humanities", 2, 195
"Critical Reading and Writing in Education", 2, 195
"Critical Reading and Writing in Pure and Applied Sciences and Medical Sciences", 195
"Critical Reading and Writing in Science and Technology and Medical Sciences", 2, 195
"Critical Reading and Writing in the Disciplines", 2, 195, 210, 231n25
"Critical Reading and Writing in the Social Sciences", 195
"Critical Reading in the Social Sciences", 2
critical thinking, 211, 220; in "English for Academic Purposes" (FD10A), 162; role of in academic writing, 8; in "Use of English" course, 90, 95
Critical Thinking, Reading and Writing (Barnet, Bedau), 155
critical writing, 190, 191, 211, 220
Crowley, Sharon, 148, 151–52, 227
current traditional rhetoric, 98, 144, 148, 152
Currey, George, *English Grammar for the Use of Schools*, 62

Curry, Mary Jane, 209
CXC examinations. *See* Caribbean Examinations Council (CXC)

D
Darnell, George, *An Introduction to English Grammar Consisting of a Graduated Series of Easy Lessons in Language*, 62
Delpit, Lisa, 73
democratization of education, 81, 120–21
Departmental Reports, 124–25, 131, 134, 138, 147, 157, 174, 176
Department of Language, Linguistics and Philosophy: "English for Academic Purposes" (FD10A), 158; graduate writing courses, 146, 173–74, 176; Jamaican Language Unit, 146, 176; "Language and Ethics" (LG20A/LANG2001), 174; "MA in English Language", 176–77; "The Art of Public Speaking" (LG30A/LANG3001), 174; WAC pilot project, 146, 177–85; "Writing in the Disciplines" (FD14A), 145, 166
Department of Language and Linguistics, 147
Department of Linguistics and Use of English: renamed as Language and Linguistics, 147
Developing Reading Versatility (Patterson, Adams), 155
Devonish, Hubert, 69, 70, 72, 198; *Language and Liberation*, 103
diagnostic proficiency test, 193; gatekeeping function, 124, 127, 129, 130, 231n16
Dialects, Englishes, Creoles, and Education (Nero), 40
differentiated instruction, 209–10, 228
digital technologies, 191, 211, 221
discipline-specific conventions, 8, 17, 211, 220–21; academic language acquisition, 28–29; documentation style, APA vs MLA, 162, 163–64; recognition of disciplinary differences, 105–9; situatedness of terminology, 26, 229n3; transparent disciplinarity, 22–23; unfamiliarity with as barrier, 15–16
discipline-specific instruction, 17, 145, 161, 181, 185, 217; disciplines as language communities, 178, 207; student initiation into, 210–11; and visible rhetoric, 187, 191, 205–11; "Writing in the Disciplines" (FD14A), 166–67, 172–73
discourse, traditional modes of, 151
discourse community, 229n3; academia as single discourse community, 31, 103–5, 116, 156–66, 185
discourse of transparency, 10, 25, 44–45, 209; historical roots of, 59–68
discourse theory: modes-driven approach of language behaviour, 97–98
Discoveries in Academic Writing (Leonhard), 155
discursive chauvinism, 219
Dobrin, Sidney, 154–55
documentation style, APA vs MLA, 162, 163–64, 173
Doughty, Peter, 96
Douglass, Frederick, 60
Downs, Douglas, 172, 213, 218, 221, 222, 223
drafting, in process approach, 151
Draft Strategic Plan 2007-2012 (UWI), 7
Drayton, Kathleen, 44, 46, 52, 61, 62, 64, 197
Dyche, Caroline, 56, 117, 118, 122, 142, 156, 204; correspondence with secondary-level teachers, 129–30; English language education policy, 40; failure rates in proficiency test, 132, 133–34; "Fundamentals of English" (UC010), 124–25; "Report on English Language Proficiency Requirements for UWI Mona Undergraduate Study", 128–29; sociolinguistic content, 148; sociopolitical role of written English, 16–17, 154; "Why English?" Conference, 141

E

Ebonics, 72
editing, 90, 151
education, democratization of, 81, 120–21, 137
elaborate codes, 99
electronic forums, 191, 211, 221
"Elementary English" course, 124
elitism, and expansions in education, 140–41
elocution, 62, 89
eloquence, Hiley's definition of, 62
Elsasser, Nan, 36, 120, 122
Emig, Janet, 151
employers, complaints on language deficiencies of graduates, 18
English Creole, 69
"English for Academic Purposes" (FD10A), 148, 193, 231n18; and audience, 161; competences developed, 159; course changes and revisions, 162–65; course description and objectives, 158–60; course workload, 166; documentation style, 162, 163–64; essay topics, 160–61, 231n21; focus on exposition, 157–58, 161–62; grading issues, 162–63, 165; grammar instruction, 159, 165; introduction of, 144; merger with UC10A course, 164–65; as required course, 156–57; staffing issues, 157, 231n20
English for Academic Purposes Study Guide (Lalla), 155
English Grammar for the Use of Schools (Currey), 62
English language: acquisition of, 197; colonial views of, 45–46; CXC examinations, 68, 230n12; diglossic language relationship with Creole, 68–69; distinctions between variations, 104; and failure rates, 12–13; influence on attitudes to writing, 73; institutional expectations, 194, 228; lexical relationship to Creole, 5–6, 69–71; linguistic imperialism of, 172; as mark of education, 44; social prestige of, 5–6, 17, 154; Standard Jamaican English (SJE), 73; student weakness in, 1–2, 3, 37; as "white talk", 50, 230n8
English language proficiency test, 2, 14, 121; categories of results, 134; challenges to, 131–32; comparative pass rates, 132–34; exemptions from, 129; and phasing out of "Fundamentals of English" (UC010), 131
English Language Proficiency Test Information Guide, 135–36
English Language Section (ELS, Mona): adaptation of US programmes, 8; business communication course, 175–76; course coordinators, 8; diagnostic test, 124; English language proficiency test, 2, 14, 121, 123; faculty comprising, 8, 9; foundation "English Language" courses, 8; quality assurance review, 37, 190, 194–95; reassessment of writing courses, 41–42, 190, 195, 231n24
essentialism, 27
"Essentials of Good Writing" course, 101
ethics, 136, 141; "Language and Ethics" (LG20A/LANG2001), 174–75
evaluation, 155, 162, 165: and formative vs summative writing, 19, 114–15; terms, 12; and transparency conceptualization, 26, 91–92, 212
excellence: exclusionary standards of, 32–34, 129; UCWI emphasis on standards, 48–49, 55–56; vs social equity, 23, 75, 88–93, 126–30. *See also* gatekeeping function
exposition, 195; in "English for Academic Purposes" (FD10A), 157–58, 161–62; and marginalization of writing instruction, 185; as universalist genre, 144, 145, 151
expository topics, 148

F

faculty development programmes, 212–13
Faculty of Arts and General Studies: "Language: Exposition and Argument"

(UC120), 157; proficiency test exemptions, 127–28, 231n16; Use of English Conference proposal, 110–11
Faculty of Arts and General Studies, Cave Hill: "Report on Faculty Review 1986/87", 18–19, 112–13
Faculty of Medical Sciences: "English for Academic Purposes" (FD10A), 157
Faculty of Natural Sciences: "English for Academic Purposes" (FD10A), 157; exemptions from "Use of English", 101–2, 103
Faculty of Pure and Applied Sciences: WAC pilot project, 146, 178–80
Faculty of Social Sciences (Mona): advanced writing course, 16; disparity in student language requirements, 16; "English for Academic Purposes" (FD10A), 157; "Essentials of Good Writing" course, 101; exemption from "Use of English", 101; WAC pilot project, 178–80
faculty-specific courses, 205, 207
Faigley, Lester, 152, 170
failure rates: of Creole-influenced students, 12–13, 58, 63, 128; in CXC English language, 129; language as obstacle to literacy, 74; in "Use of English" course, 91–92
Fanon, Frantz, 51, 230n9
Farrell, Thomas J., 100
Federation of West Indian Islands and Guyana, 80
Fergus, Howard, 50
Ferguson, Charles, 69
Fields, Linda, *Writing in English*, 155
Figueroa, John, 47, 56, 83, 94
first-year writing courses, 199; institutional awareness of writing development, 40–41; and oversaturation, 213; Russell's critiques of, 215–17; in sequential writing programmes, 221–24; and transfer of knowledge, 213
Flores, Juan, 202
Forbes, Curdella, 212

formalism, 128, 144; and critical reflection, 32–33; formative vs summative writing, 19, 114–15; and process approach, 185; WAC pilot project, 146
formative vs summative writing, 208
Foster, David, 35, 40–41, 53, 208–9, 213–14, 224; cross-national research questions, 45; one-draft writing, 154–55
foundation courses: "English for Academic Purposes" (FD10A), 156–66; reassessment of writing courses, 195; as required courses, 156; "Writing in the Disciplines" (FD14A), 166–73
Freedman, Aviva, 171
Freire, Paulo, 32–33, 217
"Fundamentals of English" (UC010), 147, 185, 193; comparative pass rates, 131–34; conflict over, 126–27; decision to phase out, 130, 131, 140; development of, 122–26, 140; introduction of, 14, 36, 118, 120; staffing issues, 125
"Fundamentals of English" post-2004 (UC010), 134–36
Fundamentals of Good Writing (Warren, Brooks), 86, 98
funds of knowledge, 199, 219

G

Gardner, W.J., 60
gatekeeping function: of diagnostic proficiency test, 124, 127, 129, 130, 193, 231n16; of general composition courses, 33, 121; as policy of exclusion, 129
General Certificate of Education (GCE) examination, 51–53
general writing instruction: foundation courses, 156–66; in postprocess theory, 215–16
"Generation 1.5", 72
genius, association with writing, 43–44, 46–47
Glazier, Teresa, 160; *The Least You Should Know About English*, 155
Gordon, Shirley, 60, 61, 67

grading issues, 226–27; of communicative competence, 97–98, 116; "English for Academic Purposes" (FD10A), 162–63, 165; MOCAS scheme, 153, 165; in process approach, 154–55; universalist writing, 152–53; untaught aspects of writing, 90, 91, 144
graduate students, as writing consultants, 138
graduate writing courses, 146, 173–74; "Advanced Academic English Language Skills" (LG600/LANG6099), 176; "Advanced Writing in English", 176
grammar: foreign instructional materials, 61–62; grading issues, 90, 91; grammatical/mechanical error identification, 106–7; language challenges, 95–96; and language deficiencies, 10–13, 15, 129–30, 197–98, 226; and mechanical correctness, 13; parsing, 62, 114; remedial instruction, 96, 100; teaching of as discrete subject areas, 62; Writing Centre, and remedial instruction, 153–54
grammar fatigue, 114
Grammar of the English Language with the Principles of Eloquence and Rhetoric (Hiley), 61, 62
great leap theory, 99–100
Greek, teaching of, 67
Greenberg, James, 199
Guild of Students, 131
Gunner, Jeanne, 38

H

Hail and Interpellate narratives, 38–39
Haitian Creole-speaking students, 15
Hall, Anne-Marie, 219
Harding, Vivienne, "Proposal for Restructuring of UC120", 148
Harvard College, *Shaped by Writing* (film), 179
Havelock, Eric, 99
Henry-Wilson, Maxine, 13

Hesse, Douglas, *Simon & Schuster Handbook for Writers*, 155, 168
Hicks, Geo, 64
Hiley, Richard, *Grammar of the English Language with the Principles of Eloquence and Rhetoric*, 61, 62
Hodge, Merle, *The Knots in English*, 155
Holding, Rheima, *Revisiting Tertiary Education Policy in Jamaica*, 13
Horner, Bruce, 203, 204
Hunte, Christopher, 49
Hymes, Dell, 43, 44

I

Inkster, Robert, 98
inspectors, 63–67, 197
instant writing, 154–55, 163
Institute of Education, 96
institutional expectations: English language acquisition, 194, 228
Instructional Development Unit, 213, 232n29
interlingual innovation, 202
International English Language Testing System examination (British Council), 140
Inter-University Council for Higher Education in the Colonies, 48–49
An Introduction to English Grammar Consisting of a Graduated Series of Easy Lessons in Language (Darnell), 62
Irish National Readers, 61
Irvine, Patricia, 36, 120, 122
Irvine Committee, 55
Ivanic, Roz, 27

J

Jamaica: as British Crown Colony, 5; colonialism, and transculturation, 4–6, 43; Constitutional language rights, 70; diglossic language relationship, 68–69; linguistic behaviours, 6; misconceptions about language, 44–46; national language policies, 73–74

Jamaican Creole. *See* Creole language
Jamaican Creole Syntax (Bailey), 104
Jamaican education system: Caribbean Advanced Proficiency Examination (CAPE), 21–22; and colonial views of language, 45–46; and English language proficiency, 5–6, 53; English superintendents' observations, 63–65; focus on the oral, 62; foreign instructional materials, 60–62; free education, introduction of, 81; influence of England on, 5, 59–60; institutional responsibility for writing development, 11, 13–14, 18–19, 93–95, 111–14, 193, 198; island scholarships, 47–48, 53; knowledge in writing vs knowledge of writing, 53; *Language Education Policy*, 73–74, 225; neglect of Creole language in public education, 68, 71–72, 73; overseas programmes, 35; public elementary education, 5, 59–63; recommendations for literacy teaching at lower levels, 136–37; *Report of the Task Force on Tertiary Education*, 120, 137; *Revised Primary Curriculum*, 74; student preuniversity preparedness, 21–22; teacher training colleges, 67. *See also* secondary education
Jamaica Talk (Cassidy), 104
Jones, Carys, 26

K
Kennedy, Mary Lynch, *Writing in the Disciplines*, 168
Kent, Thomas, 215
Kerrick, John, 66
Keys for Writers (Raimes), 155
King, Eric (David), 36, 54, 57, 85–86, 96–97, 98, 111; "Some Proposed Modifications", 108–9
Kirszner, Laurie, *The Brief [Holt] Handbook*, 155
The Knots in English (Hodge), 155
knowledge, transfer of, 213

knowledge creation: academic socialization model, 23, 229n2; interconnectedness of writing and learning, 34–35, 36, 37, 76, 121–22, 173–74, 186–87; and knowing, 29–30; relationship to language, 44–46; role of writing in, 27, 40–41

L
Lalla, Barbara, 160; *English for Academic Purposes Study Guide*, 155
language: code-switching, 64–66, 70–71; conduit model of, 25–27, 82, 86–87; and context, 43, 44–45; Creole continuum, 69–70; diglossic relationship of in Jamaica, 68–69; interconnections of in society, 225; interlingual innovation, 202; linguistic homogeneity, 31; linguistic inventiveness, 201–3; metacognitive awareness of differences, 204; modes-driven approach of language behaviour, 97–98; in postcolonial situations, 72–73; prestige value (or stigma), 104; relationship to knowledge, 44–46; restricted codes, 99, 230n13; school language vs vernacular idiom, 64–66, 73; separation from learning, 121–22; teaching implications of blurred boundaries, 9; theory of first-language acquisition, 28–29; as transparent recording, 87; visibility of, 77, 101–3; and writing development, separation of, 66–67, 75–76
"Language and Ethics" (LG20A/LANG2001), 174–75
Language and Liberation (Devonish), 103
"Language: Argument" (UC10B), 147; argumentative essays, 150; course design, 149–50; reading to write, concept of, 149; rhetorical considerations for argumentative discourse, 149–50
language deficiencies, as reflection on university, 17–19

Language Education Policy (Jamaica), 73–74, 225
"Language: Exposition" (UC10A), 149, 150
"Language: Exposition and Argument" (UC120), 147; course description, 147, 148; influence of US writing research, 150; process approach to writing, 150–53; "Proposal for Restructuring of UC120", 148; split into two courses, 149; topics covered, 147–49; use of by Faculty of Arts and General Studies, 157
"Language: Style and Purpose" (UC10A), 147, 164–65, 172
Latin, teaching of, 67
Lawrence, Jasmin, 148
Lea, Mary, 26, 27
The Least You Should Know About English (Glazier), 155, 160
Leonhard, Barbara Harris, *Discoveries in Academic Writing*, 155
LePage, Robert, 57–58, 81; linguistic survey of British Caribbean, 50–51, 230n8
Lerner, Neal, 138
Lewis, W. Arthur, 79, 80–81
Lillis, Theresa, 22, 25, 25–27, 66, 91, 209–10
linguistic codes, orality-literacy debate, 230n13, 230n14
linguistic imperialism, 43, 45–46, 172, 227
linguistic inventiveness, 201–3
linguistic prejudice: of colonial administrators, 45–46, 59; of content faculty, 145; in "Use of English" course, 90; "Writing in the Disciplines" (FD14A), 170
literacy, as function of specific community, 227
Locke, John, *Essay Concerning Humane Understanding*, 25
logic lecture series, as examination of language, 56–57
London Matriculation Examination, 51, 52
low stakes writing, in WAC, 177–78
Lu, Min-Zhan, 203, 227
Lunsford, Andrea A., 66

M
Magnus, Ken E., 103, 127
Maimon, Elaine, 31
"MA in English Language", 176–77
Mandell, Stephen, *The Brief [Holt] Handbook*, 155
Manion, Christine, *A Writer's Guide to Oral Presentations and Writing in the Disciplines*, 168
Manley, Michael, 59, 81
Massachusetts Institute of Technology, 96
Maxwell, I., 48–49, 82
Maxwell, Peter, 71–72
McLaren, Ingrid, 184–85
McNenny, Gerri, 141
McQuade, Donald, 102
mechanistic process stages, 151
media, literacy crisis in higher education, 1–2, 3, 10–13
Merrill, Yvonne, 38, 169, 199, 207, 208, 210, 216, 227
Mico College, 67
middle class, 36, 50, 78, 80, 118; expansion of, 81; professional, 77, 80
Miller, Carolyn, 206–7
Miller, E., 61, 68
Miller, Susan, 16, 17, 24
Miller, Thomas, 32, 38, 54, 61, 62, 169, 193, 199, 207, 208, 210, 216, 227
MOCAS scheme of grading, 153, 165
Moore, Schontal, 153–54, 163
Morris, Mervyn, 71
Muchiri, Mary, 137
myth of transience, 10, 101–2, 184; interconnectedness of writing and learning, 34–35, 36, 37, 76, 121–22, 173–74, 186–87; and language development, 63, 64, 189, 190; in logic lecture series, 57; social context of error, 20–22; in social-political dynamics, 21, 74; and "Use of English" course, 109–15, 117, 130; and work of literacy, 141
myth of transparency, 10; academia as single discourse community, 31, 116;

disciplinary excellence, 32–34; and transmission of pedagogy, 22–23; transparent recording, 23–27; writing instruction as remediation, 27–30. *See also* transparent disciplinarity

N
National Association of Teachers of English (Jamaica), 71–72, 125
National Council of Teachers of English (US), 138
nationalism, and regionalism, 79–80
The National Language Policy, 142
Nero, Shondel, 73, 74; *Dialects, Englishes, Creoles, and Education*, 40
Nettleford, Rex, 5, 47, 48, 79, 80, 137
neutrality, 160
Newman, Margaret, 168, 173
North, Stephen, 138, 139

O
objectivity, 160
one-draft writing, 154–55
one-semester courses, concerns over, 196
Ong, Walter, orality-literacy debate, 99–100, 230n14
oral communication skills, 174–75
oral formulaic thought, 99
orality-literacy debate, 99–100, 230n14
oral reading, 62
Ortiz, Fernando, 4
Outcomes Statement for First-Year Composition (Council for Writing Program Administrators), 211, 220–21, 223
Owens, R.J., 83, 86, 90, 94–95, 105

P
Parker, Paul, 48, 49–50, 51, 52, 82
parsing, 62, 114
Patterson, Becky, *Developing Reading Versatility*, 155
Pereira, Joe, 204; "Report on English Language Proficiency Requirements for UWI Mona Undergraduate Study", 128–29
Perspectives on Argument (Wood), 155
persuasive writing, 23–27, 185; in "English for Academic Purposes" (FD10A), 160; and rhetorical organization, 27
Petraglia, Joseph, 215
Piaget, Jean, 96
plagiarism, 173
plural nature of academy, 183; visible rhetoric, and social equity in, 205–11
plural writing processes, 215
Pollard, Velma, 71, 73
postprocess theory, 215–16
post-secondary education: recommendations for literacy teaching at lower levels, 136–37
Pratt, Mary Louise, 4
preuniversity system: institutional responsibility for writing development, 18–19, 93–95, 111–14, 192; teaching methods, 107
prewriting, in process approach, 151
Priestly, Raymond, 55
process approach to writing, 144, 150–53, 208–9, 220; criticism of, 154; and formalism, 185; instructional materials, 155–56; process philosophy, 152; stages of, 151; at UWI, 151–52
process knowledge vs. conceptual knowledge, 29–30
process writing, 8. *See also* process approach to writing
Professorial Discourse Analysis, 41
proficiency test. *See* English language proficiency test
proofreading, in process approach, 151
"Proposal for Restructuring of UC120", 148
"Proposals for Upgrading Students' Proficiency in English" (Shields), 123–24
public discourse, 216

Q
quality assurance review, 37, 190, 194–96

Quintilian, 1, 8–9, 54
Quirk, Randolph, *The Use of English*, 96–97

R
racelessness, 50–51
Raimes, Ann, *Keys for Writers*, 155
Ramsay, Paulette, 139, 166, 167, 170, 171; *Blooming with the Pouis*, 155, 231n19; "Language and Ethics" (LG20A/LANG2001), 174–75
reading (processing) competence, 159
Reading and Discrimination (Thompson), 90
"Reading and Writing about Literature" (LITS1007), 211–12
reading to write, concept of, 149
reasoning, and use of logic in academic writing, 56–57
recommendations for teaching: adoption of rhetorical stance, 198–99, 223–24; differentiated instruction, 209–10, 220, 228; distancing of colonial conceptions of language, 227; empowerment of students, 227–28; first-year writing, and development of cross-curricular aptitudes, 214–24; general introductory course about writing, 216–19; grading issues, 226–27; ongoing writing development, 211–14; sequential writing courses, 218, 221–24; teaching of writing studies, 221; terms for discussing writing, 196–98; transcultural sensibilities, code-meshing and translingualism, 200–205; visible rhetoric, and social equity, 205–11
recursive thinking, 154–55
regionalism, and nationalism, 79–80
remedial instruction: of faulty grammar, 96; and myth of transparency, 27–30, 76, 77, 190; options for fulfilling, 131; and role of tertiary education, 10–11, 14; stigma of, 212; as student credit, 109–10; view of in university setting, 44, 78, 128–29; and visibility in language,

101–3; writing as generalizable skill, 10, 24, 27, 109–15, 117, 215; at Writing Centre, 153–54
Report of the Task Force on Tertiary Education, 120, 137
"Report on English Language Proficiency Requirements for UWI Mona Undergraduate Study", 128–29
responsibility for writing development. See academic writing; content faculty; Creole-influenced students; Jamaican education system; *Outcomes Statement*
restricted codes, 99, 230n13
revision, 90, 151
Revisiting Tertiary Education Policy in Jamaica (Holding, Burke), 13
rhetoric: academic disdain for, 54–55; Hiley's definition of, 62; transcultural rhetorical approach to writing, 37–38, 189, 198–99, 200; visible rhetoric, 23, 37–38, 205–11
rhetoric and composition, 8, 38
rhetorical knowledge, as outcome of writing instruction, 211, 220
rhetoric of transparent disciplinarity. See transparent disciplinarity
Roberts, Peter, 16, 72, 94; *Writing in English*, 155
Roberts, Vivienne, 54, 79
Robertson, E., 101
Robertson Ian, 67, 69, 75, 200
Robinson, Leslie, 108–9
Robotham, Don, 20, 90; "Changing a University", 17–19
Rodriguez Connal, Louise, 200
Rogers, Paul, 212
Rose, Mike, 1, 25, 141, 227; myth of transience, 10, 20–22, 24, 229n2
rote learning, 62
The Royal Reader Series, 61
Russell, David, 53, 208–9, 210, 224, 227; academic language acquisition, 28–29; activity system of plural writing processes, 215; conflicts in

acquisition of writing, 22–23; cross-national research questions, 45; on discipline-specific instruction, 183–84; exclusionary standards of excellence, 32–34, 206; on first-year writing courses, 215–17; knowledge creation, 229n2; and myth of transience, 38, 143; one-draft writing, 154–55; persuasive writing, 23–25; social class, and linguistic homogeneity, 31; on WAC model, 167; on writing as generalizable skill, 10, 27, 215; on writing as indication of genius, 43–44; writing development, factors affecting, 35
Rutz, Carol, 184

S
Saltz, Laura, 156
school language vs vernacular idiom, 64–66, 73
School Inspectors, Reports of, 63–67, 197
Schools Council Programme in Linguistics and English Teaching, 96
scientific method, and persuasive writing, 25–27
Scott, Eileen, 136
secondary education: foundations of English usage, lack of, 11, 13–14; institutional responsibility for writing development, 18–19, 93–95, 111–14, 192, 197; role of in preuniversity preparedness, 21–22, 67; and role of tertiary education, 13–16
sequential writing courses, 214–24
Shaped by Writing (film, Harvard College), 179
shared vocabulary, development of, 196–98
Shaughnessy, Mina, 21, 65, 123, 142
Sheils, Merril, "Why Johnny Can't Write", 11
Sheridan, Thomas, 62
Sherlock, Philip, 5, 47, 48, 55, 79, 80, 137
Shields, Kathryn, 104, 114–15; "Proposals for Upgrading Students' Proficiency in English", 123–24

Simmons-McDonald, Hazel, 200; *Writing in English*, 155
Simon & Schuster Handbook for Writers (Troyka, Hesse), 155, 168
slaves and slavery, access to education, 60–62
Smit, David W., 143, 183, 214
Smith, R.T., 93–94
Smitherman, Geneva, 226
social class: and linguistic homogeneity, 31; lower income homes, 120; middle class, 81; and racelessness, 50–51
social equity: and visible rhetoric, 205–11; vs disciplinary excellence, 23, 75, 88–93, 126–30, 205; and writing development, 191
social mobility, and education, 77, 81
sociolinguistic content, 103–5, 142, 148
Sommers, Nancy, 156
speaking competence, orality of, 159
spelling, 12, 89, 91; grading issues, 90, 91; and language deficiencies, 15
Spellmeyer, Kurt, 217
Springer, Hugh, 55
"Sprinting Over the Long Distance" (Chevannes), 13–16
Sterling, John, 61
Sternglass, Marilyn, 141
Sterry, C.E., 63
Stone, Carl, "The Threat of Mediocrity", 12–13
Street, Brian, 26, 99, 230n14
Strickland, R.B.: writing as assumed instinct, 34, 35, 45, 58, 65, 66–67, 74–75
student cohorts, changing needs of, 95–96
student intake and quality/quantity controversy, 7, 11–13, 110–13
Students' Right to Their Own Language, 11, 72, 104, 117, 142
student writing: basic writers, described, 123; corrections, teacher methods of, 66–67; Creole interference in, 104–5; errors of expression, 123, 125–26; failure rates, 91–92; final year level of English proficiency, 112–14; intelligence

student writing (*continued*)
of mistakes, 21, 65; lack of logical insight in, 57; language deficiencies, 14, 15, 20–21, 122–26, 197, 225–26; of linguistic orphans, 36, 122–23; media criticism of, 1–2, 3, 10–13; MOCAS scheme of grading, 153–54; and myth of transience, 20–22; organizational and analytical skills, 212; pseudo-scientific view of, 1; punctuation, 91; remedial grammar instruction, 96, 100, 153; science students, 89; sociopolitical role of written English, 16–17; structural faults of, 116; weakness in English language writing, 58; writing miscues, categories of, 88–90

Sullivan, Robert, *An Attempt to Simplify English Grammar with the Observation and the Method of Teaching It*, 62

summative vs formative writing, 19, 114–15, 208

Survey Courses, introduction of, 77

T

Taylor, Monica, 138, 165, 167, 171, 176, 197

teacher training, recommendations for literacy teaching, 137

teacher training colleges, 67

Teaching Language and Literacy (Craig), 39–40

team teaching, 171

terms for discussing writing, 196–98

TESOL Convention, 226

"The Art of Public Speaking" (LG30A/LANG3001), 174

theory of the great divide, 99–100

"The Threat of Mediocrity" (Stone), 12–13

Thompson, Denys, *Reading and Discrimination*, 90

Thompson, Mertel, 88–89, 90, 150

Tobin, Lad, 151

traditions, knowledge of, 1, 39

transcreation, and linguistic inventiveness, 201–3, 204

transcultural rhetorical approach to writing, 37–38, 41–42, 191, 198–99, 200, 224–28

transculturation: of colonialism, 4–6; of Jamaican Creole, 200–205

transfer of knowledge research, 149

translingualism, 38, 203–5, 226

transparency, myth of. *See* myth of transparency

transparent disciplinarity, 10, 78; discipline-specific conventions, 22–23, 26, 229n3; rhetoric of, 34–35, 75, 190

transparent recording: and myth of transparency, 23–27; vs visible rhetoric, 22

Trimbur, John, 203, 213, 223

Trinidad: University of the West Indies regional campus, 6

Troyka, Lynn Quitman, 141; *Simon & Schuster Handbook for Writers*, 155, 168

Turner, Joan, 26, 91, 100–101; conduit model of language, 25–27; discourse of transparency, 25, 209–10

U

United Kingdom: academic language acquisition, 31; Oxbridge tradition, 2, 54–56; quantity/quality controversy of increasing enrolment, 18; university system, 6; "Use of English" course, 82; visible language research, 100–101; writing research, 10, 28

United States: basic writing programmes, abolishment of, 142; composition, staffing issues, 84; criticism of process approach, 154; duality of equity and excellence, 33; influence of US writing research, 148, 150–51; literacy crisis in higher education, 11; "new elitism", 121; non-standard dialects and languages, 72; "open admissions" policy, 2–3; quantity/quality controversy of increasing enrolment, 18; writing programmes, 8

universal educated discourse, 216

universalist writing, 144–45; development of at Mona, 147–56; grading issues, 152–53; influence of British research, 151; influence of US research, 150–51; instructional materials, 155–56; process approach, 150–53; rhetorical norms of, 27, 149–50

University College of the West Indies (UCWI): affiliation with University of London, 6, 47, 49, 79, 80–81; criticism of English Oxbridge tradition, 54–56; curricular changes, 80–81; development of local leaders, 43, 48; emphasis on excellence, 48–49, 55–56; English character of, 49–50; enrolment increases, 79; establishment of, 47–49; full university status, 82; general degree programmes, 82; institutional relevance to West Indies, 79–82; liberal education tradition of, 50; logic lecture series, introduction of, 56–57; London Matriculation Examination, 51, 52; matriculation requirements, 2–3, 51–53; modes of instruction, 53–55, 230n10; Oxbridge tradition, 2, 54–56; residential requirement, 2, 3, 49; writing instruction overview, 2; yearly cost per student, 80–81. *See also* University of the West Indies, Mona (UWI)

University of London, 96; affiliation with UCWI, 6, 47, 49, 79, 80–81; A-level requirement, 52–53; London Matriculation Examination, 51, 52

University of the West Indies, Barbados, 6

University of the West Indies, Mona (UWI): academic literacy crisis, 1–2; categories of students, 123; change in cohorts, 6–7; course structure and administration, changes to, 131; *Draft Strategic Plan 2007-2012*, 7; English language proficiency test, 2, 14, 121; enrolment levels, 77, 81–82, 120, 132; evening programmes, 3, 36, 78, 79, 81; financial arrangements for courses, changes in, 130–31; Hail and Interpellate narratives, 38–39; institutional responsibility for writing development, 18–19, 93–95, 111–14, 192, 197; language-based foundation courses, 2; myth of transparency, 34; "new elitism", 121; nonresident students, 36, 78, 81; part-time courses, 3; regional campuses, 6; semester system, 147; student intake and quality/quantity controversy, 7, 11–13, 110–13; Survey Courses, 77; transition from UCWI, 6–7; writing instruction overview, 2. *See also* academic literacy courses; English Language Section (ELS, Mona)

University of the West Indies, Trinidad, 6

The Use of English (Quirk), 96–97

Use of English Conference, 110–11

"Use of English" course, 37, 144, 185, 192; aims of, 85, 96–98; as applied language course, 3; class size, 85; collaboration, 102, 105–9, 116; components of, 89; course design, 88, 96–98; critical reading, 115; emphasis on exposition, 98; English proficiency component, 93; evolution of, 77–79; exemptions from, 101–3, 109; faculty attitudes towards, 96, 117–18; faulty assumptions on writing, 100–101; focus of, 115–16; formalist concerns, 106–7; influence of academic backgrounds on teaching approach, 98–99; instructional approach, 83–86; introduction of, 36, 82–87; language, definition of, 97; as "Language: Argument" (UC10B), 147; as "Language: Style and Purpose" (UC10A), 147; and myth of transience, 117; naming of, 94–95; opposition to, 126; *problems* vs *requirements*, 105–9; promotion of, 100; recognition of disciplinary differences, 105–9; recommendations for restructuring, 92–93; "report writing", 109; school English vs survey courses, 93–95;

"Use of English" course (*continued*)
sociolinguistic content, 103–5, 118; staffing issues, 84–85; "study method", modifications to, 107; survey vs service course, 119; visible language, and remediation, 100–103; writing as generalizable skill, 109–15, 115
"UWI Mona Writing Centre Mission", 181–82

V
Vélez-Ibáñez, Carlos, 199
Villanueva, Victor, 1, 41, 50–51
Vygotsky, Lev, 28, 96

W
WAC pilot project, 146, 194, 199; collaboration in, 180, 182, 183–84, 186; disciplinary writing principles, 182; faculty participation, 178–80, 183–84, 186; improvements in writing, 186; recommendations for, 180–81; and social construction of knowledge, 178–80; support and funding of, 184; universalist orientation of, 179; "UWI Mona Writing Centre Mission", 181–82; and WRITE symposium, 179–80; "Writing Centre Pilot Proposal", 181
WAC reform movement, 177–78
Waldo, Mark, 28
Walker, Joyce, 89–90, 107–8, 109
Wardle, Elizabeth, 172, 213, 218, 221, 222, 223
Warren, Robert Penn, *Fundamentals of Good Writing*, 86, 98
Wells, Peter, 16
West Indian Committee of the Commission on Higher Education: Caribbean literacy, 46, 116
West Indies Group of University Teachers, 93–94
White, Edward, 140, 213
white planter class, views on education, 5, 47, 59–60

"Why English?" Conference, 141
"Why Johnny Can't Write" (Sheils), 11
Whyte, Millicent, 47
Widdowson, H.G., 226
Wignall, Mark, 11
Williams, Eric, 54, 56, 80
Wilson, Don, 204; "Report on English Language Proficiency Requirements for UWI Mona Undergraduate Study", 128–29
Winch, Christopher, 16
Winford, Donald, 69, 88, 104, 107
Wood, Nancy, *Perspectives on Argument*, 155
A Writer's Guide to Oral Presentations and Writing in the Disciplines (Manion), 168
writer's journal, 162–63
WRITE symposium, 179–80, 218
writing across the curriculum, 2. See also WAC
writing (production) competence, 159
Writing Centre: ambiguity in provision and management of, 137–40, 231n17; funding, 139–40; goal of, 137–38; as paid service, 139; physical layout, 138–39; remedial grammar instruction, 153–54, 159; resources available, 139; "UWI Mona Writing Centre Mission", 181–82; and WAC pilot project, 179
"Writing Centre Pilot Proposal", 181
Writing in English (Simmons-McDonald, Fields, Roberts), 155
writing instruction: and academic literacy crisis, 1–2, 3; attitudinal change toward, 144, 157; comparisons to international teachings, 3; content faculty involvement in, 207–8; cross-curricular, absence of, 38; as developmental, 191; within disciplines, 217; discipline-specific instruction, 17, 75, 103–5, 143; evolution of at Mona, 120–22; exclusionary standards of excellence, 32–34; for ex-slaves, 61; faculty responsibility in, 183–84; first-year courses, 40–41; foundation

"English Language" courses, 8; general composition courses, gatekeeping function of, 33, 121; Hail and Interpellate narratives, 38–39; implication of factors beyond secondary level, recognition of, 15; influence of US composition in, 142; as interdisciplinary discipline, 214; and knowledge creation, 9; language as transparent recording, 87; outcomes for, 211; persuasive writing, 23–27; place of in higher education, 34; Priestly's comments on, 55; rationale of, 136; as remediation, 10–11, 14, 22, 27–30, 36, 44, 76, 78, 96, 100, 128–29, 190, 212; rhetorical approach to, 219–20; and role of tertiary education, 13–16; as separate from disciplinary knowledge, 10; summative vs formative writing, 19, 114–15, 208; and training of thought, 95; transcultural rhetorical approach to writing, 37–38, 41–42; tutoring, 93, 96; at UCWI, 43; 'writing to learn' vs 'learning to write', 167. *See also* foundation courses

"Writing in the Disciplines" (FD14A), 193–94, 210; and CAPE Communication Studies examination, 166, 170, 231n22; conception of, 166–67; course description and objectives, 168–69; discipline-specific instruction, 166–67, 171; documentation style, APA vs MLA, 173; factors affecting lack of course success, 167–68, 172–73, 185–86; linguistic prejudice, 170; social sorting in, 170

Writing in the Disciplines (Kennedy), 168

writing portfolios, 8, 150–51, 160, 162–63

writing research: academic language acquisition, 28–29; authorship, compromising of, 16; code-meshing, 38, 200–205; critical reading, 96–98; discourse of transparency, 10; influence of US writing research, 148, 150–51; institutional awareness of writing development, 40–41; myth of transience, 10; transfer of knowledge research, 149; translingual approaches to teaching, 38

Writing Research Unit Council, 96

writing samples, and writing development, 15

writing to communicate, 177–78

writing to learn, 177–78

The Written Word (Anderson), 96

Wynter, Hector, 58

Y

Young, V.A., 204

www.ingramcontent.com/pod-product-compliance
Lightning Source LLC
Chambersburg PA
CBHW021821300426
44114CB00009BA/267